THE POLITICAL ECONOMY
OF REGIONALISM

THE POLITICAL ECONOMY
OF REGIONALISM

edited by

Michael Keating
and
John Loughlin

FRANK CASS
LONDON - PORTLAND, OR.

Published in association with the Robert Schuman Centre
European University Institute, Florence

First published in Great Britain by
FRANK CASS & CO LTD
Newbury House, 900 Eastern Avenue
London IG2 7HH, England

and in the United States by
FRANK CASS
c/o ISBS
5804 N.E. Hassalo Street, Portland, Oregon 97213-3644

British Library Cataloguing in Publication Data

A catalogue record of this book is available
from the British Library.

ISBN 0-7146-4658-X (hardback)
ISBN 0-7146-4187-1 (paperback)

Library of Congress Cataloging-in-Publication Data

The political economy of regionalism / edited by Michael Keating and
John Loughlin.
      p.   cm. – (Cass series in regional and federal studies)
   Includes bibliographical reference and index.
   ISBN 0-7146-4658-x (hardback). – ISBN 0-7146-4187-1 (pbk.)
   1. Regional economies. 2. Regionalism. I. Keating, Michael,
1940–   . II. Loughlin, John. III. Series
HT388.P65   1996
330.0–dc20
                                                          96-20554
                                                             CIP

Typeset by
Barbara Ciomei

Printed in Great Britain by
Bookcraft (Bath) Ltd., Midsomer Norton, Avon

Contents

PART TWO: CASE STUDIES

List of Contributors

EDITORS

Michael Keating is Professor of Political Science at the University of Western Ontario, Canada. He previously worked at the University of Strathclyde, Scotland, where he is now Visiting Professor. He has taught in universities in the United States, Spain and France and has been Visiting Professor at the European University Institute, Florence, and Senior Visiting Fellow at the Norwegian Nobel Institute. With John Loughlin, he is joint director of the European Consortium for Political Research Standing Group on Regionalism. He is author or editor of fifteen books and many articles, most recently *The European Union and the Regions* (with Barry Jones) (Oxford University Press, 1995), *Nations Against the State. The New Politics of Nationalism in Quebec, Catalonia and Scotland* (Macmillan, 1996). The latter has also appeared in Spanish (Ariel) and French (Presses de l'Université de Montréal). Currently, Michael Keating is working on a book on regionalism in Europe.

John Loughlin is Professor of European Politics and Jean Monnet Professor of European Political Economy at the University of Cardiff, Wales. He is joint founder and managing editor of *Regional and Federal Studies: an International Journal* (London:Frank Cass) and is joint convenor (with Michael Keating) of the European Consortium of Political Research Standing Group on Regionalism. Formerly Associate Professor in Public Administration at the Erasmus University, Rotterdam, he was Visiting Professor at the European University, Florence, Italy, and at the European Institute of Public Administration, Maastricht, in 1994. Among his recent publications are (editor) *Southern Europe Studies Guide* (London: Bowker Saur) and (editor with Sonia Mazey) *The End of the French Unitary State: Ten Years of Regionalization in France, 1982-1992* (London: Frank Cass). His book *Governance and the New Regionalism* (London: C. Hurst) will appear in 1997.

CONTRIBUTORS

John Bachtler is Director of the European Policies Research Centre, University of Strathclyde, Glasgow, UK.

Richard Balme is Professor of Politics in the Institut d'Etudes Politiques at the Université Lumière Lyon 2, France.

David W. Conklin is Associate Professor in the Western Business School at the University of Western Ontario, London (Ontario), Canada.

Howard Elcock is Professor of Government in the School of Social, Political and Economic Sciences at the University of Northumbria at Newcastle-upon-Tyne, UK.

Liz Fulop is Associate Professor of Management in the Department of Management at the University of Woolongong, Australia.

Frank Hendriks is Lecturer in Public Administration in the Department of Law at the University of Tilburg, The Netherlands.

Brian Hocking is Professor in the School of International Studies at the University of Coventry, UK.

Barry Jones is Head of the Politics Section in the School of European Studies at the University of Wales, Cardiff, UK.

Bernard Jouve is a Researcher in the Laboratoire R.I.V.E.S. at the Ecole Nationale des Travaux Publics de l'Etat, Vaulx-en-Velin, Lyon, France.

Winnie Lem is Associate Professor in the Department of Comparative Development Studies at the Trent University, Peterborough (Ontario), Canada.

Pierre Martin is Associate Professor in the Department of Political Science at the Université de Montréal, Québec, Canada.

James Mitchell is Senior Lecturer in the Department of Government at the University of Strathclyde, Glasgow, UK.

Francesc Morata is Professor of Government and Administration in the Department of Political Science at the Universitat Autónoma de Barcelona, Spain.

B. Guy Peters is Maurice D. Falk Professor of Government in the Department of Political Science at the University of Pittsburgh, PA, USA.

Simona Piattoni is Lecturer in the Institute of Social Science at the University of Tromsø, Norway.

Roland Sturm is Professor of Politics in the Department of Political Science at the University of Erlangen–Nürmberg, Germany.

Urlan Wannop was Professor of Regional Planning at the University of Strathclyde, Glasgow, UK

Colin H. Williams is Research Professor in the Department of Welsh at the University of Wales, Cardiff, UK.

Introduction

MICHAEL KEATING and JOHN LOUGHLIN

The 'regional question' is once again on the social science and political agendas in Europe and North America. In Europe, the slogan 'Europe of the Regions', originally meaning a federal Europe with a reduced role for nation-states (Loughlin, 1994), has become popularized and expresses an enhanced role for European regional policy as well as a new role for sub-national regional and local authorities. This raising of the profile of regions in Europe has been given institutional expression by the 1993 Treaty of Maastricht which created the Committee of the Regions (CoR), with representatives from regional and local authorities, as an advisory body alongside the Economic and Social Committee (ECOSOC). In North America, too, the regional question has been raised in both the United States and Canada where it has consequences for the federal systems there.

What is also significant is the form the 'regional question' takes today. Twenty years ago, when students embarked on research on this question, they did so either from a political science perspective which was concerned with 'national' or 'ethnic' minorities who, according to both liberal and Marxist theories of the state and society, should have disappeared from advanced capitalist societies (Smith, 1981; Gellner, 1964, 1983); or, as economists or geographers, they were concerned with the development of national regional policies and their effects on the economic and social life of regional populations (Vanhove and Klaassen, 1987; Molle, 1990). Only rarely were these two questions related to each other. Today, the regional question is still concerned with these issues but the perspectives and context have changed. From about 1985, social scientists began to look at regions from the point of view of accelerated European integration, the growth and implementation of structural action funds (including regional policy funds), and the mobilization of regions within a broader political game across Europe. In Europe, these processes have been given impetus by the Single European Act (1987) leading to the setting up of a Single Market in 1993. In

North America, the new context is provided by the North American Free Trade Agreement (NAFTA) signed in 1989, and the ongoing crisis of the position of Quebec in the Canadian federation.

However, analysis of the regional question is still bedevilled by a lack of clarity in the concepts that are used, not least in the use of the term 'region' itself. Before presenting some thoughts on why the regional question has re-emerged onto the political and social science agendas in this particular form, it will be useful to give a short summary of the ways in which the various terms may be understood (Keating, 1988b; Loughlin, 1994, 1996b). First, it is necessary to distinguish 'regions' as the term is used in International Relations and early European integration literature, where it refers to groups of countries, such as 'Western Europe', 'North America', 'South East Asia', and 'regions' understood as territorial entities below the level of the nation-state and sometimes crossing nation-state boundaries as in cross-border regions. When scholars such as Ernst Haas debated European integration in the 1950s and 1960s and spoke of 'regional integration', they meant the integration of Europe as a whole, not regions within Europe. In this book, the term 'regions' is used primarily in the second sense.

However, even when used in this sense, there are problems of definition. The term may be used in four principal ways, all of which are relevant to the problematic of this book. What all four have in common is that they refer to territories, but they differ in the way that territory is conceived.

Economic Regions

These are territories defined according to economic characteristics or criteria such as industrialized/deindustrialized, urban/rural; or sectoral: steel producing, ship-building, tourist-oriented. These may also refer to territories designated by national governments for economic development. However, a more recent manner of defining economic regions that is relevant to this book is based on the notion of new emerging economic regions marked by local or endogenous development and sometimes related to economic globalization, technological changes and shifts in the factors of economic production (see below). This phenomenon, while new, harks back to the old Marshallian idea of industrial districts. To some extent, these new economic regions are outside the control of existing political and administrative institutional arrangements.

Historical/Ethnic Regions

These are territories marked by the presence of human societies sharing histories and cultural/linguistic features different from that of the dominant culture of the nation-state in which they find themselves. Sometimes these groups define themselves as nations or nationalities (Smith, 1981). The collapse of the Soviet Union and its satellite states has shown that these groups survived in the East despite the attempts of the Communist regimes to suppress them. However, Spain, Italy, France, the United Kingdom, Belgium and even the Netherlands and Germany possess such minorities. Some of the political formations found within these groups, particularly in Spain (for example, the Basque ETA movement) and the United Kingdom (the Scottish National Party), espouse a nineteenth-century concept of nation-state nationalism and have raised their demands for recognition to such a level that the nation-state has had to respond with distinct political or administrative arrangements. In North America, too, there is a variety of such groups including French-speakers in Quebec in Canada and in Louisiana in the United States, as well as native Americans who are not primarily organized on a regional basis. In Canada, the problems of the coexistence of the various peoples, and especially of Quebec and the rest of Canada, are still far from resolved and the break-up of the Canadian federation cannot be ruled out. Yet many contemporary minority nationalist movements have recognized the limitations of sovereignty and traditional statehood and are seeking new forms of recognition and autonomy within a more interdependent world and continental order (Keating, 1996b).

Culturally distinct regions have in recent years been attempting to develop a model of regional economic development where their cultural distinctiveness is regarded as giving them a competitive advantage over their competitors. Movements of cultural defence thus link up with ideas of endogenous development theory, as this model attempts to preserve features such as the regional language and culture while at the same time providing both sufficient employment for young people and a rich cultural life for the inhabitants of the region and those whom it hopes to persuade to invest in the region. Catalonia and Quebec are two examples of this approach.

Administrative/Planning Regions

All states define territory for the purposes of policy-making or simply for gathering statistics. France created administrative or planning regions in the late 1950s when it regionalized the national plan. In recent years, even highly centralized states such as Ireland and Greece have set up administrative entities at the regional level for the purposes of meeting EU criteria for the implementation of EU regional policy funds (Loughlin, 1996; Papageorgiou and Verney, 1992). In England, the ten Standard Regions exist almost exclusively for this purpose, although a number of Integrated Regional Offices were established in 1994 to co-ordinate the regional activities of a number of central government departments. However, such regions have no political function in the sense of possessing an elected council or assembly to which a regional executive may be accountable.

Political Regions

Political regions differ from the above in that they possess democratically elected councils or assemblies who in turn choose an executive accountable to the electorate through them. In other words, they have fully-fledged regional governments. However, there is a wide variety of political and constitutional situations with regard to such governments. These range from the situation of federal states such as Germany and Austria which possess powerful *Länder*, and Belgium whose linguistic communities and economic regions have replaced the central state in many of its functions, to the rather weak French *régions*, which, although they do possess regional governments, must compete with the existing *départements* for occupation of the meso-level of decision-making space (Loughlin and Mazey, 1995). In between are the Spanish Autonomous Communities and Italian Regions. Smaller European states have not followed the path of setting up regional government, despite a currently prevailing notion that there is a general tendency in this direction.

In order to complete the conceptual clarification necessary for understanding the complexity of the regional question today, we will conclude this section by distinguishing regionalization from regionalism. This has been expounded in greater detail elsewhere (Hayward, 1969; Loughlin, 1994). It will suffice here to say that regionalization refers to a process whereby national governments or the EU define regional policies for, or impose them on, regions. In other words, it is a process whereby something is done to regions and is often top-down, centralizing and technocratic. Much national and EU regional policy falls into this category. Regionalism, on the other hand, is an '-ism': it refers to an ideology and to political movements which demand greater control over the affairs of the regional territory by the people residing in that territory, usually by means of the installation of a regional government. It is essentially bottom-up, decentralizing (of political power), and political. The two phenomena do not always coincide and may even be in conflict, as happened in France in the 1960s where government regional policies, which excluded significant sections of the regional populations, provoked widespread regionalist responses in some regions such as Brittany, the French Basque Country and Corsica. EC regional policy was a form of regionalization but, since the 1988 reforms and the introduction of the principle of partnership, an element of regionalism has entered into it. Part of the confusion surrounding the slogan 'Europe of the Regions' results from failing to distinguish between these two processes. While keeping these processes analytically distinct, however, we recognize that there is a close link between them. State and European policy initiatives have often provoked mobilization on the ground as state and regional actors contend for control of the development project (see Keating in this volume).

We may now turn to the question of why the regional question has assumed such importance in recent years and particularly from 1985 onwards. There are three principal sets of reasons for this development: (i) economic changes on a global level; (ii) political developments and (iii) changing policy aspects of territorial politics in Western states.

ECONOMIC CHANGES

It is possible to distinguish a number of distinct periods in recent economic history since the Second World War. The first period is that of economic reconstruction and development, with American financial aid through the Marshall Fund, which occurred in most European states between about 1950 and the oil crisis of 1973. This was a period of unprecedented prosperity marked by almost full employment, an increase in material well-being and the setting up of welfare states providing a wide range of benefits to citizens whose 'needs' were defined in an increasingly generous manner. This period was also marked by the Keynesian belief that governments could bring about economic development and prosperity through intervention in the economy and society. Regional policy was adopted by many Western governments within this framework: what social policy did for individuals or categories of individuals lagging behind a level of equality, regional policy would do for territories lagging behind the most advanced areas (Vanhove and Klaassen, 1987). Although European integration was proceeding slowly during this period, the European Community felt no need to develop its own regional policy. There were a number of reasons for this. First, of the original six EEC states, only Italy and France had important regional problems and the latter country, during the period of Gaullist grandeur, was reluctant to admit this. Second, the prevailing European economic policy at this time was based on the notion of the free market. There was little conviction that Europe itself should intervene directly in an economic sense, especially with regard to regional policy and this was left primarily to the member-states. It was also felt that the growing wealth of European societies would automatically 'trickle down' to the weaker regions.

However, the post-war boom ended with the oil crisis of 1973, although it had already begun to falter before this with rising levels of inflation and growing unemployment. This led, in the late 1970s and early 1980s, to a backlash led by politicians such as Margaret Thatcher and Ronald Reagan who were elected to power with programmes that promised to 'roll back the state'. This New Right neo-liberal agenda was to some extent based on the monetarist economic theories of Friedman and Hayek and the anti-bureaucratic theories of Niskanen. The reforms inspired by these theories were most ruthlessly and systematically applied in the United Kingdom by Mrs Thatcher. In this country, there have been radical overhauls of the civil service, whose numbers have been drastically reduced, and central government has imposed important reforms on the health service, local government and education. However, under Thatcher, the United Kingdom, far from having a weakened state, has become one of the most centralized countries in the West. Most other Western countries adopted aspects of these reforms although not as systematically as the British (Loughlin and Peters, in this volume).

Regional policy, as an aspect of neo-Keynesian macro-economic planning, was one of the first policies to be seriously cut back in most European countries with some exceptions such as the then West Germany. However, it was at this time, as national governments abolished or scaled down their regional policies, that the EC began to develop its own regional policy and, in 1975, set up the European Regional Development Fund (ERDF). At first, the new policy was little more than an attempt at harmonizing national policies where they existed and ensuring that national regional policies were not attempts at creating unfair market advantage, and its piece-meal and inadequate character was severely criticized by those who sought a more effective policy approach to the regional question.

The Single European Act setting up the Single Market was passed in 1987 and the Maastricht Treaty on Political and Economic Union in 1993 formed the background for a dramatic heightening of the salience of the regional question in Europe. Spain, Portugal and Greece were now members and feared that the drive toward a single market might be harmful to their less developed economies and particularly their peripheral regions. Italy, the UK and Ireland had similar fears. The outcome of the negotiations leading to the drawing up of the Single European Act was an enhanced regional policy (Marks, 1992). However, the growing importance of EU regional policy is not simply a result of horse-trading between member states. It is also based on economic arguments connected with bringing undeveloped sectors of territory and human resources into the productive cycle (Hooghe and Keating, 1994).

This growing awareness of the importance of regions for the economic development of national societies, and indeed of European society as a whole, coincides with another development in economic thinking. This is the notion that with economic globalization, that is, the creation of world-wide markets and the internationalization of factors of production linked to new technological developments, new economic regions are emerging as the key territorial units of economic activity. Within this perspective, nation-states are no longer adequate units within which to frame economic activity. They are too small for the global aspects and too large for the regional dimension. However, one problem for existing political regions is that their territorial boundaries do not always coincide with the boundaries of the new economic regions. Indeed, these regions may cross national boundaries. To some extent, the European Commission has recognized these developments and put forward a proposal, in its documents *Europe 2000* and *Europe 2000+*, to adopt a new approach to spatial planning which should become an EU responsibility rather than a national one.

POLITICAL CHANGES

The most dramatic political change in recent decades concerns the nation-state itself (Keating, 1988b; Loughlin, 1994, 1996b). Basically, the old nineteenth-century concept that the nation-state should have absolute sovereignty over all affairs that happen within the national territory is no longer valid. What used to be defined as domestic issues, including policing, financial and economic issues and environmental questions, have an increasingly transnational character. The solution to these problems lies in international co-operation and a recognition of international interdependence. This is true of even large states such as the US, Germany and Japan which are not capable of operating alone in an increasingly complex and interdependent world. It is true *a fortiori* of the member states in the European Union which have all voluntarily ceded aspects of sovereignty to the supranational institutions of the Union. The nation-state is also changing from within through processes of administrative reform (often linked to the neo-liberal reform agenda mentioned above) by which it attempts to shed many of the functions and responsibilities (and expenses) accumulated through the building up of welfare states. Although not all states have carried out this programme to the same extent and outcomes have varied according to state tradition (Loughlin and Peters, in this volume), all Western states and many of the new states which have emerged out of the old Soviet empire have felt obliged at least to pay lip service to this fashion. The result of these changes has been the redefinition of the relations between the public and the private, between the state and society.

However, other forces, this time of a territorial nature, have served to redefine the nation-state: it has been claimed that in recent decades there has been a general process of decentralization, or to put it another way, the 'rise of the meso' (Sharpe, 1993; Balme,

1995), with some exceptions such as the United Kingdom, Ireland and Greece. Although these claims are somewhat exaggerated, it is true that a number of states have instituted stronger levels of subnational government: Belgium has become a fully-fledged federal state (Delmartino, 1993); Spain, as part of its transition to democracy, adopted a system of autonomous communities (Morata, 1992); and France, in 1982, instigated a process of decentralization which included upgrading its regional councils to regional governments (Hainsworth and Keating, 1986; Loughlin and Mazey, 1995). Most of these reforms have been carried out for reasons internal to the states involved. However, the increasing 'Europeanization' of the member states of the EU has also to some extent led to a 'regionalization' of their administrative and policy-making systems, even if this is simply to gain a position of competitive advantage with regard to access to European structural funds (Marks, 1992). There is some evidence that even the highly centralized (and centralizing) states such as the UK, Ireland and Greece have been led to introduce regional levels of administration. The UK has set up Integrated Regional Offices, Ireland has established Regional Development Offices (Loughlin, 1996); and Greece has introduced Regional Administrations for the purposes of the implementation of the Integrated Mediterranean Programmes of the EU. Although these latter developments are far from constituting regional governments, they do illustrate a general tendency and the importance of the European framework in which policy now occurs.

These trends have led to greater decentralization even in the absence of constitutional change (Courchene, 1995). Free trade within North America has had important regional implications, as Conklin explains in this volume. American states and Canadian provinces have become more important actors in economic development as their respective federal states have retrenched. NAFTA, however, does not establish political institutions at the continental level, as is the case in Europe, or even a political space for regional action. Nor does it provide incentives to regional co-operation. On the contrary, by simply opening up markets, it encourages competition among places for investment and market shares. So while there has been economic integration, this has not served to erode political borders (Keating, 1996b).

The new context of the nation-state has led to the emergence of new interest groups mobilizing around a regional problematic

(Marks, 1992). First, there is the phenomenon of intraregional mobilization. This refers to a process whereby regional governments have attempted to gather together forces (private and public sector actors) within their region with a view to competing in the wider international context of economic globalization mentioned above. Many regions and sub-federal provinces and states now attempt to market themselves as attractive locations of inward investment. Furthermore, many of these sub-national entities have signed agreements with other states or sub-national governments to promote co-operation and trade. Strictly speaking, only national governments are able to conduct foreign policy although in some federal states, such as Germany and Belgium, the sub-federal units may conclude treaties with equivalent bodies in other states on matters on which they have competence. There now exist in Brussels many regional information offices which do represent a considerable investment on the part of sub-national entities. Another form of mobilization that has developed is inter-regional mobilization. This involves either multilateral links among regions and states within countries, as has occurred in France and the US, or the creation of bodies such as the Association of European Regions (AER) which represents over 200 European regional and local authorities (some English counties play an important role in the organization). The AER defines its mission as explicitly political and attempts to raise the profile of regions and local authorities. Other transnational regional groupings have a more specific orientation related to a geographical feature (for example, the Assembly of Cross-Border Regions or the Conference of Peripheral Maritime Regions) or an economic function (for example, the Traditional Industrial Regions – RETI – network which groups together industrialized regions – in effect, these are industrial regions in decline). Although these associations are, in constitutional terms, simply private interest groups, they have an important function of creating networks and providing exchanges of information among their members.

Political parties too have responded in some measure to the new 'regional imperative'. The great families of political parties are usually organized on a national basis according to socio-economic or ideological criteria (such as Socialist, Conservative, Liberal, Christian-Democratic). However, sometimes 'national' parties also have a territorial dimension and it is common to find certain parties having strongholds (or lacking them) in particular regions. There also exist specifically regionalist or minority nationalist parties. These regionalist and nationalist parties are primarily concerned with their own regions. However, on occasion, where they also are represented at the state level, they may hold the balance of power. As the traditional parties at the national level fragment, this heightened strength of regionalist parties is sure to grow. Furthermore, in Europe the existence of regional funds from the European Union, and the growing importance of both Europe and the regional levels of governance, mean that political parties of all kinds will invest greater resources at these levels.

POLICY CHANGES: THE NEW TERRITORIAL POLITICS

Trends in public policy making have produced a disjuncture between policy making and political institutions. There is a substantial literature to the effect that policy processes can better be understood through an examination of 'networks' and 'policy communities' which span tiers of government and the public and private sectors (Marin and Mayntz, 1991). In such a world, it might appear that policy and politics have been 'deterritorialized', especially given modern communications technology and the rise of global corporations. We do not share this view. Rather, we see a reconfiguration of political space in which territory continues to feature largely. We have noted above the importance of regions as spaces for the action of states and for political mobilization, economic change and cultural defence. Territory also remains an important principle of political legitimation and one of the few challengers to the monopoly of the market as a principle for legitimation in the contemporary world. We do not, however, see a world in which regions take the place formerly occupied by states. There is no consistent definition of regions across Europe or North America or even within individual states. In many instances, two or more levels of mobilization and legitimation compete, as when a large city exists within a region – the rivalry between the city of Barcelona and the Generalitat of Catalonia is an example. There the definition of the region itself is in contention. There are institutional rivalries in federal systems, where federal governments may use regionalism as a way of undercutting or by-passing the federated units. The issue of regionalism in Australia cuts across the constitutional division of powers, as Fulop shows in this volume. In the United States, too, regions rarely coincide with states. Similarly in Europe, the three levels of the EU, the member states and regional governments may conflict over the definition and control of political space. We do not see a new territorial hierarchy to replace the old. Rather there is a variety of institutional arrangements and forms of political mobilization across Europe and North America. The 'variable geometry' Europe is likely to be accompanied by 'variable geometry' states and regions.

Clearly, this is important for regions where mobilization has involved building networks within regions and across national boundaries. As was remarked at the beginning of this introduction, the regional question is studied today largely as a problem of policy formulation and implementation. The new political role of regions, at least in the European case, is related to the opportunities opened up as a result of enhanced European regional policy. The policy analysis approach may therefore be highly relevant for analysing these developments.

However, the principal limitation of the policy approach is that it tends to downgrade the importance of institutions. Largely as a result of debates concerned with 'bringing the state back in' (Evans et al., 1985) and neo-institutionalism (March and Olsen, 1984), it is now recognized that institutions do matter. This is particularly the case on the continent of Europe where there is a strong tradition of public law and where the state defines itself as beginning with a capital letter (l'Etat, el Estado, lo Stato, etc.). Thus, it may not be sufficient simply to build regional coalitions, as is happening today in England, if these do not exist within an institutional framework of regional government. In other words, while networks are important and do influence policy-making, sometimes crucially, it is equally important as to whether these networks can also call upon the services of regional governments. In concrete terms, a German *Land* or a Canadian province, with all the constitutional, political, financial and administrative resources that it possesses, is a much stronger player in the political game than even a Spanish autonomous community and, *a fortiori*, an English regional association such as the North West Regional Association (Burch and Holliday, 1993). Within this context, there is a crucial distinction to be made between federal and non-federal states from the point of view of the resources available to sub-national political authorities. The German and Austrian *Länder* and the Belgian linguistic communities and regions may, in certain instances, enter into formal treaty relationships with political entities outside their national territories and, indeed, may even participate at meetings of the EU Council of Ministers.

The chapters in this book focus on regions and the nexus of economic, cultural and political change. They look at the influence of economic change on politics and of politics on economic development. They recognize that the impact of global change is mediated by local structures to produce a variety of outcomes.

We would like to thank a number of individuals as well as institutions who contributed to the production of this book: Yves Mény, Director of the Schuman Centre, European University Insitute, Florence; the Social Sciences and Humanities Research Council of Canada; the Council for International Canadian Studies; the British Council; the European Consortium for Political Research; the Department of Public Administration, Erasmus University Rotterdam; the School of European Studies, University of Wales, College of Cardiff; Jörg Mathias, Research Assistant at the School of European Studies, Cardiff; and Nichola McEwen. Most of all we would like to thank the contributors to the volume who presented papers at the initial conference at the University of Western Ontario and at an ECPR Workshop in Madrid. We would equally like to thank the other participants in these events whose papers have appeared elsewhere.

PART I

THEORETICAL AND COMPARATIVE ISSUES

1

The Political Economy of Regionalism

MICHAEL KEATING

REGIONS AND REGIONALISM

Regionalism in western industrial societies covers a complex and varied set of phenomena, to the extent that some observers have doubted whether the concept has any analytical value at all. Yet, in its varied and changing form, it returns regularly to the political agenda. After a period in which it went out of fashion, it has returned again in the 1990s as states and political and social actors adjust to changes in the global and continental economic and political orders.

From a strictly empiricist and positivist perspective, it might seem logical, before discussing regionalism, to define what is a region. Yet region, like the related concepts of state and nation, defies descriptive definition. It takes different forms in different places and refers to a variety of spatial levels. Moreover, in most states, the region is a contested area, both territorially and functionally. Spatially, it exists somewhere between the national and the local and is the scene of intervention by actors from all levels, national, local, regional and now supranational. Functionally, it is a space in which different types of agency interact and, since it is often weakly institutionalized itself, a terrain for competition among them. Definitions of regions are also value-laden, since they reflect different conceptions of their political character and potential. Some represent them as mere administrative divisions, to be defined in functional terms. Others see them as reflecting communities of interest; some regions define themselves as historic nations or harbour movements with nationalist aspirations.[1] Political entrepreneurs themselves seek to shape the definition of region to reflect their values and interests.

This paper examines the process of regionalism and region-building from the various perspectives and concludes that, while the theme of regionalism is increasing in importance, there is an increased differentiation between types of region and their potential. First, it examines regionalization as state policy, a top-down phenomenon and the way in which this was increasingly politicized, the problems of institutionalization and the subsequent decline in regional policy. Then it looks at regionalism as political demands, or bottom-up regionalism. Finally, it considers the problem of regionalism in the context of global economic change, continental integration and the changing scope of the nation state.

REGIONS AND STATE POLICY

Regional anti-disparity policies emerged in western Europe in the postwar era as an extension of Keynesian macro-economic management. They followed both an economic and a political logic (Biarez, 1989; Keating, 1988b). Economically, the aim was to rectify what were seen as market imperfections in the allocation of resources. Capital tended to flow to central places close to markets, a tendency exacerbated by technological changes which liberated newer industries from their ties to raw materials and waterways. This produced higher levels of unemployment and lower regional incomes in depressed regions, together with overheating and inflationary pressures in the booming areas.

In a pure market economy, adjustment would be automatic. Workers would have to move to where the jobs were, or accept lower wages in order to attract capital to them. This happens to a large extent in the USA, where mobility is seen as normal and proper. In Europe, there was considerable migration into the industrial areas, notably in Italy and Spain. Yet moving the workers was not seen as the only appropriate solution and in some countries it was rejected almost entirely. Partly, this was for economic reasons, to avoid the costs of congestion and stress on housing markets in booming areas, and to exploit available space in the depressed regions. Political incentives existed to favour a policy of work to the workers rather than vice versa. One is the existence of trade unions and nationally negotiated wage rates in several sectors. This prevented wages falling in poorer regions to attract capital and lower-value-added types of production. There is also a more general expectation in European culture, sustained especially by social democratic and some Christian democratic values, that citizens should be entitled as far as possible to equal living standards irrespective of where they live. Citizenship has increasingly been given a substantive social and economic content, with the state responsible for more than mere protection of life and limb. Nation-building and consolidation were also seen to imply a commitment to equalization of living standards, especially where there were historic problems of national integration or separatist pressures. Class settlements reached after the war, and the need to incorporate the working class into the political nation, also limited the ability of governments to pursue policies of wage differentials or involuntary mobility. The political weight of poorer regions themselves also counted. In a nationalized and centralized political system, poorer regions are able to use their political weight to compensate for their economic weakness. This, of course, is a variable, depending on the importance of regions to the national governing coalition, their political marginality and their potential for disruption or separatism. More generally, regional policy was a means of securing the consent of poorer regions to the constitutional state order and the government of the day. Socially, it could relieve the burden on the welfare state, promote social integration and prevent marginalization of groups and places.

Governments therefore adopted a series of diversionary policies. The main instruments were: grants and incentives to private investors to locate in development regions; restrictions on investment in booming locations; the diversion of public-sector investments into development regions; public infrastructure investment in advance of need, to create favourable conditions for growth.

For governments, this could be presented as non-zero sum, with advantages for all. Poor regions could gain investment, jobs and increased living standards. Prosperous regions gained from the moderation of inflationary pressures and pressures on infrastructure and housing markets. The national economy gained from additional production, using idle resources and being able to sustain a higher level of aggregate demand without encountering resource constraints or inflationary pressures. Policy was seen as marginal, not affecting mainstream economic policy or putting in question the basic outlines of national demand management. It was seen as essentially short-term since, when economic conditions equalized, active policy would no longer be necessary. A pattern of self-sustaining growth would be established and regions could then be left to look after themselves while contributing to national economic growth. They would cease to be special regions and be reintegrated into the national economy.

Diversionary policy in its early phases was largely depoliticized and technocratic. Initiatives were in the hands of the technical bureaucracy. Gradually, however, it became more sophisticated and interventionist, with other policy measures to accompany diversionary incentives. Rather than focus on blackspots defined by levels of unemployment, policy was addressed to more broadly defined regions. Growth poles were selected within regions at the locations with the best potential for development, rather than just those with the worst problems. Planning frameworks were developed to link diversionary policies to sectoral initiatives and local land use planning. This required a greater institutionalization of policy and attention to the political and administrative mechanisms for its implementation. Local political, administrative and economic elites were increasingly drawn in as partners in the development project. This led to a greater politicization and made the policy area and its funds an object of increasing contention. Central state intervention had in many cases destabilized existing networks of territorial representation and exchange, leading to a crisis of territorial representation and the emergence of new movements of regional protest (Keating, 1988b).

In the 1980s, the traditional model of diversionary policy experienced something of a crisis. One reason was the experience of policy failures, such as the 'cathedrals in the desert', expensive projects which did not link effectively to their local and regional economies, produce spin-off jobs or stimulate a regional multiplier effect. In many cases, regional policy was given inadequate administrative means, consisting of grants and incentives without the necessary co-ordination, monitoring and follow-up. Linkage to sectoral policies and to local land use planning was not always ideal, despite the efforts of states to modernize their local government structure to facilitate this. In some cases, the failure was political, either of will or the result of corruption and patronage. After all, if regions did succeed in achieving self-sustaining growth, they would no longer need regional aid and a powerful instrument of clientelism and patronage would be lost.

More generally, the opening of European and international markets has led to a shift of priorities on the part of national governments. Instead of putting resources into backward regions, they feel increasingly compelled to favour their most dynamic sectors and locations in order to maximize national competitiveness. The increased international mobility of capital makes it more difficult for governments to steer investments, since a firm prevented from investing in its preferred location is able to choose from a variety of European and world sites and no longer feels constrained to go to a development region. EU policies on industrial subsidies and incentives restrict what governments can do, although there are exceptions in the case of approved development areas. Hence governments have moved to sectoral rather than regional aid, guided by national considerations. As the commitment to full employment has been abandoned, social problems, including the management of unemployment, have been separated from mainstream economic management. Social priorities themselves have also been redefined, as has the spatial geography of need. Urban problems have emerged within regions which are, overall, prosperous, so spatial problems have become more complex and policies inconsistent.

THE POLITICS OF REGIONAL POLICY

Early regional policies tended to be undertaken by national governments, pursuing national and partisan goals and acting in a rather centralized fashion. From the 1960s, governments began to involve regions themselves more as they institutionalized the policy. There was a need to involve local collaborators in the design and implementation of national strategy if it was to be effective. There was also a desire to stimulate and tap the energies of dynamic economic elites in the regions, including business leaders, modernizing farmers, trade unionists and professionals – what the French came to call the *forces vives*. By institutionalizing regional policies, it was also hoped to link them more closely to other spatial initiatives including land use planning and social priorities. There were two modes of institutionalizing regions.

The first might be described as neo-corporatist. Regional economic elites are co-opted into advisory and executive institutions and invited to co-operate with the state in the pursuit of regional development strategies. In this way, policy can continue to be depoliticized, the policy community restricted and the agenda kept rather narrow. In France, Italy and the United Kingdom, advisory committees, including business, trade union and local government representatives along with academic and independent members, were established to work with local offices of national government in devising and implementing regional development strategies.

Neo-corporatist institutions at the regional level were not a great success. There were tensions between the state's view of regions and desire to integrate them into national policy priorities, and demands from within regions themselves. There was an ambiguity in the role of private sector and regional actors, expected to provide a distinct regional input to strategy while administering central government policy. The institutions lacked powers and resources of their own, and the central state was not always able to deliver on its own undertakings. So, with the increased politicization of the issue, these institutions have either atrophied or developed into elected regional governments. In Italy, they rapidly developed into the regional governments which had been promised in the postwar constitution but put on ice for 20 years; the special agencies, however, continued in existence for much longer. In France, the process was slower but between 1972 and 1986, elected regions came into being to replace the old CODER. In Britain, the process stalled in the late 1960s and regional institutions atrophied until the last remnants were abolished by the incoming Thatcher government in 1979. In Germany, regional government already existed in the form of the *Länder* but these were brought into the regional policy process from 1970. In Spain, there were technocrats in the Franco regime who wanted an institutionalized regional policy, but such was the paranoia of the regime about Catalan and Basque nationalism that the very word region was almost taboo.

The new institutionalization shifted the basis and context of policy. It had been a largely technical matter, handled by central bureaucratic elites. Local politicians merely had to wait for what the French called the 'manna' to descend on them. Now the process became more politicized as the political and social implications of development and change came to impinge on the work of local governments. Once local and regional interests were brought formally into the process of policy making and implementation, it became apparent that regional preferences and priorities were not always consistent with those of governments.

REGIONALISM FROM BELOW

Regional demands include cultural issues, questions of autonomy, social priorities and differences in emphasis on economic matters. Some territories are historic nationalities with a memory of independent statehood or separatist demands. Others are culturally or linguistically distinct. Diffusionist and assimilationist theories of the 1950s and 1960s tended to argue that these cultural and political differences were evidence of retarded modernization and would disappear in the face of market integration, social assimilation and the uniform state (Shils, 1975; Smelser, 1966; Lipset, 1985). Where assimilation was not possible, there might be separatism, which would equally tend to create integrated nation states (Deutsch, 1966). Elsewhere (Keating, 1988b) I have argued at some length against this view, which tended to reflect the bias of metropolitan scholars, and have insisted that territorial politics is a permanent feature of the modern state. There is no necessary connection between modernization, however that is construed, and the consolidation of a particular nation state. Historic memories, traditions and solidarities can be political instruments used in the pursuit of contemporary objectives.

Another element in bottom-up regionalism is the pressure for democratization and participation in the face of the centralizing state. From the 1960s, there was a revival of interest in minority languages and culture. This included people in traditional sectors and peripheral regions whose way of life was threatened by the advance of the homogeneous market and of the centralizing welfare state. It also included middle-class urban professional elements who had rediscovered traditional languages and cultures.

Finally, there was a series of crises in traditional sectors of industry and agriculture from the 1970s. These were now increasingly seen in spatial terms, as regions had been mobilized by the very policies of the national government and encouraged to view their problems and articulate their demands in regional terms. Coalitions of territorial defence emerged to fight to preserve existing sectors threatened by modernization or European competition. The result was a crisis of territorial representation in several states in the 1970s, as the postwar model of territorial management broke down and policies and institutions for governing regions were increasingly contested.

Three types of regionalist politics then emerged, in rather uneasy alliance with each other and subscribing to a vaguely defined set of slogans to indicate common concerns. First, there was a defensive regionalism, tied to traditional economic sectors and threatened communities, and committed to resisting change. This was a marked feature of rural areas, such as the *arrière-pays* of Languedoc and of declining industrial areas, such as west-central Scotland in the 1970s. Second, there was integrating regionalism which sought to modernize the region with the aim of re-inserting it into the national economy but without making claims for continued regional distinctiveness or cultural promotion. This was evident in north-east England and in some of the urban-based territorial notables of France. Third, there was autonomist regionalism, which sought to construct a distinct path to modernization on a programme which could combine autonomy, cultural promotion and economic modernization. This emerged especially in territories with historic claims to nationality. These are conceptual distinctions. Any given movement has to play on one or more of these elements in order to maximize its appeal. The French Communist Party, once it adopted regionalism, tried all at once. Yet there are basic contradictions in the three approaches at the level of policy and practice and over time, one or other conception tends to dominate. It is in the difficulty of combining these three modes of regionalism that the weakness and decline of many of the regionalist movements of the 1970s can be understood. At the same time, they need to play on the economic, cultural and political dimensions of regionalism, bringing them together into a coherent appeal. This is easier when the movement is at the stage of protest than when it has to shape policies and programmes.

These types of regionalism all existed in relation to the state to which their demands were addressed. From the 1980s, a new type of regionalism has developed, in which the international context is more important and which is marked by competitive growth rather than consensual management. This regionalism is dominated by the economic dimension, and has had important effects in restructuring political relationships.

THE CHANGING CONTEXT: REGIONS IN AN OPEN ECONOMY

The most significant element in the new context for regionalism is provided by globalization. This rather general term refers to trends in the economy, in culture and social relations but, more specifically, to changes in the nature of capitalist production. Capital has become more mobile both within and between countries. This reflects changes in the technology of production, which make it less dependent on natural resources or locational factors. It also reflects changes in capital markets, which allow money to be moved around freely, as well as state policies, which have tended to the abolition of controls on capital movements. At the same time, the rise of the multinational corporation has allowed for rather rapid switches of production between states as well as regions.

Trends to globalization in the economy do not mean, however, that space has ceased to be a factor in economic development or in politics. Local and regional factors are important in economic development and innovation, and it is the combination of factors in particular places which governs the relationship of a territory to the global market and provides the conditions in which capital can be attracted. Attention has also moved to examining the conditions in which indigenous development and entrepreneurship can occur, so lessening the dependence of regions on footloose capital. So the relationship of the region to the market has generated a new series of political issues. With the retreat of the national state from territorial economic management, local and regional governments have attempted to mount their own development strategies. The context for the new regionalism is not merely, as in the past, the nation state; it is the continental, and even global economy.

THE CHANGING CONTEXT: POLITICAL RESTRUCTURING

In the political sphere, there have been two important developments. On the one hand, governments have been decentralizing functions and spending choices (but not always resources) to regional and local governments. Where they have not decentralized to sub-national governments they have done so in favour of the markets. On the other hand, there have developed continental free trade regimes, such as the European Union (EU) and the North American Free Trade Agreement (NAFTA). These changes have impacted on the power of national states to manage their economies. They have also helped change class relationships within states.

There are two contradictory hypotheses on the combined effects of devolution upwards to international regimes and downwards to regional and local governments: that they will serve to weaken the nation state; and that they will strengthen it. They may weaken it by reducing its functional capacity, resources and decision-making autonomy. On the other hand, they may enhance the autonomy and effective power of state elites by offloading the more burdensome and less gratifying tasks, or providing an external support system for small states which might otherwise not be viable. The European Union has allowed national governments to hive off responsibility for agricultural adjustment, restructuring in coal and steel and, more recently, monetary and fiscal rectitude. Critics have charged that both the EU and NAFTA serve to entrench the neo-liberal agenda of deregulation, markets and privatization favoured by existing governing elites, with local and regional communities left to bear the burden of change. In this way, overload is reduced and the problem of governability addressed. Instead of being managed by the central state, territories could be left to look after themselves.

Which of the two hypotheses is substantiated is a matter for empirical research, but certain factors can be identified. In the short term, devolution upwards and downwards may enhance the autonomy and authority of state elites – presumably they would not otherwise engage in the exercise. In the longer term, they may not be able to control the processes they have set in train. New actors and networks may emerge to create a new political game. It is also important to bear in mind the simultaneous functional retreat of the state in the face of the market and the precise form which continental integration is taking. In both North America and Europe, it involves the surrender and not the merely pooling of power by national governments. The proposed European central bank, for example, is to be independent not merely of national political control but of political control altogether.

There are divergent interpretations of the political logic of continental economic integration. Canadian and Mexican opponents of NAFTA insist that economic integration will lead ineluctably to political integration and the loss of national identity. Canadian and some American labour interests insist that it will undermine the capacity of governments not only to steer the economy but also to provide social protection. Supporters of the agreement, including Quebec nationalists, deny this.

The European Union, by contrast, is explicitly intended to link economics and politics, and provide the basis for a new political order. Yet the nature of this new order remains unclear. For some, the Union represents a form of internationalism, a transcending of the nation state. There is little evidence for this point of view. On the contrary, the Union is a regional political-economic system set up precisely to enable Europe to compete more effectively against the rest of the world. Others see the Union as the basis for a new state, the culmination of those integrationist and diffusionist trends which are credited with creating the existing states from their component parts. This interpretation is also questionable. The European nation state as we know it was the product of a specific time and place, in a specific global context. This time and place is not late twentieth century western Europe, subject to all the eroding effects on nation states examined above. Rather, the Union, along with other continental organizations, represents a new form of political order in which authority is dispersed and sovereignty shared. This will be a variegated order of states and regimes with overlapping institutions, responsibilities and memberships. This creates a new type of politics, in which the old simplicities of national political systems are challenged by new modes of representation and exchange. Given the weak institutionalization of NAFTA, this is much less true in that case, though there are still opportunities for sub-national action.

Equally important is the context in which devolution upwards and downwards is taking place - in particular, the increased mobility of capital and the rise of neo-liberal ideas in economics. This has had enormous implications for the relationship between capital and public authority, whether at national, regional or supranational levels, and between capital and labour. States can no longer effectively control capital movements and fear that any limitation on the prerogatives of capital will drive investors into rival countries. National policies have thus switched from a concern with regional balance within the state to the need to promote national competitiveness in global markets and to attract capital by offering the best sites and opportunities.

The state has not faded away, or even retreated. Rather, it has been penetrated by new influences, whether supranational, sub-national or sectoral. Hierarchical control has given way to complex patterns of negotiation. Borders are permeable and frontiers lose their significance as non-state actors can communicate across space. Policy-making is less a matter of authoritative allocation than of negotiation and adjustment among actors within complex networks and policy communities, many of which are global in extent (Mlinar, 1992). The state is no longer the privileged arena in which policy differences are negotiated and resolved, but is merely one of a number of such arenas. It ceases to be a place where the diverse aspects of policy are mediated and integrated. Instead, economy, social integration and culture are discrete fields of policy, with their own communities, networks and rationales. Collective action is still necessary but increasingly escapes the purview of the state, custodian in the past of the 'general interest' (Crozier, 1987). The several domains of action previously accommodated by the nation state have increasingly become divorced. So systems for policy-making are divorced from territorially defined institutions, systems for representation and democratic legitimation. These in turn may no longer correspond to forms of collective identity. As Touraine (1992) notes, the social world is divided into a sphere of international competition in which the state is allied with business or subordinated to the international market; one of consumption, dominated by the individual; and one of defensive identity. This fragmentation of the political and social world provides the context for new forms of politics in which not only substantive issues but the arenas in which they are to be resolved are contested.

Social and political interests seek to conduct politics in arenas and on ground favourable to themselves. Labour is less mobile than capital, confined by national labour markets and regional factors. Because of the vulnerability of regions to capital mobility and disinvestment, especially where one employer accounts for a large proportion of the local labour force, labour movements have increasingly focused on local struggles but have sought to retain the protection of the national state. Labour movements have also clung to the nation state because it is the basis for the welfare system. National solidarity provides the rationale for redistributive policies and the social safety net. National governments are able to mobilize resources for welfare spending on a broad tax base. Labour movements have, as a result of the postwar social settlement, been incorporated into national level politics. All this is threatened by globalization as national governments are tempted to cut back on welfare provision in order to reduce the social overheads of producers. As a result, it is labour which is now among the most stalwart defenders of the nation state and of national protectionism.

Capital, on the other hand, is more internationalized and tends to support free trade and deregulation. It resists anything which might divide markets. This is a historic shift from the late nineteenth and early twentieth centuries when, broadly speaking, capital was national and dependent on the state, and labour tended to favour local action on the one hand and global free trade on the other. Yet to draw the broad conclusion that globalization favours capital and nationalism favours labour, as some have done, would be a gross simplification. On both sides of the industrial class divide there are exceptions. Some sectors of industry are closely tied to the national state and continue to seek and enjoy protection.

Social movements too have chosen their ground, or had it chosen for them. Many social movements have local bases because of the difficulty of organizing at a broader level. An exception might be the environmental movement, which has had some success in organizing at local, regional, national and international levels.

Political parties have also sought to take politics to the level most favourable to their policy priorities and where their support bases are stronger. Parties of the social democratic left have moved away from centralization to support decentralization and regionalism, despite the tensions which this might cause with their base in organized labour (Keating, 1992a). They have increasingly supported European integration as a way of controlling the internationalization of capital. Parties of the right, with their mixture of economic liberalism and social authoritarianism, have generally supported European integration while being wary of regional decentralization.

All of this might seem to presage the end of territorial politics, the dislocation of social and economic processes and a disintegration of space as anything more than a topological category. Yet in some places, a new form of politics has emerged, focused precisely on territory and new relationships between it and social, economic and political change. This is not happening everywhere, which is one reason why talk of a Europe of the regions, or of the cities, is so misleading.

THE NEW POLITICS OF REGIONS: THE COMPETITIVE IMPERATIVE?

There has been a reconfiguration of politics at the regional level around the theme of growth and regional competitiveness. We have moved from a system in which regions could be managed within national politics to one in which they are increasingly competing with each other in an international context. The focus has at the same time moved from diversionary policies to the need to exploit regions' indigenous potentials. In an open economy, they are forced to compete for investment and tax base, a phenomenon also observed at the level of cities (Peterson, 1981). Regions are especially prone to competitive growth politics given their close association with development and planning in the post-war era, and their functional competences, which very often are focused on these matters.

Common effects of growth politics have been observed at both the urban and the regional level (Dunford and Kafkalis, 1992; Kantor, 1995; Logan and Swanstrom, 1990). Studies note that it changes political relationships, and that a focus on economic development tends to increase social inequality, since resources are diverted away from social programmes to those activities which promote growth. Development politics thus can lead to the marginalization of various social groups; or a model can be adopted which integrates them and reconciles development with distributional demands. These groups may be defined by class, gender, race or culture. Competition in the international market place may also weaken local and regional cultures, including minority languages. This can undermine collective identity and thereby social solidarity and cooperation. The search for investment and development at any price can also lead to a neglect of environmental considerations.

The focus on growth and competitive development alters the terms of political debate. Where policy can be defined as 'development', it can be presented as non-zero-sum, representing a higher or general interest since it adds to total output. It thus becomes difficult to criticize. Redistributive policies, on the other hand, appear to be zero-sum. Projects which make reference to development and are presented in terms of the values and rhetoric of the market also carry a special legitimacy, enhancing their appeal to politicians. Development has another political advantage in that the more narrowly policy is defined, the easier in general it is to mobilize resources and measure success. Convention centres and other mega-projects carry an identifiable price tag (although one which inevitably seems to increase in the process of building) and their effects are rather visible. When policy is seen more broadly to include social and cultural aspects, its definition and the measurement of success are much more difficult. So there is a tendency to narrow the political agenda and the definition of development goals.

To say that regional politics is increasingly dominated by the competitive pursuit of growth, however, is less enlightening than might first appear. One difficulty is the elusive nature of development as an objective. Even in strictly economic terms, policy may have multiple objectives, including promotion of employment, enhancement of the tax base, increased productivity, maximizing inward investment, local innovation and entrepreneurship. These may conflict with each other, as do, at least in the short term, increasing employment and raising productivity. When the definition of development is expanded to include social and environmental objectives and the distribution of the fruits of growth, objectives become still more complex. The balance of these objectives will vary from one case to another, according to the composition of the dominant coalition, so that it is not possible simply to examine a series of indicators across different regions and compare performance. Even if it were possible to measure outputs accurately and produce comparative data, we could not attribute these to policy measures without controlling for all other possible causes (Keating, 1995).

Further, it is only at the analytical level that we can separate economic development from other objectives being pursued by social and political actors. These include social integration and redistribution, cultural development and identity, and environmental considerations, indeed all the pressures of 'bottom-up' regionalism already discussed. Any given proposal or development project is likely to involve all four aspects, which is why development is so contested and not subject to a single measure of success.

Despite the rhetoric of competition, development, whether understood in a narrow economic, or a broader sense, also involves co-operation. Businesses compete with each other within the region, but may co-operate to promote the region as a whole. Localities within a region compete with one another, but need to co-operate in promoting common regional interests. One of the secrets of international competitiveness on the part of regions may be an ability to exploit external economies of scale in industrial districts (Harrison, 1992; Ritaine, 1989), and to accumulate social capital in the form of traditions of co-operation and the production of public goods (Putnam, 1993). Social integration may not be a mere costly burden but may be conducive to economic growth. Traditional culture may similarly not be merely a brake on economic success but a resource, giving a region a specific niche in the international market place as well as sustaining social solidarity and encouraging the production of public goods. If they fail to reconcile these needs, regions risk fragmentation and reduction to complete dependence on the market.

We can postulate two models of regional development, a virtuous one and a vicious one. In the virtuous model, there is a successful programme of economic development. Social integration is secured and marginalization avoided. Culture and identity are safeguarded. The environment is conserved. These serve to create social capital and public goods which in turn favour economic growth. In the vicious model, the region is subject to the disintegrating effects of the international market. Growth is narrowly defined and socially divisive. Cultural identity is destroyed or fragmented and the environment neglected, in favour of development of any sort. This in turn reinforces dependency, discourages the formation of social capital and public goods, which in turn adversely affect growth. Whether regions are able successfully to reconcile these needs and to mobilize around projects for development depends on their social construction, institutions and resources, and on patterns of social relations within the regions.

THE CONSTRUCTION OF REGIONS

One way of approaching the new constellation of interests is through the idea of 'meso-corporatism'. This, however, is charged with difficulties. Corporatism itself is a difficult concept to operationalize since, while it focuses on the relationship between government and private actors, it does not in itself contain a theory about the power relationship. Consequently, it can be used to describe anything from the subordination of private actors to the state, to the capture of the state by private actors. Nor does it in itself contain a theory of the state, a critical problem given the transformations which the state itself is undergoing. Applied at the 'meso' level, between the central state and the localities, these difficulties are magnified. It is difficult to know what to describe as the state at this level, since it is a meeting place for various types of state intervention. Nor is it easy to identify the social partners who would have the ability to deliver consent to policy at this level. This, as noted above, was one of the problems which beset the 'neo-corporatist' efforts of the 1960s. Neither local and regional governments nor the decentralized arms of interest groups command the authority to enter into binding arrangements (Anderson, 1992).

Stone (1987, 1989), writing about cities, has noted that the 'urban regime', that is the constellation of public and private actors who make policy, varies from one case to another. The same may be said for the regional level. Another way to get at this is to see the development project in particular places as the outcome of a process of political and economic interaction within development coalitions. A development coalition (Keating, 1993c) is here defined as a place-based inter-class coalition of political, economic and social actors devoted to economic development in a specific location. It may include locally-based and non-local business interests, trade unions, local and national politicians from the locality, regional and local bureaucracies, as well as locally-based national bureaucrats, and neighbourhood and social movements. This is not a theory of regionalism, but merely an analytical framework which allows us to identify the actors and roles in development policy. It recognizes that no agent has the powers and resources to undertake a programme of development itself. Policy is made and formulated within networks; but this otherwise vague concept needs to be given substance by identifying the actors, their interests and their relative power. Development policy is not a given, but depends on the relative weight of these interests and the external environment, with its constraints and opportunities.

The potential actors within a development coalition include private business, trade unions and social movements concerned with distributional or non-material issues. Regional and local governments and agencies of the central state also figure. It is through the interaction of these within a given context that regions are defined and policies framed.

Regions are dependent on private business in two respects. One is the external dependence which arises from the need to attract capital and which may lead regional actors to adopt pro-business stances. In a capitalist system, owners of capital are privileged since they are able to make the claim that their self-interest corresponds to the public good, in investment and growth (Lindblom, 1977); this applies at local and regional level to an increasing extent as regions compete to attract and retain investment. The other is internal dependence, which arises from the ability of business to intervene in the regional political process, through political parties, links with the bureaucracy or special agencies (discussed below). To talk of business as an undifferentiated entity is, of course, an over-simplification. Small and locally-based businesses may have more of a stake in the well-being of the region than large multinationals which can withdraw their capital more easily. Business interests will be favoured to the degree that emphasis is placed upon economic growth and competition. Business also has the advantage of having at least a minimal level of organization and spare resources, allowing it to intervene selectively and provide side-payments to potential opposition groups (Stone, 1989).

Trade unions have varied in their response to development politics. Generally, in western countries, they have lost membership and political influence. As suggested above, they tend to favour settling issues in the national political arena, where they are better integrated. They do not favour dividing the labour market regionally and see inter-regional competition as a means of putting downward pressure on wages. Yet in many cases, they have joined regional development coalitions seeking to promote and defend local and regional employment. Since they do not command vital resources and are weakly organized at the territorial level, they have tended to be junior partners. It might be hypothesized that, where trade unions are actors in the regional development coalition, whether directly or via a social democratic party, policy will be focused more on the needs of employment than simply on capital attraction, and that there will be a stronger social dimension.

Representatives of movements concerned with social and environmental issues have even greater difficulty in asserting their priorities as stress is placed upon competitive growth. This is why they have often tended to defend the national welfare state and national regulation, or to seek stronger supranational regulation. On the other hand, it is at the local and regional levels that many social and environmental issues take concrete form. Yet the altered terms of discourse engendered by the focus on development produces a bias against social spending unless social advocates can frame the development project so as to include these considerations.

Alternatively, they may be reduced to accepting side payments from the development coalition as the price of acquiescence. Cultural issues are similarly difficult to press in the face of competitive pressures. Advocates of cultural spending and policy are thus often forced to tie their demands into the development agenda. Culture as economic development finds a more receptive audience than culture for its own sake.

INSTITUTIONS

Regional institutions are important in defining the issues, in mobilizing resources, in providing differential access, in mediating interests and in implementing policy. Where regional boundaries are broadly drawn, they may better be able to integrate policy sectors and spatial priorities, and to internalize costs and benefits of public policies. Where regions are fragmented into competing jurisdictions, on the other hand, there is a danger of wasteful competition, as localities seek to export costs and capture locally mobile capital. Public choice theorists, stressing the benefits of competition, tend to favour such fragmentation (Parks and Oakerson, 1989; Schneider, 1989). Those concerned with the need for cooperation take the opposite view. Where elected regional governments exist, development is likely to be more politicized. Depending on the structure of regional institutions and such factors as the party and electoral systems, they may be open to a wide variety of influences. Development may thus be defined in broad terms, to include distributional issues, environmental concerns and cultural matters.

The other characteristic institutional form is the special purpose agency. Such agencies may be able to accumulate specialized knowledge and skills, engaging in institutional learning and focusing on one task. This is particularly important in regional development, which is less a matter of administration than of promotion and stimulation of activity. Entrusting regional development to agencies may also be a means of depoliticizing anew the development function, in two senses. First, it may help to remove political manipulation and clientelist practices by placing decisions in the hand of technical experts. Of course, this is not always achieved, since agencies can be captured by patronage machines. Depoliticization in a second sense involves the separation of economic development from social considerations, with agencies devoting themselves single-mindedly to the former. This narrows the political agenda and passes the social costs of change onto other agencies. Agencies are also a means of promoting public-private partnership. Partnership has come to be almost universally valued, but more rarely analyzed as a form of political restructuring which both reshapes the political agenda and shifts the locus of control of public resources. This also favours private-sector assumptions and practices of commercial secrecy, and leads to the abandonment of public-sector principles of universality and equity in favour of selectivity and opportunity.

Central government policies continue to influence the structure of opportunities available to regional development coalitions, and state agencies may be directly involved in regional-level policy. In Britain, for example, selective intervention by central government development agencies with rather modest resources has succeeded in changing priorities and perceptions and inducing local actors to modify their own behaviour in order to capture their share of central resources. So, instead of engaging in comprehensive territorial management as in the past, states can effect change by selective and rather inexpensive forms of intervention in the regional and local policy arena. Similarly, intervention through the European Union structural funds, involving even smaller amounts of money, has encouraged new forms of partnership and mobilization. Indeed, this is an explicit aim of the Union in its structural interventions.

RESOURCES

Policy outcomes are governed by the composition of the development coalition, but also by the availability of resources. These include financial and technical resources, and may be available from regional governments and agencies, the private sector or via the intergovernmental system. In regions which are attractive to the market, private-sector resources may be available. In others, access to national governments or supranational bodies may allow the substitution of intergovernmental for private-sector resources and reduce dependence on private capital. This depends on the availability of such resources, the ability of regional actors to penetrate the intergovernmental system to obtain them and the terms on which they can obtain them. In systems where the central state retains a large degree of autonomy, such as Britain, intergovernmental transfers may be used to restrict regional choice in policy. In states where central government is penetrated by, or dependent on regional and local elites, such as France, intergovernmental transfers may enhance regional autonomy by lessening dependence on the market. A great deal of attention has been given in Europe to the structural funds of the European Union, which have become an object of contention among European, national and regional actors (Marks, 1992). While the sums involved are small, they are seen as giving regions greater autonomy from national government and the market; in practice, they tend to be fairly tightly controlled by national governments.

CIVIL SOCIETY

Just as important as institutions in moulding projects for regional development may be the nature of the regional civil society and its ability to promote consensus on development and distribution, and to regulate competition and co-operation. Indeed, with the retreat of the state, civil society becomes all the more important. This is a complex of social and economic relations integrating the territory while differentiating it from the wider state society. Territorial societies were at one time assumed to belong the *Gemeinschaft* society, founded on personal and kinship relations rather than the market or law, and doomed to disappear with the expansion of the nation state. The international market might be assumed to be even more inimical to traditional forms of community. Yet there also exists a more modern type of territorial identity rooted not in affective forms of community but in structured patterns of co-operation and exchange. This type of territorial community does not require political and social homogeneity but is consistent with a vigorous internal politics (Mabileau *et al.*, 1989). In both the economic and political spheres, it provides a balance of co-operation and competition. A territorial community can thus become a space for social interaction, within which politics has its place. Agnew (1987), calling this simply 'place', distinguishes it from community in the affective, monolithic sense. Place he sees in terms of three elements: locale, the settings in which social relations are constituted; location, the geographical area encompassing the settings for social interaction as defined by social and economic processes operating at a wider scale; and sense of place, the local 'structure of feeling'. Balligand and Maquart (1990) similarly distinguish between *espace*, a purely geographical notion, and *territoire*, which includes the pattern of economic, social and political relations within it. Putnam (1993) shows how, given the right type of civic community, patterns of co-operation can be self-sustaining.

Such a rational form of territorial identity can provide the social cohesion necessary to bridge individual and collective forms of rationality. Reduction of territory to a mere set of exchange relationships (as described in the public choice literature) provides no basis for economic or social exchange other than simultaneous and reciprocal benefit to identifiable beneficiaries, and poses a whole range of collective action problems. At the level of production, a sense of territorial identity and strong networks can overcome external diseconomies and provide collective economies of scale. It can also provide the rationale for the production of public goods, investment in the future and deferred gratification, neither of which occurs spontaneously in a purely individualized market. On the distributional side, a sense of common identity may encourage the attribution of rewards in a manner seen as legitimate. It may also help integrate cultural concerns into the development project. It thus encourages positive-sum outcomes from political and economic interaction.

Co-operation in this manner represents rational self-interest on the part of individuals. Yet the co-operation does not come about because there is a mutual interest in it. Providing the link between individual and collective are institutions and practices which encourage competition or otherwise. These are rooted in historical experience and socialization. The transmission of civic and political traditions over time is well attested (Todd, 1990; Putnam, 1993) though the mechanisms are poorly understood. Internationalization of markets and communication has not eroded place in this sense. On the contrary, the uneven impact of national and global forces in different locations has served to enhance its importance. It is precisely in places that the often conflicting pressures of global economic forces, distributive justice and cultural specificity have to be managed, providing for distinct forms of local politics.

Historic nationalities may be able to provide the social cohesion necessary to project the territory in the new context and prevent social disintegration. After all, these were among the historic tasks of the nation state. So minority nationalism, far from disappearing under the pressures of modernization, may be strengthened as it provides a focus for the new territorial politics. Some territories may thus be able to find their own routes to modernization, using traditional identity as an instrument in this. On the other hand, where minority nationalism is based not on civic identity but on an exclusive and ascriptive idea of group membership, it may merely promote social disintegration.

CONCLUSION

Regionalism has been described from the top down and the bottom up, as state policy and as regional demands. Regions have been a significant political arena in which a variety of interventions occur, but increasingly they can be seen as actors in their own right. To speak of regions as actors, of course, runs the risk of reification, unless we specify how such actors, or systems of action, are constructed. They are constructed in a variety of ways but increasingly have come to be defined by projects for economic development, within a changing economic order. Regions constructed in these ways may be identified at different spatial levels. In some cases, mobilization for development has occurred at the level of cities or city-regions. In others, the process is organized around regional institutions or federal units. In some instances, there are rival development projects by urban and regional elites, with the very definition of region continuing to be politically contested. Development policy can no longer be presented in the technocratic, consensual terms in which national diversionary policies were presented in the 1960s. In some instances, it has become highly politicized. In others, there are continued attempts at depoliticization through special agencies or differentiated access to policy influence; or by a discourse which presents development as something which cannot be contested.

   In the past, regionalism was largely contained within the nation state. Previous crises of territorial management, in the late nineteenth century, and in the 1960s and 1970s, were largely resolved by compromises between state elites and regionalist forces. The new regionalism of the 1990s transcends the nation state, as the old state-region dynamic gives way to a complex set of relationships among regions, states, international regimes and the global market. Some regions have strong institutions and a sense of identity. Others are fragmented territorially or riven by social divisions. The retreat of the state, and its decreasing ability to manage the spatial economy or integrate productive with distributional considerations, raises the importance of regions. Some are better equipped than others to fill the gap. This raises at least two important normative questions. First, it threatens an increase in inequality between regions and within those regions which cannot secure a social consensus. Second, the divorce of policy-making, which has disappeared into complex intergovernmental and public-private networks, from systems of democratic representation and cultural identity, threatens democratic accountability and undermines the basis of social solidarity. Only a few regions and stateless nations may have the ability to manage these consequences, projecting themselves in the international and continental economy while maintaining their social and spatial integrity.

NOTES

1. With all due deference to my fellow-Celts, and my Québécois, Catalan, Gallego and other friends and colleagues, I use the term 'region' here in a generic sense. This is not to deny the nationalist aspirations of the above places, but to place them in a broader, political economy framework.

2

State Traditions, Administrative Reform and Regionalization

JOHN LOUGHLIN and B. GUY PETERS

One of the most common features of public affairs during the 1980s and 1990s has been administrative reform, which differs from simple administrative change and incremental adaptation by being planned, intentional and, sometimes, systematic (Caiden, 1990). Countries that appear to be models of superior economic and political performance – Japan and Singapore are examples – have engaged in significant reform efforts (Krauss and Muramatsu, forthcoming; Quah, 1987) along with those of less commendable records of performance. Even in those countries that have adopted no significant administrative changes possible reforms have been on the political agenda, and political and administrative elites to some degree have had to justify their lack of greater reform activity. One of the most important reform efforts in most western states has been some form of regionalization (Loughlin, 1994). This has happened at the level of the European Union with the enhancement of regional policy since 1985 and the introduction of the principles of partnership and subsidiarity in the Single European Act of 1987 and the Treaty on Political Union signed at Maastricht in 1993. Political regionalization (the granting of decision-making powers to regional governments) has occurred in individual states such as Spain, France, Italy and the Netherlands and is on the political agenda in the UK, with Labour promises to implement devolution to Scotland and Wales and the English regions. Administrative regionalization, largely as a result of pressures from the European Commission in relation to the implementation of Structural Action Funds, has occurred in Ireland, Greece and is being encouraged in Portugal, although none of these countries is keen on developing a political form of regionalization.

Given the ubiquity of administrative reform, and particularly of the regional variant, and the diverse settings in which it has occurred, the obvious question is why. Clearly, the motivations for reform may be very different depending on the concrete conditions of particular countries but also on the period in which reform has occurred. We might distinguish three periods marked by some overall tendencies. First, the period of economic boom which lasted from about the mid-1950s until the oil crisis of 1973 necessitated reforms which were designed to improve the management of expansion. During this period, rational utility techniques of public management were introduced in several Western states to improve effectiveness. This period saw the development of regional policy as an aspect of macro-economic planning and the territorial dimension of welfare state social policy. The second period coincides with the economic recession of the 1970s and early 1980s. While still concerned with management techniques, reformers, often from the New Right school of thought, were now preoccupied with the management of contraction and sought to improve efficiency. The catchphrase of this period was 'rolling back the state'. This also applied to national regional policies which were among the first state interventionist policies to be cut by neo-liberal governments. Finally, the current period, from about the mid-1980s, marked by modest economic recovery, economic global restructuring, and the solution to recurrent economic problems such as inflation, has seen an attempt to rethink the role of the state. There is now a greater willingness than in the previous period to accept state intervention in the society and the economy, but the nature and functions of the 'state' have considerably changed. This period has also witnessed the revival of regional policy, at least in Western Europe, and now at the EU level. Regions have also found a new voice and 'regional studies' have experienced a new lease of life.

The stimuli behind administrative and regional reforms in a variety of countries may be divided into two kinds: global socio-economic and political changes that affect all countries; and individual sets of circumstances peculiar to particular countries. To some extent, the reforms may be merely the current 'fad and fashion' of government (Peters, 1990) or there may be more fundamental reasons motivating the adoption and diffusion of similar innovations in so many settings. What do governments believe they are achieving when they invest in one or another reform initiative? Further, are the reforms as implemented as similar as they appear to be when viewed across countries? It may be that the same nominal reform is being interpreted very differently in different political systems, or at least within different families of political systems, and consequently the evaluation of what constitutes success or failure may also be very different. This is particularly the case with regional reforms given the many ways in which the term 'region' may be understood (Loughlin, 1994).

This chapter attempts to examine reform efforts in light of different national experiences and state traditions. Underlying the analysis is the idea that administrative reform should be understood as yet another example of the importance of social constructionism as a means of understanding the public sector (Best, 1989; Gusfield, 1989). That approach has been used primarily to understand specific policy issues rather than these organizational and procedural issues, but it should also be applied to an understanding of issues arising within the structure of the state itself.

The chapter is also closely akin to the 'new institutionalism' in the social sciences (March and Olsen, 1984, 1989; Ostrom, 1991). More specifically, the assumptions are similar to those of 'historical institutionalism' which argues that there are very long-term and pervasive effects of institutional choices (Ashford, 1986). From this perspective, the values and understandings contained within state structures in different countries will be among the principal influences on how the state and its component parts function. That influence will extend to the success or failure of reforms. Certainly there will be some impacts of formal structures on the outcomes of the reform process, as well as some immediate influences arising from the partisan and ideological composition of governing coalitions and the role of interest groups, but the enduring values and traditions of public institutions are conceptualized as the basic parameters within which these more immediate factors operate.

There appear to be at least two ways in which these values can play a role in administrative reform. One is through defining what reforms are compatible with the political system in question. So, for example, reforms in personnel policy such as 'pay for performance' appear entirely compatible with the values of countries such as the United States that are individualistic and oriented toward personal competition (Bellah, 1986; Girvin, 1989). Reforms of this sort would be less compatible with the institutional values of the public sector of, say, Germany with its greater status orientation (Lohmar, 1978). These values are not, of course, immutable and the long tradition of wage solidarity in the Scandinavian countries appears to have been broken in favour of pay for performance (Laegreid, 1994; Sjolund, 1994).

The other and more subtle influence of values on reform efforts is through the interpretation of the reforms. The same reform can mean very different things in different contexts. Take, for example, the idea of 'Next Steps' or the creation of largely autonomous executive agencies in British government (Jones, G., 1989). As devised by the Thatcher government, this was a means of breaking the power of the traditional ministries and their civil servants and forcing the public sector to be more efficient. The same reform, with the same name (when translated), has been adopted in the Netherlands without much of the anti-statist ideology. Here it is more a means of strengthening the policy formulation role of the ministries by removing some of the day-to-day implementation responsibilities; the idea is to make administration 'smaller but better' (Kam and Haan, 1991). This cross-national difference in motivation and interpretation points rather clearly at the need for a more careful examination of the ideological and conceptual interpretation of administrative reforms, especially when viewed in comparative context.

All too often, administrative reforms have been looked at as virtually context-free and as being homogenous across countries. They have been considered in terms of their managerial implications substantially more than in terms of their relationship to broader cultural, social and political values. Those common omissions in the research on reforms, therefore, have created the need to think more carefully about the broader relationships and to examine the existing knowledge base in light of those relationships. It may be that reforms that are reasonable in one context are not reasonable in the least in others.

There is also a need to examine the nature of the multiple political and cultural environments of reform as well as the economic conditions within which it occurs. If this task can be done successfully, not only would it provide a broader interpretative framework for the reform process, but it also might provide some ideas about contextual factors that may make some reform initiatives successful and other less successful. It is probably too much to hope for a clear set of contingency statements that might be used to advise decision-makers, but even some tendency statements might be a positive contribution to administrative reform.

STATE TRADITIONS

Having made the argument that state traditions and institutional values can play an important role in the interpretation of administrative reforms, including regionalization, we then need to identify what those traditions are and what they entail. As in historical institutionalism (Steinmo, Thelen and Longstreth, 1992) policy choices analysed from this perspective will be 'path dependent'. That is, final outcomes will be heavily dependent upon initial conditions (Krasner, 1988). Further, we will need to identify some aspects of those traditions which may play a role in the adoption and success of reforms. To do this may require lumping together some individual states that would certainly differentiate themselves from one another along many dimensions. That having been said, however, we will be arguing that there are sufficient similarities and common features to use these traditions as categories for analysis. Even then, we will attempt to nuance the interpretations as much as possible to take into account important national differences.

THE FOUR TRADITIONS

We will look at four distinctive state traditions among the developed democracies and at some of the defining characteristics of each (see Loughlin, 1994).[1] By tradition, we mean sets of institutions and cultural practices that constitute a set of expectations about behaviour (Perez-Diaz, 1993). Again, we should note that these are generalities and there are differences within each tradition. Further, the four traditions will not necessarily be different on all dimensions so that there may be sufficient similarities to permit successful transplantation of reforms from one set of countries to another. There may be other factors that permit or prevent successful transplantation, but the existence of common factors will certainly be conducive.

The four major state traditions in Western Europe and North America are as follows:

1. Anglo-Saxon (no state)
2. Germanic (organicist)
3. French (Napoleonic)
4. Scandinavian (mixture of Anglo-Saxon and Germanic)

TABLE 1

STATE TRADITIONS

	Anglo-Saxon	Germanic	French	Scandinavian
Is there a legal basis for the 'state'?	no	yes	yes	yes
State-society relations	pluralistic	organicist	antagonistic	organicist
Form of political organization	limited federalist	integral/ organic federalist	Jacobean, 'one and indivisible'	decentralized unitary
Basis of policy style	incrementalist 'muddling through'	legal corporatist	legal technocratic	consensual
Form of decentralization	'State power' (US); local government (UK)	co-operative federalism	regionalized unitary state	strong local autonomy
Dominant approach to discipline of public administration	political science/sociology	public law	public law	public law (Sweden); organization theory (Norway)
Countries	UK; US; Canada (but not Quebec); Ireland	Germany; Austria; Netherlands; Spain (after 1978); Belgium (after 1988)	France; Italy; Spain (until 1978); Portugal; Quebec; Greece; Belgium (until 1988)	Sweden, Norway, Denmark

Source: Loughlin (1994)

Boxes such as this are inevitably simplifications of complex realities. However, a useful distinction to help in interpreting it is between a dominant logic and a subordinate logic in the organization of social systems. A dominant logic refers to the most important systemic characteristics which influence all other parts of the system. A subordinate logic refers to the characteristics of a sub-system which may or may not challenge this dominant logic. In France, for example, the dominant logic is the tendency towards centralization and uniformity summed up in the phrase 'the one and indivisible Republic' also known as Jacobinism (Hayward, 1983). However, there are subordinate logics competing with this such as various kinds of regionalist and federalist movements. A federalist logic is not compatible with the Jacobin logic in the sense that the Jacobin state cannot at the same time be a federation. However, there can be a compatibility between a Jacobin logic and a regionalist logic providing the latter is not an expression of federalism. Thus, the 1982 Socialist decentralization reforms in France had a strong regionalist element, at least in the legal texts, but were described as a new kind of Jacobinism: the unity and indivisibility of the Republic would be better assured by decentralization and regionalization (Loughlin and Mazey, 1995). The point is that any one state may contain features from another major state tradition. Italy, at the time of unification, was divided between those who advocated a Germanic and those who advocated a French constitutional structure. The Netherlands inherited a Napoleonic state structure based on a centralized state, provinces and municipalities, but the actual administrative culture since the Thorbecke constitution of 1848 is more influenced by the Germanic organicist state. What the box provides are the dominant logics of state traditions applied to a particular state rather than the full complexity which would also include subordinate logics.

The fundamental difference to be noted is between the Anglo-Saxon and the continental European traditions. In the former, the state as such does not exist as a legal entity but rather one speaks of 'government' or 'government departments'. In the latter, by contrast, the State (with a capital letter: l'Etat, lo Stato, el Estado, de Staat, der Staat, etc.) is an overarching entity capable of entering into legal contracts with other moral persons (such as regions, communes, universities). It is true that a weak form of this exists in the Anglo-Saxon tradition in the form of the 'Crown' (states in the

British tradition) or the 'Constitution' (United States). But this is very different from the continental European State.

The Germanic State

One of the most clearly identifiable state patterns is that of countries in the Germanic tradition, including much of continental Europe and perhaps Japan (Dyson, 1980; Gluck, 1985). In this tradition the state is a transcendent entity, with any particular regime and government of the day being but one manifestation of that more permanent but less tangible entity.[2] Furthermore, despite the inevitable division of government into a number of departments and agencies, the authority of the state is not really considered divisible or bargainable. Indeed, many political systems within the Germanic tradition are federal, with a number of governments at several levels each expressing the authority of the state. A citizen in this tradition is not an atomistic individual but rather is a member of an essentially organic society that exists in a more or less formalized relationship to the state. This social reality is perhaps best indicated by the prevalence of corporatist patterns of representation in these systems (Lehmbruch, 1991; Kraemer, 1955).[3] It is further manifested by the characterization of Germany by Katzenstein (1987) as a 'semi-sovereign state', given the inter-penetration of state and society.

The central defining characteristic of the state in this tradition is that it is a *Rechtsstaat*, a legal state. Although the state is invested with exceptional authority and potential power, it remains constrained by its own laws; it is semi-sovereign in this way as well. The law then becomes a more or less tangible manifestation of the state and is the central expression of the authority inherent in that state. The importance of law within this state tradition was apparent during the Third Reich when a totalitarian regime felt compelled to follow the legal niceties when implementing its racial and political edicts (but see Laux, 1986). There is little doubt that the same outcomes could have been achieved by other means, but attaching legitimacy by the use of legal forms apparently was considered important for the success of these policies.

Similarly, in this tradition the servants of the state – civil servants – are in many ways more than simply public employees and are to some degree personifications of the power and centrality of the state. This relationship to state power is in part manifested through the importance of legal training as the qualification for civil servants. It is further manifested in the constitutional status of the civil service and the continuity of its basic forms through several major regime transformations. A final indicator of the central importance of the civil service to the state is the concern manifested about any possibility of radical political activity on their part (Braunthal, 1990). In short, because the state is so central to political life, the servants of the state must also have a very firm moral and legal foundation.

From the point of view of regionalism, the relevant factor in the Germanic state is the prevalence of a federal mode of decentralization. Although it is sometimes argued that federalism was imposed on Germany by the victorious allies following the former's defeat in the Second World War, the roots of German federalism lie deep in the history of the country. To some extent, therefore, contemporary German federalism links up once again with an older tradition following the unusual centralization under the Weimar Republic and Nazi periods of history. However, contemporary German federalism, sometimes called co-operative federalism, has developed unique characteristics particularly in the division of labour between the legislating *Bund* (federal) level of government and the implementing *Land* level of government. Within this division of labour, regional policy was largely the prerogative of the *Landesregierung*, although in co-operation with the *Bundesregierung*.

Although there is a sub-*Land* level of regional government, in contemporary European territorial politics the *Land* is usually classified as the regional level of government. This arrangement has come under some strain as a result of the implementation of European regional policy which has had the effect of transferring some of these regional policy prerogatives to the federal state. This was one of the reasons behind the support for a notion of a 'Europe of the Regions' by the German *Länder* and for their strong support for the setting up of a Committee of the Regions by the Treaty of Maastricht. However, federalism and regionalism sit together uneasily in modern Germany and the relationship between them has not yet been fully worked out. A similar process might begin to happen in the case of Austria which has recently joined the European Union.

Anglo-Saxon Traditions

The state tradition in the United Kingdom, the United States and in Anglo-American derivative systems is in many ways the antithesis of the Germanic tradition. Stillman (1991), for example, describes the United States as a 'stateless society'. That statement is perhaps hyperbolic and may represent the end of the continuum even within this category, but it does express something important about the nature of the state in the Anglo-American systems. Whereas in the Germanic tradition the state and society are in essence conceptualized as a part of one organic entity, they are more separable within the Anglo-American tradition. Indeed, the state most commonly is conceptualized as arising from a contract among members of the society to create that entity and the boundaries between state and society are therefore more distinct.[4] This having been said, that boundary is perhaps more flexible and bargainable than would be the case in most other state arrangements, given that contract rather than natural law serves as its basis. In this tradition, there is a high tolerance of what may be termed 'administrative eccentricity': anomalies such as the separate regimes of the Channel Islands and the Isle of Man which are 'associated' with the United Kingdom; the special status of Scotland and Northern Ireland within the UK; the coexistence of common law and French state traditions dating from the *ancien régime* in Canada (Quebec) and the US (Louisiana). At another level, such anomalies would not be tolerated in a French Napoleonic state.

Just as the position and role of the civil service are central in the Germanic tradition, the absence of such a clearly identified position of this institution is characteristic of the state in the Anglo-American tradition. This position does not mean that the civil service will be irrelevant in government or policy making, as it certainly has been relevant in the United Kingdom and Australia (Campbell and Halligan, 1992). The absence of a clearly defined constitutional role for the civil service is manifested in part through the separation of politics and administration in a good deal of thinking about governing in the Anglo-American tradition. This is most clearly seen in the United States, but there is some strand of this thinking in all the systems. It is in large part for that reason that issues of politicization have been most important in the Anglo-American democracies (Benda and Levine, 1988), and that there has been greater concern about possible bureaucratic dominance of government and public policy (Peters, 1992).

One of the important manifestations of the relative lack of *étatiste* sentiment within the Anglo-American systems is the degree of internal regulation of administrative action. Certainly, all political systems legally restrain the activities of their civil servants, but the general cultural lack of acceptance of the legitimacy of this institution in many Anglo-American systems has been associated with apparently excessive amounts and detail of internal regulation (DiIulio, 1994). Similarly, deregulating the public service has been a common form of reform in these systems (Barzelay, 1992; Skelcher, 1993), although more often motivated by an attempt to make the public sector managed more like a private business rather than a desire to enhance the power of the state and its bureaucracy.

Although most states in this tradition adopted forms of regional policy in the 1960s and 1970s, there have been few attempts to set up regional governments as in the countries of southern Europe and Belgium. In North America and Australia there exist federal systems which do allow a degree of decentralizaiton. However, the nature of Anglo-Saxon federalism is rather different to the brand found in continental Europe, including Germany and Austria. Basically, in the Anglo-Saxon tradition, federalism is a method by which government is limited and the rights of individuals and groups in society are protected against government. In other words, it is a way of preventing the emergence of a State (in the Hegelian or Rousseauesque senses). The possible exception here may be found in Quebec which follows French state traditions. All this means that regional governments, as emanations of the central government, or as creating regional bureaucracies, are foreign to this tradition. However, it will be interesting to watch developments in the United Kingdom where the British Labour Party, now in a strong position to win the general election in 1997, has promised to set up some form of regional government in England alongside a parliament for Scotland and an assembly for Wales. Whatever happens, such bodies will still have no constitutional protection such as exists in Italy, since they may be abolished overnight by an act of the Westminster Parliament.

Napoleonic States

The Napoleonic state is found in France and in several southern European states which developed those patterns during the imposition of French rule in the nineteenth century, or by emulating the example of the French state (Loughlin, 1993).[5] Like the Germanic tradition described above, the authority of the state has been conceptualized as being unitary and indivisible (Hayward, 1983). Indeed, one of the principal justifications for the formation of the state in the particular form in which it has been designed and evolved was to overcome divisions within the civil society and to create a nation. Thus, although France is often regarded as the exemplar of the nation-state, historically at least it is more accurate to describe it as a state-nation. This is also true of many countries in the so-called Third World which emerged from colonialism with state forms but with societies deeply divided along tribal lines. In the French case, nation-building was largely, if not completely, successful while in other countries such as Spain and Belgium, the process basically failed. At most, the integration that was created through this process was artificial, but it did, for a time, effectively paper over the divisions in societies. Such a conceptualization of government would naturally be associated with a highly centralized state structure, using instruments such as prefects (Bernard, 1983) to ensure the uniformity of policy throughout the political system.

Although there are similarities between the Napoleonic and the Germanic conceptions of the state, there are also some interesting contrasts. The most obvious is that, although both traditions have a rather unitary conceptualization of the state and its authority, one approach appears to feel the legal framework emanating from this source of authority is sufficient to guide action by policy-makers. The Germanic tradition therefore permits, or even encourages, federal solutions to the spatial questions of governing. The French approach to governance appears to rely substantially more upon the direct imposition of the authority of the state over its citizens. This choice of authority patterns may reflect assumptions, perhaps justified, of the difficulties of governing a population with a number of significant historical social cleavages and a cultural antipathy (at least historically) to government authority.[6] Those assumptions about society and the need for state authority appear even more fully justified in the cases of Italy and Spain (Furlong, 1994; Perez-Diaz, 1993) and also in Portugal and Greece. Thus, there is a strong contrast in state–society relationships in both traditions: the Germanic manifests a deep inter-penetration of both state and society; the Napoleonic tradition is characterized more by antagonistic relations.

The centralized power position of the state in the Napoleonic tradition is reflected in its role as a central actor in the social and economic development of the country. This role has been most pronounced in France, but can also be observed in the other systems within this tradition. Working within this tradition, the elite formed within the public sector constitutes an all-purpose elite for the entire society (Suleiman, 1978; Kessler, 1986), with frequent movement back and forth between the sectors. Further, the development of the private economy has been influenced by government planning and by the power of publicly owned corporations. This role for the Napoleonic-style elite is in contrast to the Germanic tradition. Although the state in that tradition also has played a major developmental role, it tends to maintain somewhat greater separation between the public and the private sectors.

Another feature of the centralization of the Napoleonic state is manifested in the relative fragility of constitutional regimes. As Hayward (1983) once argued, constitutions have been 'periodical literature' for the French and although the state *per se* has persisted, regimes have changed by relatively dramatic upheavals, rather than by gradual accretion as in most Anglo-American systems.[7] This character was likened by Huntington (1968) as being similar to his praetorian model of political change, in which change is sporadic and revolutionary rather than incremental. This pattern tends to invest too much in one particular set of ideas and rulers to be able to respond effectively to environmental changes.

If a Napoleonic state wishes to decentralize, it tends to follow a regionalized unitary state model. The prime example of this was in Italy which, in its 1948 Constitution, developed a model of two kinds of region: 'special' (the linguistically or geographically distinct areas) and 'ordinary' (the rest). However, the Jacobin state still retained legal and financial control over the regions which have established themselves only slowly (the ordinary regions came into operation only in 1970). The Italian approach was followed by Portugal in its 1974 constitution although only the 'special' regions of the Azores and Madeira Islands have come into operation. The ordinary regions are still dormant. In France, regional bodies have existed since the 1960s but it is only with the decentralization reforms of 1982 that regions have been upgraded and are now equipped with democratically elected regional councils and governments (Loughlin and Mazey, 1995). To some extent, the Italian model has been followed as there now exist four different kinds of regions in France: ordinary regions, the DOM-TOM regions, Corsica which has a *statut particulier*, and Paris (Hintjens *et al.*, 1995). Spain, in its 1978 constitution, was influenced by the Italian model and recognized what amount to 'ordinary' and 'special' ACs (Autonomous Communities) or at least two tracks – a fast and a slow one – to the gaining of full status as an AC. Those on the 'fast track' were the three historic nationalities of the Basque Country, Catalonia and Galicia, and also Andalucia which was recognized as having special needs.

Scandinavian States

The final state tradition in this categorization is perhaps the least homogenous, although there is substantial internal variation in every one. The four major Scandinavian countries have at one time or another been united in a variety of configurations under the Danish or Swedish crowns. That common historical background, however, has evolved into somewhat different governing patterns. For example, the Swedish and Danish systems and their state traditions would appear somewhat similar to the Germanic pattern outlined earlier. The Norwegian state, on the other hand, has not been nearly the strong central source of authority as that of the others; in some ways it has evolved to be more similar to the Anglo-American tradition, with a contractual basis for defining the relationship of the people and their government. The state in Finland appears to fall somewhat beyond the Swedish in terms of the authority of the regime, with a state nominally similar to that of Sweden strengthened to meet the challenges posed by the necessity to maintain its existence in an awkward environment during the second part of the twentieth century.

Although there are marked internal differences, there are also some important common patterns in the Scandinavian states. One of these is that there is a *Rechtsstaat* tradition as was identified in the Germanic tradition. The Norwegian adage that 'with law we shall build our land', going back to the Vikings, clearly indicates that aspect of the tradition. As in the Germanic tradition, law is the most common educational background of civil servants (Lundquist and Stahlberg, 1983) and legal restraints are usually conceptualized as being sufficient to gain compliance of civil servants and political leaders; they are still in many ways *embedsmannsstats* (Seip, 1964).

Thus, public policy can be implemented through highly decentralized organizations without the elaborate degree of internal regulation that might be expected in the Anglo-American tradition. Hiring of civil servants, for example, can be decentralized as in most Germanic countries without the need for the central personnel agencies common within the Anglo-American tradition.

As well as their structural and legal characteristics, the state in the Scandinavian countries tends to be defined substantively more than is true in other systems. In particular, the Scandinavian states are welfare states, with extensive commitments to the social and economic well-being of their populations. This means in turn that even if the state does have some existence that extends beyond any simple contract with its population at one time, it also has extensive responsibilities as well as extensive rights as it deals with those populations. These rights are political as well as social and economic, so that there is a strong participative ethic in the society and government. In particular, those participative rights exist in and for the local governments in the country (SOU, 1992).

The Scandinavian states are characterized as decentralized unitary states where local government has been called upon to play a key role in the politics and policy of an advanced welfare state. However, these states have recognized regional diversity in a number of ways and have permitted the setting up of regional governments with a high degree of autonomy. Examples are the rights accorded to the Swedish-speaking minority in Finland and the statutes of autonomy granted to the Faroe Islands and Greenland. Nevertheless, the regional problem in Sweden and Finland will become more salient since the accession of these two countries to the European Union in 1995. Already there are attempts by the new member states to reshape EU regional policy to their advantage and policy actors are already examining possible regionalization within their territories. This is especially important given the geographical vastness of the countries and the existence of large areas of tundra in the North.

We now turn to a number of reforms which, although not all directly related to regionalization, have been part of the 'fad and fashion' of administrative reform in the 1980s and 1990s, and have important consequences for the territorial dimension of governance.

PRIVATIZATION AND DEREGULATION

The most fundamental form of reform in the public sector has been to remove a function from the public sector entirely, or to eliminate a set of public regulations that have influenced behaviour in a sector of society (Feigenbaum, 1994; Wright, 1994). Thus, the slogan 'rolling back the state' sums up what is perhaps the most striking 'fad and fashion' of reform in the 1980s and 1990s: privatization under various guises and attempts to introduce what is conceived as the discipline and efficiency of private sector conditions into the public sector. All western countries have attempted to introduce such reforms but with widely varying degrees of commitment and 'success' (Wright, 1994). Governments appear to have found it easier to get into areas than to get out of them. Further, once a function is privatized, governments often find that they must begin to regulate the function because of its economic characteristics, for example, a natural monopoly. Thus, if there is any commitment at all to collective choice, as opposed to simple reliance on the market, the state will remain involved in these policy areas.

Even when the state does not choose to privatize a service fully, it may attempt to impose market logic and market discipline on that service. This has been done through the creation of 'internal markets' in the public sector in a number of settings (OECD, 1993). For example, in the National Health Service in the United Kingdom, management has attempted to separate purchasers from providers in order to use price and other aspects of the market as mechanisms to control the behaviour of physicians, hospitals, and other participants in the provision of health care. There are any number of analyses pointing to the artificiality of these arrangements (Bartlett, 1991), but they do represent an innovative approach to the management of a large and potentially unwieldy public service.

What is important from the point of view of regionalism is that this particular set of reforms may spill over into the territorial aspects of the state. This may take a number of forms. First, while national governments adopt a neo-liberal approach and attempt to slim down their activities and expenditure, sub-national governments, within certain constraints, may be able to retain a neo-Keynesian perspective and retain a number of functions abandoned by the national level. Examples of this are the UK where the Thatcherite policies applied to England were adopted in slightly modified forms in Scotland, Wales and Northern Ireland. Similar situations arose in Germany where individual *Länder*, ruled by the SPD, could modify the policies promoted by the centre-right coalition that formed the federal government. Another consequence, which occurred in France, was that the decentralization reforms of 1982, which were based on the principles of democratization, regionalism and administrative streamlining, simply became a means by which the central government divested itself of certain burdensome and financially expensive tasks. The point here is that, where significant sub-national levels of government exist, a complex policy-making system emerges in which policies based on quite different logics (for example, neo-liberalism and neo-Keynesianism) may co-exist, albeit not always peacefully.

EMPOWERMENT

Another aspect of managerialism in the public sector has been the movement to 'empower' workers in public sector organizations (Kernaghan, 1992). Interestingly, the notion of 'empowerment' may have its roots in very different political traditions. On the one hand, it was a common theme of the New Left in the 1960s and 1970s who mounted a critique of the modern state seen as repressive and over-bureaucratic. The alternative to the authoritarian state was a society and political system based more on 'participation', 'self-government' and *'autogestion'*. On the other hand, the libertarian right remained suspicious of any involvement of the state in the affairs of citizens who were seen primarily as individuals governed by self-interest and relating to each other in market-type conditions. Thus, clients of public services should be viewed as customers and those who provided these services were conceived as simply managers who were also driven by self-interest. The New Right's solution was to reduce the number of services provided by the state and to commercialize those that remained.

These positions were a reaction to the tradition of public management based on a hierarchical, Weberian model, with lower-level employees expected to follow the directions of their superiors. This was in part a function of the chain of command flowing out of doctrines of ministerial responsibility. That is, if a minister were to be held responsible for the actions of the public employees in his or her department then there should be some direct linkage between the minister and those employees. Further, the hierarchy has been conceptualized as a means of ensuring that decisions made at the bottom of the organization conform to legal and administrative rules. As well as having important humanistic values that have been well-recognized in management theory, empowering the lower echelons in public organizations also permits governments to reduce the number of middle managers and therefore to reduce the total costs of government.[8]

The concept of empowerment has not been confined to the workers in administrative organizations but also has been extended to include the clients of those organizations. This reform is closely related to the 'customer driven' orientation in policy discussed above, but also has a somewhat more participative orientation than that set of ideas. That is, while the customer approach usually is conceptualized as an external guide for action for the organization, the empowerment approach tends to involve clients directly in the management of the organization. The empowerment of clients, combined with the simultaneous empowerment of lower-echelon workers, may establish the setting for substantial conflicts over which group really has the power over decisions affecting the clients.

DECONCENTRATION AND DECENTRALIZATION

According to Sharpe, there has been a 'general trend toward decentralization' in most western countries since the 1970s, the most important exception being the United Kingdom, which witnessed an increased centralization under Mrs Thatcher (Sharpe, 1980; 1993). However, it is important to distinguish different kinds of decentralization. What Sharpe had in mind was a political decentralization by which political power was transferred from the central government to lower levels of government. This may have taken the form of the creation of regionalized unitary states such as Italy, and France, and in some cases, federalized states such as Germany and Austria. Some regionalized unitary states such as Belgium have become fully-fledged federal states while others such as Spain appear to moving in the same direction (Burgess, 1986). This kind of decentralization differs from administrative deconcentration which involves simply transferring some administrative tasks to lower levels of government but without a corresponding transfer of political decision-making power.

Administrative deconcentration was characteristic of France before the decentralization reforms of 1982 (Mazey, 1986).

The deconcentration option is today best represented by the 'Next Steps' initiative in the United Kingdom (Kemp, 1990), with related changes in other countries such as the Netherlands (Kickert, 1992), Canada (Aucoin, 1988) and New Zealand. Instead of large, conglomerate departments, the emerging picture of government is one of multiple small organizations, each delivering a single service or a limited range of services. These newly created organizations also have been granted a good deal of autonomy and are expected to respond to market considerations when that is possible.

The option of decentralizing decisions to sub-national governments is in some cultural contexts regarded as radical, even more radical than reforms such as Next Steps. Further, given the fiscal pressures that represent a significant part of the background for the spate of administrative reforms during this period, moving decisions away from central control may appear an even more risky undertaking. Local governments may have different political (and fiscal) priorities than does central government and, if given the latitude, may undermine the policy choices of central government. This is perhaps the principal reason why the United Kingdom under Mrs. Thatcher chose to centralize policy determination (Rhodes, 1992) while most other countries were decentralizing rather rapidly.

CONCLUSION

This paper has been an exploration of the relationship between broad state traditions and administrative reform. It focused in particular on the reforms related to regionalization. Four distinct state traditions were identified which formed the historical path trajectory within which reforms take place. This historical context, and in particular the state tradition in which a reform occurs, to a large extent determines the outcome of the reform. In the case of regionalization, it is clear that each tradition will encourage or discourage particular forms of this. The Germanic tradition often takes the form of federalization although in some instances, such as the Netherlands, it might take the form of strong local governments. The French tradition allows regions to be set up, but these are usually under the control of the central state with the possibility of a few exceptions (the 'special' regions). The Anglo-American tradition is more flexible and allows for a much wider diversity of institutional arrangements, ranging from full federalism, as in the United States and Canada, to the peculiar form of centralized unitary state that exists in the UK. The Anglo-American tradition tolerates administrative anomalies such as the peculiar arrangements of Scotland in the UK or of Quebec in Canada. The Scandinavian tradition has a long history of decentralized government in which counties and cities perform important welfare state functions. The county often plays the role of the region in these countries.

There is a great deal of additional research that needs to be done to make a strong case for this important linkage between state traditions and administrative reform outcomes. Most importantly, the characterizations of the state traditions presented here are brief and do not do justice in the subtleties of each, or to the internal variations within each. In particular, it would be useful to differentiate those aspects of the tradition that have a direct impact on administration from those more related to political life in general. Even that differentiation, however, may speak a good deal about the different traditions, with public administration being central to the Germanic and Napoleonic traditions; bureaucracy is more marginal within the other two traditions, especially the Anglo-American.

As well as having relevance for a retrospective understanding of recent reform efforts in the developed democracies, this form of analysis could have relevance for understanding administrative life and administrative change more generally. For example, some of the same state and administrative traditions described here have been imported into, or imposed upon, countries of the Third World and may have an influence on the capacity of those countries to develop economically and politically. For example, although their record is far from perfect, the experience of Latin American countries, whose model of the state is derivative from the Iberian and Napoleonic tradition, appears to be somewhat more supportive of successful development than is true for the other traditions. In part, the patrimonial linkage between state and society within this tradition has done a better job of coping with the problem of making personal and societal needs congruent than has been true in most other settings.

To be able to make more definitive statements will require more precise specification of both the dimensions within state traditions and the characteristics of reforms that would be related to those traditions. What is perhaps the most interesting finding of all in this paper is the number of instances in which reforms successfully have gone against the grain of their state traditions, as we have characterized them here. This may point to the extent to which these traditions may be mutable under international pressures and the diffusion of ideas. The finding may also point to the usual conclusion of papers of this sort – the need to do additional research.

NOTES

1. For an approach that tends to lump together a number of state traditions that are treated as distinctive in this analysis see Silberman (1993).

2. This is not dissimilar to the distinction in Easton's (1965) theoretical writing between 'system' and 'regime'.

3. This remains true, albeit in a somewhat diminished form, even after fiscal problems and ideological shifts have made this form of representation less acceptable in many political systems.

4. The contractual concept is expressed rather clearly by T. Jefferson in the American Declaration of Independence, as well as in any number of other political documents found within this tradition.

5. The support of France for Piedmont as the central actor in the unification of Italy appears to have played a role in the adoption of the French-style state in Italy.

6. We should note here that the choice of state tradition cannot be made independently of the social and political situation within which governance must be exercised. The social system that Napoleon sought to overcome clearly shaped his conception and the interpretations that have ensued within that broad tradition.

7. The pendulum nature of the swings from more authoritarian to participatory conceptions of governing is perhaps indicative of the need for a strong state to restrain the ideological tensions that exist within the system.

8. The Gore Report in the United States, for example, advocates cutting public employment by over 200,000 positions, most of which would be middle-management positions.

3

Regional Policy and European Governance

RICHARD BALME

INTRODUCTION

The European integration process questions territorial politics and policies within the member states in two different ways. First, the economic aspects of integration, with the Single European Act in 1986 and the Single Market in 1993, change the relations of capital and labour and create new types of territorial polarization. Second, the political aspects of integration, with the increased powers of EU institutions and the development of regional policy, exert a more direct influence upon territorial politics within the member states. National governments and bureaucracies face dramatic geo-economic changes amplified or created by the integration process, which often make previous public policies obsolete. They are also constrained in their adaptive strategies by the normative and administrative pressures of new European regulations and policies.

The most striking part of this process may be seen in the regional reforms and the controversies on regional institutions which have appeared on the political agendas in most European countries during the last decade, most notably in France, Italy, Spain and Belgium. Aside from questions of administrative or economic efficiency, the implications of these reforms suggest new forms of 'governance' as a result of the creation of a European polity. Governance is understood here as the capacity of political institutions to articulate, through public policies and democratic representation, conflicting trends within the political process. These contradictions may arise among divergent or conflicting interests, as is generally assumed by behaviourist and functionalist approaches to politics, but also between different temporalities involved with public policy (short-term versus long-term objectives), and between different levels of social organization (micro versus macro-levels of politics). Whereas government refers to sovereignty and political autonomy, governance refers to social mediation and institutional interdependence (Mayntz, 1993, Scharpf, 1993). The emergence of regional issues and the idea of a 'Europe of Regions' as a feature of the political debate suggest new modes of governance to tackle sectoral, temporal or micro–macro contradictions. The generalization of multi-level public policies and of meso-regulations of governmental activities are indicative of a new European mode of governance. The development of this European governance is brought about by European public policies among which the regional policy of the EU can be assumed to have the most direct effects upon regional politics and policies within the member states. To assess the main features of European territorial governance, we therefore analyse the political interdependencies created by the policy-making process and the implementation of EU regional policy. We first consider the cognitive frame justifying this policy, calling for public interventions at the European level and defining its conceptual tools. We then turn to policy-making to show how regional policy has progressively gained in autonomy with regard to the intergovernmental process and how this can be seen as significant for the development of public policy at a supra-national level. Finally, we question the idea of the development of meso-government as a policy style initiated or encourged by the implementation of EU policies, characteristic of a mode of European governance.

THE SYMBOLIC MAKING OF PUBLIC POLICY: MAPPING THE NEED FOR TERRITORIAL GOVERNANCE

The basis on which the regional policy of the EC was founded, and the reason for its development, was to reduce spatial disparities within the Community. Yet the scale of the member states has little significance and statistics supplied by the different national administrations are not easily comparable with one another. It has thus been necessary to devise a common procedure with which to evaluate territorial inequalities, a task taken on by Eurostat, the Statistical Department of the European Community. These disparities have been observed at 'regional' level, a level which lies midway between national and local government levels and which reveals the difficult nature of regional policy.

Considerable problems arise from the classification of regions simply as statistical units – NUTS (nomenclature des unités statistiques). There is no easily definable socio-economic regional entity which can be methodologically isolated according to empirical criteria. It is thus necessary to use existing administrative divisions. It was hoped, or at least suggested, that these socio-economic territorial units would find their own institutional level quite 'naturally', independently of all cultural constraints and national political contexts, but this clearly has not been the case. National data are often not comparable, since each country has its own idiosyncrasies in the production of administrative statistics, with large discrepancies between the countries of northern Europe and those of southern Europe. The 'regional' map thus became no more than an artefact. This is not to say that the expertise produced no data or misrepresented regional economies: the aims of the specialists were precisely to draw up the most reasonable approximations. But this attempt to measure territory also created a representation which concretized as an economic reality (the market on a European scale) a division into territories whose aim was pre-eminently political (the historical development of territorial administration in the member states). In other words, it presented territories that had been created over a period of time and through the constraints of history, culture and politics as if they were areas defined by the fluidity and spontaneity of economic exchange. Paradoxically, the question of the role of institutions in regional development, and thus in the evolution of inter-regional differences, was overshadowed by such a representation, even though the categories themselves were created on an institutional basis.

The 'permanence of the diagnosis' of territorial inequalities established by the Commission's periodical reports progressively changed the spirit of regional policy. According to these documents, in the ten most underdeveloped regions, which are concentrated in Greece and Portugal, the average income per inhabitant is less than a third of the average income of the ten most advanced regions. These inequalities are estimated to be 'at least twice as great as those that exist in the United States' (Commission of the European Communities, 1991: 5).

There is thus a degree of scepticism and disenchantment which today imbues the tone of comments on territorial policies at

European level. Regional policy as an accompaniment to European reconstruction is not challenged. The liberal approach to integration, based on the capacity to encourage spontaneously an improvement in standards of living and to produce more social equity, is being called into question when applied to territory. The opening up of frontiers will not significantly reduce the most flagrant regional inequalities and European programmes seem to be very limited, if not totally powerless, in their ability to curb such trends. In shifting from a reduction in spatial disparities within Europe to their alleviation, regional policy remains legitimate but alters its logic, in that it gives rise to and appeals to a very different type of motivation. It is necessary to stress the normative dimension of such a perspective and note that comparing regions as far apart, economically, in terms of per capita Gross Domestic Product (GDP) as Luxembourg and the Greek islands, to take an extreme example, is doomed to fail.

Actors involved in EU regional policy have aspirations of both a utopian and a normative nature. The idea of convergence does indeed presuppose that a reduction in the gap between standards of living in the regions is both possible and desirable. Its achievement, however, is fraught with difficulties. It involves, or would involve, changes in behaviour, in lifestyles and even in cultures, and would be a long and hazardous process, laden with serious consequences. The gradual awareness of the constraints on such aspirations, however well-founded, is compounded nowadays by the acknowledgement of the permanence and the strengthening of not only the North-South divide, but the East-West divide too. Convergence will have to be polarized, basically around central Europe, with an extension along the Mediterranean coast, popularized by the image of the 'blue banana' and the Mediterranean Arc (Sortia *et al.*, 1986; Brunet 1989). The economic geography of the Union shows clearly that we risk marginalizing rural areas and regions along the Atlantic coast. This fear of territorial fragmentation sometimes takes on a much more political aspect, as with state federalization in Belgium, for example, or as in Italy, with the League movements in the northern regions. It has also been reinforced by disturbances at the international level in eastern Europe since 1989 and the uncertainties that this introduces into strategies for enlargement, and also by difficulties in intergovernmental processes to ratify the Maastricht Treaty. European territory has become an important geo-political issue, perhaps more obviously so today than since the difficult times of the Cold War. EU regional policy is obviously not competent to address all these problems, but it is nevertheless very much affected by such a situation because of the much more crucial and pertinent measures expected of it. Policies which reinforce European integration on a territorial level appear to be economically and politically necessary, yet also more difficult to achieve.

Territory is thus 'highlighted' by scientific and administrative expertise. It is perceived and displayed according to a perspective which defines it as a political issue. We should perhaps question the origin of this principle of territorial equality in the European context. The liberal inspiration behind the movement for European integration in no way imposes such a direction, and would even appear to contradict it. Decisions on regional policy development are based more on political than on economic criteria and are linked more closely to European construction at inter-state level than with concerns that relate strictly to regional economy.

REGIONAL POLICIES AS AN INSTITUTIONAL COMPROMISE

Regional policy has been built up only very gradually as a form of legitimate intervention by European bodies (Lajugie *et al.*, 1985; Mawson *et al.*, 1985; Pascallon, 1990, Keating and Jones, 1995). The latest phase of European regional policy developed through the Structural Funds reforms in 1988, the aim of which was to remedy the relatively wide scattering of Community intervention. After the signing of the Maastricht Treaty, Structural Funds were renewed for the period 1994-1999. The setting up of regulations regarding these funds was included in negotiations for the 'second Delors package' and these were adopted on 20 July 1993 (Commission of the European Communities, 1993). The fund was awarded 141 billion Ecus for this period and largely followed the outline of the 1988 reforms, though with some amendments. The first concerns the question of zoning. The new regulations took into account the post-1989 political context, by classifying the eastern *Länder* and East Berlin under objective 1. The notion of 'under-developed area' was thus extended to areas which were suffering economic problems or difficulties, but which were not necessarily peripheral in the geographical sense of the word. Thus, by extension, other regions, such as the Scottish Highlands in the UK, Hainaut in Belgium and the region of Cantabria in Spain, were listed under the same objective, thus redefining the idea of peripherality or economic under-development. The objectives themselves were subjected to a re-evaluation: the new objective 4 was to carry out tasks assigned to the European Social Fund (ESF) in the Treaty, in particular, to 'facilitate the adaptation of workers to industrial transformations and to changes in systems of production'; objective 5a retained its original aim of adapting agricultural structures linked with agricultural policy reform, but to this was added the task of helping in the modernization and restructuring of the fishing industry, in which it would be supported by the specially created Financial Instrument for Conversion in the Fishing Industry (IFOP). This territorial and functional readjustment in no way interfered with the continuation of the reform programme, especially in relation to funding. The Edinburgh summit provided for 70 per cent of all Structural Funds in 1999 to be allocated to objective 1. Regulations stipulate that for each of the four member states targeted by the new financial instrument for cohesion (Spain, Greece, Ireland and Portugal), the increase in credits should enable them to double their commitments in real terms under objective 1 and the Cohesion Fund between 1992 and 1999. For the regions concerned, this represents a further doubling of European funds, the second since the introduction of the reform in 1988. With regard to procedures, the new regulations were intended to strengthen existing methods by simplifying the development phase and reaffirming the principles of additionality, partnership and evaluation.

The gradual introduction of these new procedures shows up several revealing features in relation to the evolution of public policies at European level. First, the effect of the enlargement of the Community from six to nine, 12 and then 15 countries, coupled with growing economic integration, and in particular the prospect of a single market and monetary union, has led to a clearer statement on EU regional policy. The enlargement of the Union appeared to be a decisive factor in the short term, since regional policy is to a large extent the product of negotiations between member states and between the different EU institutions. For a combination of political and ideological reasons, the governments were, on the whole, not eager to see the emergence of a supranational public field of action. Throughout the history of European integration, integration itself was itself supposed to produce long-term economic convergence among the member states. The indicators originally selected to estimate regional disparities, that is, mainly the per capita GDP or GDP per employed person, reflect a notion of convergence based much more on economic development than on revenue transfer. The political management of territory, however, has been a decisive element in the compromise which allowed the entry of the UK in 1973, Greece in 1981, and Spain and Portugal in 1986. The entry of Austria, Finland and Sweden has also been accompanied by a series of such measures, at least with regard to the northern Scandinavian countries, and the creation of IFOP has to be considered in this perspective too. Over and above these specific goals, regional policy is above all an institutional arena, a place of mutual concessions representing the means rather than the ends of European integration. We may even doubt the specifically regional nature of these interventions, since eligible areas are so concentrated in some borderline cases (Greece, Portugal and Ireland) that intervention is in fact a barely disguised form of national integration policy (Delfaux, 1989). This undoubtedly explains the relative importance of these policies, which accounted in 1994 for one third of the EU budget, second only behind the Common Agricultural Policy, and a long way ahead of energy, industry or environmental protection policies. This aspect of 'compromise' not only defines EU interventions on regional issues, which appear as if they were an imperfect product, the result of an assortment of many influences. It also defines public policy as negotiation, as a bargaining process, a relatively stable and organized transaction founded on an interdependence of resources, yet retaining a certain degree of flexibility enabling it to adapt to fit the goals and the form of the exchanges. From this point of view, public action is a vital factor if political interaction is to endure and, in this case, regional policies contribute to formalizing and institutionalizing the intergovernmental cooperation required for EU construction. We must note that the complex negotiations that govern European integration take regional issues into consideration in the question of enlargement.

The second feature of regional policies is that they are based on a classification which effectively puts labels on regions, labelling as defined by the term used in the sociology of deviancy, producing a form of interactive stigmatization which can have serious political consequences. In setting out the criteria of eligibility for Community policies, a classification of regions is drawn up whereby territories are arranged into an ordered hierarchy through a process of qualification and disqualification. This classification is not static or fixed, but dynamic and constantly evolving. As a result of concentric EU enlargement, the categories which form the basis of regional policy change and thereby modify the relative position of the regions in the European hierarchy. From an economic point of view, the Single European Market has transformed this large area which, until now, was formed by the juxtaposition of territories whose activities were, for the most part, polarized according to national development models. It has now become a more or less integrated whole, on a European scale. In this new perspective, regional issues are now defined according to international rather than simply national competition. The Paris region, for instance, is now in competition with Greater London, the Rhône-Alpes region with Piedmont or Lombardy, south-west France with the whole of southern Europe. Indeed, this economic interdependence is the aim of EU regional policy. The emergence of this new scheme of things, however, has given rise to, and objectivized, various forms of political interdependence: between rich and poor regions, in relation to the transfer of resources; between Community policy 'target' regions which discover that they have a common interest in their relationship with Brussels; between regions which have been disqualified according to European guidelines and feel prompted to challenge the criteria and act to try and change them. After the Community increased its membership to 12, the regions of southern France, for instance, instead of having the status of rich regions among the most disadvantaged of the Community, were classified as poor regions among the better off. They were therefore declassified according to the Commission's eligibility criteria, even though their economic performance had not shown any radical transformation, and with the *Délégation à l'Aménagement du Territoire et à l'Action Régionale* (DATAR), they demanded the creation and the renewal of the Integrated Mediterranean Programmes (IMPs). More recently, the classification of the Avesnes, Douai and Valenciennes districts under objective 1 was claimed by France because they bordered on the Hainaut region in Belgium. Similarly, co-operation among the Atlantic regions exists mainly to obtain EU programmes, to which they feel entitled because of their increasing marginalization, which is ignored by existing measures. Theirs is for the most part a symbolic attempt at self-presentation, the invention of their 'Atlanticity' a label to define and legitimize their inclusion among the applicants for European intervention. The important fact is that these interactions bear witness to a much wider range of relationships between the regions and between regions and EU institutions. Regional policy has broadened the economic interdependence brought about by the opening up of frontiers and has converted it into political interdependence. In this way too, it is an institutional construction.

The third important characteristic of regional policy is its progressive differentiation. The political dynamics of the enlargement of the Community, although crucial in the decision-making process that saw regional policy emerge, do not adequately explain the scale of regional policy development. In other words, its budgetary evolution, especially the repeated doubling of the Structural Funds, has gone far beyond the resource transfers that it represented between member states (Marks, 1992). Community procedures have begun to escape national control, with the suppression of quotas and, as a result, the development of so-called Community Initiative Programmes, which evade the additionality rule. In the 1988 Structural Funds reform and in all the new regulations that followed the Maastricht Treaty, there is clearly a change in philosophy relating to Community regional policy, given some impetus by the Presidency of the Commission which assigned it a less compensatory and a more directly active role in the convergence process. These changes in no way invalidate the predominant vision of the DG XVI (Directorate for Regional Policies), which inclines more towards a 'northern' development concept, based on private initiatives, than on territorial development after the French, Italian or Spanish models, which lean more towards public interventionism (Célimène and Lacour, 1991). There is no doubt that EU policy is increasingly autonomous in relation to the territorial policies of member states. The implications of this are considerable. It must also be stressed that national or regional policies (in the *Länder*, for example) which support companies within the member states often conflict with EU competition policy implemented by the DG IV. National or regional authorities are thus deprived of an important territorial managerial tool, and at the same time are forced by the additionality rule and the uncertain nature of European aid to intervene using different methods. This normalizing process, sanctioned by the application of regulations and Community law and by access to financial support from Brussels, seems to be leading to a modernization and a relative convergence of territorial policies in the member states. It affects, in particular, the form, the definition and the treatment of territorial issues which are no longer considered without reference to Europe.

Lastly, the incremental development of regional policies produces new sectoral and inter-sectoral dynamics. In other words, it groups together, under a territorial label, forms of public action which are still in the preparation stages and whose legitimacy at European level is still in doubt, but which may gradually become differentiated. Hence the European Social Fund (ESF) is listed under regional policy action, whereas objectives 3 and 4 are not subject to a definition of restrictive intervention zones by eligibility criteria. There is reason to believe that this is a social policy in disguise and may at some time in the future unmask itself and dissociate itself still further from regional policy procedures. Moreover, the Cohesion Fund set up at Maastricht has borrowed the attitudes and the organizational skills of regional policies and has applied them in a national arena. Such funds will be taken into account in the additionality evaluation of the implementation of the Structural Funds. This fund finds its justification, however, in the prospect of monetary union, and in this respect, it can be seen as a bridge thrown between regional policy and a possible future macro-economic policy. When territorial questions are at issue, regional policies represent the necessary compromise between member states to enable European construction at international level to take place 'horizontally'. Among themselves, member states and the European institutions define 'vertically' the division of labour in the sphere of public action. This gradual differentiation and its sectoral implications make it a crucial element in the institutional construction of Europe.

MESO-GOVERNMENT AS EUROPEAN GOVERNANCE

We may examine the place of the regions in a political Europe and the effects of their new relationships with the central echelons through an analysis of three trends in regionalization – federalism, or the region as a 'founding' unit; regional culturalism, or the region as 'demander'; planning, or the region as 'recipient' – often combine to produce a specific historical configuration (Mény, 1982 and 1984; Morgan, 1986). These are ideal types, but can be illustrated empirically by concrete cases, in Germany, France and Spain, for example. In each of these cases, the historical dynamics involved, which also represent reasons for action for the parties concerned, are potentially affected by the process of EU construction. The case of France demonstrates how the process affects an essentially functional form of regionalization (Balme and Le Galès, 1993; Balme and Jouve, 1993). Federal or semi-federal systems are also affected as they have the problem of legislative bodies which are distributed over three levels of a hierarchy instead of two and which require a redefinition of relationships between the state and the regions. Lastly, it is clear that when national construction is challenged by separatist movements, these movements can look to the European set-up for a justification of their demands by bypassing the nation state or by subsidiarity, for instance. Thus, all aspects of regionalism and regionalization are potentially affected by Community integration.

While the development of the Union undeniably affects social territorial constructions within each member state, the global effects are more difficult to define. It is possible to envisage a whole range of scenarios: central administrations or governments may become weakened or may be consolidated in their intermediate position between the regions or local authorities and the European bodies. When we observe the situation, however, we see a more complex reality which varies from one country to another, often subject to conflicting trends and where the definitive form is still quite uncertain. Empirical analyses agree on the importance in all countries of central administration in the implementation of Structural Funds. This is because of the Commission's lack of administrative capacity and that of the regions, when these exist. It must be stressed that Greece and Portugal, which are very much concerned in regional policy as they are classified entirely under objective 1, are deprived of effective territorial organization at regional level. There is no 'natural' equivalence between regional policy and regionalization. Central governments and administrations can thus not be considered as marginalized by Community regional policy and indeed they sometimes gain in influence over the regions, as in France, in Spain (Morata, 1991) and, at least until the implementation of the Structural Fund reform, in Germany (Malanczuk, 1985; Gestenlauer, 1985). Policies to reduce regional disparities in the member states are also directed and occasionally created under the influence of Community programmes, though they may also be upheld to only a minimum degree, as in the UK. The 1993 regulations apply the additionality rule in order to stipulate that European commitments cannot fulfil their target of doubling their finances unless the member states concerned maintain their contribution at a level at least equivalent to that contributed for the earlier period. The regions have also extended their prerogatives, since the German *Länder* and, more recently, the Belgian regions are in association with federal bodies to create Community policy. They are, however, in a very different position in relation to Community policies (Keating and Jones, 1995). European funding may always be welcome in periods of recession and when national territorial development policies are withdrawn, but the regions which are most differentiated have more influence in Brussels by virtue of their legal and organizational skills. They are also more aware of constraints imposed by Community legislation and policies which can have more of an effect on local policies when these are more highly developed. Thus the German *Länder* are somewhat reluctant in the face of requirements made by the Commission in relation to their own development policies and the heavy burden being imposed on them (Anderson, 1990). Overall, the effects of Community policies are diverse, as a result of the differences in politico-administrative systems. It is possible to envisage a movement of limited convergence, where regional autonomy is supervised in those areas where it is strongest and reinforced in those areas where it is weakest, thus producing in all cases an improved integration between the centre and the periphery. We should also note that a 'Europe of regions' seems to be taking on a dual aspect: first are those regions which occupy a central place economically and are strongest institutionally and involved in all Community policies (typical of this category are the western *Länder*, Lombardy or Catalonia); second are the peripheral regions (the French overseas regions, Ireland, Greece and Portugal), where the state is still decisive in allowing access to European regional policy. It is the diversity and the polarity of these two issues which now defines the context in which regional institutions can be associated in Community policies.

Comparative analyses also agree on the importance of trans-frontier and inter-regional co-operation and the development of transnational pressure groups to defend regional interests before the Community institutions in Brussels or Strasbourg (Charpentier and Engel, 1992; Goldsmith, 1993; Mazey and Richardson, 1993). We have room here only to mention briefly the rapid expansion in the number of offices opened in Brussels by the regions or by local governments and the creation in 1988, in response to requests by the European Parliament, of the Consultative Council for Regional and Local Authorities, the forerunner of the Committee of the Regions set up by the Maastricht Treaty. In the very hypothetical case of a Europe of regions competing directly with central governments, it is tempting to see in this the forerunner of a European Senate, integrating the regions. Such an eventuality would come up against far too many institutional problems (disparities in the status of the European regions) and political problems (resistance from the Council) for it to be feasible in the short or medium term, but nevertheless, these changing trends are significant. The change in scale of exchanges and economic interdependence means that all the political certainties that were forged in the context of the nation states are now thrown back into question, while the entire territory and public policy networks undergo reorganization (Keating, 1991; Streeck and Schmitter, 1991).

Territories are obviously larger and as a result of this phenomenon, regional and local institutions have had to enter into relationships of competition and exchange which extend beyond the traditional hierarchical forms of public action. Public policy networks now have three important characteristics: they are situated at meso-government level, midway between the central bodies and the strictly local governments and they often place the region or the regional echelon in a key position. They are horizontal: more and more frequently, they are bringing together different local governments, often from a range of different levels, and involving them in co-operation procedures; they are usually joined by socio-economic actors or private enterprise, thus producing networks which contain a mix of interests. Third, they are subject to a process of internationalization, reaching beyond state borders and contributing to the complex and still incomplete system of relationships between actors involved in EU construction and their institutionalization. These networks are thus an important subject of study, not only in order to understand recent developments in local government but also to look at the phenomena of territorial integration and disintegration in the context of the nation-states and lastly to interpret the dynamics of European institutions and the European political system. In its European dimension, territory is now perceived as an area for collective action, competition and co-operation between local institutions, and where vital functional expectations are now invested in the regions. The 'Europe of regions' is a many-faceted and controversial reality. It is currently gripped by the notion of subsidiarity. Debates around this subject are evidence of controversial interaction, through which relationships between member states and Community institutions are being negotiated and as a result of which public action is being redefined in each country, especially in relation to territorial organization. In this respect, meso-government, understood as an institution-making process, may be analysed as one of the main characteristics of a European mode of governance.

4

New Dimensions of Regional Policy in Western Europe

JOHN BACHTLER

INTRODUCTION

Over the past two decades, the approach to regional economic development in Western Europe has become increasingly complex. Once the preserve of national governments alone, regional policies are now operated by a wide range of institutions at regional, national and European levels through a diverse mix of instruments and addressing manifold objectives. Regionalization, policy integration, strategic planning, partnership, networking and evaluation are some of the newer trends being advocated or implemented in recent years.

This chapter reviews the shifting form and substance of European regional policies over the past ten to 15 years. It begins with an account of trends in the regional policies undertaken by national governments within selected Western European countries, followed by a discussion of the growing importance of the regional policy of the European Union (EU) – the Structural Funds. Thereafter, the chapter examines some of the key themes in regional development at the regional level, concluding with some critical comments on the future evolution of regional policy within the EU.

REGIONAL POLICY IN THE MEMBER STATES

During much of the post-war period, since the early 1960s in particular, regional policy has become a permanent feature of the policy landscape of every Western European country. The rationale has been highly varied: the excessive growth of capital cities, prevention of rural-urban migration, maintenance of settlement patterns and associated socio-cultural traditions, promotion of infrastructure in underdeveloped areas, and the reduction of unemployment in areas of industrial decline.

Traditionally, the goals of regional policies were concerned mainly with inter-regional equity, reducing spatial disparities in income, unemployment, levels of public service and educational opportunities. In part this continues to be the case. The regional policies of the Nordic countries, for example, emphasize the importance of balanced regional development, particularly to maintain settlement patterns and associated socio-cultural traditions in the northern parts of Norway, Sweden and Finland. In France, also, the objective of equity remains important; the latest French framework law for regional policy explicitly targets the reduction of geographical disparities in living standards with the objective of ensuring 'equal opportunities' throughout the country. Similarly, in Germany the 'equalization of living and working conditions in all parts of the country' is enshrined in the Basic Law of the Federal Republic.

Over the past ten to 15 years, many Western European countries have reoriented the objectives of their regional policies. Efficiency goals have become paramount, and regional policy is increasingly concerned with optimising the contribution of regional resources to the creation of economic growth by promoting competitiveness and reducing unemployment (Prud'homme, 1994). This applies, in particular, to smaller Western European countries – Austria, Denmark, Netherlands, Switzerland – where the competitiveness of national economies in the international environment has become the primary policy objective.

These shifts reflect the changing global economic context. The internationalization of production, associated with organizational and technological changes, has been characterized by a major rationalization of manufacturing industries, high and nation-wide unemployment and (latterly) widespread insecurity of employment. Geo-political developments (European integration, German unification) present new maps of regional problems and disparities. Few regions or localities have escaped the pressure to restructure, to diversify or to improve competitiveness (Bachtler, 1995a).

The changes in regional policy objectives have also been influenced by trends in political thinking. Since the start of the 1980s, many Western European countries have implemented policies of economic liberalization, deregulation and privatization. The priority given to controlling inflation, associated with public expenditure constraints, has reduced the extent of state intervention, characterized by the elimination or diminution of many subsidy programmes. Large-scale, direct support to enterprises has fallen out of favour; in its place, governments have emphasized improvements to the 'business environment' such as lower taxation and less regulation.

The new economic and political environment has placed great strain on regional policy in many countries, especially in northern member states of the European Union. First, in conditions of high and nation-wide unemployment, at the start of the 1980s and again in the early 1990s, the economic rationale for retaining a redistributive regional policy has sometimes been questioned. In Denmark, for instance, regional aid to enterprises was abolished in 1991, while in the UK, since 1983, the British government has stated the rationale for regional policy to be social rather than economic, concerned with reducing regional imbalances in unemployment in view of the undesirable social consequences. Elsewhere, there have been major cutbacks in expenditure on regional policy in Belgium, Finland, Ireland, the Netherlands and Sweden. (By contrast, in southern Europe, regional policy expenditure has tended to increase, supported by receipts from the European Union.)

Second, regional policy has been applied more selectively. Reductions in expenditure have mainly arisen from a more discretionary application of regional aid to private firms. Major subsidy programmes have been eliminated in most Western European countries over the 20 years, especially those providing large scale capital grants. A particular casualty has been so-called 'automatic' aid – subsidies provided automatically to firms fulfilling specified eligibility conditions. In their place, financial incentives have become increasingly 'discretionary', giving policy administrators more control over the award of regional aid in line with policy objectives and budgets. Regional subsidies have also been focused much more on specific types of sectors and enterprises (for example, new start-ups) and on investment projects that create substantial numbers of jobs. In recent years, they have also been targeted at projects providing some clear added value to the regional economy in terms of technology, product innovation, employment quality or other improvement of regional competitiveness (Bachtler and Michie, 1994; Yuill et al, 1995).

The most visible evidence for the growing selectivity of aid is in the 'spatial coverage' of regional policy. At the start of the 1980s, regional policy was implemented over large parts of Western European countries, in certain cases covering 30 to 40 per cent of the national population of individual countries. Although such widespread coverage is still a feature of some southern European countries, in northern EU states the maps of 'assisted areas' have shrunk considerably – the average population coverage is now less than 25 per cent - and are focused much more on the worst regional problems, usually measured in terms of unemployment rates.

A third trend has been the growing concern with the impact of regional policy. Against a background of public expenditure constraints, greater attention has been given to value-for-money considerations in the design of policy measures (for example, more precise and stringent job creation targets) as well as in the administrative procedures for policy implementation, such as the assessment and monitoring of applications for regional aid and emphasis on the 'clawback' of misspent aid. More resources have also been devoted to policy evaluation and the assessment of the efficiency and effectiveness of regional aid.

In assessing the above trends in regional aid, one further contributory factor should be noted: the influence of the European Commission. Under the competition policy provisions of the Treaty of Rome, the Commission is allocated powers to monitor the provision of state aids and to take action against impediments to free trade and competition. Over the past ten to 15 years, these powers have been exercised increasingly by the Commission's Directorate-General for Competition Policy (DG IV) in the field of regional aid. In its efforts to create a so-called 'level playing field' for competition in the EU, aid ceilings have been established for different regions, new subsidy programmes are rigorously scrutinized, and some countries have been forced to reduce the coverage of their assisted areas or their award rates, to amend the eligibility conditions of certain programmes and to improve the transparency of the aid provided. These actions have contributed significantly to a certain 'homogenization' of regional aid across the northern EU member states: most now only have a high value subsidy programme available as part of regional policy (Bachtler, 1990; Wishlade, 1993).

Although financial subsidies or incentives still form the mainstay of many regional policies, there has been increasing interest in other types of measure, particularly those suitable for improving the 'business environment'. This term encompasses 'hard' factors like physical infrastructure as well as 'soft' factors such as information networks, collectively contributing to the maintenance and enhancement of regional competitiveness and the establishment of a 'creative milieu'. Key features would appear to include amenity (including high-quality health and education services), physical and telecommunications infrastructure, education and training to improve regional strengths in entrepreneurship, management and innovation, and an information and contact-rich environment, especially innovation networks (Bachtler, 1992; Steiner and Sturn, 1992; Prud'homme, 1994).

REGIONAL POLICY OF THE EUROPEAN UNION

While the regional policies of many Western European countries have faced cutbacks over the past decade, the regional policy of the European Union has flourished. In the Treaty of Rome, the founders of the European Communities committed themselves to reducing regional inequalities among the member states, but it was only with the accession of the UK, Ireland and Denmark that a mechanism – the European Regional Development Fund (ERDF) – was established specifically for this purpose. With the rise in unemployment across the EC during the late 1970s and early 1980s, the resources allocated to ERDF and the parallel European Social Fund (ESF) grew significantly, placing pressure on the (then) project-based system for administering expenditure. It was also increasingly recognized that regional policy instruments needed to be co-ordinated more effectively, concentrating resources on regions in greatest need and with the most serious problems of structural adjustment.

The impetus for reform was the accession of Spain and Portugal, at the start of 1986, which considerably widened regional disparities across the Community. Additionally, the ratification of the Single European Act in 1987 required a commitment to the economic and social cohesion of the Community as part of the completion of the Single European Market. In consequence, a major reform of the Community's main regional policy instruments – the Structural Funds (ERDF, ESF and European Agricultural Fund: Guidance Section) – was undertaken in 1988. Structural policy was to be transformed into an instrument with 'real economic impact'; a multi-annual approach for expenditure planning was introduced to assure member states of the stability and predictability of Community support; and structural policy was to be implemented on a 'partnership' basis involving not just the European Commission and member states but also relevant regional authorities. Further, EC regional policy was to be compatible with other relevant Community policies (for example, competition policy, environment policy), and Community measures were to represent 'additional' expenditure to what the member states would otherwise have spent (Bachtler and Michie, 1993).

The reform of the Structural Funds also defined five types of objectives for the Funds:

(1)   development of lagging regions;
(2)   conversion of regions in industrial decline;
(3)   combating long-term unemployment;
(4)   increasing youth employment;
(5a)   adjustment of agricultural structures; and
(5b)   development of rural areas.

The first 'programming period' under which the reform operated lasted from 1989 to 1993. In the interim, the Maastricht Treaty on European Union (EU) upgraded the importance of EU regional policy, establishing economic and social cohesion as one of the 'pillars' of the Community structure. The demands on the Structural Funds also increased as the economic climate worsened, many regions experiencing severe recession conditions and pressure for structural adaptation. A revision to the Structural Funds in 1993 saw additional resources being allocated to EU regional policy, new financial measures (including a Cohesion Fund for the poorest member states) and a new 'objective 6' for sparsely-populated areas in the new Nordic members of the EU (Finland and Sweden) (Bachtler and Michie, 1994).

The impact of these trends in EU regional policy has been profound. First, the regional policy of the European Union has become a very significant area of policy. Second only to agriculture in the EU budget, EU spending on regional policy will exceed ECU 20 billion per year by 1999. In some southern EU member states, it is estimated that the Structural Funds account for three to four per cent of GDP (Commission of the European Communities, 1992; 1995).

Second, the conduct of EU regional policy is reshaping the conduct of regional development in individual member states. This applies, in particular, to the 'cohesion' countries (Greece, Ireland, Portugal, Spain) where the principles and operational procedures of the Structural Funds dominate the economic development effort at national and regional levels. However, it is also evident in other member states. A recent review of regional policy in Germany has widened the scope of national regional policy in order to enable it to co-finance Structural Fund measures more effectively.

This highlights the key distinctions between the 'action areas' of national and EU regional policies. Whereas in several northern EU member states, national regional policies are mainly concerned with promoting productive investment (business development) and infrastructure, Structural Fund operations may encompass not just aid to firms and local infrastructure but also human resource development, urban regeneration and environmental improvement, research, innovation and technology transfer and community development.

Third, the reforms of the Structural Funds have given the European Commission a highly influential role in regional policy-making. The designated areas within which the Structural Funds operate are defined according to EU criteria. In some cases (for example, UK, Germany) these may differ considerably from national assisted areas. Also, the implementation of the Structural Funds requires member states to submit regional plans and programmes for Commission approval. Such plans have to fulfil a complex range of criteria, and they may, following negotiation with the Commission, be subject to extensive changes with respect to priorities and the allocation of expenditure. The Commission also implements its own 'Community Initiatives', designed and implemented to meet EU priorities (Bachtler, 1995b; Bachtler and Michie, 1995).

Not surprisingly, the increased influence of the European Commission in the field of regional policy has been a source of tension with some member state governments. The regional policy priorities of the Commission are not always shared by member state authorities, especially the degree to which the scope of the Structural Funds has been broadened into areas such as human resources, information and advice, education and healthcare. EU regional policy has also been perceived as bureaucratic. Even small regional programmes require detailed planning, appraisal and negotiation and the establishment of special institutional structures and systems for spending and monitoring EU expenditure.

Perhaps the most damaging source of conflict between the European Commission and the member states concerns the interpretation of 'subsidiarity' and the appropriate locus for decisions on regional policy issues. Under EU regional policy, regional authorities have assumed a higher profile in the design and implementation of Structural Fund programmes. In some countries, this reflects the prevailing institutional structure; in Germany, for instance, the *Länder* have the constitutional responsibility for regional economic development. In unitary member states, this is not necessarily the case, and some national governments consider that their authority is being challenged by the Commission's promotion of greater regional participation in economic development. In the UK and France, for example, EU funding is seen by local authorities as providing both resources and the legitimacy for action in areas previously strictly constrained by central government.

This conflict of interests is evident in the case of Community Initiatives. These initiatives provide a means by which the EU can respond to special regional problems, particularly emergency or unforeseen difficulties such as defence closures. However, Community Initiatives frequently originate in lobbying by regional interests such as steel, coal or shipbuilding closure regions. The Commission may thereupon design a Community Initiative and then consult with member states regarding its introduction. At this point, even member states which are seriously opposed to an initiative claim that it is politically difficult, if not impossible, to reject proposed spending in their country. They may then find themselves implementing a measure to which they do not subscribe.

Taking a broader view, some member states find that their regional development approach is, on the one hand, subject to the growing influence of EU regional policy, designed and administered according to EU criteria, while at the same time their domestic regional policies are increasingly constrained by EU competition policy through the state aid controls noted above (Bachtler, 1990).

REGIONAL POLICY IN THE 'REGIONS'

Much of the discussion so far has focused on the national and European levels of government. However, one of the most interesting and universal trends across Western Europe over the past decade has been the regionalization of economic development. National governments are not only sharing responsibility for regional development with the European Commission, they have also seen powers taken on by sub-national authorities and agencies.

As noted above, some (federal) countries have constitutions that allocate legislative and administrative responsibilities for regional development to lower levels of government. This applies in Belgium, where the Walloon and Flemish regions each have their own regional development policies, sometimes implemented under their own regulatory procedures. It is also true of Germany, where the *Länder* have the lead responsibility for regional development but share the co-financing and planning of regional policy with the federal level in a 'joint task'. Similarly, in both Austria and Switzerland, the states develop their own development plans or concepts, co-ordinated and funded jointly with federal government.

These federal arrangements are mostly long-standing. More recent are the initiatives of other countries to regionalize parts of their economic development competencies. To a certain extent, this is reflected in the devolution of powers for regional and industrial development to regional authorities. This is evident in the Netherlands (where there has been a transfer of responsibilities to the provinces), Spain (Autonomous Communities), Sweden and Norway (counties). An alternative approach is the deconcentration of responsibilities, transferring powers to the representatives of central government in the regions, as in Finland or the UK. A common feature of both trends in most countries is that the regionalized responsibilities tend to be restricted to administrative functions – the implementation rather than the design of policy.

The regionalization of central government activities has been accompanied by a further important trend - the growth of regional institutions, established from the 'bottom up' by regional and local authorities to initiate and promote economic development within the region or locality. The majority of regions now have a diverse range of public and quasi-public authorities and agencies engaged in a wide variety of economic and social development functions. An increasing number of such agencies are community-based, voluntary organizations, especially in the social and environmental fields.

Three features characterize the trend towards regionalization. The first is the regional differentiation of economic development strategies. Whereas the 'traditional' model of regional development was one of central government operating standard regional policy measures across all the assisted areas of a country, this model is being replaced or supplemented by region-specific economic development strategies designed and implemented by regional and local organizations to suit local conditions. Although there are often common features – the promotion of inward investment and tourism are standard elements – the more sophisticated approaches are 'grounded' in the particular strengths and weaknesses of individual regions with a tailored mix of interrelated measures.

In some cases, such strategies are built around target sectors or industrial 'clusters' (as advocated by Michael Porter). The Tampere Region in central Finland is typical of many Finnish regions with a regional development strategy being designed around three interlocking sectors – mechanical engineering, IT and healthcare – which are perceived to offer a competitive advantage for the region. Measures for business development, infrastructure, employment and training, and exporting and marketing are specifically oriented towards the needs of these sectors. A similar focus is evident in several Dutch regions, such as Arnhem-Nijmegen or South Limburg (logistics, producer services).

In part, there appears to be a renaissance of 'strategic' thinking and planning in the field of regional development. This has been strongly influenced by EU regional policy, which requires regions to formulate strategies based on an analysis of regional deficits, the definition of regional goals and priorities, and the quantification and appraisal of objectives. However, it is also evident elsewhere. Austrian regions are being offered financial subsidies to adopt a more co-ordinated approach to regional development planning and, in Germany, a recent regional policy review encouraged sub-*Land* levels of government (districts) to take more responsibility for regional development by drafting their own 'regional concepts' that could qualify for state funding.

The German approach is based on an effective initiative pioneered in North-Rhine Westphalia during the late 1980s. Under the *Zukunftsinitiative Montanregionen* (ZIM) (future-oriented initiative for coal-mining regions), financial assistance was provided for sub-regions and localities to initiate development plans or concepts, in particular by involving new 'actors' – such as universities, chambers of commerce, local communities – in the development process. Within an already devolved economic development system, it marked a further decentralization of responsibility with a view to tailoring strategies more closely to local needs (Waniek, 1993).

The second feature of the regionalization process is institutional co-operation. There is increasing evidence that participants in the economic development process are working more closely together – both vertically, between different levels of government, and (more commonly) horizontally, among economic and social development actors within the same region or locality. Experience has shown that, in some cases, it is easier for governmental organizations to work more closely together at the regional level than at central government level where the political and administrative resistance to power-sharing is greater. National governments, as in Finland or the UK, have encouraged this process by locating the regional offices of different government departments in the same building or by creating 'one stop shops'. The UK government has recently taken this process one stage further by 'integrating' the resources and responsibilities of four government departments into single, regional government offices and a Single Regeneration Budget.

A third aspect of regionalization is the growing interest in networking, both internally within a region and externally. It has been argued that a fundamental element of the new model of regional development is the mobilization of regional resources around new regional innovation networks that involve a high degree of vertical and horizontal collaboration among firms and the close involvement of a wide range of public and private organizations specializing in business information, consultancy services and technology transfer. The Italian region of Emilia-Romagna is most often identified as the exemplar of effective formal and informal regional networking, tapping a broad 'collective intelligence' to promote regional innovation (Cooke and Morgan, 1991; Morgan, 1992).

The internationalization of markets, sectors and firms has propelled regional authorities to become more outward looking in their economic development thinking and planning. Links between regions or municipalities are being established on a more sophisticated basis than the early city/region 'twinning' initiatives - to attract inward investment, to promote the acquisition and transfer of technology, to facilitate training and skill enhancement and to support inter-firm linkages between enterprises. Within a more integrated European Union, regions have also found common political and economic purpose, based on their common advantages (for example, the 'Four Motors' – Baden-Württemberg, Lombardy, Rhône-Alpes and Catalonia), shared economic development problems such as peripherality (Atlantic Arc) or industrial conversion (RETI), and their geographic location (Baltic Rim, Alpe-Adria) (Bachtler, Waniek and Michie, 1995).

CONCLUSIONS

The above discussion illustrates that regional development in Europe is in a state of flux, with dynamic processes of change at regional, national and EU levels. There is a widespread, if not universal, pressure for structural adaptation within regions and localities. New forms of regional development are being introduced or revived. Different institutional structures and organizational systems are emerging, and the relationships between levels of government and between 'actors' within regions are changing.

These developments give rise to several questions or issues. The first question is whether the resources available for regional development are adequate for the challenges of economic and social restructuring. Compared to the scale of structural change in many regions, the levels of unemployment and the severity of urban decay and social exclusion, the resources devoted to regional development appear inadequate. In many countries, following anti-inflationary policies and attempting to reduce budget deficits, expenditure on regional policy has been falling since the early 1980s. At EU level, resources for the Structural Funds have increased enormously since 1988, but measured against the extent of regional disparities, they are marginal outside the 'cohesion' countries on which the majority of expenditure is concentrated. Employment data for regional development measures at regional, national and EU levels reveal the limited numbers of jobs (relative to the scale of unemployment) that current policy expenditure is able to generate.

Second, the trend towards regions becoming more self-reliant may have many positive virtues, but there is a danger that regionalization may be seen as a substitute for central government action. Regions have a major role to play in improving their economic development conditions, but central government retains a key role in mobilizing resources, reconciling conflicting interests and preventing competitive outbidding. There is a potentially destructive dimension to the increasing competition among regional authorities for a limited pool of foreign investment whose permanence and economic and social contribution may be questionable (Amin and Tomaney, 1995). In this context, not only does the nation state retain an important function in the regional interest, but there is a growing requirement for international action in areas such as state aid control and foreign investment.

Finally, within Western Europe, the relationship between the EU and nation states in the field of regional policy is in need of review. Depending on the outcome of discussions over EU enlargement at the 1996-97 InterGovernmental Conference, such a review has always been anticipated since the EU appears unlikely to be able to extend its current regional policy to potential new member states in Central and Eastern Europe. Additionally, there are growing concerns among several member states with respect to key aspects of EU regional policy, notably the 'executive' role of the European Commission in the design and implementation of regional development programmes. These concerns will have to be addressed if the key principles of EU regional policy, and the commitment to EU economic and social cohesion, are not to be endangered (Bachtler, 1995a).

5

Regionalism: An International Relations Perspective

BRIAN HOCKING

Approaching regionalism – where this refers to subnational territorially-based social, political and economic phenomena - from what might be termed an 'international relations' perspective prompts several questions. Firstly, why should one engage in such an exercise? After all, is not regionalism, in its various definitions, perceived in terms of domestic rather than international politics? The answer to this, as to similar propositions regarding the analysis of human affairs in an increasingly inter-linked world, is that our traditional disciplinary boundaries no longer accord with the structures and processes which they seek to describe. This is particularly so where the boundaries separating what have been regarded as discrete arenas of political activity are concerned. It is not so much that 'international relations' can provide startling new perspectives on this issue. Rather, its characteristic preoccupations with the nature of the international system and the patterns of interaction within it have become increasingly intermeshed with those on the 'domestic' side of the disciplinary divide and are therefore essential to an understanding of them. If this appears to be evasive, then it reflects the fact that the author has spent much effort in teaching and research arguing that our understanding of political processes require a relaxation of the international-domestic divide (Hocking and Smith, 1990; Hocking 1993).

A second issue relates to ideas and definitions. The term 'region' in the context of international relations has traditionally denoted sub-areas of the international system, such as 'South-East Asia', the 'Middle East', etc. Whereas these traditional designations have not historically implied homogeneity within a region, more recently, they have to some extent overlapped with another expression of 'international' regionalism, that of regional cooperation; for example, the Association of South-East Asian Nations, the Carribbean Community, the Asia-Pacific Co-operation initiative and, of course, the European Union. In the context of the post-Cold War environment, regionalism has come to acquire an added significance in terms of the suggestion that we are witnessing the emergence of a new order based on three economic regions, Europe, North America and the Asia-Pacific region (Garten, 1992; Thurow, 1993).

Such usages are quite clearly distinct from those generally employed by, say, economists, sociologists or political scientists, where the focus is on aspects of sub-state phenomena. Here, of course, we confront one of the essential characteristics marking out the study of international relations, namely its focus on the nation-state, traditionally viewed as a unitary actor within a 'state system' to which it has lent its name. This 'state-centric' view of international relations (to which we shall return) sees nation-states as largely undifferentiated entities whose relationships are mediated by national governments. In this view, internal characteristics of states, such as territorial allocation of power, lie within the 'black box' of national systems and remain, at best, secondary factors to the central concerns of international politics.

But the study of international relations embraces a diversity of approaches and 'state-centrism' finds itself under attack from a number of quarters. The international system is now often portrayed as a 'mixed-actor' system wherein national governments are by no means dominant actors on the international stage. Moreover, their international policies are the product of complex domestic forces. In this context, 'internal' regionalism assumes a significance in understanding how nation-states behave as international actors. Along with other factors, such as the functional distribution of power at the centre (between Congress and the White House in the US, for example), it can help to determine the foreign policy behaviour of national governments, and thereby the level of conflict and cooperation in the international system. A recent example can be found in the pressures directed by Florida on the Clinton Administration as Washington sought to develop a policy response towards events in Haiti.

As a result, considerable interest has developed over recent years regarding the growing international involvement of subnational territorial entities, such as the constituent governments of federal states.[1] This has grown as changes in the global economy have impacted on domestic interests, encouraging them to take an active role in trade promotion, investment attraction and, more recently, in trade policy. Broadly speaking, however, the focus of concern is with what might be described as the 'localization' of international relations in general terms, where this is understood to reflect a growing interaction between localities in all their forms – cities, local government, regions – and their international environment. Bearing this in mind, the aim here is to examine briefly some of these perspectives, with the objective of identifying where the phenomemenon of regionalism fits within them.

THE REALIST PERSPECTIVE

As noted above, one of the most pervasive features of international relations has been its focus on the state as the dominant actor in the international arena. The assumption that states interact with one another through governments which express the 'national interest', that is, that international politics is concerned with the pursuit of power and that the chief issue on the international agenda assumes the form of military security, tends to make the international activities of regions and other localities appear at best an irrelevance to the 'real world' of international politics, or at worst a dangerous aberration. Here, the key assumption is that the central requirement in the conduct of foreign policy is coherence and that this, in turn, demands strong central control. In this sense, foreign policy is assumed to be something qualitatively different from domestic policy, drawing its peculiar requirements in part from its association with the very symbols of statehood. Consequently, any development which challenges this assumption will be regarded with suspicion, not least by policy-makers. Thus, depending on the precise circumstances, the growing international involvement of states/provinces in federal systems has been a phenomenon which central policy-makers have usually regarded as needing to be kept within strict bounds. One reason for this, of course, is that internal coherence is regarded as one of the intangible dimensions of national power; anything that reduces it provides an advantage to actual and potential adversaries.

The emphasis on the importance of coherence extends beyond the requirements of foreign policy, however. At the systemic level, the preservation of order has placed considerable emphasis on the coherence of the state for the maintenance of international legal norms. As Bernier has noted in his study of the implications of federalism for international law, there is an essential incompatibility between the two, underscored by the fact that 'recognition of the division of competence inherent in federal states would have meant a serious encroachment on one of the most basic principles of international law, that of state sovereignty' (Bernier, 1973).

In another sense, regionalism threatens the international order by de-stabilizing it. An obvious example lies in the re-emergence of regionally-based nationalisms and demands for national self-determination in central and eastern Europe which have become an integral part of the emerging post-Cold War order. Elsewhere, regionalism in China, for example, is regarded as a potential threat to stability, especially were this to be reinforced by the regionalization of the military.

LOCALIZATION AND INTERDEPENDENCE

Set against the realist/state centric image of international politics is that which focuses on the effects of economic interdependence, technological change and enhanced communications. These have at once created the opportunity, the desire and the need for localities to adopt an international perspective and for central governments to encourage the controlled involvement of regions in specific areas of external relations. The broad dimensions of what Keohane and Nye term 'complex interdependence' are familiar, and emphasize the decreasing capacity of the state to act as a coherent entity whose collective interests can be represented and expressed by a central authority (Keohane and Nye, 1972; 1988).

On the one hand, the expanding agenda of world politics has resulted in a diversification of the channels through which governments conduct their business, as reflected in the proliferation of international contacts between departments traditionally regarded as 'domestic' elements of the bureaucratic structure. On the other, a broad spectrum of groupings, governmental and non-governmental, interact across national boundaries, thereby producing a complex web of relationships which embraces sub-national actors.

Underpinning these trends are two developments which both reflect and help to explain them: the expanding agenda of foreign policy and the diminishing distinctions between domestic and foreign policy. Not only have economic and technological changes broadened the spectrum of issues on which international politics turns, but traditional distinctions between 'high' and 'low' politics, and the assumption that the former is represented solely by issues relating to military security, appear far removed from reality. Where economic interests are affected by the international environment, and where issues (such as ethnic and human rights matters) stimulate an enhanced interest on the part of domestic groups in influencing events outside and across national boundaries as well as within them, so traditional distinctions between the realms of public policy and foreign policy become hazier. Moreover, issues relating to foreign economic policy usually display the political characteristics of bargaining and compromise more often associated with domestic policy.

These processes have helped to produce the major structural changes which Daniel Bell equates with post-industrialism, for there is an obvious link between economic and political structures. As Greer has noted, in the beginning, foreign policy was the policy of cities (Greer, 1967). The emergence of the nation-state and industrialization witnessed a growing centralization which, in turn, is being reversed with the decline of industrial societies: information societies, like agricultural societies, tend to be decentralized. At one level, therefore, the international economy is becoming increasingly integrated whilst many individual polities are becoming more and more fragmented. In this process, regions and other localities are finding that the traditional national boundaries and their own points of interface with the international system no longer accord.

Change in the international agenda – now associated with the post-Cold War environment but in fact often debated long before the apparent demise of bipolarity – has helped to reinforce such developments. From a predominant concern with East-West relations in the early post-war era, new threats in the shape of inflation and unemployment were emerging in the late 1960s and the 1970s. While the 'high politics' of the Cold War agenda had reinforced the perception of foreign relations as the responsibility of central government, the international realities of the 1970s seemed to cast doubt on the possibility and wisdom of centrally-contrived solutions (Brown, 1988). The politics of scarcity, epitomized in the energy crisis which dominated the 1970s, were part of a new scenario in which both the impact of international events on domestic interests and the incapacity of national governments to respond to them were emphasized.

Change in the security agenda also affected the spatial context in which 'new' modes of security could be achieved. Alongside a proliferation of political actors mobilized by events in the energy sector, regions, whether as producers or conservers of energy, were impelled to take a close interest in this vital policy sector, 'creating new energy councils, communities and task forces to deal with energy issues and to coordinate policy' (Hughes, 1985). Just as national governments became increasingly engaged in 'resources diplomacy', so did sub-national levels of government, creating situations in which external and internal political factors became more closely entwined. This was to extend beyond the energy sector to other areas, notably food, as 'food power' and 'food security' became prime concerns with the dramatic changes in food markets seen in the 1970s and 1980s (Cooper, 1986).

As manifestations of growing sub-national concern with the international environment increased, its consequences became more marked. Elazar has suggested that the growth of scarcity was instrumental in reinforcing the role of sub-national governments as polities. In the case of the USA, Reagan's 'new federalism' enhanced the standing of the states by reinforcing externally-generated scarcity with its own internally-generated scarcities which demanded policy responses at the state level (Elazar, 1986). Significantly, policy vacuums at the federal level were often as much reflections of international as domestic events. Apart from the need to establish footholds in overseas markets and to attract foreign investment, state governments were required to respond to the problems posed by oil prices and petrol shortages and, in another area, the lack of a federal policy to deal with growing numbers of South-East Asian refugees.

The consequences of these developments, however, were more complex than a mere strengthening of the role of regions and their representative political structures, such as the constituent units in federal systems. First, they helped to reinforce long-standing differences of interest towards foreign economic policy. On the one hand, differences between resource-owning regions such as Alberta in Canada, and resource consumers (such as Ontario) reinforced more traditional, but no less significant differences between those regions favouring free trade and those favouring protection. Central government responses – for example, those of the Trudeau government in the energy area – often served to reinforce inter-regional differences as well as to enhance tensions between the national government and those non-central governments who believed that their interests were being sacrificed to the benefit of other regions (Doern and Toner, 1985; Granatstein and Bothwell, 1990).

REGIONS AS INTERNATIONAL ACTORS

Within the context of a pluralistic or 'mixed actor' international system central to the interdependence perspective, there is a need to appreciate the particular qualities of actors in terms which complement the traditional attributes of states: sovereignty, territory and population. In the case of regions and their political structures, this presents obvious difficulties, firstly because of their sheer variety in terms of a number of significant criteria. Thus, the degree and nature of decentralization within the political system, the pattern of centre-region linkages, and the resources that regional authorities are able to deploy in the pursuit of their policy objectives will each help to determine the character of the region as an international actor. Of obvious significance as a determinant of a region's international involvement are the linkages that it has with the international system and here, a major variable is clearly geography. [1]

Where territorial proximity encourages the development of transnational and transgovernmental links between regional authorities in neighbouring states, as in North America and in areas of Europe, then international involvement will be enhanced. Hence, the image conjured by the prime minister of Baden-Württemberg of a 'Europe of Regions', as represented by the relationships between his own region and those of Rhone-Alpes, Lombardy and Catalonia, the so-called 'four motors of Europe' (Goodheart, 1991). Another example is to be found in the Regio Basiliensis where Basle, isolated from the rest of Switzerland by the Jura mountains, shares boundaries in the Rhine valley with Germany and France, endowing it with particular concerns regarding Swiss policy towards European economic integration (*Financial Times*, 1991).

However, territorial contiguity of itself may not lead to cross border regional activity. Despite the trans-border concerns of certain Austrian and (formerly West) German Länder bordering on states of the former Soviet bloc, such matters as environmental pollution had necessarily to be pursued through traditional diplomatic channels because of the unwillingness of the authorities in these states to allow issues to be managed at a lower level. This, of course, contrasts with the intense cross-border links between US states and Canadian provinces.

A second problem in categorizing regions as international actors lies in the fact that they are complex actors which do not fit easily into the accepted taxonomies of international relations literature. For example, as Elazar suggests, some regions – especially in federal systems such as Canada and the US – are 'polities' in the sense that they are more than mere sub-divisions of central government. They may be political arenas in their own right, possessing decision-making capacities certainly, but having in addition a sense of collective identity related to a territorial area which provides them with qualities attaching to sovereign states. And yet, somewhat paradoxically, they are also able to capitalize on what Rosenau sees as the inherent strengths of 'sovereignty-free' actors because they do not have the responsibilities of sovereign states (Rosenau, 1988). This places them in quite a different category from that usually conveyed by the term 'transnational' actor. Rather, they are political settings within which regional interests develop and pursue their goals at various levels of political activity, often in co-operation with agencies in both national and sub-national tiers of government.

Nor does the term 'transgovernmentalism' – where this is taken to denote international linkages between agencies of central government – serve to describe accurately regional international activities. Quite clearly, non-central government departments do interact with other bureaucratic agencies at international, national and subnational levels; but they can do so as representatives of interests quite distinct from, and in opposition to those of central government.

This underscores the fact that regional authorities have at their disposal a range of strategies through which they can pursue their own concerns, and those of their domestic constituencies, within the international system. Adapting Keating's typology of channels of influence available to European regional interests and governments in their dealings with the European Union, we can see that regions can pursue their international interests in two basic ways (Keating, 1985): by exerting influence on national governments to project their interests at the international level, and by using their own resources to act directly on the international stage.

Similarly, regionally-based domestic interests have at their disposal several routes for influencing external policy, some of which may involve regional political structures:

- through national governments via regional agencies;
- directly through national governments;
- directly through regional agencies;
- directly to the international system without any intermediaries.

From this it can be seen that regions can be both 'primary' international actors, pursuing their own and their clients' interests by direct international action and 'mediating' actors, using national routes to achieve their aims. The availability of these routes to international activity, the patterns of relationships between non-central and national political arenas and domestic interests in their various forms means that regional authorities are 'hybrid' actors, possessing some of the qualities associated with nation-states as well as non-state actors. In this sense, they transcend this traditional distinction common to international relations analysis.

LOCALITIES IN A 'BORDERLESS WORLD'

Closely linked to the interdependence arguments are those which focus on the effects of the globalization of the international economy on regions and localities more generally. Taking a general overview, the perspective offered here is one in which the forces of economic globalization help to redefine the relationship between localities and their national settings. For example, the internationalization of the US economy has had the effect of alerting regions to the effects of international trends on regional economies and to stimulate inter-regional trade promotion and foreign investment competition. Whilst there is now a marked tendency for state governments to cooperate on a regional basis in the area of trade promotion, attempts to persuade foreign firms to locate in a particular state have generated battles as state governments seek to outbid each other in offering incentives (Glickman and Woodward, 1988). Robert Reich, in a frequently-cited example, has pointed to the success enjoyed by the US forklift truck manufacturer, Hyster, following its announcement to the five states and four countries in which it operated that some plants were to be closed. This threat produced $72.5 million in aid from the various jurisdictions (Reich, 199).

Furthermore, conflicts of economic interests both between and within regions are exacerbated, thereby creating additional pressures on national trade policy. West Virginia offers one such example. Here, the trade issue is central to the state's future but its economy is so structured that conflicting messages emerge from its representatives. On the one hand, West Virginia depends to a considerable exent on exports: 20 per cent of its output is exported compared to the 12 per cent national average. At the same time, however, it has experienced heavy job losses in the steel, glass and petrochemical industries as a result of foreign competition. Not surprisingly then, there has been a divided response towards US foreign trade policy from state politicians, with some advocating protectionist measures whilst others argue that enhanced competitiveness is the solution to growing import penetration and the trade imbalance.

This is part of a broader change represented by the emergence of what is seen as a new geopolitics underpinned by geoeconomic forces (Cohen, 1994). Noting the relationship between developments in the global and national economies, Ohmae has recently refined his 'borderless world' thesis to embrace the concept of what he terms 'region-states' whose essential characteristic is that their 'primary linkages ... tend to be with the global economy and not with their host nations' (Ohmae, 1993). Thus region-states are seen as 'natural economic zones' which may be located within national borders (Catalonia or northern Italy) or across national boundaries, for example Hong Kong and southern China or the 'growth triangle' comprising Singapore and adjacent Indonesian islands. But they perform a particular function which is of growing significance in the post-Cold War world of international regionalization, namely as points of access to centres of economic activity.

The significance of this role reflects the changing strategies of international business faced with the challenge of operating in the global economy. Increasingly, it is recognized that the logic of access to the global marketplace requires the integration of global and local perspectives. Thus Kapstein argues that rather than 'establishing transnational structures with global ownership, global employment and global products', large corporations are becoming increasingly sensitive to their home bases (Kapstein, 1991-92). The argument is sustained by Michael Porter's thesis that leading firms have stable ties with specific regions which offer them an environment from which they can develop global strategies:

> Internationally successful industries and industry clusters frequently concentrate in a city or region, and the bases for advantage are often intensely local ... While the national government has a role in upgrading industry, the role of state and local governments is potentially as great or greater (Porter, 1990).

In terms of gaining market access, Ohmae has pointed to the advantages experienced by Nestle and Proctor and Gamble in penetrating the Japanese market through the Kansai region rather than Tokyo, where competition is far more intense. In addition, the growth of economic groupings such as NAFTA, or their strengthening, as in the case of the EU's Single Market programme, is likely to enhance the significance of such access regions or cities. In the case of the latter, Kresl has noted the effects of the lowering of national borders in Europe on the role of cities and regions, and the growth of competitiveness between them as they redefine their relationships in the European and global, rather than the national, economic space (Kresl, 1992). Hence, cities such as Amsterdam and Lyon become important 'gateway' cities within the global economy and develop appropriate strategies in pursuit of such roles. Such a redefinition of roles, of course, may come about through developments within the framework of the 'traditional' military-security agenda. The Greek government, for example, has identified a potentially significant role for Thessaloniki in northern

Greece as a hub for trade and communications as the war in the former Yugoslavia has deprived Serbia of its Adriatic ports (Hope, 1992).

The consequences of such developments have been variously regarded. At one extreme, regionalism has been seen as involving the creation of new political entities which are detaching themselves from national jurisdictions. In this vein, Garreau's 'Nine Nations of North America' argues that north-south regional forces are creating nine distinct regions cutting across the boundaries of Canada, the US and Mexico (Garreau, 1981). To other students of cross-boundary regionalism, however, its significance is by no means clear. One study of the linkages between British Columbia and Washington state concludes that the picture they present is 'not exciting nor even terribly interesting' (Rutan, 1988). Similarly, an examination of Quebec-New York and Quebec-New England relations suggests that neither has entailed even the hint of the development of supranational loyalties to the transborder region (Lubin, 1988).

Rather than 'detachment' from the national setting, the impact of global economic forces is more likely to involve the 'relocation' of a region within its national and international space. Again, this can be seen in the North American context following the Canada-US Free Trade Agreement and the North American Free Trade Agreement (NAFTA). The gradual integration of the Canadian regions into the global and North American economy, suggests Simeon, has both redefined the relations between the regions and between region and centre (Simeon, 1991). The result is that north-south linkages are weaker; Ontario auto workers have less interest in the welfare of British Columbia forestry workers because their primary markets lie elsewhere. Moreover, the economic underpinnings of the 'federal bargain' look less relevant than once they did. Similarly, in the negotiations leading up to the signing of NAFTA, it was clear that the US states contiguous to the Mexican border had a clear interest in the successful outcome of the negotiations.

Whatever the precise relationship between the region and the central government, the impact of relocation is likely to create tensions, partly due to fears that the national government is losing control and partly because local economic policies may no longer fit with the economic frame of reference of the centre or its political concerns. The latter, as Ohmae notes, may lead governments towards policies of control over regional initiatives adopted in the name of protectionism, whilst the global economic orientation of a region may impel it in quite a different direction. The situation, of course, is not the zero-sum game that this image suggests. Kincaid has pointed out that regional entities and their peoples have dual interests – as consumers and as citizens. Consumerism leads towards the global environment in pursuit of economic development; citizenship tends towards the national framework in which the region is located (Kincaid, 1993). The precise implications of regional relocation will depend to a considerable extent on how these twin forces interact with one another.

REGIONALIZATION AND THE POLICY PROCESSES

As indicated in what has gone before, perspectives on the impact of regions and localities on the processes through which policies with a pronounced international dimension develop will be governed by judgements as to their significance and legitimacy. However, it is hard to deny the fact that the forces outlined above have modified considerably the way that foreign economic policy is conducted. One major factor here is to be found in the desire of localities to gain a voice in the shaping of such policy. The non-central governments in federal systems, for example, have been anxious to promote their regional economic interests in the context of the Tokyo Round and Uruguay Round of the GATT negotiations (Hocking, 1993). But additionally, as the trade agenda has moved beyond a primary focus on tariff barriers and towards non-tariff barriers, such as public procurement, so the concerns of regional economies and their representatives are alerted (Weiler, 1994). Furthermore, national negotiators have realized that this interest is essential if progress on trade negotiations is to be made. In this sense, the problem may be more one of encouraging an informed involvement of regions in such negotiations rather than excluding them.

There is, however, a more general issue here that touches on the manageability of government and the demands and expectations generated within political systems. This is reinforced by the enhanced intermeshing of the foreign and domestic components of public policy identified above. Thus, the growing international involvement of localities reflects the fact that national governments find it increasingly impossible to serve community interests from a single centre of power. Frequently, complex problems simply do not respond to master-plans devised at the centre; attention has to be paid to the specific needs generated by local conditions and interests. Large central bureaucratic structures often lack the knowledge and flexibility to do this.

While responding to the problem by decentralization may resolve specific issues, it is likely to reinforce demands for more autonomy and greater freedom for local jurisdictions to operate internationally, where this is perceived to be necessary. This linkage between central government ineffectiveness and local international involvement has been well-summarized by Seyom Brown:

> In some countries where the national government is ineffective in dealing with the concerns of subnational communities and especially where such communities are concentrated in particular provinces or localities, provincial or local governments have been asserting themselves, not only as agencies of advocacy for the cultural and human rights of the aggrieved communities, but increasingly as their economic agents in the global market place, negotiating trade and investment arrangements with similar subunits of government in other countries (Brown, 1988).

On the more specific, foreign policy level, confidence in central government management has also declined. In his survey of local foreign policies in the USA, Shuman points to growing disenchantment with the Reagan administration's policies on arms control in Central America and towards South Africa as major factors in the development of what he terms 'citizen diplomacy' in the 1980s. Given the perceived requirements for the conduct of foreign policy – coherence, continuity and bipartisanship – this is not infrequently regarded as a particularly serious dimension of the diminution of control exercised by national governments. Yet it can also be perceived as another indication of the growing intricacy of the processes by which public policy is managed. 'The last thing an overworked, underfunded executive branch needs is direct micromanagement of thousands of local investment, cultural exchange and border coordination activities.' (Shuman, 1986–87).

BEYOND FOREIGN ECONOMIC POLICY

It is the development of complex policy environments in which domestic and international political arenas are increasingly interlinked that have made traditional notions regarding the nature of foreign economic policy appear far less sustainable. Increasingly, the conduct of public policy involves not the predominance of any one political arena, but a frequently bewildering network of linkages between those arenas through which actors relate to each other in a variety of ways. In other words, policy-makers are required to operate increasingly in a 'multi-level' political environment spanning subnational, national and international arenas, where the achievement of goals at one level of political activity demands an ability to operate in the others.

As a result, strategies for accomplishing external policy goals demand that national negotiators engage in international and domestic diplomacy simultaneously, pursuing a 'multi-layered' diplomacy as they seek to balance domestic – including regional – interests with pressures from the international environment (Putnam, 1988). Because the outcomes of such negotiations will depend on the degree to which negotiators in one country are aware of the social, economic and political forces determining the stance of other governments, the significance of regional structures and interests is enhanced. This can be seen in various international economic negotiations, including those connected with the shaping of the European Union's Single Market Programme (SMP) (Hocking and Smith, 1994). The demands for creative responses to the challenges presented to outsider governments by the SMP have resulted in the development of diplomatic strategies which bring together a variety of actors in differing locations. As roles and relationships are redefined in consequence, so are notions regarding the fundamental nature of foreign policy and how it is managed. In particular, attention is likely to turn to the establishment of 'linkage mechanisms' between the centre and regions, enabling each to gain access to the resources of the other (Hocking, 1993: 175-81).

FOREIGN POLICY LOCALIZATION: COUNTERING 'STATE IDEOLOGY'

For a number of writers, the significance of the growth of foreign policy localization lies in the challenge it poses to traditional conceptions of international relations, particularly state-centric assumptions outlined above. In arguing the need to counter what is often referred to as 'state ideology', various writers, approaching the problem from differing perspectives, regard political activity within subnational arenas as a way of transcending the dominance of the nation-state.

One dimension of this approach is stimulated by the impact of social activism focusing on issues which span the domestic and international arenas, including global poverty (particularly famine), disarmament (especially nuclear disarmament), human rights and environmental pollution. A range of issue-specific groupings have arisen around these problems. At the same time, broader social movements (such as the women's movement) have increasingly focused their attention on international concerns. One of the most prolific writers in this vein, Chadwick Alger, has pointed to the growing number of people (albeit a small minority of national populations) who 'think globally and act locally', a slogan which has two linked dimensions. On the one hand, there is the belief that national foreign policies can be affected by dealing with the local dimension of global issues – creating local nuclear-free zones is one example. On the other, the emphasis rests on direct action, employing resources under the control of a local or regional authority, for example, in pursuit of a stated goal. Many such authorities divested themselves of shares in companies with South African interests. In other words, localization as activism is directed towards affecting policy both at home and abroad, and rests on the perception that people 'are growing in their comprehension of how the foreign policy of states affect their local community and are attempting to mobilize local action in response to those policies' (Alger, 1988).

Decentralization encourages individual involvement in international issues, whilst the pressures that stem from individual demands produce an inclination on the part of central administrations to respond to and involve people at the local level. However, it should not be assumed, as Rosenau notes, that all individual involvement in international issues is mediated through groups. The phenomenon of what he terms 'leaderless publics', whose opinions and interests are aggregated by such means as newspaper reports and public opinion polls, can influence the character and content of public policy in the absence of mediating group actors (Rosenau, 1990).

Alger and others see such developments as qualitatively different from mere pressure-group politics directed towards issues that transcend national political communities. Whereas they might embrace traditional populist forms, there is - to use a phrase employed by Walker and Mendlovitz – 'a sense of something new' (Walker and Mendlovitz, 1987). The newly emerging social movements possess a 'willingness to articulate alternative ways of knowing and acting that puts the claim to politics as usual into serious question'. A number of writers see the rise of social activism at the local level as symptomatic of a new form of politics which challenges old assumptions and practices. Social activists, whether in the peace, environmental or women's movements, have succeeded in 'bypassing legal and territorial definitions and bringing new constituencies into the political arena around new definitions of the issues and content of politics' (Sheth, 1983).

The stimulus towards internationalization comes from two directions. Firstly, action groups recognize that local power structures gain much of their power from the national and international power structures to which they are linked, thus requiring them to involve themselves in politics at the global level. Secondly, national governments, as the representatives of traditional political structures and the guardians of the international order of which they are part, are aware of the transnational processes through which both might be undermined. Especially within the states of the Third World, activist groups are challenging the elites in their own societies, and thereby threatening to project domestic political stresses and strains onto the international stage. From both directions, a rejection of the basic features and structures of modern politics is turning the local into the international and vice versa.

REGIONALISM AND WORLD ORDER BUILDING

From this viewpoint, localization offers the prospect of, and may be a prerequisite for establishing, a new world order based on greater equality and justice. Central to this perspective are the writings of the dependency and world systems theorists who have linked patterns of exploitation at the global level to the locality. Just as such linkages offer analyses and explanations of what Johan Galtung refers to as 'structural violence' produced by exploitation both domestically and globally in terms of the human individual, so the remedies for such a condition are seen in terms of self-reliance achievable in part through local action (Galtung, 1980).

To take one example, Alger has suggested that the disparities of wealth that characterize North-South relations require a new model for action on the part of the peoples of the Third World which operates outside the traditional assumptions of inter-state relations, and more specifically, which asserts that the interests of the South can be advanced only by LDC governments acting either individually or in coalitions. One major reason why, according to Alger, there is a 'need for new norms and institutions for local and regional participation in foreign policy-making of national governments' in this area is to be found in the links between LDC governments and the transnational economic forces that impinge on local and regional communities. Consequently, the latter, in order to protect themselves, need to take direct action against these forces, developing in the process linkages with individuals and groups in both Third World and industrialized states who share common interests. In particular, developing collaborative arrangements with local groupings in developed countries would help to fragment the latters' power, thus making the relationships between the strong and the weak in the international system more symmetrical.

Adopting a broader and more ambitious perspective, other observers envisage a future world order in which localities assume a key role. Galtung draws a picture of a future world which comprises small, self-reliant communities, territorially based but interlinked, held together by a network of non-territorial groupings and presided over by a world central authority serving 'the double function of *articulating* problems and conflicts and *solving* them' (Galtung, 1980). To take another example, Richard Falk's image of a new world order assigns a central role to the politically aware sectors of society who would exert pressures on governmental elites at the national level to transform the present international structures into the supranational system represented by his 'Preferred World Polity' (Falk, 1987).

It is the uncertain juxtaposition of description and prescription which opens the proponents of this alternative ideology to criticism. If advocates of state-centrism can be accused of describing a world which no longer exists, then those who identify the growing role of individuals and groups can equally be accused of describing a world which has not yet arrived. Apart from a tendency to identify patterns in what are diverse phenomena, often interest and activity in international affairs are equated with influence over outcomes. There is a distinction to be made between the actions of a small, articulate elite, acting on the principle of 'thinking globally and acting locally', and mass consciousness-raising and policy-affecting activities which embrace and involve significant sections within local and regional communities.

Furthermore, it can be argued that those seeking a greater recognition of the potentialities of linkages between micro and macro politics fail to take account of the major obstacles which confront individuals seeking to operate at the international or transnational levels. Returning to the example of Alger's advocacy of transnational linkages between localities in the Third and First Worlds, the obstacles to the development of the requisite political skills amongst the peoples of the South would appear, to say the least, a barrier to such a strategy. To be fair, Alger and others do recognize the inherent difficulties for local institutions when challenging macro institutions; but it is an inherent premise of the counter-ideology that to accept such arguments regarding limitations on the scope of local foreign policy involvement constitutes a self-fulfilling prophecy and simply underscores the continuing dominance of the ideology of the state.

Of course, it should not be assumed that there is an automatic linkage between enhanced public awareness of global issues and the desire to act internationally. Not only do individual capacities vary, but so do attitudes and beliefs regarding the appropriateness of local involvement in international affairs. Both Alger and Shuman point out that local administrative bodies vary in their attitudes towards involvement in international issues. Thus, whilst many subnational authorities around the world have been active in declaring themselves nuclear-free zones, some have consciously rejected such moves on the grounds that they relate to issues outside their area of responsibility. Furthermore, it is not necessarily the case that individuals who have international concerns choose to achieve their goals by linking the micro and macro levels of politics. This is but one strategy and stands alongside those which involve individuals working at the international and national levels, for whom the involvement of the locality is peripheral to their concerns.

As noted above, events since the end of the Cold War present a further challenge to the image of a more peaceful world structured on local/regional territorial identities. How to manage a potential proliferation of regions seeking national self-determination, and how to find alternatives to territorial modes of accommodating aspirations and redressing grievances which create sources of destabilization in the international system, has become one of the most pressing issues on the international agenda (Halperin, Scheffer and Small, 1992).

CONCLUSION

Rather than offering an 'international relations' perspective on the phenomenon of regionalism, this discussion has sought to demonstrate that there is a variety of views, both descriptive and prescriptive, relating to the impact of the diffusion of territorially-based power within national settings on both the macro and micro levels of international politics. This manifestation of a broader tendency towards the localization of international relations, closely related to the processes associated with globalization, can be seen in the context of the erosion of the boundaries traditionally regarded as separating arenas of political activity and the disciplines which seek to analyse them.

At one level, the localization of international politics is interpreted as a rejection of 'traditional' international relations, particularly realist assumptions with their state-centric focus. Regionalism is seen as part of a new pattern of global politics characterized by linkages within and across national boundaries that elevate the significance of individuals and the localities in which they live. One consequence of this is the creation of more participative forms of international politics. For some this is part and parcel of the oft-heralded demise of the nation-state. Hence, in the case of the European Union, a 'Europe of the Regions' is seen by some as offering a re-structuring of political power, whereby the nation-states will be squeezed between the processes of subsidiarity on the one hand and the growing centralization of power in Brussels on the other.

From another broad perspective, however, these developments are more accurately seen as one aspect of the modification of traditional international politics, reflecting a far more complex domestic and international environment. In this context, regions, alongside cities and other non-central governmental actors, assume their place in an ever more intricate multi-layered policy milieu. Their relationship with central governments is equally complex. Rather than standing in opposition to the centre, far less symbolic of the decline of the nation-state in some zero-sum contest, the internationalization of regions represents the emergence of policy processes in which subnational actors are capable of fulfilling a number of diverse roles. Some of these will create tensions with the centre, as the sub-national, national and international levels of political activity intermesh and interests differ; others will suggest a mutuality of interest between centre and region in pursuit of goals relating to the international environment.

NOTES

1. Among the growing literature on the international activities of non-central governments in federal states can be found: John E. Kline, 1983, *State Government Influence in U.S. International Economic Policy*, Lexington: Lexington Books. There are a number of collections of papers on various aspects of the theme. Taking them in order of publication, they include a collection of articles published in the American journal devoted to federalism, *Publius* (14[4] Fall 1984). Two years later, the journal of the Canadian Institute of International Affairs, *International Journal* (41[3] Summer 1986), focused on the theme 'Foreign Policy in Federal States'. The latter has a broader geographical focus and a more issue-oriented approach. As its title suggests, the next collection to appear was concerned with the contacts between non-central governments in different nation-states: Ivo. D. Duchacek, Daniel Latouche and Garth Stevenson (eds.), 1988, *Perforated Sovereignties: Trans-Sovereign Contacts of Subnational Governments*, New York: Greenwood Press. As with much of the literature, there is a strong North American emphasis here, but it is supplemented by some European material. A much broader survey is to be found in Hans J. Michelmann and Panayotis Soldatos (eds.), 1990, *Federalism and International Relations*, Oxford: Clarendon Press. Alongside some useful analytical articles, the volume covers the major federal systems with contributors varying in their approach but frequently adopting a legal-

constitutional perspective. Finally, there is a collection of papers given at a conference in Australia House, London, in March 1992: Brian Hocking (ed.), 1993, *Foreign Relations and Federal States*, London: Leicester University Press. Here, the aim is to focus more on the policy processes and to look at the impact of non-central government international activity on the management of foreign relations.

6

Territory, Identity and Language

COLIN H. WILLIAMS

THE POLITICIZATION OF SPACE

Conventionally, scholars of political regionalism treat territory as a passive element bounding regional activities and as a container which gives physical meaning to socio-political action. This is a limiting view of territorial considerations which plays down the substantive implications of change in the spatial structure of Europe. I want to examine some of the considerations which prompt the development of regionalism by questioning the relationship between key socio-spatial patterns and processes of linguistic and cultural reproduction within communities pressing for regional autonomy.[1]

A critical feature of European history has been the relative lack of congruence between population distribution patterns and the political organization of space. Territorial sovereignty was initially determined by church and dynastic settlements following periodic warfare which legitimized some cultures and alienated others in the construction of the 'territorial nation-state'. State-formation in the period of chauvinistic nationalism and state expansion – circa 1789– 1919 – involved the institutional denial of minority rights, initially justified on religious grounds and more recently on grounds of 'national' integration. As capitalism penetrated into ethnically differentiated peripheries, the survival of outmoded cultures was considered anathema to the realization of a fully integrated national market, and a barrier to participation in a developing world system. Virulent 'nation-states' sought to integrate their regions through core-periphery economic development. Citizenship was promoted through policies of compulsory education in the state language, conscription into the armed forces and mass socialization. New state-controlled domains structured the range of identities which were to be recognized and sanctioned in the public realm.

It has been argued that 'if the nation represents a mode of moulding and interpreting social space, "nationalism" as ideology and movement may be viewed as the dominant mode of politicizing space by treating it as a distinct and historic territory' (Williams and Smith, 1983). Three consequences follow from the 'national construction of social space'. First is the increase in society's control over and ability to manipulate the environment. Both majority and minority communities seek to activate their respective environments as a resource for their collective goals. This includes population transfers as nationalist elites 'purified' their ethnic territory: witness the Greco-Turkish exchanges after 1922, the German border areas between the two World Wars, or ethnic cleansing following the break up of Yugoslavia (Magas, 1993; Glenny, 1993; Williams, 1993a). Less tragically, it also involves questions of in-migration into linguistically endangered areas such as Friuli, Brittany, Euskadi, Wales and Ireland, where the consequences of regional development, tourism, strategic state defence and energy installations pose dilemmas for cohesive ethno-linguistic communities.

A second consequence has been the 'hardening of space', the filling out of power vacuums and the utilization of all areas for social benefit and communal power. National elites have been unremitting in this task of nation-building and state-integration. The vanquished in the struggle between the state and nation harbour other 'regional/national' level solutions to this enduring conflict (Héraud, 1963, 1971; Fouéré, 1984). Such elites have sought 'to present to the world the face of a united and mobilized community securely based throughout a compact territory, which brooks no external interference or internal subversion, and which is able to unleash a collective energy for development that can utterly transform its environment and deter aggressors' (Williams and Smith, 1983).

Third, there has been a growing 'abstraction of the land' that has given new meaning as the environment becomes reinterpreted to suit the exigencies of the day. This is evidenced in the zest for linguistic revivals, in the rewriting of history textbooks about a particular homeland, in the manner in which populist writers and artists have reinterpreted society's relationship with nature, in ecological protest actions and in the whole movement to understand our origins, whether that be in the scientific search for archaeological remains or in the experiential search for authenticity in the 'return to nature' movement.

There is a new self-consciousness about the environment which is tapped by government and by the leadership of communities who feel threatened by a centralizing state apparatus and the ever-voracious economic imperative of resource extraction and exploitation by commercial interests. The land has become a new battle-ground between the local and the universal, the indigenous and the exogenous. Territory is a significant source of symbolic and resource power. Its possession and control is often deemed vital to the survival of indigenous cultural communities.

As Williams and Smith observed, within these three trends,

> ...the ideals of autarchy, boundary, homeland and nation-building have found concrete expression ... in the democratic movement for popular sovereignty over a given territory, itself an abstraction and reinterpretation of government and state as these evolved in early modern Europe ... The net result has been to deliver exceptional political power and cultural control into the hands of zealous nationalist elites and their parties, a power and control that they have utilized to effect perhaps the most radical transformation in society's relationship with its environment since the Neolithic revolution (Williams and Smith, 1983).

Geographers have traditionally focused on territory, symbolic places, boundaries and frontiers, access to resources, population movement and strategic locations, rather than upon ideology or the processes for ethnic-conflict resolution. Recently, the inter-relationship of globalization and localism, holistic and ecological ideas, and reformed conceptions of space occasioned by telematic revolutions have figured strongly. There has also been a concern to differentiate between regionalization, identified as the regional application of state policy and regionalism, defined as the attempt to optimise the interests of a region's population through the manipulation of the political process.

A key concern is the relationship between territory and identity at all levels in the spatial hierarchy. Realist and neo-realist conceptions of the international order regard the territorial state and its concomitant of 'national citizenship' as fixed entities. However, this privileging of the territorial state in the literature on international political economy has been much criticized by geographers, most effectively in John Agnew and Stuart Corbridge's work *Mastering Space* (1995). They argue that 'a changing global economic geography is exploding the fixity of the territorial state and is thereby creating a trap for those who want to build timeless models upon rapidly shifting foundations'(Agnew and Corbridge, 1995). They also wish to confound the market ideologues who assert that transnational liberalism has re-defined '*the market* as the arbiter of the just and the true' (ibid.). Setting aside technical arguments as to whether or not truly open and competitive markets allow real people equal access to, and 'just' rewards from, the market place, it follows that if the inexorable trend is toward a global market then we need countervailing institutions to regulate the operation of multinational corporations, to guarantee the rights of 'global citizens' and to give meaning to the localized effects of global processes.

Agnew and Corbridge have called for a discussion of the 'new *representational* spaces that are resistant to some aspects of the emerging world order' (ibid.). I conceive political regionalism as forming part of this representational space. Its geographical discourse influences how we perceive regional communities by treating them as coherent socio-spatial places. This chapter's focus will be ethnic-regional movements concerned with the defence of unique territorial identities.

POLITICAL REGIONALISM

The power of regionalism and nationalism lies in their ability to mobilize people on the basis of their historical occupation of a cherished environment. Despite nationalism's potential for destruction it can also provide a beguilingly complete socio-cultural framework for political and economic action. Anthony Smith has phrased its allure thus:

> Nations derive their profound hold over the feelings and imaginations of the people because they are historically embedded. They are rooted in older and more long-lasting

ethnic ties, myths and sentiments from which these modern nations draw much of their emotional and cultural sustenance and much of what makes them distinctive, even unique. If nationalism is the normalization of the unique, then we should not be baffled by its global power. It satisfies the dual craving to preserve what is felt to be a collective self and all its special culture values, while inserting that self as a political community into the community of nations by endowing it with the standard attributes of the nation (Smith, 1993).

The defence of territory figures both as a context for socio-political processes and a repository for a threatened group identity. Hence the concern with an accurate definition of the nation and its territory so as to realize a new basis for political legitimacy, usually in the call for some form of autonomy. The most virulent form of political regionalism in the EU today is ethnic separatism, as manifested among elements (usually a fraction of the elite) of the Basques, Bretons, Catalans, Corsicans, Flemish , Scots and Welsh. These enduring nationalist movements act as a counter to the general thrust of globalization and integration so redolent of the so-called 'post-modernist, New World Order' (Williams, 1993a). But they also signify an awareness that their political pressure is essential if their nations are to benefit fully from the new opportunities that are emerging within the new European order.

Ethnic and Territorial Separatism

Theories of separatism generally describe the separatist claim as a search for collective equality. It involves a complex set of grievances which are packaged under convenient headings such as territorial defence, language recognition, economic development, and social justice. In multi-ethnic polities, ethnic separatism often derives from an acute concern over the erosion of a group's identity and resource base. Separatists assert that ethnic discrimination can only be halted through the separation of their territory to form a sovereign state co-equal with all other states. Regionalists assert that one need not go so far as to break up the state but insist that its internal affairs should reflect its plural character. However, both regionalists and separatists pose similar challenges to the territorially fixed nature of monopolistic sovereign space.

Figure 1: Politicoterritorial Processes 4. Separatism

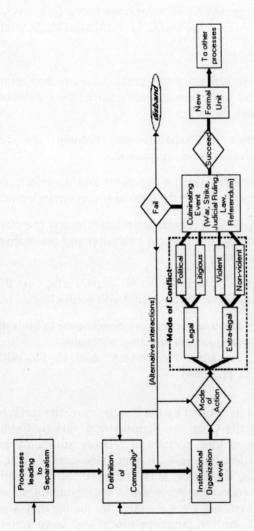

Source: Whebell. 1988. and Williams. 1994.

* Community means "Politicogeographical community" - it may be formal (bounded) or informal, and may be revised in successive "passes".

Figure 1 charts the process by which the preconditions of separatism are triggered into the emergence of a separatist movement. It is taken from C. F. J. Whebell's (1988) analysis of political territory and has been illustrated with reference to Biafra, Quebec and Euskadi in Williams (1994). The geographical process is related to a larger theory of separatism based on the writings of J. R. Wood (1981), A. Orridge and C. H. Williams (1982), which sought to account for:

1   the preconditions of separatism, namely the factors which are necessary (but not necessarily sufficient) for the beginnings of separatist alienation;

2   the bases of separateness, namely the materials of distinctiveness and uniqueness;

3   the rise of separatist movements and the effectiveness of their attempts to achieve the goal of sovereign independence;

4   the response of central governments, and the effectiveness of their attempts to prevent secession and maintain the integrity of their states;

5   the direct precipitants of separatism, in the form of confrontational development and conflict issues;

6   the likelihood of success, with reference to both domestic and international factors affecting outcomes.
(Wood, J. R., 1981; Orridge, A. and C. H. Williams, 1982; Williams, C. H., 1984).

This is best illustrated by the Basque case, though it has purchase in explaining the Corsican, Flemish and various Celtic cases. The Basques enjoyed long periods of relative autonomy prior to their incorporation into the Spanish state; elements of their institutional distinctiveness, the *fueros*, survived until fairly recently and were used as evidence of a prior claim to legitimate statehood. Their language and culture were deemed unique for they were unrelated to any Indo-European language group and were among the oldest surviving elements of civilization in Europe. Under the impress of state-building, non-Spanish elements were ruthlessly eradicated, producing a deep resentment within the Basque community. State oppression was confirmed during the Spanish Civil War and sustained thereafter when Spanish forces were regarded as constituting an internal colonial military occupation.

The creation of Euskadi ta Askatasuna (ETA – Basque Homeland and Liberty) in 1957 reinvigorated Basque nationalism. A particular combination of the defence of traditional cultural values, rapid industrialization and opposition to Spanish internal colonialism nurtured violence as a movement strategy (Clark, 1979, 1984). The three issues which animate autonomy are common to most contemporary regionalisms, whether separatist or not. They are a concern for the survival and promotion of a unique culture, its language and attendant social institutions; a concern to influence the direction of economic change, so as to cope with de-industrialization and regional economic decline; and a concern with political representation which maximizes democratic accountability.

Spain has experienced a startling transition from Francoism to representative democracy. It is neither a regionalized unitary state nor a federal state but a hybrid form incorporating features of both. However, the development of the European Union has provided a new context for relations between Madrid and the historic nations and regions (Loughlin, 1996). If separatism is contained through political accommodation, we are still left with the significance of the ethno-linguistic issue in Euskadi and Catalonia; for the post-Franco reforms designed to introduce Eusquerra and Catalan to new domains – for example, education, commerce, the media and the law – have been less effective than anticipated in assimilating both Spaniards and North Africans into the new 'nationalist' social order.

The territorial nation-state, though fiercely criticized, is a near-permanent political feature and in consequence structures the degree of regional autonomy available to sub-state nationalities. Separatist pressures were curbed by the ability of central states to respond to regionally-based demands for tariff protection. Keating (1992b: 54) identifies an important shift in that 'peripheral nationalists have moved from demanding protectionism to support for free trade'. Regions have created an alternative agenda with a renewed sense of purpose and economic direction which has much to do with promoting the regional identity as the basic building block of European history. A 'Europe of the Regions' vision is still a long way removed from regional economic reality, yet despite the apparent impracticability of the desire for regional autarky, it is still one of the most powerful visions of a refashioned Europe.

The ethno-regional challenge to the nation-state

The nation-state is being challenged by a number of forces both from above and below. Two trends influence the capacity of ethno-linguistic minorities to re-negotiate their role in the European division of labour. The first is the weakening of national economic sovereignty and the transfer of economic powers from state legislatures to the European Commission. Despite current difficulties with the ERM and post-Maastricht negotiations, the EU has developed an integrated management of its constituent economies with new policies on competition, trade, monetary exchange rate, science and technological research, and to a lesser extent, its foreign policy. At the regional level, agreements such as the 'Four Motors' programme linking Baden-Württemberg, Rhône-Alpes, Lombardy, Catalonia together with Wales and Ontario, help to sustain an element of additional political-regional dynamism. For lesser-used language speakers in Catalonia and Wales, more economic autarky can slow down out-migration and language shift, thereby easing one of the key determinants of ethnic antagonism. Such moves represent a broader structural pattern seeking to by-pass aspects of central state authority and build-up regional-level power. We may not need to establish a *de jure* federal Europe if regions increasingly operate as members of a *de facto* federal Europe.

Because conventional political authority is increasingly shared among a number of units within the political system, the absolute nature of the territorial nation-state can no longer be sustained as if it were a closed system. Pooled sovereignty, permeable borders, Community-wide socio-economic and environmental policy-making, freedom of movement and to a lesser extent shared foreign policy through inter-related agencies such as the Western European Union, NATO and the OSCE all characterize the contemporary state system and render it more inter-dependent, both with respect to member states and to subordinate constituent regions. However, increased integration and mutual dependence is not without its own structural strains which pose new challenges which we shall examine.

MOVEMENT, REGIONAL DEVELOPMENT AND CULTURE

Geographers have a long established interest in migration, population displacement and territorial adjustment. The major ethnic question facing western Europe at present is the effect of the collapse of the bipolar system on the New World Order. There are at least two contradictory processes at work. The first is the opening up of Europe to democratic ideals and representative politics, which follows the advance of social democratic capitalism eastward and its creation of new markets, resources and social organizations. The second is a reaction which serves to close, limit and protect the 'national' character of states. The resulting tension which hinders the full and free movement of people, ideas and goods is a major source of ethnic tension.

Two issues are pertinent: one which focuses on how ethnicity and race are handled, the other on how regional dependency is managed. They used to be treated as quite separate entities but are now linked in the wider question of defining Europe. The mobilization of social movements concerned with ethnic identity, class, gender, environmentalism and animal rights might have led one to assume that the 1960s ethnic revival would have been matched by greater racial tolerance within a multicultural Europe. MacLaughlin (1993) argues that ethnicity and race are being used in different ways to categorize groups and to structure policies which 'defend' the integrity of Europeans. Within sections of the media and the political scene, 'ethnicity' is increasingly used to construct a positive, quasi-biological identity which links a particular group to a specific place. Race, in contrast, is used as a classificatory category to reflect primarily, if not exclusively, negative tendencies of dissociation and exclusion at state and EU levels. Race has come to 'signify a set of imaginary properties of inheritance which fix and legitimate real positions of social domination or subordination in terms of cultural differences between native and foreigner in the European Community' (MacLaughlin, 1993). Approximately 30 million people entered Western Europe between 1945 and 1975, forming one of the largest migratory movements in modern history. At present, there are an estimated 13 million legally settled non-Europeans and approximately 2 million 'illegals' within the EU. In times of economic difficulty, race can once again be used as an exclusionary category in any of the European 'shatterbelts' and there has been a growing incidence of racial victimization and a resurgence of neo-nationalism, fascism and crypto-communism (Williams, 1993a).

In an open society which values social justice, accommodation and mutual tolerance, there is a problem if the gains of autochthonous ethno-linguistic minorities are won at the expense of other minorities, rather than in tandem with them. Keating (1992a) places some hope in the construction of a far more secularized territorial identity, where new forms of class relations between capital and labour and between political and bureaucratic elites may develop at the regional level. He argues that such an identity would be 'more open to newcomers with a capacity to assimilate immigrants without making them pay too high a price. A political culture emphasizing bargaining, compromise and accommodation will also be an advantage in the new conditions over one in which adversary politics is the norm' (Keating, 1992a).

A second issue concerns regional dependency characterized by the exploitation of natural resources, such as water and oil, or a wild and rugged landscape; or of human resources, when a well-educated, but relatively poorly paid, labour force is exploited in the service sector, with its seasonal and tourist-dependent characteristics, in areas such as Brittany and Wales. This perception can stimulate violence as in Euskadi, Northern Ireland and Corsica. Conventionally, the state responds by seeking to develop the dependent region so as to reduce inter-regional economic disparities and manage potential conflict through a judicious mix of directed capital investment and social equalization. However, such interventionist planning often weakens the very essence of a region's distinctiveness and spawns counter-movements dedicated to cultural maintenance.

Regional development policy is weak in relation to the multi-ethnic basis of planning and it is only recently that we have a fledgling literature on planning for lesser-used languages. Cultural considerations are often considered less relevant than economic and political concerns in the development process. Because planners treat culture as an essentially private matter, linguistic and religious considerations are hardly ever made explicit in regional development plans. This is not surprising, for the planning and development process normally serves state-wide rather than indigenous needs. Conventionally, the minority cultural group is portrayed as being traditional and in need of development. Reformist state attempts to integrate the minority region into the national economic space are predicated upon the assumption that development will lead to a reduction in the gap between the regional minority and the state majority, between tradition and modernity. Regional economic development becomes one of the prime instruments of this transformation process. Often viewed as statist in its perception and formulation of the problem, it adopts a managerialist perspective on cultural relations.

Interest groups and local authorities in Catalonia, Euskadi, Ireland and Wales have come to recognize the effect which planning decisions have on cultural reproduction. They have drawn lessons from Quebec where after the Quiet Revolution of the 1950s, modernization and secularization led to rapid economic development which changed the cultural attitude of the *Québécois* towards economic enterprise and transformed their role in the North American division of labour. Language legislation reinforcing French in the workplace, in government and private sector agencies and in education, sport and entertainment have strengthened the language's purchase in the provincial economy. Quebec represents an advanced technologically sophisticated society which is conscious of its role within *la francophonie* (Williams, 1994).

CASE-STUDY: WALES

Generally, it is the ideological, electoral and constitutional aspects of political regionalism which receive detailed scrutiny in Quebec, as in our European examples, and excellent accounts of its impact are available in Young (1995), McRoberts (1995) and Keating (1988b). I want to set aside such considerations so as to focus on socio-cultural issues which prompt political regionalism as a response to the struggle for Welsh identity.

Wales is a bi-cultural nation but much of the pressure for regional political control is economic in origin, though often expressed through discourses on culture and national territory. A central issue is whether or not a viable Welsh culture can survive without its own heartland as a resource-base. A summary of the principal census findings (1991) suggests that the Welsh-speaking population of 510,920 (18.7 per cent) continues to decline, albeit at a modified rate; that it is predominantly ageing; that it is concentrated in proportional terms in the north and west; that it shows encouraging signs of growth among the younger age groups, particularly in the industrial south and east; that this growth can be largely attributed to the development of Welsh-medium education in such areas in combination with the wider revival of interest in the language and

TABLE 1
REGIONAL DIMENSIONS AND INDICATORS

	Area '000 sq km	Population 1992 (m)	% Growth rate p.a. 1981-92	% Employment 1991* agriculture	% Employment 1991* industry	% Employment 1991* services	% Unemployment rate 1993	Average gross weekly income per household	Private cars per '000 population 1990	GDP pc 1991 Index
South-East	27.2	17.70	0.4	1.2	25.4	72.5	10.2	407.3	388	117.3
East-Anglia	12.6	2.09	0.9	4.0	29.2	66.3	8.1	350.2	409	100.4
South-West	23.8	4.57	0.7	4.6	29.0	65.6	9.5	346.5	401	94.3
East Midlands	15.6	4.06	0.5	2.7	38.0	58.5	9.5	344.4	341	97.1
West Midlands	13.0	5.28	0.2	2.1	39.1	57.7	10.9	304.2	377	92.4
North West	7.3	6.40	-0.1	1.5	33.3	64.6	10.7	317.1	325	90.4
Yorkshire & Humberside	15.4	5.00	0.2	2.5	34.8	61.7	10.3	303.2	313	91.7

TABLE 1 (CONTINUED)
REGIONAL DIMENSIONS AND INDICATORS

	Area '000 sq km	Popu-lation 1992 (m)	% Growth rate p.a. 1981-92	% Employ-ment 1991* agri-culture	% Employ-ment 1991* industry	% Employ-ment 1991* services	% Unemploy-ment rate 1993	Average gross weekly income per household	Private cars per '000 popula-tion 1990	GDP pc 1991 Index
North	15.4	3.10	-0.1	1.7	34.9	62.0	11.9	285.1	284	90.5
Wales	20.8	2.90	0.3	3.1	32.7	62.9	10.3	294.6	328	85.1
Scotland	78.8	5.11	-0.1	3.0	30.2	65.9	9.7	313.7	280	95.8
Northern Ireland	14.1	1.61	0.4	4.5	28.0	66.4	13.9	281.3	281	81.1
UK	244.1	58.0	0.3	2.3	30.9	65.9	10.3	342.9	352	100

* Figures derive from annual European Community sample survey on Labour Forces, and definitions may differ from those used in the UK statistical series.

Source: Regional Trends, 1994; Spooner, 1995

its institutionalization in many aspects of public life; that following the passage of the Welsh Language Act (1993) and the establishment of the statutory Welsh Language Board, Welsh is increasingly identified with government support and set for an increase in use as a working language for the heartland region. However, in common with many other linguistic minorities in Europe, Welsh speakers face a difficult economic situation and find it almost impossible to find adequate employment within predominantly Welsh-speaking regions, which atrophy because of the out-migration of the young, fecund and well-educated and the in-migration of non-Welsh-speaking residents, who are attracted by a variety of factors.

All left-of-centre parties in Wales argue that devolved self-government will narrow the persistent inter-regional differentials which characterize the British economy. As is evident in Table 1, Wales under performs *vis-à-vis* more dynamic British regions with a very low GDP per capita 1991 index and average gross weekly income levels per household. Influential structural arguments hold that such disparities derive from the regional mode of production which reflects Welsh dependency and regionalism is a predictable response to external control. I want to add a fresh dimension by asking questions which are internal to Welsh society. By so doing, I hope to illustrate elements and predispositions which encourage regionalism. The most controversial claim is that Welsh economic performance is due to an inherent lack of enterprise which is culturally determined.

Certain European regional and local authorities are now examining the role indigenous culture can play in encouraging sustainable development. For the first time the relationships between culture and business formation, product innovation, risk-taking and enterprise are being systematically analysed. It is assumed that if one can understand the inner workings of a culture, strategic intervention can direct under-performing regions to become more concerned with economic success and indigenous development. Minority cultures are described in a dichotomous manner as being either essentially innovative or dependent. Given its poor economic performance, the Welsh-speaking part of Wales is characterized as a dependency culture and in need of development. What socialization processes pre-dispose individuals and cultures to gravitate towards or away from entrepreneurial business skills and acumen?

Self-doubt and an ambiguous relationship towards English ideas, culture and practice pervade many of the criticisms of the under-performance of predominantly Welsh-speaking regions which in turn, are a spur to demands for autonomy. Influential theories, such as 'internal colonialism' (Hechter, 1975), posit that a cultural division of labour operated to the disadvantage of the 'minority'. Others argue that this misrepresents Welsh-speakers for they are part of the mainstream, being identified as 'ethnic' only from the dominant-centric perspective of the state's elite (Bellin, 1989).

Put simply, does Welsh culture reproduce a negative self-image in relation to an entrepreneurial business spirit because it is a subordinated culture? If so, does this reflect a deeper lack of confidence based upon an uncertain identity? Or is this myth of conquest a perpetuation of internalized power differentials? Revisionist historians argue that culturally determined dependency theories ignore centuries of structural discrimination which systematically excluded Welsh interests from mainstream economic development.

Faced by a declining territorial base and a limited private sector, are there any structural determinants which necessarily confine the use of Welsh to public-sector domains? If there are, what is the relationship between a minority language and a public-sector career path? Does this perforce increase the dependence of the language on local and central state agencies? And if so, with what consequences for the relative autonomy of Welsh speakers seeking to reproduce their culture? (Williams, 1989b).

These issues affect the supply and demand of Welsh-speakers in employment and condition our attitude to Welsh in the private sector. Unless Welsh can break out into the private sector, there is a danger that cumulative factors will restrict its use to marginal domains. If employment opportunities in public domains remain static, then successive generations will be under-employed if they wish to use Welsh in their careers, and this we know from the experience of Quebec and Euskadi leads to increased frustration and conflict.

Infra-structural factors

The struggle for the development of a fully functional bilingual society has dominated the post-war agenda. Many Welsh speakers believe that they are engaged in a national struggle for cultural survival and choose employment which in some way is both community-oriented and socially responsible, such as education or the health services. The real challenge is to determine the relationship between individual motivation and social agencies. This is the issue of holistic versus individualist explanations of culturally-influenced actions and beliefs. There is a real difficulty in relating individual perceptions and actions to aggregate structural features of a socio-economic nature. Are many Welsh speakers in the public sector because it is one of the limited domains available to them to function in a developing bilingual environment? If so, does this small, yet critical mass of employment opportunities unduly influence others to follow in their footsteps? The context of Welsh employment is critical for we need to ascertain the impact of a wide range of features, including the physical and social communication system, which structure material cultural reproduction. Heartland employment is heavily dependent upon farming and extractive industries which are shedding labour. What effect does this have on community involvement, the viability of scattered rural settlements, labour training and skill acquisition? Also the size of companies in Welsh-speaking areas is limited, leading to narrow regional economic diversity and an undeveloped urban network wherein alternative sources of employment in the service sectors might be provided.

The limited research suggests that Welsh-speakers favour self-employment, which may reflect its greater availability in rural areas. The 1981 census suggested that 15.8 per cent of the Welsh-speaking population were self-employed, as opposed to 9.2 per cent of those who do not speak Welsh (Chapman et al., 1990), and that the differential was greatest in Clwyd and Dyfed. In contrast, English speakers constituted a greater proportion of the self-employed in Gwynedd and Powys. Clearly far more than linguistic variables are at work here and relate to the particular localized nature of economic diversification in these counties.

Negative attitudes which tend to denigrate the ability of Welsh speakers to innovate and to show enterprise were identified by Gahan (1989). Success in business was projected as occurring outside Wales and there was a lack of entrepreneurial Welsh-speaking role models in business, together with a reluctance to take risks and a higher incidence of insecurity and fear of failure (Beaufort Research, 1991). Welsh-speaking parents were unlikely to encourage their children to consider a career in business and assumed that one needed an unduly large amount of capital to start a business. Students were generally more favourable to business activities, including self-employed ventures, attending Welsh-medium post-graduate business courses and supporting services designed to integrate Welsh-speakers more effectively into the world of business and commerce.

The real difficulty in interpretation is 'whether the relative lack of enterprises created and owned by the Welsh people, and Welsh-speakers in particular, owes more to the in-built social and psychological propensities of the Welsh, or should be explained instead in terms of the structural nature of the Welsh economy and society?' (Carr, 1992). Though culture is significant, there are class differences also to be considered, for middle-class Welsh-speakers are differentially concentrated in the bilingual public sector, particularly in Gwynedd, while English incomers are over-represented in the private sector managerial classes (Morris, 1989). This reflects a dependency culture which ties Welsh-speakers into the local state and interventionist employment-generation agencies such as Menter a Busnes confirm this disparity by their very existence (Williams, 1989). It has been argued that the Welsh express collectivist community values rather than individualistic ones. If one merely celebrates the private profit syndrome and ignores the social responsibility of capital, this will lead to inter-group tension and exacerbate indigenous-exogenous divides. Because of Wales's radical political heritage, any attempt to instil a general enterprise culture will be interpreted as reproducing the ideology of the present British Conservative Party.

The logic of uneven development too often ignores peripheral collectivities and/or renders their categorization as a separate social grouping within the state as irrelevant to the real materialist explanation for structured inequality. We need to relate macro-level theorizing to specific examples of those who least benefit from the development processes and incorporate conceptions of struggle, conflict and dissonance into an explanation which does not assume that social cohesion and state integration are a necessary consequence of the maturing of capitalism. This would involve examining the ideological basis of Welsh culture to ascertain how messages relating to business, enterprise, political representation, regional development and planning are constructed and diffused.

Wales represents a case where the decline of the traditional productive base of formerly cohesive regions and the acute sense of crisis over its national culture and associated territory produce a broad consensus of the left that greater regional autonomy would serve the twin purposes of economic regeneration and democratic accountability. As with Brittany, Catalonia, Flanders and Scotland, it represents a particular configuration where regional innovation has also led to a renewed sense of confidence in European-level institutions and networks.

GLOBALIZATION, TECHNOLOGY AND ACCESSIBILITY

If we shift attention away from territorial heartlands and towards more technologically-influenced definitions of space, it becomes evident that a major source of conflict will be the differential access to information space and power networks that groups enjoy. The technological trends underpinning European integration suggest four outcomes in relation to the interaction of language, ethnic identity, territory and the state system. First, mass communication technology has reinforced the dominance of English. This has led the French, German and Spanish languages to re-negotiate their positions within the educational, legal and commercial domains of an enlarged Europe. Fears of Anglicisation ushering in greater North American and Japanese influence has stimulated the following four propositions: that the EU educational system should encourage all students to acquire two foreign languages; that a first foreign language should be obligatory; that English should be taught as a second foreign language, but never as a first; and that less information and cultural loss would occur if the principle of multilingualism could be instituted in most supra-national public and governmental affairs. These propositions may engender sympathy but they are unlikely to become policy and even less likely to weaken English-language hegemony.

A more immediate fear is that autochthonous language groups, such as the Basques, Bretons, Irish and Welsh might be further marginalized in an increasingly complex and competitive social order. Their only hope lies in establishing regional bilingualism as the dominant pattern. Limited success in introducing bilingual practices in education, public administration and the law offer some hope. Ironically, some groups are witnessing the erosion of their traditional strength in heartland areas and key cities while simultaneously harnessing the potential of mass communication and electronic networking.

Third, there will be increased pressure on local and metropolitan authorities to provide mother-tongue education and other public services to the children of mobile workers and their families in multicultural cities such as Milan, London, Paris and Frankfurt. This is set to become the major policy issue within public administration if a fully functional EU is to be realized.

Fourth, there will be a demand at the Union level to provide resources for the instruction and occupational integration of the children and dependants of non-EU migrant workers and refugees. An inability or a refusal to provide such public facilities, especially in education, health services and community care will undoubtedly increase ethnic tension and call into question the nature and direction of the multicultural character of the EU itself.

A more virulent expression of such tensions will be the continued importation of non-European conflicts into the multi-cultural cities of the Union. Globalization implies that the safety valve of relative insulation from other countries' problems and issues no longer operates in a 'nationally bounded' manner.

Ethnic mobilization is so often a surrogate for issues such as political struggle, economic deprivation and psychological adjustment that the salience of identity is likely to increase as western Europe avers a more open, pluralistic society. Our major challenge is interpreting the gap between formal political units and the social behaviour of increasingly autonomous and individualistic citizens. This is doubly difficult in a fluid environment which poses the following questions about the nature of European politics:

- Will the new European identity be national, federal, regional, racial or some combination of these?
- What effect will the enlargement of the EU have on the management of ethno-linguistic and regional issues? English has been strengthened by the admission of Nordic members but there is no agreement as to whether other major languages are necessarily weakened by enlargement.
- Will ethnic identification increase or decrease with political-economic integration?
- How will political organizations, especially metropolitan authorities, cope with the increased diversity of their constituent citizens and the newly enfranchized rights of cultural pluralism?

- What role will territory and place have in structuring the life chances of hitherto discriminated-against minorities? Will we have a hierarchy of disadvantage aggravated by global economic changes accelerating the dependence of the poor and racially distinct?
- Who controls access to information within the mother tongue and the working languages of European minorities? Are they destined to occupy a more dependent role because of superstructural changes favouring dominant groups, or will they achieve relative socio-cultural autonomy by adopting mass technology?
- How permeable are the new frontiers of the European Union? To what extent will border tensions spill over into Community states and with what effect on the grand design of 'opening up the frontiers of Europe'? Will we have a situation of internal openness allowing permeability and external closedness seeking impermeability?
- What role will intractable ethnic conflicts play in triggering major regional clashes and how will the security architecture of Europe react to such conflagrations?
- How will deterritorialization effect the construction of regional identities and corresponding regional spaces?
- Most intriguing of all is to ask what effect globalization will have on the regional-local infrastructure upon which European ethnic minority groups depend?

The plight of threatened cultures has become a world-wide concern, as we recognize that many forces contribute to the apparent homogenization of so many peoples. The closure of time and space implies that the traditional solution to many problems in the past, namely relocation, no longer offers a means of coping with an external threat. Linguistic minorities cannot migrate so easily to avoid the penetration of a majority group. In consequence, 'the higher the level of globalization the narrower the scope for "escape alternatives".   In this sense globalization is also a kind of totalitarianization of world space' (Mlinar, 1992).

Globalization involves a hitherto unprecedented interdependence at the world level, in which widening circles of domination and dependence are accelerating the effects of uneven development, both internationally and within long-established states. The transfer of manufacturing from peripheral Europe to Asian or Central

American states mirrors today what happened in the textile industry of north-west Europe in the mid-nineteenth century. Core-periphery differentials are maintained because surplus regional capital is re-invested elsewhere. Galicia, Wales and Ireland find it difficult to sustain vibrant ethno-linguistic communities in the face of out-migration, relative deprivation and regional infrastructure decline. Regional development aid is only partially successful in improving infrastructure and employment prospects, as such interventions often accentuate cultural assimilation and regional dependence.

Second, there is the overcoming of temporal and spatial discontinuities in 'real time' communication and economic transactions which are increasingly independent of the limitations of specific locations.

Third, there is the penetration of a globalization process which is not merely the sum of its constituent parts, but has a simultaneity of both increased uniformity and increased diversity. New possibilities re-awaken or give ·birth to alternative identities, practices and preferences. Nowhere is this more evident than in the cultural infrastructure of world cities, suffused as they are with multicultural choices and exotic consumption, quite distinct from most of the state's remaining territory. In such a milieu, emerging or re-born linguistic identities are nurtured and expressed. So also are their opponents who wish to impose a pristine cultural order on dissenting ethnic activists, resulting in tension, hostility and racial/ethnic violence.

Fourth, the superficial current of homogenization throughout the world and the apparent inexorable development of a uniform global culture deserves particular scrutiny. Deeply embedded in the growth of modern technology is the question of language choice so that the spread of English contributes to the link between globalization and post-modernity. Many European minorities, despite being bi- or tri-lingual, face extreme pressures as a result of super-structural changes.

Fifth, there is the counter-current of increased religious and/or ethnic identification and confrontation within and across national frontiers and often in violent and emotional forms (Mlinar, 1992; Williams, 1993). Political movements within linguistic minority regions have been persistent in their assertion that it was their forced incorporation into an alien state system which was the cause of so many of their woes. It is significant that so many ethnic leaders co-align themselves with nationalists, regionalists, ecologists and liberals in calling for a re-structured Europe which will promise to give due attention to group rights and to the economic welfare of historically disadvantaged minorities. Thus the role and future of the nation-state constitutes one of the prime questions to be analysed within a globalization perspective.

Globalization also influences cultural patterns and modes of thought because as a constant interactive process it is always seeking to break down the particular, the unique and the traditional in order to reconstruct them as a local response to a general set of systematic stimuli. This is the threat of the deterritorialization of society and space. For cultural conservatives and ethnic defence activists, such processes are anathema to their existence for they signal a relative loss of power, of cultural autonomy and ultimately, of course, of absolute decline *qua* language death.

The collapse of both space and time demand a fresh appreciation of global interdependence, for we have been quick to characterize the advantages which accrue to well placed groups and regions. We have been less careful to scrutinize the impact such transitions might have on minorities and the disadvantaged. These would include the denial of human rights and the attack on religious beliefs in an increasingly secular social order. They may also impact on the process of deterritorialization and its obligation to redefine spatial relationships; on the old certainties of global strategic relationships; on the nature of the state and its legitimizing philosophy of national self-interest enshrined in the sovereignty of the citizen; and on the direction of world development and our common hopes and fears as we face a succession of global environmental crises.

Globalization, thus conceived, is an ideological programme for thought and action. As with modernization, it is not merely an account of how the world is changing but also a prescription for how it should change. As yet, we do not have global economic change; rather, we have macro-regional functional integration in western Europe, North America and to a lesser extent, in parts of South and East Asia. But the cumulative impact of these trading blocks is to establish a new regime whereby barriers to capital, trade, influence, the race for resources, uniform product standards, manufacturing and technology transfer are all reduced. Social and cultural change are deeply implicated in this world vision, and we have enough evidence to recognize that some groups and regions will be advantaged and others marginalized as globalization is entrenched in the world system. However, it is neither an inevitable nor an uncontested process. Fragmentation and dissolution so often follow periods of aggrandisement. How do minorities cope with these new challenges and opportunities and how does the recent strengthening of the European Union influence the impact of these diverse processes in selected regions?

European Consolidation

Logically, if globalization and interdependence can enhance the productive capacity of majority 'nation-state' interests, they can also be harnessed to develop the interests of lesser-used language groups. The EU has harmonized state and community policies so as to strengthen its majority-language regimes. But the wider question of the relative standing of official languages makes political representatives wary of further complicating administrative politics by addressing the needs of roughly 50 million citizens who have a mother tongue which is not the main official language of the state which they inhabit. Recent expansion of the EU has increased the difficulties in translating multi-cultural communication and guaranteeing access to information and hence power for all groups. The real geo-linguistic challenge is to safeguard the interests of all the non-state language groups, especially those most threatened with imminent extinction.

The past decade has witnessed an improvement in the formal position of many lesser used languages. The most significant development was the establishment of the European Bureau for Lesser Used Languages in 1984. Located in Dublin and Brussels, this small but effective organization has sought to co-ordinate and nurture inter-linguistic experience and transfer good practice from one group to another (O'Riagain, 1989; Williams, 1993b). Other initiatives involve the Conference of Local and Regional Authorities of Europe with its Charter on European Regional and Minority Languages. Politically, the most important reinvigorated actor is the Conference for Security and Co-operation in Europe which has increased its involvement in minority group rights since 1989. Although still evolving as the re-constituted Organization for Security and Co-operation in Europe (OSCE), it has detailed the rights and obligations of both minorities and host governments throughout Europe (Williams, 1993a).

Some minorities face a brighter future if they can use this international spur to democratic participation in public affairs, encouraging representation within decision-making bodies at all levels from the local to the supra-state level. However, reliance on this form of supra-structural definition of rights could provide a false dawn of optimism, if it is not also accompanied by a parallel sub-structural reform of many aspects of life in multi-cultural societies. It is essential that experiments in language planning regimes such as those currently undertaken in Euskadi and Wales be fully honoured and funded by the local state. Because these are 'true *Abstand*' minority languages (Trudgill, 1993), what happens to the struggling minority in these two countries is a predictor of the linguistic fortunes of other groups, including those such as Norwegian and Danish who are bolstered by their own state, but nevertheless face the same external competition from languages of wider communication.

Two final implications remain. The first is that several leading industrial conglomerates are seeking to construct a defensive alliance by building a 'Fortress Europe' against US and Japanese multinational competitors. This is the economic equivalent of the earlier discussion which highlighted the right-wing construction of new racial frontiers for Europe.

A second inter-regional trend which has accelerated since the demise of centrally planned economies in central and eastern Europe is cross-border co-operation. This transforms previously suspect or fragile strategic regions into pivotal nodes in an expanded European network of communication and trade. Such change emphasizes how geography and place are periodically reinterpreted and transformed. Vulnerable strategic minorities, such as the German-speakers in the Alto Adige/South Tyrol, are now in a stronger position to re-build their relationship with geographically contiguous majorities to the north. Once again, they can serve as a bridge between the Romance and Germanic culture areas and trade regions. Similarly, the Friulian-Slovene corridor now offers a strategic gateway to central Europe as it did in the days of the Austro-Hungarian Empire. Whether economic development will invigorate the Friulian language in that borderland region, or more powerful neighbouring languages will re-establish themselves, is an open question.

CONCLUSION

All of these issues influence the fortunes of political regionalism. Cumulatively, these trends will enhance the productive capacity of European economies, but they will also strain the public finances of responsible local and regional government. During economic downturns, the refusal to honour any of these initiatives is likely to antagonize those interest groups who anticipate that they are an integral part of the realization of a multilingual Europe.

Globalization is an imperfect and developing process, an ideology and programme which challenges the current order. Together with European integration, it changes the context within which civil society is mediated, posing a threat to the conventional territorial relationships and simultaneously opening up new forms of inter-regional interaction such as cable television and global multi-service networks. Ethno-linguistic minorities have reacted to these twin impulses by searching for European-wide economies of scale in broadcasting, information networking, education and public administration. They have also established their own EU institutions and bureaux and entered new alliances to influence EU decision-making bodies. They believe that by appealing to the superstructural organizations for legitimacy and equality of group rights, they will force the state to recognize their claims for varying degrees of political/social autonomy within clearly identifiable territorial/social domains.

It is claimed that such developments constitute the dawn of a 'Europe of the Regions' but this is premature, despite the emergence of a new regional actors. The nation-state remains dominant and is likely to gain further prominence if it becomes the filter through which increased regional-level mobilization from below is mediated or alternatively, the instrument by which top-down regional development and social equalization policies are enacted within an enlarged European Union. In one of the ironies of history, it could be that the expanded super-structural organizations and the emerging regional-level actors both contribute to the renewal of a reformed, decentralist nation-state posing as the only truly representative instrument of a multi-cultural civil society. The critical test of European democracy is how well it can harness the material and political advantages of enlargement and globalization without sacrificing the identities and ambitions of constituent minorities on the altar of political-economic integration.

NOTES

1. I will not be referring to the policies of particular political parties pushing for regional autonomy, preferring to concentrate on the general theme of regionalism and ethno-linguistic concerns for identity in a rapidly changing environment.

7

Regional Planning and Urban Governance in Europe and the USA

URLAN WANNOP

INTRODUCTION

Although few stable arrangements had been established in the US, European regions were increasingly a focus for new approaches to strategic planning and governance in the 1980s. England's dissolution of metropolitan local government in 1986 was the major exception to a European trend which was better matching local governance to the spreading scales of regional economic and social affairs. But even in the two conservative countries of the US and the UK, there was a real awakening to the potential of effective regional planning in the 1990s, when the pressures of urban growth and political tendencies were reinforcing aspects of regional governance.

WHAT KIND OF REGIONAL PLANNING?

Like kinds of region, the kinds of regional planning are various. The long-involved US academic and regional planner, John Friedmann, has said that 'regional planning' is often used as a phrase to describe a congeries of more or less unrelated activities, giving his own definition as: 'regional planning is the process of formulating and clarifying social objectives in the ordering of activities in supra-urban space – that is, in any area which is larger than a single city' (Friedmann and Weaver, 1979).

Economists and political scientists commonly take regional planning to mean initiatives in balancing resources to modify disparities in economic conditions and standards of living as between different regions of a nation, otherwise referred to as inter-regional or regional economic planning. However, this paper deals primarily with what is often called intra-regional physical planning, which attempts to resolve strategic issues allied to problems of growing metropolitan cities, spilling population and their economic and social relationships, and raising political disputes beyond their administrative boundaries.

Although most frequently associated with cities and metropolitan areas, this kind of intra-regional planning has also arisen in sparsely populated regions with enduring problems of depopulation or of changing rural economies. It has sometimes been closely allied to economic planning, as in the work of the regional economic planning councils existing in England between 1965 and 1979, or in British cases such as the West Central Scotland Plan of 1974 or the Strategic Plan for the Northern Region of 1977, or in the roles of the *Conseils Régionaux* in France and most notably that for the Nord–Pas de Calais.

Also, of course, intra-regional planning may sometimes be wholly advisory, as with the English regional economic planning councils, or executive, as in the case of Scotland's Strathclyde Regional Council (1975-96), or the Spanish autonomous regions. It has sometimes taken the form of a government agency with resources and selective executive responsibilities, as with the Highlands and Islands Development Board in Scotland or the Appalachian Regional Commission in the US. Its scale has ranged from a population of 18 million for the London and South East Regional Planning Conference, four million for the Nord–Pas de Calais, to under 200,000 in the Highland region of Scotland, although these are all regions of similar surface area.

RECENT REGIONAL DEVELOPMENTS

The Europe of Regions in Flux

Enlarging the scale of local or sub-national government was widespread in Europe in the 1980s, with the notable exception of the United Kingdom and some specific exceptions such as the cancellation of co-operation of levels of government in the region of Greater Copenhagen (Bours, 1993:110; 126). The trend included the introduction of varieties of metropolitan local governance for strategic planning, as in France and Italy. In the early 1990s, regions were being established in Portugal and were being considered for the purposes of strategic planning and regional development in Hungary and Poland; they were also an implication of possible EU membership for the Scandinavian countries.

Experience has greatly varied in this Europe of regions in flux. Almost 200 years of Napoleonic prefectoral administration in France was counter-balanced in 1986 by the introduction of elected regional councils. In the Netherlands, a highly structured system of national governance and planning was adapting in the 1990s to metropolitan reorganization of local government for the Rijnmond. In Spain, much of the centralized authority of national government has been devolved to the *juntas* for the autonomous regions formed by 1983. But elected regional authorities established from 1970 in Italy were enmeshed in the bureaucratic and political corruption of Italian government, being marginal players in events. At an extreme, over 40 stable years of the German *Länder* represent as significant a level of regional governance as ever attempted in Europe.

Above the metropolitan level, five kinds of scale enlargement have been seen as afoot in the Union (Council of Europe, 1991):

1 addition of member states to the EU;
2 enlargement of state territories, as in Germany;
3 insertion of a regional layer, as in France and Italy, or the adoption of the 71 European Statistical Regions;
4 deletion of a layer of governance and transfer of some functions to central government, as extensively in Britain;
5 amalgamation of lower levels of governance, as in Sweden, Denmark and in parts of Britain, or new arrangements for metropolitan co-operation, as in the Netherlands or Italy.

The forms of regional governance have differed considerably. Major regions have become a full level of regionally elected governance in France, Italy and Spain. Belgium has effectively adopted federal government as has existed in the German *Länder* since 1949. Regional reform has customarily added a tier of governance rather than displacing one. And the metropolitan areas of Europe have been at the cross-roads on the routes to reform of regional governance, located at the junction between demand for local responsibility and the opportunities for economic initiative and efficiency to be gained through regional management.

There has been relatively little regional empowerment in some cases; the 13 Greek administrative regions legislated for in the late 1980s (Georgiou, 1993) were headed by government appointees; they were only a small step in devolving the highly centralized Greek administration, although matching the EU's expectation that its aid programmes would be monitored within the regions benefiting. Similarly, the Republic of Ireland launched eight regional authorities in 1994, nominated by the constituent counties, co-ordinating government services in the regions and being responsible for monitoring the implementation of EU programmes. While antipathetic to elected or to representational regional governance of any consequence, the UK government nonetheless significantly reorganized departmental affairs in the English regions in 1994, the new co-ordination going some way to bridge the wide gap between the UK and the European Commission over the principle of regional economic planning.

Beyond the EU, the collapse of totalitarianism in eastern Europe in the autumn of 1989 brought a demand for popular representation and local community control. But running alongside the urgency for economic reform which required centralized action, there was a vacuum between the contradictory processes of decentralization and of centralization (Welch, 1993). Thus, some form of regional governance was an obvious means to fill the gap between the levels of priority for immediate action.

However, as ethnic divisions led to bloody struggles, particularly in the former Yugoslavia and the Soviet Union, and as Czechoslovakia divided into new republics, resilient regional cultures emerged and the regional issue inevitably resurfaced. A variety of mechanisms of regional local self-government developed in the 14 new republics of the reconstructed Soviet Union (Ushkalov, 1993). A level of regional self-government was added in the Ukraine. Various regional unions arose in Russia, where regional soviets were given equal status with central state organizations, being permitted to make agreements with other Russian regions and republics and to settle administrative and territorial structures within their regions (Lysenko, 1993).

Poland came to debate whether the country's 49 provinces should be displaced by at least eight, but as many as 12 to 14, regions (Regulski, 1993). Hungary rationalized its local government system after 1991 by affirming seven prefectoral regions, each containing either two or three counties of diminished status; left at issue was whether or not prefects' functions as state officials would be displaced by the succession of elected regional governments. Czechoslovakia's system of local and regional governments emulated that of the Soviet Union prior to 1989. However, subsequent abolition of the ten regional committees led to calls for new regions or for up to five republics to bridge the governance gap, but division of the country in 1993 into separate Czech and Slovak republics took precedence over sub-national reform.

The regionalization of Europe has been matched by the progressive rise of new transnational groupings of regional representatives. The rise of these groups ran with the spreading sense of the arbitrariness of most national boundaries to the contemporary economic geography of Europe. The reality of the geography of common interests was expressed by a principal European bank: 'The economic interests of cities like Milan, Frankfurt, Paris and London have far more in common with each other than any of them has with, say, Cornwall, Limousin or the Mezzogiorno. They might form a rather stable monetary union of their own, if it were practicable.' (Credit Suisse First Boston Bank, 1992). A group of regions formed in 1986 comprising the Rhône-Alpes from France, Baden-Württemberg from Germany, Lombardy from Italy and Catalonia from Spain became known as the 'Four Motors of Europe', a club of rich men.

The number of clubs to which some regions belong almost defies credibility. A relatively late enthusiast for inter-regional co-operation, Catalonia not only joined in European networks but made co-operative agreements with Wales, the State of Illinois and with the Provincial Government of Buenos Aires in Argentina. Lombardy had international agreements to co-operate with regions in China and Canada (Borrás, 1993).

Amongst peripheral European regions fearing the consolidating economic strength of the core metropolises of Europe, the new groupings reflected a strong measure of self-protection. The long-standing geographers' view of a 'Golden Triangle' across parts of France, Germany, Britain, the Benelux countries and Italy was succeeded in the 1980s by the odd image of the 'Blue Banana' - a favoured arc of rapid economic growth stretching from Lombardy through Switzerland, southern Germany, the Benelux countries, northern France and south east England. Both images may have been trite and flawed in parts, but they had significant political resonance. As EU policy increasingly emphasized the economic potential of metropolitan regions in and near the 'Blue Banana', even the sunrise economies of the northern Mediterranean felt the need to assert themselves; significantly, in 1993, the Assembly of European Regions drew its president from Spanish Catalonia and its vice-president from adjoining French Languedoc-Roussillon.

So new associations of regions formed new spheres of common political interest across Europe, in a shifting mosaic of often overlapping regions. Overlaps reflected different purposes and terms of definition of the various groupings. The Regional Policy Directorate's report on *Europe 2000* (European Commission, 1991) defined eight supra-national regional groups:

- Atlantic Regions (UK, Ireland, France, Spain, Portugal)
- Central Capitals (London, Bonn, The Hague, Brussels, Luxembourg, Paris)
- Alpine Regions (Germany, France, Italy)
- West Mediterranean Regions (Spain, France, Italy)
- Central Mediterranean Regions (Italy, Greece)
- North Sea Coastal Regions (UK, Netherlands, Germany, Denmark)
- Inland Continental Regions (France, Spain)
- East Germany

Although the Commission remains without any formal responsibility for spatial planning, it has been led to it by awareness of how widely and significantly European territory is being restructured by the forces of economic change and of an enlarging Union with an open market. Regions are affected by the changed effectiveness of EU policies and as national boundaries have ever less significance to investors, economic forces and would-be migrants in Europe, issues of strategic and regional planning increasingly escape the control of individual national governments.

Arguing that member states have common interests in this new geography, the Commission has investigated possible strategic and regional impacts. Studies in spatial planning have joined others on inter-regional and inter-urban networks, cross-border co-operation and urban pilot projects. After initial studies into European demographics up to the year 2015, urbanization and the functions of cities in Europe, new industrial location factors and the spatial impact of the Channel Tunnel, the Commission in 1991 came to an appraisal of demographic and urban trends in *Europe 2000*, and launched a Committee on Spatial Development to systematically exchange information and fill out the framework for planning of *Europe 2000*.

Priorities in regional plans in Western Europe have shifted greatly since 1945. Post-war reconstruction and satellite communities to relieve metropolitan congestion were priorities up to the late 1950s, when came the advance of the economists with policy hypotheses to exploit the potential of the peripheral regions. In the 1960s, growth centres studded regional plans in both Europe and the developing countries. Growth centres and regional economic planning then fell into disrepute in the later 1970s. Political critics accused them of being Trojan horses for the advance of international capitalism, economists found them to be of variable and sometimes disappointing performance, and sociologists found them to work against the best of liberal ideals.

The United Kingdom; Against European Convergence?

In the UK, it was commonly supposed in the 1980s that regional planning and governance were lost causes. By the early 1990s, however, it was clear that a progressive revival of the regional dimension was under way. This was true in strategic physical planning and also in varied aspects of government administration. Despite continuing antipathy to elected regional local government or assemblies, the Conservative government was being forced to accept that regional issues and top-heavy centralized government demanded regional dimensions to physical, social and sometimes economic policy. In 1994, a much strengthened co-ordination of the government's departmental offices was introduced in the English regions. Although in 1996 the government was to abolish Scotland's most populous regional councils, this was a less considerable regional retreat than many critics supposed.

The abolition of the Greater London Council (GLC) and English metropolitan county councils in 1986 misled many about the strategic trend. Although the strategic capacities of the metropolitan county councils were greater than those of most of the arrangements by which they were replaced, the councils were conceptually flawed and inherently unstable. All had been much smaller than their recognizable city regions, and they had to strike arrangements for strategic co-operation not just with surrounding shire counties but also between two metropolitan counties in the case of north west England.

But the post-1986 metropolitan arrangements have been as unstable as those before. Strategic problems have been acted upon no more convincingly than previously, and the continuing strategic hiatus has been criticized by industrial, commercial, financial and other widespread interests in the private sector, as well as by parliamentary committees and opposition politicians.

So the motivations for reinforcing forms of English regional administration from the mid-1980s were many and different, and some developments were as politically expedient as was the abolition of the GLC and the English metropolitan councils. But without there being any coherent or real government enthusiasm for regional administration and planning, there came an appreciable flow of regional initiatives. A regional dimension was confirmed in health administration; it was being threatened for the police; it was introduced for higher education in Scotland and seemed inevitable for school administration in England; and it was introduced in urban regeneration and was anticipated in the allocation of EU regional funds in England. When, in 1994, England was for the first time completely covered by standing conferences of planning authorities, this was primarily a response by government to pressures by house-builders for regional planning to ensure a sufficient supply of building land.

However, the supposed streamlining of governance for metropolitan England in 1986 left many gaps and rough edges in the system of local government. When proposals for reorganization of the English shire counties were completed by the Local Government Commission in 1995, they sustained widespread inconsistencies of discretion and capacity. The parallel proposals for Welsh and Scottish reform also harked back to fragmented government of the kind which, for much of the twentieth century, had plagued coherent metropolitan development and inhibited an efficient economic infrastructure.

Notably, there were still no convincing signs of the government sustaining an effective vision, substantial strategy or dynamic planning for metropolitan London. Such flagships as the government helped launch seemed leaky and accident-prone: the Docklands enterprise was a lesson in clumsy and unbalanced strategic planning; the East Thames Corridor project seemed insufficiently substantial to bear comparison with urban projects in many non-capital cities in other countries; and the protracted story of deciding on terminals and entry routes for the Channel Tunnel rail link was a comedy in many parts without a convincing conclusion.

Government's reinforced regional co-ordination of urban regeneration policy in England from April 1994 had real potential, overseeing spending previously managed exclusively by the four Departments of Employment, the Environment, Trade and Industry and Transport, and combining 20 previously separate budget headings. This was far from a simple managerial initiative to redress years of disjointed regional planning and budgeting in England. It had two significant advantages for government. It disguised large cuts in funding of between 20 and 80 per cent amongst the 20 budgets unified in the Single Regeneration Budget (Shiner, 1995). It also disguised the fact that the European Commission had called for a single programme document from each region competitively bidding for EU Funds. Such was the rationality of this aspect of the UK's regional revival.

The United States

During the 1960s, the whole governmental structure of the United States was changed by the impact of rules for federal funding leading to sub-state regional councils of government being voluntarily interposed between local and state governments (Advisory Commission on Intergovernmental Relations, 1982). The councils of government became eligible for planning funds under the Housing and Urban Development and the Demonstration Cities and Metropolitan Development Acts, and for economic development under the Public Works and Economic Development Act. Federal grants for transportation and other public facilities were conditional upon metropolitan planning. Health planning and law enforcement councils were among the variety of regional initiatives instigated by federal funding policy. By 1971, another 18 federal programmes were helping fund regional councils across the US.

Councils of government were not an instant means of comprehensive planning for the fragmented metropolitan and regional governance of the US. They could be seen as the 'weakest kind of alliance conceivable ... from which a participant may withdraw without citing cause. It is not a body politic or corporate, nor could it by any reasonable definition of the term be called a government' (Martin, 1963). As to the metropolitan planning agencies, the Joint Center for Urban Studies (1964) expected them to be severely handicapped by insufficient power to control development, lack of clear statutory direction and small and uncertain budgets. This foresight was later confirmed by Rondinelli:

> From a traumatic decade emerged a painful lesson: the most widely accepted principles and assumptions of American planning theory proved inadequate to meet the complexities of implementing urban and regional development policy ... Attempts to require comprehensive planning in federal housing, transportation, regional economic development, anti-poverty, and community development programs have not succeeded. (Rondinelli, 1975)

In 1961 there had been only 36 councils of government, but by 1978, there were 659 councils nationally, of which 292 were metropolitan; 44 councils operated in regions with over one million population, but most had less than a quarter of a million. By 1980, almost the entire US was covered by regional planning organizations of some form.

But the councils generally had little or no power, their priorities greatly varied and they had only a weak popular base. The first transformation of a council of government into a directly elected metropolitan government was in 1979 in Portland, Oregon. In a region of over a million people, the Portland Metro was still the United States' only directly elected regional government in the 1990s, although some (DeGrove, 1991) felt it had yet to realize its full potential. It was responsible for strategic planning, operating the transit system and disposing of solid waste, with a limited range of other functions.

During the 1970s, the US anticipated the European trend of the 1980s, as regional groupings formed not just within states but between them. As growth rates sharply diverged across the US (Markusen, 1987), three political coalitions were formed in the Southern Growth Policies Board, embracing 12 growing states, the Northeast-Midwest Congressional Coalition, combining 17 states with problems of severe economic adjustment, and the Policy Office of the Western Governors, covering 11 states on the old western frontier.

When the Reagan and Bush administrations severely cut federal aid to the metropolitan US in the 1980s, regional planning was left to the states or to local areas. All except two of the 12 big federal block grants were fed through the states, which tended to spread them more evenly and to disconnect them from metropolitan or regional planning (McDowell, 1985). Although metropolitan planning generally subsided, the Department of Transportation still put much federal financing of urban transportation planning through regional councils in metropolitan areas. Yet regional collaboration became generally perfunctory. Where remaining, it had to sell its merits and its services to the local governments subscribing to it.

Councils' duties to the federal government were progressively eliminated and the limitations of this kind of regional planning could be seen as it subsided in the 1980s. It was said to have sought impracticable comprehensiveness, to have been slow and unresponsive, very expensive, and to have demanded large amounts of often outdated information for cumbersome data processing routines. Councils of government were generally too fragile to implement contentious proposals and although ambition produced some comprehensive and visionary plans, these were often rigid and unyielding (McDowell, 1985).

Nor did the movement to councils of government carry over into a widespread reorganization of local governance. Metro Portland and the metropolitan governments for Dade County, Florida and Nashville, Tennessee were exceptions. Inner cities were reluctant to succumb again to the white majorities which the incorporation of suburban districts would have implied, and the suburbs were reluctant to share the costs of regenerating the inner cities.

But although suspected by local politicians and difficult to sustain when described as regional planning, a process of the kind was increasingly pursued by a minority of states under the guise of 'growth management'. From the 1970s onwards, this was a philosophy to direct urban and allied growth so as better to conserve resources from environmental pressures. The first wave of growth management ran from 1970 to 1978 (DeGrove, 1991), with a second wave emerging in 1985 to run from Florida on through New Jersey, Maine, Rhode Island, Vermont, Georgia and Washington state. The plans were often under-funded and troubled by ambiguous political support, but they showed that regional planning was a growing concern for state governments.

Those states asserting a regional, strategic planning role were mostly on the Atlantic or Pacific coasts. California, the Pacific North West and the tourist economies of the New England states demanded preservation of their best landscapes. Hawaii asserted itself as a state planning authority because of the rapid loss to building of its fertile agricultural land. Vermont was pressured by development and urban growth was drowning Florida, where the Governor's 1989 task force on growth management advised that the doubling of the state's population since 1970 required strategic urban policy to combat future urban sprawl. Georgia sought to avoid the fate of nearby Florida. Maine's coast had become an asset of greater profit through tourism than through fishing. Californians feared being cut off from their beaches and coast, and Oregon was anxious to hold back debasing 'californication'. New Jersey was already the most urban state in the US and in the path of the still consolidating Bos-Wash megalopolis lay Rhode Island. By 1992, 13 states had legislated for state-wide or special area land-use planning and not only in coastal or mountain regions, but increasingly where transportation gridlock and housing spread beyond metropolitan areas into extensive suburban regions.

The state programmes of growth management of the 1980s had six characteristics (DeGrove, 1991). They focused on: strategies for funding and implementation; balancing environmental protection and economic development; increased emphasis and state funding for affordable housing; matching infrastructure to the impacts of development; mandated strategies for implementation; rural and wetland protection.

Growth control sailed on murky waters. The 1988 report on *LA 2000: A City for the Future* was criticized as a 'manifesto of a new regionalism', based on rationalized growth management within a regional goals consensus but assuming an economy of endless growth: 'There is no consideration whatsoever of possible contradictions within this perpetual growth machine' (Davis, 1990). The contradictions soon surfaced in the Los Angeles riots of 1992 and a failing Californian economy.

Was growth management a real revival of regional planning? Certainly not equally in the eight states actually implementing their growth management legislation. Some adopted centralized scrutiny of locally prepared growth management programmes, while others involved regional bodies in the process of analysis and approval (Gale, 1992).

But the rise of states' growth management programmes reinvigorated regional planning in new clothes. In 1991, federal encouragement to regional planning revived through the long familiar but indirect route of transportation planning. The Intermodal Surface Transportation Efficiency Act reformed federal transportation grants, demanding state-wide as well as the metropolitan transportation plans required since 1962.

WHAT MOTIVATES REORGANIZATION OF REGIONAL PLANNING AND GOVERNANCE?

An Imperative

In almost every country, the pressures for regional planning and forms of regional governance have persisted too widely and repetitively to be likely to go away. But neither does it seem that pressures are likely to be often met by fully stable regional arrangements. Reorganization and adjustments are endemic features of regional planning and governance, whatever their various motivations.

A drive for coherent planning of metropolitan growth, regional transport strategy and resource management has lain behind much regional reorganization. Need to resolve political tension between neighbouring local administrations has commonly been bound up with ostensibly technocratic aims. Although metropolitan local government may have been most often reorganized on the argument of economic and administrative efficiency, politics has normally suffused the scene. Party politics has been an overwhelming motivation in some reform, as with the advantage for the Conservative Party allegedly underlying both the creation of the Greater London Council in 1965 (Young and Garside, 1982: 308) and its abolition in 1986. Demand for regional planning at least and regional governance at most has come from the highest levels of industry and commerce, and from environmental interests. The economic case for regional planning has been most convincingly put by the private sector, as by the Bay Area Alliance in California or the Confederation of British Indistry (CBI) for metropolitan London.

Barlow (1993: 136) overlooks the factor of partisan politics in describing regional governance as having three common stimuli: administrative regionalism, where central governments have devolved functions to regional offices and may also have borrowed functions from local government; sub-national elected governance, particularly for cultural or ethnic regions; and metropolitan governance, in the face of a globalizing economy and competition between metropolitan areas.

These factors and that of partisan political advantage leading to the introduction of particular forms of metropolitan and regional planning and governance will mix differently at different places and at different times. The sole aim of efficient and sensitive co-ordination of interrelated aspects of governance is likely to have been relatively rare, but political crises of some kind seem to have been a frequent stimulus. UK governments have turned to regional planning in wartime, when established systems could not cope with the speed or directness or authority which emergencies required, and they have turned to it at times of economic crisis, as in the early 1930s and the early 1960s. Similar responses have occurred in the US. Regional planning has commonly been a means by which governments have declared a special political concern by going over and above established administrative arrangements; it can be used to overcome defects in local government or to by-pass it; and it can be a means of asserting central control over provincial affairs.

The regional structures of government administration consolidated in the UK in the 1990s were rooted as much in the government's party political attack on local government in the 1980s as in any spontaneous espousal of regional co-ordination. Regional administration and agencies had become functionally necessary as a consequence of progressive transfer of power from local to central hands.

The Depression between the world wars brought pressures for governments in the US and the UK to be seen to attempt to alleviate poverty and unemployment in decaying regions. Regional planning was based primarily on initiatives to foster industrial growth, a populist approach graced in the 1960s by emerging economic theories which were variants on Perroux's strategy of 'growth poles'. The increasingly evident external diseconomies of metropolitan locations for industry made decentralization policies palatable to most UK politicians, aided by governments' post-1945 acceptance of the long argued case of social reformers that overcrowded and poorer city dwellers should be enabled to spill out to green field estates and new towns. More wealthy citizens who had earlier moved to the suburbs were reluctant to co-operate in this leapfrogging strategy. So governments were led to look to reform of fragmented metropolitan governance. British reform of metropolitan governance in the 1970s was driven by experience of battles over urban renewal and growth in the 1950s and 1960s, perhaps more bitterly experienced in the Greater Manchester and West Midland metropolitan regions than in London and the south east.

Industry and business retain a significant interest in regional planning in parts of the US and a new interest emerged in the north west and south east regions of England in the 1990s. In most countries, it is governments which dominate in regional initiatives, with five common grounds for intervention, as evidenced by the case of the UK:

1 to assert government authority in significant affairs of long-run political interest such as Scottish Enterprise, Scottish Homes and English Partnerships;
2 to cover for a political crisis such as the regional development programme for north east England in 1963 and wartime measures to organize industry or civil defence;
3 to overcome stalemates in local government over strategic urban growth, for example the sub-regional planning studies in metropolitan England in the late 1960s and early 1970s;
4 to manage national assets, for example the national parks, and the Countryside Commission, and coastal planning;
5 to spread pressures on central administration, for example regional offices for the government's ministries, regional management of the National Health Service and regional boards for the Arts Council.

Hogwood explains the persistence of a regional dimension in UK administration since the Second World War largely in terms of governments' progressive accumulation of what had previously been local authority functions (Hogwood and Keating, 1982). In Europe, continuous regional restructuring has been described as the outcome of the interaction of four processes: of changes in economic systems of production and services; of the behaviour of multi-national corporations; of people's lifestyles and their composition into labour markets; and of political reactions to economic restructuring (Hansen, 1990).

In the 1980s, a new dimension was added to structures of politics and regional planning in European countries, when the European Commission made the role of regions and of regional planning a prime issue in the Union's development. Several principal and overlapping factors were thereby mixed in pressures for the reorganization of regional and metropolitan planning and governance in Europe. They were: the changing context of the European Union; continuing growth of demand for housing and continuing residential dispersal, spilling over city and metropolitan boundaries into the areas of peripheral local governments; the restructuring of economic and social affairs associated with a progressive shift of industry, warehousing, hospitals and other historic urban activities to suburban or out-of-town locations; change in political issues and in the balance of power between central and local government; restructuring of the way in which local services are delivered; and the redistribution of voters and the trend – exemplified in the UK – for a reducing number of 'marginal' councils and parliamentary seats.

The changing context of the European Union

In the early 1990s, even tendencies in the UK were converging with the EU's sustained pressure for more considered regional planning. The government's reinforced control of local affairs and planning was only manageable by an intermediate tier of central administration, with or without the appointment of allied government-financed agencies. This trend and its potential to match EU ambitions for regional programming became even more obvious, as the UK linked EU funding to a new Single Regeneration Grant, co-ordinated through the government's regional offices.

Urban Population Growth and Dispersal

Population growth and spread has destabilized governance in many European and US metropolitan areas. Even when some metropolitan populations have reduced, smaller households have commonly spread a wider demand for houses. With many of the costs of servicing the dispersed people falling still on the central city of the metropolitan regions, financial concerns as well as civic status prompt city councillors to seek compensation. In the UK, the Netherlands, Italy and a few other countries, local government boundary extensions have been feasible, sooner or later. But local governments have been less malleable elsewhere, in France in particular, as in the US.

Restructuring of Economic and Social Affairs

In the restructuring of regions, the dispersal of industry, social affairs and some business has generally followed the deconcentration of population, but there have been cross-currents. The central city focus has been reduced for homes and for manufacturing, but reinforced for most high-level financial, business and administrative functions. This has significantly affected the spatial distribution of public costs, income and common interests in airports, surface transport, exhibition and conference facilities and other regional goods.

The spreading nature of metropolitan regions has been reflected in the way in which UK governments have progressively redefined the region centred on London. In the Second World War, a London region of some seven million people was assigned its own Regional Commissioner. At the war's end, this London region was combined with four counties into a London and South Eastern region of 11 million people. In 1974, a new South East region was created, incorporating 13 counties and over 17 million people.

Comprehensive regional and metropolitan planning has dampened some of the damaging forces of restructuring in the UK and some European countries, unlike in the US where very fragmented local governments have induced development to local gain but metropolitan disadvantage, not least to the private sector which has often been a prime mover for regional planning.

Changing Central–Local Government Relations

In France, the new regional councils gained less authority in the 1980s than had been previously expected, but the direction of transfer of discretion was down from central government. In Spain, the direction was also strongly towards regional discretion, but in the UK, the direction was opposite; intervention of central government to disturb settled relationships with local government reached unprecedented heights under the Conservative government of the 1980s. The inner city issues to which that government gave priority in this period led it to intervene directly in local affairs through urban development corporations, task forces and other initiatives in fields in which local authorities had led the way for a hundred years previously.

Restructuring of the Delivery of Local Services

Technical and policy changes have consequences for the appropriate scale of administration of local services, which may be altered also by changes in the discretion permitted by a higher level of governance.

Privatization has had impacts which have made Britain's two-tier system of local government rather less viable than when it was designed in the early 1970s. While through competitive tendering, opting-out of schools from local government control and other means, the scope and size of local government affairs was reduced, the capacity to negotiate a programme and budget with local electors was curtailed by expenditure restraints, including the ceiling set on local taxes.

Voter Redistribution and The Reduction of Marginal Constituencies

From the 1970s, there has been a consolidation of persistent majorities for either the Labour or Conservative parties amongst British local authorities and parliamentary constituencies. Marginal majorities have become fewer. Selective emigration of the better-to-do from the principal cities excluded the early possibility of Conservative control being restored to many urban areas, leading to abolition of the Greater London Council and English metropolitan government in 1986. After the abolition of the GLC, the alternative to parliamentary and ward boundary changes – which were beyond government control – was a combination of policies to privatize the inner city and to increase the Conservative voting residents of selected London boroughs. Gerrymandering the distribution of voters where gerrymandering of boundaries is impracticable is a strategy familiar to politicians in many countries.

What Circumstances Achieve Changes in Governance?

In the British experience, there have been two dominant grounds for local government reform. Governments have wished for rationalization and greater efficiency and effectiveness, as represented in the national reforms of the 1970s, 1980s and 1990s, and in occasional localized reforms in and outside London. Governments have also been opportunistic in seizing party political advantage, as in London in 1963 and 1986, in the abolition of the English metropolitan county councils in 1986 under the cloak of 'streamlining the cities', and in the reorganization in Scotland occurring in 1996.

Better metropolitan but not better regional planning was certainly a purpose of English reorganizations of the 1970s, together with advantage for local Conservative party interests. But the metropolitan reorganizations by a later Conservative government in 1986 had no mind for strategic planning at all, and the reforms of Scottish local government in 1996 put no significance upon planning at either the metropolitan or regional scale.

It can be argued that the British reorganizations of the 1970s were no longer appropriate to the 1990s and that the major English metropolitan and Scottish regional councils were obsolete in the terms in which they were created. The scale of enduring issues of physical regional growth had outgrown not only the metropolitan areas, but also several of the larger standard regions originally defined over 50 years before. The areas and responsibilities of the GLC and the metropolitan councils were unbalanced, as many had long foreseen. And the Scottish system of regional councils was due for reconsideration after some 20 years of changing political and economic circumstances, particularly affecting the metropolitan-centred Strathclyde region.

The strategic obsolescence of English local government, in particular, could have been at least partially overcome by effective local alliances. But the English regional conferences of planning authorities have seemed always less direct and effective than the best examples of regional authorities in other countries. The Joint Regulations Act for the Netherlands reinforced the ability of local governments to work together over mutual interests, thereby adapting their administrative territory without need for structural reform. The West German *Länder* managed growing cross-boundary interests by standing conferences of ministers. Although nearly unique in the US, the Twin Cities Metropolitan Council in the US had more potential to plan effectively than any English regional planning conference.

In the US, seven principal stimuli recurred and mixed in different proportions at different times in the various outbreaks of regional planning and co-operative regional governance. They were: problems of enduring fragmentation of local governments in the most urbanized parts of the US, under pressures of development affecting regional issues from water supply and sewage disposal to traffic gridlock; the economic interests of industry and commerce, from Chicago in 1910 to the Bay Area of the 1990s; national political crises, from the Depression of the 1930s and the New Deal to pressures of war-time, and on to problems of economic adjustment as in the northern states' Rustbelt in the 1970s; resource development, as typified by river basin planning from the Tennessee Valley to the Columbia River from 1933 to 1945 and more recently on the Atlantic and Pacific seaboards; environmental movements, from the Sierras Club to the Greenbelt Alliance of the Bay Area; times of advancing federal intervention and support in cities and metropolitan regions, coupled to the rise of new techniques for strategic land use and transportation planning; and times of retreat in federal intervention and support for the cities and metropolitan regions, with a relatively increased state role in regional planning (Wannop, 1993).

MODELS OF REGIONAL PLANNING AND GOVERNANCE

The Variety of Regional Planning and Governance

Few regions of governance have the stable homogeneity of the regions described in traditional geography. Regions of governance are driven by factors of politics or economic dynamics, in constant flux. This is likely to be particularly the case in metropolitan regions. As political issues will always spill over the boundaries of such dynamic regions, regional issues are, in essence, those which an individual piece of a larger mosaic of governance cannot solve internally.

Our definition of regions relates to many forms of planning and governance, as it does to a variety of regions. It embraces plans of comprehensive scope and idealistic ambition like the Clyde Valley and Greater London plans of the UK in the 1940s, as well as bureaucratic and barely visible processes of regional collaboration, such as the Association of Bay Area Governments in the region of San Francisco or the conferences of south-east England planning authorities continuous since the 1960s. At an extreme, our definition would cover the study of the future of the Yangtze Valley, completed by the China Academy of Urban Planning and Design in 1990 and certainly one of the largest of cases of regional planning anywhere.

In the contemporary era of economic unions of nations, we have also seen how the old definition of regions as being smaller than states has been overtaken by the European Commission's recognition of supra-national regions.

Different models for regional planning arise within different traditions of governance, as Clout explains:

> ...national approaches to regional development then diverge from one another for three main groups of reasons. First, regional problems are in themselves highly varied and more importantly, have been perceived in different ways by government institutions and planning bodies. Second, national systems of administration, government and planning vary enormously at the institutional level. Third, national schemes of regional management vary in their stage of evolution. (Clout, 1975)

A selective range of models by which regional planning can proceed, directly or indirectly, includes:

1 regional assemblies with very significant executive responsibilities and legislative authority, such as the Spanish autonomous regions, including Andalusia and Catalonia;
2 regional assemblies with lesser resources, such as the regional councils of France and Italy;
3 regional local government, for example Strathclyde Regional Council in the UK;

4   metropolitan local government, such as the metropolitan county councils of England 1974-86;

5   directly elected single-purpose planning authorities on the German metropolitan model, such as that in Hannover;

6   standing conferences, on the US model of councils of government or the English model of the 1990s, for example, the Delaware Valley Regional Planning Commission and the London and South East Regional Planning Conference;

7   associations of local government investing appreciable authority in a mutual organization, such as the *Siedlungsverband Ruhrkohlenbezirk* in Germany;

8   consultants or an *ad hoc* team appointed to meet a specific strategic crisis, as for regions of Britain like the West Midlands or Humberside which, in the 1960s and 1970s, were expected to face major urban growth;

9   regional offices of a higher government, such as the Scottish Office and regional offices of government in England or the *Regierungsbezirke* of the German *Länder*;

10 governments' regional development agencies on the model of the *Etablissement Public Foncier Nord-Pas de Calais* or the Scottish Enterprise and Welsh Development agencies;

11 regional planning commissions with substantial government authority, acting either directly, like the COPLACO agency planning for Madrid prior to the introduction of the Madrid Junta, or indirectly, like England's regional economic planning councils of 1964-79;

12 regional planning commissions within a sub-national level of governance, amongst which the Twin Cities Commission for Minneapolis/St Paul is distinctive in the US.

The larger variety of contexts for regional planning and of forms of governance which could be described cannot be simply typified without neglecting significant distinctions. An adequate typology would have to recognize the widely different stimuli and substance of regional planning. Similarly, a categorization of forms of regional governance would have to recognize whether each had a role limited primarily to the exchange of information, or including proposals for strategic policy, or extended as far as the allocation of resources and to direct implementation.

Voluntarist, reformist and business groups were a main stimulus to regional planning in the early twentieth century. They remain so in parts of the US and they re-emerged in France and the UK in the 1990s. Some groups have arisen through popular environmental concern, while others have represented interests of commerce and industry. Professionals in urban and regional transportation planning have sought and initiated regional planning, and administrators in centralized bureaucracies have supported regional administration, as in the UK in the 1980s and 1990s. But political initiatives have been the prime stimuli to regional planning, arising from crises of various kinds and at various levels of governance. Central crises have arisen from regional threats to governments' electoral futures, from demographic trends implying exceptional demand for urban growth, from wars' implications for civil defence or emergency administration, or from regional pressure for political devolution. The crises may be more localized, lying in particular local political circumstances or a lack of capacity among particular local governments effectively to fulfil regional needs; or long-term growth management may call for semi-permanent arrangements for regional planning to forestall recurrent local crises.

External extra-governmental groups have been significant in the experience of regional planning. Some have been simply sources of regional data and intelligence, while others have been advisory or advocacy groups from which plans or policy ideas have stemmed. In the region of San Francisco, the Bay Area Council has, over many years, combined some of the US's top industrial and financial interests with the Greenbelt Alliance defending the environment, forcing regional issues onto political agendas.

DO REGIONAL PLANNING AND REGIONAL GOVERNANCE INVARIABLY FAIL?

Where there has been an erratic history of regional planning and governance, as in the UK, their real performance has been poorly observed and analysed. Comment has dealt more in hypothesis and ideology than in empirical observation. Regional planning has had predictably strong support amongst professional planners (Royal Town Planning Iinstitute, 1986), whereas its merits have been denied by many politicians. Regional governance has divided the major political parties in the UK and academics have given it slight support and some strong criticism.

The case against regions is characterized by Jones (1988), who dismissed regional government for the UK as 'redundant and dangerous', describing it as 'a fashion' drawing functions from central and local government, having its own tax, being directly elected - and never tried in Britain. Such criticisms neglect both the experience of much of mainland Europe and such cases of regional governance in the UK as that of the Strathclyde and Highland Regional Councils in particular. By not considering whether a regional scale could be adopted for local government rather than adopting a new level between it and national government, criticism commonly neglects possible variants in forms of regional governance.

So the argument against regional strategy commonly incorporates fallacies and misconceptions. The case against regional governance has much to commend it in parts but it tends to distortion in the whole. For although the limitations of some forms of regional and metropolitan governance tried in the UK and the US have been substantial, the need for regional arrangements of some kind is better reflected by their recurrent revival than by their frequent dissolution. Both the critics and supporters of the regional dimension may have expected too much of it. It may have been damned by opponents for falling short of unrealistic standards, while its supporters may equally have aimed too high.

The record of evidence across Western Europe and in the US (Wannop, 1995) shows that only in ignorance can it be argued that regional planning is not in demand or that metropolitan regions cannot be a sufficiently effective basis for governance. The context may commonly be unstable, but there can be no question about the permanence of regional issues in planning, or of continued initiatives towards forms of governance which can handle them.

Among the regional experiences of Europe, the German *Länder* and Spanish autonomous regions, as fully as in any country, match scale of governance with the capacity for direct and effective regional planning. Neither system has been perfect, being inevitably prone to strains within the regions. The metropolitan system in Britain between 1974 and 1986 was, however, much further from perfection and was ripe for reform.

Advances in the concept of regional planning and the most outstanding of strategic planning decisions commonly occur outside any formalized system of regional governance. They have occurred at political heights, often at the interstices of established systems of governance and frequently through *ad hoc* initiatives, consultants' reports and other often transitory sources of advice and policies.

This irregular and occasionally obscure context for decisions on regional planning reflects the frequently transitory nature of significant regional issues. The flexible region is not always matched by similarly flexible governance.

Matching and permanent arrangements for regional governance are clearly not essential for effective action in regional planning. Although stable arrangements for regional governance may potentially ease the way to effective implementation, regional planning of the traditional physical kind is not of itself a sufficient argument for regional governance. The relative significance of different regional issues varies –over time – between such matters as regional highways, rapid transit, housing overspill, inner-city regeneration, major industrial development and other topics – and different organizational and political ways of dealing with these may be appropriate at different times.

Eight characteristics summarize the nature of regional planning:

First, it is often a mercurial concept. It is frequently ephemeral and more like a guerrilla operation than mainstream public administration. Some of its advocates have wished too much to institutionalize it, and some of its critics have failed to appreciate its irregular nature.

Second, much has been highly successful. Some plans, like those for Greater London (1944) or the Clyde Valley (1946) in the UK, have been profoundly influential. Planning in the Ruhr and Paris regions has been similarly effective. Where it has seemed to fail, it has often been because it was not followed up by an appropriate context for action or, as in the 1970 Strategic Plan for the South East of England, because it proved to be technically flawed.

Third, because regional planning so repeatedly emerges, it is evidently an enduring necessity between levels of government and agencies of administration. It arises in different places at different times, in different forms and with varying intensity in often changing circumstances.

Fourth, regions are inconstant. Their size, composition and shape fluctuate with changing political circumstances and with the changing dynamics of social and economic geography.

Fifth, no sooner are planning or administrative arrangements fixed for any region than new regional issues arise around its borders. Regional issues are often political in origin and are certainly political in their implications. Thus, no perfect system can be devised for regional planning and governance, and any regional planning arrangements tend to instability;

Sixth, while regional planning conferences or councils of largely equal partners are invaluable for monitoring, interpreting and exchanging information, they are commonly inept at resolving strategic policy. Leverage on those who implement a strategy is normally essential to resolving one which is coherent and far-sighted.

Seventh, the need for comprehensive redirection of most regional strategies is infrequent and the timing is irregular. The proper role of many strategic teams is to report and then to self-destruct. The time cycle of strategy-making does not match that of implementation.

Finally, the technical methods appropriate to regional planning must be sensitive to its characteristics. An exceptional degree of risk surrounds much regional planning strategy, because it commonly looks to longer time-horizons and a more complex context for its implementation than do most other kinds of development planning.

THE FUTURE FOR REGIONAL PLANNING

The Regional Dilemma

Regions are dynamic and no longer only parts of separate nations, but now often transcend national boundaries. From the commencement of the Channel Tunnel, the Region Nord-Pas de Calais and Kent County Council have co-operated in a joint pilot action programme presented to the EU for training, economic development and tourism, to be followed by a joint cross-border development programme. This kind of regional co-operation was far short of significant regional governance, but it was one of many such regional links between territories of member countries of the EU and stretching also into eastern European countries seeking EU membership around the end of the century.

The spreading mosaic of regions has created an underlying dilemma for the EU's approach to regions. One EU categorization defines regions in terms of industrial similarities and, by 1992, the Union fostered 37 different networks linking widely separated local or regional economies. A quite different EU categorization recognizes eight supra-national regions including Alpine Europe and the Maritime Periphery. Yet another EU categorization fits all countries into a three-level European NUTS classification. Some countries have no formal governance arrangements at any of the three levels, and the NUTS classification accordingly suffers by anomalies and arbitrary amalgamations of administrative areas which have no meaning in the country in question.

The EU illustrates the dilemma of drawing regional patterns. This is considerably due to the inevitability that economic regions do not always make suitable regions for the purpose of regional planning and of regional governance. Economic regions may not correspond with acceptable political regions. Thus, the Europe of regions is a confused scene.

Metropolitan or regional governance?

Part of the case for dismissing the possibility of metropolitan area governance in favour of regional governance is the development of regional cities, whereby some cities which once dominated their hinterlands have now become dominated by them in important respects (Self, 1982). Self also argues that effective regional government would better match an accompanying level of unitary local government. Particularly among politicians representing the status quo, there is criticism that regional governance must inevitably be distant, lacking an electorate with any inherent regional loyalty.

The professional case for formalized arrangements for regional planning and governance has been argued by planners to rest on three principles (Royal Town Planning Institute, 1986): the evolving and spreading complexity of the social and economic structures of most metropolitan urban regions and of many rural regions; direct electoral accountability by extending the responsibility of locally elected representatives over a wider range of public services; and the merits of distributing resources to bring a considered balance between local aspirations, efficiency and equity within the regions.

But does regional governance necessarily imply remoteness, weak popular participation and lack of accountability? Bennett (1989) identifies four criteria for acceptable participation:

1 identity: maintaining community interest and mutual support between individuals and groups within areas;

2   legitimacy: the extent to which administrative decisions are
    accepted by individuals or groups;
3   penetration: the effectiveness of administration for individuals
    or groups;
4   distribution: the degree of redistribution from those who have to
    those who have not.

In contemporary economies, a large scale of sub-national
governance can be argued to be commonly justified on all these
criteria. Long resettlement of metropolitan populations to new
towns and commuter villages creates two significant scales of
identity for substantial numbers of people, who have a regional as
well as a local community identity. In urban regions particularly,
legitimacy cannot be merely the sum of many local responses to
wider problems; there are wholly proper differences of interest to be
raised between participants at local and regional levels. Penetration
certainly requires local sensitivity, but fragmented governance will
tend to be inequitable governance.

But if very local government cannot by itself satisfy the criteria
for acceptable participation, an exclusively top-down approach in
strategic matters is likely to be similarly insensitive. In larger
countries, central government is too high above the regional level
and local governments are too numerous for governments to
arbitrate for all issues with a regional dimension. Also,
governments' quasi-judicial role in planning and the proper
interplay of local and central considerations are prejudiced by
unifying regional planning in government hands. This does not rule
out, however, indirect regional planning through a planning
commission or some other form of intermediary.

With the spreading hegemony of key functions of major
metropolitan centres and the dispersal of other activities within
their widening hinterlands, previously separate regions may
overlap as specialist and complementary services are accentuated.
As notable a regional concept as the Randstadt was becoming
obsolete in the 1980s, when the Netherlands government saw it
being replaced by a Central Netherlands Urban Ring, including two-
thirds of the Dutch people (Faludi, 1994). Also, new regions may
emerge, as they have in the corridor of the M4 motorway between
London and Bristol in southern England.

In these circumstances, metropolitan areas have commonly
become quite arbitrary areas. They may be a relatively appropriate

level for operating some infrastructure services, but will be too narrow a focus for much significant sub-national strategic physical and economic planning.

EUROPE: THE NEW REGIONAL PLANNING AND THE EUROPEAN FUTURE

The new Europe will remain dominated by the large metropolitan regions, even as tertiary services displace secondary manufacturing as the major employer in national economies. But scenarios of the future metropolitan and regional structure of Europe can be as varied as the ways in which the current structure can be interpreted. The 1980s concept of the 'Blue Banana' metropolitan axis from London to Milan, curving through Brussels, the Ruhr and Zurich, has since been distorted by new regional groupings and shifting alliances. Marine issues faced by Baltic countries and by those around the Aegean and Black Seas will link current and prospective Union members. Berlin's enhanced significance for the European economy will further distort the perceived shape of the 'Blue Banana'. Other regional forces will bear on regional economies and alliances.

Some of the proliferating networks among European cities and regions may have little more than social value, entertaining civic officials and exchanging schoolchildren. But they are argued to have economic as well as political and cultural importance (Berg and Schaafsma, 1991). Networks induce exchange of information, helping participants to be among the first to gain significant knowledge. This is as true for those in public administration as for those in industry and in commercial multi-nationals. And the intersections of networks are favoured locations in the competition between city and metropolitan economies; here is fertile ground for multinational companies, for international organizations, for research institutions, for marketing and for regional distribution and services.

Regional networking has been supposed to be economically significant not only in mutual support and exchange between regions across Europe, but also within regions. It has been formalized since 1964 in the regions of France and has been a significant feature elsewhere, as in Baden-Württemberg and Emilia-Romagna. In France, not just internal politics but also the advantages of scale in international competition were reflected in 1994 when government was encouraging the regions to co-operate for added economic strength, as with the *Grand Sud* consortium of as many as five *conseils régionaux*.

Belatedly, the idea of networking became explicit in some UK initiatives of economic and social rehabilitation in the 1990s, beginning with the City Challenge scheme and extending to the government's Single Regeneration Budget for the regions in 1994. The British regional economic planning councils of the period 1965-79 had been only a pale reflection of the kinds of regional network between industrial, business, research, training, labour and social interests formalized in some other European nations. Fifteen years of erosion of such networks had occurred in the UK during the era of confrontational political ideology in the 1980s. The privatization of so many public services did not help the possibility of the UK emulating the economic success of regional networks elsewhere in Europe, credited with having a real part in some exceptional economic growth (Bachtler, Downes and Yuill, 1993; Cooke and Morgan, 1991). The UK also lacked the local networking force of the Chambers of Commerce in France or of the regional business associations of Italy.

In eastern Europe, some have looked to their countries being absorbed into a Europe of comprehensively structured regions, taking a rapidly growing role in an institutionalized system of European planning. This new regional planning has been seen as not merely the allocation of resources from the centre, as in the past; it would arise from within the regions. It would be 'innovative, strategic and pluralistic planning' (Kuklinski, 1993).

After its *Europe 2000* appraisal, the Commission expected to proceed to complementary regional programmes among member states. Regular review of the European Regional Development Fund containing national and regional planning objectives would influence the Union's priorities for its own programmes. It would also be a potential means of reinforcing the Union. A European statement would be prepared, identifying national policies and programmes affecting other Union members and indicating Union development priorities. The new Committee of the Regions and Local Authorities would be employed to advise the European Parliament in all this and the Parliament would assume a decision-making role equivalent to that of the Council of Ministers (ARL/DATAR, 1992). 'A regional development policy for Europe ...

must put forward a comprehensible and credible approach to the future spatial distribution of activities on the Continent. It must also suggest concrete programmes of reorientation with respect to the available resources' (Ibid).

Institutionalizing regional planning within a European framework raises the dilemma already posed. No uniform pattern can be drawn to serve all the purposes of regional planning in Europe equally well. Yet, as Kuklinski (1993) suggests, revised analysis would be required to develop a comprehensive regional system across the new Greater Europe. But member states have not waited for the Union to develop their regional structures. Late in 1992, Belgium agreed that its historic schism would be further rationalized by creating directly elected parliaments in Flanders and Wallonia.

Out of the turmoil of experience and progressive understanding of the developing impacts of the international economy, new priorities for regional planning are still being formed. After long practice in newly industrializing countries, Friedmann and Weaver (1979) came to argue that although traditional regional planning might continue for many years, the cutting edge of professional thinking and practice now lay in helping assert regional interests against those of transnational economic forces. Regional planning had become one of the proliferating weapons of intercontinental economic defence.

The US

Consolidation of US city and county governments to reinforce the potential for effective strategy and resource allocation for combined functions has been very limited. Yet, despite the seemingly chaotic context for regional planning in such metropolitan regions as Chicago, decisions of a kind are reached by processes euphemistically described as those of an ideal pluralist democracy (Hemmens and McBride, 1993). An imperative for regional planning has remained inherent in US conditions, as the fragmented complexity of its local governments has suffered sustained pressures of development and of servicing in water supply, sewage disposal and traffic gridlock.

So although the source of the stimulus changes with national politics and preoccupations, the regional dimension persists in US public affairs. The scales and the titles change, but there is a continuing imperative for regional planning and governance. Its more rationalized future shape might come from one of three moulds (ibid.): a regional state commission like the Twin Cities Council or the consolidated Bay Area Commission proposed by interests in the Bay Area; reinforced sub-regional planning focused on county governments, which would commonly call for a regional council of sub-regional governments; or a strong regional agency with responsibilities deriving more from regional than from state government. A sustained rise of growth management must also sustain US experiments in regional planning and governance.

CONCLUSION

Metropolitan planning and metropolitan governance are likely to lose ground to wider regional approaches in the longer run. Imperatives for reappraisal and recasting of the means of regional planning and governance will persist in both Europe and the US, but any pursuit of enduring forms of these is likely to be frustrated by the dynamics of regional issues and of regional economic development. Metropolitan planning and governance will remain common enough, being an alternative in some cases, an intermediate stage in others, and a complementary approach elsewhere.

8

Restructuring, Work and Identity: Perspectives on Region, Class and Gender in Southern Europe[1]

WINNIE LEM

INTRODUCTION

In the face of major changes in the international economy and the political turbulence of recent times, many theorists have been concerned, on the one hand, to understand the complexities of economic change under late capitalism and to unravel the enigmas of cultural politics in what is often referred to as a post-modern world on the other. To apprehend the shifting contours and structures of the contemporary economy, social scientists have proposed that prevailing global economic and social patterns have undergone a fundamental restructuring since the mid- 1970s. The broad set of changes taking place world wide has been referred to variously as the end of 'organized' capitalism and the beginning of 'disorganized' capitalism (Lash and Urry, 1987; Urry 1990), or the end of industrial society and the emergence of 'post-industrial' society (Touraine, 1987), or perhaps more commonly as the end of the Fordist era of economic organization and the advent of post-Fordism (Aglietta, 1979; Piore and Sabel, 1984). While there are many similarities and significant differences in how these writers conceptualize the essential characteristics of the new economic regime that has emerged, collectively they have been referred to as theorists of restructuring. Underlying their different explanatory paradigms is a common concern to explicate the reordering of economies and societies under new structural principles.[2]

Along with the emergence of this particular academic discourse on the nature of change under late capitalism, a literature devoted to theorizing what has been termed the 'new social movements' has proliferated (Melucci, 1980; Habermas, 1981; Touraine, 1987). It has been concerned with the 'new social movements' that centre their struggles around a diversity of issues reflecting the heterogeneity of interests that prevail in a post-modern world. Broadly, these movements encompass such political forces as environmentalism, feminism, peace activism, anti-racism and ethnic nationalism. While there is some question as to how 'new' these 'new social movements' are (Weir, 1993), it is generally held that their salience reflects the condition that social life, culture and politics are no longer predominantly organized around social class. Class-based politics, so it is often held, no longer adequately address the multitude of points of contention on contemporary political agendas (Urry, 1990). As diverse as the new social movements are, a significant number of them, such as feminism and ethnic nationalism, are oriented to what are thought to be the ascribed and particularistic qualities of individual subjects. As such, they are focused on identity, revolve around defining difference and, in the case of movements based on ethnic nationalism, they in fact promote and celebrate distinctiveness. In Europe, regionalism and the cultural manifestations of regionalism have been among the forms that the new social movements have taken. The ascendancy of regionalism in this context has coincided with international efforts to create pan-European institutions in the forging of a 'Europe without borders'. Thus, various forms of regionalism have erupted precisely at a moment when the forces of globalization are at work redrawing the boundaries of political, economic and cultural spaces. In the face of these apparent countervailing forces, scholars have been struggling to comprehend the dimensions of a cultural politics which assert attachments to place, region or locality.

As a contribution to this struggle, this chapter explores some of the issues and questions raised in investigations of the nature of economic restructuring, on the one hand, and on regionalism as one manifestation of the 'new social movements' on the other. My objective is to inquire into the relationship between processes of economic restructuring and the shifting forms of collective identity which have arisen in the European context. This objective is clearly not original since, as I have mentioned, many political economists have indeed grappled with this problematic in a variety of geographic contexts (see also Jensen *et al.*, 1993). However, many current approaches to both problems, as I argue below, tend to locate their analyses at a macro-analytic level. They focus on structural transformations in the national economy, political institutions, as well as the policies of national and supra-national organizations. Although illuminating on macro-level structures, institutions and organisations, one limitation of this analytical approach is that the concrete experiences of people who work and live under such large-scale forces of change are often far removed or indeed absent from many of the current exegeses. This paper, by contrast, attempts to shift the analytical focus somewhat by drawing attention to the experiences of working people, how their lives absorb such changes, and how they attempt to define their collective subjectivity in the face of large-scale transformations in the economy and society. It adds what I would argue is a much-needed ethnographical dimension to the issues of economic change and regional identity, and, as such, the paper is based on anthropological research conducted among small scale farmers in the Lower Languedoc region of southern France.

My purpose, therefore, is to trace the relationship between the process of restructuring and the salience of regionalism by focusing on changes in the organization of production, work relations and the definition of group interests that have issued from the transformation of agriculture in a southern European context since the end of the Second World War. In exploring this relationship, I will also critically assess some of the assumptions made in theories of restructuring on how collective identities are constructed among people whose working lives are profoundly affected by large-scale change. Before proceeding, however, a comment on restructuring theory is in order. In addition to the limited emphasis placed on the 'micro' level, theories of restructuring, by and large, have been centred on the analysis of <u>industrial</u> change. Few analysts of restructuring have directed their attention to agricultural change nor indeed on the relationship between agriculture and industry. (Kenney *et al.*, 1989, is one exception.) It should be pointed out, therefore, that the discussion presented here involves the extrapolation of some of the central tenets of restructuring theory, which largely concerns industry and industrial change, to the analysis of agrarian change. In this light, the observations made in this paper are largely tentative and the conclusions, in effect, represent a series of hypotheses that may be explored in future research (my own and that of others).

The exploratory nature of this paper notwithstanding, my overall argument, consonant with the assertions of many theorists of restructuring on the question of identity and the new social movements, is that changing spatial and social divisions of labour in late capitalism have been accompanied by a fragmentation of the class identity of working people and its re-configuration into a series of diverse and particularistic identities. The most relevant of these for our purposes are those focused on locality and region. In departing from such theories, however, I argue that regional identity itself does not necessarily exclude other forms of mass identity, but is often configured and reconfigured in fact by class solidarities. I shall further argue that the hegemony of class and regional identity does in fact have the effect of effacing a politicized gender consciousness. Indeed, gender identity has been subsumed under modes of identity that are privileged by specific forces in the contexts of changing social and sexual divisions of labour in various phases of the development of capitalism.

I shall illustrate these points by reference to the Lower Languedoc region which is located in an area of France noted for its radical traditions (Loubère, 1974; Judt, 1979; Agulhon, 1982). In this area of Lower Languedoc, grape growing and the manufacturing of wines by large owners and small growers have been the mainstay of the economy since the late nineteenth century. The grapes grown in the region are used in the production of generally low-grade wines that are vinified either privately or in cooperatives, or distilled to make industrial alcohol. While grape growing tends to represent the main source of income to rural households, many smallholding families actually sustain themselves by following a variety of livelihood strategies that involve members of the household in wage-earning activities and other forms of remunerated work. The small farmers of this region have worked their land under the vagaries of an economy that has slumped and boomed for a period of at least 100 years, coinciding with the increasing penetration of capitalism into agriculture.   Over these years, a primarily subsistence-oriented polyculture became transformed into a market-oriented monoculture based on the cultivation of grapes for wine production. From the mid-nineteenth century to the present, the small farmers of the region have responded to market failures, crises of over-production and state interventions into the viticultural economy by taking up various forms of collective action to defend their livelihood. From the late 1800s and the interwar period, rural women and men were prominent actors in public and collective acts, such as strikes and protests, as well as acts of sedition against the state. However, after the Second World War, women have all but disappeared from the stage of public protest. In the past few decades, the farmers of this area have received considerable media attention, both nationally and internationally, largely for their political protests against the entry first of Italy, then later of Spain and Portugal into the EEC. The kinds of struggles that have taken place have taken on a variety of forms, from mass region-wide forms of collective protest to small-scale guerrilla-like assaults launched at specific targets at the local level. Whether mass or small scale, highly organized or spontaneous, the actions of the small-scale growers have been cited as a prominent example of Occitan struggles and regionalism (Touraine *et al.*, 1981). In this area of southern France, Occitan regionalism and regionalist discourses have come to be incorporated into the political practices of small-scale vine growing peasantry aimed at defending a livelihood. This has occurred precisely in an era in which different but related spheres of work have been undergoing a process of restructuring to the point where people's experiences of work are becoming more fragmented, discontinuous and casualized (Pahl, 1985: 245). Since the late 1960s and 1970s then, in peasant protests and in various manifestations of rural militancy, class themes, once prominent in rural struggles, have been conflated or integrated with regional themes in their efforts to defend their means of making a living. A territorial sensibility has become prominent among many of the rural inhabitants of Lower Languedoc and this sensibility pervades contemporary political practice.

A NOTE ON OCCITAN REGIONALISM

Occitan struggles can take on a radically different character depending on the interests of particular groups and organizations that espouse its demands.[3] However, in general, there has been a tendency among scholars to dismiss Occitan regionalism as politically and historically insignificant. Often it is seen as an example of the failure of regional mobilization (Keating, 1986; Touraine *et al.*, 1981). This is especially the case when Occitan regionalism is compared to other examples of European regionalism (Le Roy Ladurie, 1977; Loughlin, 1985). Because of its cultural diffuseness and lack of unity, Occitan regionalism is often considered a force of little political and historical consequence.[4] Yet, Occitan consciousness and Occitan identity, at least among the small farmers of Lower Languedoc, exists as a compelling force which incites people to take up collective action to resist state domination, *dirigisme*, and to decry the conditions which have brought about dependency on the state.   The case of Occitan regionalism is therefore provocative and engenders interest precisely for those reasons that it is often so easily dismissed. A consciousness of being Occitan pervades the political practices of small farmers of Lower Languedoc despite the absence and the incoherence of an Occitanist political movement proper.   In this light, it offers an occasion to study the question of how identities become constructed in the absence of formal institutional and organizational supports.   Furthermore, it allows us to gain some insights into how various collectivities – peasants, workers, women – respond to changing social, spatial and sexual divisions of labour within a process in which capitalism constructs new places as sites for accumulation.

PERSPECTIVES ON THE RESTRUCTURING OF CAPITALISM

Restructuring theories as a mode of analysis emerged out of the shortcomings of approaches to understanding the evolution of capitalism through a political economy based on modes of analysis generated by 'classical' scholars (that is, Marx, Lenin and Kautsky) on the nature of capitalist transformation. The dissatisfaction with 'classical' models of capitalist transformation centres on how linear, teleological, historically and nationally specific such analyses of transformation were. For example, it has been stressed repeatedly that theories generated for capitalist development were formulated when the dynamics of capitalism itself involved competition through concentration, centralization and monopoly. However, economies in Europe and elsewhere have moved from operating on the principles of highly centralized, mass and highly regulated forms of production in an old phase of capitalism to decentralized, flexible forms of production in a new phase.

In moving beyond classical approaches, then, it has been proposed that large-scale restructuring of European and indeed global economies can be periodized in terms of the two economic regimes that prevailed since the Second World War (Jensen, 1988). The first economic regime spans the years of the post-war economic boom from 1945 to the 1960s and is referred to as the 'Fordist' economic era. Fordism is considered by theorists of restructuring to be the dominant form of twentieth-century production. Under Fordism, systems of mass production, mass consumption, managed national markets, collective bargaining and centralized organization lie at the core of the economy. Moreover, four principles are combined to govern the production of commodities to allow mass production to achieve economies of scale: the standardization of products; mechanization; Taylorism; and an industrial assembly line production (Murray, 1990).

It is held by writers examining the nature of global economic restructuring that a crisis in Fordist economic structures and organization occurred in the 1970s. The cause of the crisis has been attributed to the rise in oil prices, the fluctuating exchange rates, the fall of productivity growth due to workplace militancy, falling investments, the globalization of production and competition from newly industrializing countries (Murray, 1990; Urry, 1990; Kenney *et al.*, 1989; Jensen, 1988). Industries tended to respond to the crisis by cutting down the number of employees, shifting to part-time work and introducing new technologies and relocating (Jensen, 1988; Kenney *et al.*, 1989). These changes heralded the era of post-Fordism and flexible production systems.

Under post-Fordism, economic organization involved a move away from mass production toward a system of production based on flexibility in production processes and labour. In production, flexibility or flexible specialization (Piore and Sabel, 1984) involves the manufacture of a range of specialized goods for changing markets using general purpose machinery and largely skilled labour in factory or artisan workshops.[5] In many global contexts, the search for flexibility has meant the relocation of firms often to economically depressed areas that offer the locational advantages of cheap and abundant resources, including labour to work in the relocated factories and workshops of decentralized firms. Unemployed and underemployed women tend to serve as the main pool of labour from which workers are recruited, not only because of their 'flexibility' but also because, so their employers suppose, of their limited experience of labour militancy. Both these attributes often reflect a less continuous relationship to the labour market, as women often move in and out of employment depending on demand (Jensen, 1988). In both rural and urban settings, relocation, down-scaling and the decentralization of work, combined with industrial unemployment and recession, have implied the emergence of new forms of work. They have involved the intensification of pluriactivity, homework, subcontracted outwork and the informal economy, magnifying the already uneven pattern of development in southern European countries[6]. Moreover, under post-Fordism, the state has been retreating from its managerialist role in the economy and moving toward *laissez-faire* economic policies in many European contexts, which has implied that changing work contexts are often unsupervised and under-regulated by the state.

Analyses of Fordism (and indeed post-Fordism) have focused largely on the industrial structures and very few attempts have been made to apply such analyses to agriculture or rural settings. Nonetheless, since theorists of restructuring, at a more general level, are devoted to abstracting the logic of capitalist transformation, an argument can be made for its usefulness as an analytical framework in the study of an agriculture that has been subsumed by the dynamics of capitalism. The value of employing such a framework is underscored by the fact that the trajectories of industrial development are linked with agricultural development and this continues to be the case in many national contexts[7].

It has been proposed in theories of restructuring that the salience of different forms of collective identity are directly linked to the changing experiences of work which prevail under different periods of such changes in global capitalism. It has been argued furthermore that changes in the organization of production have eroded class-based politics and mass consciousness. Mass consciousness and union activity are ineffective in protecting working people from vagaries of post-Fordist production practices, and class-based action itself is very limited in contexts where the bases of conflict are multiple, where hostilities are directed at the state, the bureaucracy, political parties, other ethnic groups, male trade unionists and so on (Lash and Urry, 1987; Urry, 1990). For our purposes, perspectives on restructuring promise a way of understanding the salience of alternative collective orientations, especially regionalism, since they focus on the ways in which 'capital makes use of particular places for varieties of production in the pursuit of accumulation' (Bagguley *et al.*, 1990). Thus, there is an emphasis on the ways in which places are called into being, transmuted and destroyed in the pursuit of accumulation. One of the places that has been subjected to various forms of transmutation is the region of Lower Languedoc, France. In the next section, I address these suppositions through a discussion of the transformations of Languedoc agriculture using the insights offered by theorists of restructuring. I will also posit some links between these developments and the salience of class, regional and gender consciousness.

RESTRUCTURING AND RURAL LANGUEDOC

In line with the perspectives offered by theories of restructuring, the development of Languedoc agriculture followed a classic pattern of capitalist development with identifiable 'Fordist' characteristics until the 1970s. This pattern involved a continuation of a process that began in the late 1800s of intensifying the commercialization of monocrop viticulture and rationalizing production systems. Regional specialization developed, both in the kind of agricultural product that was produced in Lower Languedoc and also in the quality of the product. Lower Languedoc came to be the area that produced the wine that was generally considered to be the *vins de pays* and the *vin ordinaire* of France, destined to be sold on wine markets as a beverage for the numerically increasing working class of France, or to be distilled into industrial alcohol.

Throughout this era, the state played a highly interventionist role in Languedoc viticulture. The modernization of Languedoc viticulture was encouraged in various phases through agricultural policies to make wine growing more efficient, cost-effective and progressive. The wealthier farmers and village elites welcomed and indeed invited the technological innovations and scientific management of viticulture that accompanied state planning and regulation of wine growing (Keating, 1986). However, small producers and poorer segments of the farming population felt the effects of policies which were Malthusian in nature. Despite the ostensible support offered to growers in the form of subsidies and measures to improve the quality of wines, the latent agenda was the elimination of the smallest, and therefore, those considered the most inefficient units of production[8]. In this way, the effect of state aid has a differential impact on a rural population that was divided in terms of wealth and class. For the elite, it meant profitability. For smallholders, it meant decline or the threat of decimation.

The class differences in Languedoc villages were reflected in the structural characteristics of vine cultivation. On the one hand, there were large wine-growing estates or private farms which employed a force of permanent agricultural labourers combined with part-time and seasonal agricultural workers. The labour force on these estates was made up of women and men who cultivated their own small holdings on a part-time basis. The second structure that prevailed was the family farm, operated by using the labour of family members and often neighbours in reciprocal exchange networks.

It is beyond the scope of this paper to detail the precise nature of the capitalist transformation of agriculture.[9] However, the general pattern of change can be summarized. Capitalist transformation of Languedoc agriculture brought rationalization through technological changes to farming. The advent of the tractor, as well as the introduction of biochemical inputs contributed toward achieving economies of scale as farming on the large estates became more capital-intensive. The Marshall Plan also initiated a period of intensive and rapid modernization of French agriculture after the Second World War. New capital equipment was used in the vinification of grapes and assembly lines were introduced for the bottling of wine (Loubère, 1990).

Such changes had serious repercussions on the nature of farming, the relations of work and the social and sexual divisions of labour. On the larger estates, of course, this meant the displacement of labour since agricultural work became less labour-intensive. Women agricultural labourers were the first to lose their employment. Women also came to be displaced from farm work on the smaller family-based holdings, which could, through various forms of state aid and credit arrangements, take advantage of technological changes but at a slow rate of innovation. This development then had the effect of creating a peripheral or marginalized labour force, or a 'labour reserve'. Economies of scale and rationalization also meant that efficient farms absorbed weaker ones, again contributing to the generation of surplus labour, and the dynamics of concentration and the centralization of forms of production in agriculture and industry were prevalent. Resistance to the changes brought on by the capitalist transformation of Languedoc agriculture involved class-based protests through union activity, strikes, work stoppages and acts of sedition directed at estate owners which erupted often into violent and bloody confrontations in region-wide protests (Smith, 1978).

The modernization of Languedoc viticulture then pushed a significant proportion of the rural population out of agriculture and more people migrated from the country to the city in search of employment in France's expanding industries. The extensive rural to urban migration in the post-Second World War period has led to what has been called the depopulation of the French countryside in the period of rapid urbanization in an increasingly industrialized France. This pattern of rural out-migration was, in effect, a continuation of a trend that began in the late nineteenth century, with the migration of farm workers to expanding industrial centres which produced armaments, metals, and eventually automobiles and electrical equipment. So, from about 1946 to 1968, the proportion of the agricultural population in France fell by over half. It has also been noted that in the post-war period, there was a rise in the employment of women in industry and the service sector (Jensen, 1988).

However, not all surplus labour was immediately or even eventually absorbed by industry. For those who remained in the rural milieu, making a living involved the pursuit of other forms of livelihood activities in multi-occupational or pluriactive households. Increasingly gender-differentiated spheres of work in agriculture developed in the Languedoc countryside. Women agricultural labourers, who often combined domestic work with paid employment, became more identified with reproductive work, while farm work became masculinized. Many women became involved in petty commerce or earned income by working as housekeepers, child minders, cooks, laundresses or by selling produce grown in home gardens, while working occasionally in the fields as hired labourers or part of a family labour force.

National economic development under the economic regime of Fordism intensified the processes of the differentiation of the peasantry, with a significant segment undergoing a process of proletarianization or at least semi-proletarianization. Many women were further subjected to a process of increasing domestication. Surplus labour in farm households and in farm communities in general was freed and redirected to the industries in urban centres.

In the countryside, there was an intensification of pluriactivity which, in effect, contributed to offsetting the process of peasant disintegration, at least over the short term. Because of the presence of multi-occupationality and indeed, the ability of family-based enterprises to engage in 'self-exploitation', many writers have argued that such small farms were able to hold their own under the modernizing imperatives of the French state (Duby, 1976). Nonetheless, this era is often referred to as the era of the peasant transfigured into Frenchmen (Weber, 1976) and many studies in social science declared the inevitability of the end of the French peasantry (Franklin, 1969; Mendras, 1970).

FORDIST ECONOMIC STRUCTURES AND COLLECTIVE IDENTITIES

The Fordist period is often talked of as an era of the mass collective worker. This was the era in which people's work experiences were more or less continuous, at least in the sense that French citizens were by and large able to secure employment, even in the face of declining employment in agriculture, and also secure the means for their social reproduction. This was all assured through Keynesian macro-economic policies and the state's commitment to social welfare programmes within a corporatist ideology, social transfers, family allowances and social security[10].

In line with such a suggestion, a universalistic and national orientation prevailed in many of the villages of Lower Languedoc. The local farming bourgeoisie accommodated the imperatives of the cultural assimilation and modernity project of the French state. They also accepted state subsidies and participated in the programme for agrarian reform (Lem, 1995). Amongst the small farmers, there was more opposition to the modernizing imperatives of the French state. The acceptance of subsidies to rationalize farming often meant a loss of control over the production process and its subordination to the exigencies of state regulation. To some, these processes meant extinction, since much of state policy was geared to the transformation of hide-bound family farms into modern capitalist enterprises, at least over the long term. Over the short term, capitalist rationalization meant lay offs on large estates and wage cuts, as well as the deterioration of work conditions. The claims and demands of smallholders, who worked also as agricultural labourers for protection against the vagaries of capitalist transformation, were incorporated into the political agendas of national parties of the left and as a consequence, union activity was seen as an essential component of labour action. Through the 1960s and into the 1970s, farmers adhered to rural political organizations, such as MODEF (Mouvement pour la défense de l'exploitation familiale) and CAV (Comité d'action viticole), supported by the Communist Party, which often called for massive strikes and demonstrations to protest against the threats to the smallholder economy. An example of this was the threat posed by the expansion of the European Community, as competition from wine producers in other countries would undermine the livelihood of family winegrowers in Languedoc. From the mid-nineteenth century to the present, smallholders formed the backbone of such struggles. The village elites who operated large, modern, capitalist farms seldom participated in such protests, believing the wine produced on their estates was destined for a different market than wines produced by smallholders.

Under the dynamics of economic development in the Fordist era, then, the mobilization of rural working people involved appeals to their sense of association through class. This was often articulated in terms of their self-identification as members of the working class in public collective acts, in accounts of their actions and in their descriptions of their conditions of work (Lem, 1994). What this reflected was the fact that women's and men's experiences of work were consonant with the experience of being members of the labouring class in France. The structures of domination and subordination were defined in an era in which accumulation involved concentration, rationalization, mass production and economies of scale. Further, a class-oriented identity was reinforced by a peasantry that experienced proletarianization, either directly or in a vicarious manner, through other kin and family members, those who migrated and those who worked on local estates as agricultural labourers. Household members often combined wage work on local estates with other forms of wage work throughout the nineteenth century and until the 1970s.

In this context of classical Fordist organization, the experience of work involved a situation in which almost all workers in a factory could be expected to be concentrated in one place, inside an enclosed factory setting located in specific industrial centres. In the rural context, the location of work was largely concentrated on the farm or the local estates. In both settings, the experience of being a worker involved participation in collective or team work as a member of a labour force. Moreover, while the context of work often involved the dispersal of villagers to diverse geographic settings, solidary ties often extended well beyond the immediate locality of work and often linked people in the village, and the neighbourhood, to those on the estate and even in urban industrial locations in such distant centres as Paris. In this respect, the paths of working people in the region often followed along the trajectories of those kin and members of the community who migrated. The conceptual space of work in the Fordist period in this sense was wide, extending beyond the immediate physical location of work. Moreover, as the work histories of many rural people included a phase of factory work, their direct experience was also shaped by wage work. Thus, in political struggles, Lower Languedoc farmers asserted their national identity as citizens and members of the labouring classes in France. The protests adopted a rhetoric of defending their entitlements as members of the working class. Their demands focused on protection against the vagaries of the market as they sought to bend the will of the state to intervene and regulate the often erratic market, in the interest of the labouring classes in Lower Languedoc. Languedoc history has thus been punctuated by strikes and other forms of class-based protest defending rural livelihoods against the capitalist transformation of agriculture and changes in the national economy.

In the pre-Second World War period, women were as fervent as men in their political practices and participated with them in organized public protests, as well as in spontaneous demonstrations and insurgent acts. Despite their presence in moments of conflict, however, a consciousness of women as a political group was absent. Women identified strongly with their working class position and an autonomous gender consciousness did not emerge, despite the fact that the degree of exploitation on local estates was higher for women than for men. Wages paid to female agricultural labourers were half that paid to their male counterparts. Yet, class identity tended to override any consciousness of the different conditions under which women and men worked. In Lower Languedoc, class-based identities and politics enjoyed a certain hegemony which meant the occlusion of a politicized gender consciousness. This was buttressed by the popularity of the Socialist and Communist Parties in a region noted for its radical traditions.

This national orientation and the consolidation of national class identities in many respects reflected a fragmentation of local social structures, in which the organic solidarity of small farming families was fractured through labour migration. Still, the locus of social reproduction lay only in part in the national economy and in part in the state and its Keynesian policies. A part also lay in the regional economies as migrants often maintained economic ties to farming and farm property, and social and cultural ties to locality. Migrants returned to Languedoc villages for holidays, renewed their ties to kin and often inspected property still held in the community. Thus, in this era of essentially national development, in which class identity was prominent in peasant protest, regional themes were not entirely absent in the livelihood struggles of rural working people in Lower Languedoc. Throughout the nineteenth century and through the early twentieth century, conflicts between estate owners and workers, as well as between peasants and the state, were inscribed with regional referents. Class and regional identity was often conflated. To be Occitan was also to be working class. This division between local classes was marked by a referent to regional culture. Occitan-language festivals and customs were considered essential facets of local working class culture. French-language festivals and celebrations represented facets of a culture appropriate to the regional bourgeoisie who, because they assimilated to the imperatives of capitalist development and modernization, were perceived to be in league with the capitalist class. I will return to this point later in the paper. Class themes, then, often incorporated regional themes in struggles to defend a livelihood, as discussions of the various revolts of uprisings of small farmers against the state in Languedoc suggest (J. H. Smith, 1978). This observation belies the assumption in theories of restructuring that collective identities reflect work relations in a simple and direct way. In this respect, there is some difficulty explaining the presence of regional referents and indeed, the absence of a specific gender consciousness in political practices in the Fordist era. This point is also further discussed in the next section.

POST-FORDISM AND THE SALIENCE OF REGIONALISM

In this most recent period of capitalist restructuring, the development of France has become more regionalized, with the establishment of regional poles of development and attempts to decentralize government (Keating and Jones, 1995; Loughlin and Mazey, 1995; Rousseau and Zariski, 1987). Under post-Fordism, economic peripheries and regional places have become constructed as new sites for accumulation and investment.

With the deindustrialization of urban centres such as Paris and Lyon, combined with years of recession, high levels of industrial unemployment have resulted, effectively in stemming the tide of rural out-migration. Furthermore, the establishment of growth poles and the increasing dynamism of small, often family-based firms, established in peripheral districts rather than industrial centres, helped attract labour from central districts suffering industrial decline in this new stage of capitalist transformation (Lash and Urry, 1987). It has been observed that agricultural regions throughout France, and indeed in other European regions, have experienced population increases since the mid-1970s (Sabel, 1989). This trend is reflected in many of the villages in Lower Languedoc, which have recovered from population losses suffered in the decades immediately following the Second World War. This rise may be explained by the influx of migrants to the countryside, both from urban centres and from other countries, as well as by the phenomenon of village youth remaining in the countryside in the face of declining industrial employment.

The social profile of migrants to the countryside is diverse, often spanning the spectrum from intellectuals and ecologically-minded 'hippies' seeking alternative lifestyles, to managers and technical personnel recruited to run regional firms. Still, a notable number among them are village sons and daughters who during an earlier period in their work histories left the agricultural milieu to seek employment in the north or in central districts. With the changes in the economy over the past few decades, many of those have returned to their village and their farming families, or have reclaimed farm properties to attempt to put together a livelihood in the countryside concentrating on agriculture. This regenerated commitment to farming and to making a living in the countryside has helped regalvanize the region as the territorial framework for social, political, economic and cultural activity in the face of the restructuring of the national economy. Observing these developments for France and elsewhere in Europe, it has been proposed that there has been a virtual renaissance of regional economies in the search for locational advantages which facilitate the process of accumulation (Sabel, 1989).

The restructuring of capital has implied changing labour processes in rural settings. Forms of making a living have become more diversified with the intensification of subcontracting, outwork and homework. Moreover, with the changes in the labour process for relocated manufacturing firms, domestic spaces have come to be reconstituted as workplaces for the production of commodities. Surplus labour in the regions generated from the decentralization of industrial production and from an earlier period of the modernization of farming constitute the main source of cheap labour, offering a key advantage to firms wishing to relocate. Women, already created as a marginalized and surplus labour force during an earlier phase of capitalist restructuring, often serve as the main source of cheap labour for manufacturing firms operating on putting-out systems and using networks of homeworkers. As ways of making a living proliferate and the domestication of commodity production becomes established, patterns of association in the workplace become fragmented, on the one hand, and constricted, on the other. The orientation of working people, particularly women, to a smaller universe – the household, the family, work distributors – takes place in the context of an overall fragmentation of the work experience, as the locus of social reproduction has shifted from the state to the locality and region, especially in an era of neo-liberal reform in economic policy. Furthermore, the reconstitution of the home as an isolated work-place in which women engage in the production of pieces of commodities strengthens the mechanisms for the subordination of women in the labour process through cultural and economic means. During the 'post-Fordist' period, then, local social structures experienced a period of reconsolidation as the locus of social reproduction returned to the region with the decline in Keynesian state policies.

In the light of these changes, communities of interests have come to be reconstituted in a more particularistic or local sense and political commitments come to be redefined in terms of defending a right to making a living in the region. Further, the narrowing of the work experiences of women and the intensification of the association between women and the domestic sphere mitigates against the possibility of women developing solidary ties with other women and men in collective acts of protest, as their experience of work becomes highly individualized, or hidden in underground economies stitching shoes, sewing clothes or cleaning (Benton 1990). The de-politicization of women and their absence in forms of collective protest are consequent upon the processes which engender atomization. Their work spheres and their experiences of work become constricted, oriented to a narrow and particularistic universe. In these conditions, the sense of collectivity that prevails is underwritten by sentiments and attachment to the locality, which finds its cultural expression in terms of an Occitan regional identity. An independent and autonomous gender identity, and a political consciousness which expresses and articulates the new conditions of women's subordination is again effaced by the hegemony of regional identity, under circumstances which privilege the idea of region both economically and politically.

The highly individualized and fragmented experience of work under a relocated and restructured form of production in late capitalism led theorists to assert that the currency of class-based politics had declined. However, such decline does not necessarily imply the disappearance of class-based forms of solidarity. In the case of the working people in Lower Languedoc, class identities often share a place of prominence with regional identities in struggles initiated by small farmers to defend a livelihood. When the political practices of the Occitan rural working people are interrogated, class themes noted earlier are combined with regional themes. In Lower Languedoc, many rural women and men consistently point out that the Occitan language, when it was habitually spoken before the Second World War, acted as a class marker separating out members of the working class from members of the rural bourgeoisie. The elite, the estate owners and the upwardly mobile assimilated to French national culture and spoke the national language (Cooke, 1987, for observations of similar linguistic alignments and cleavages in south Wales). While *patois*, as villagers call it, is now spoken only amongst the elderly, the idea of the Occitan language resonates with this class referent. Moreover, in contemporary political practice, Occitan identity amongst the small farmers carries a strong class referent. The small farmers of Languedoc have adopted as a slogan '*Volem viure (et trabahar) al pais*' – we want to live (and work) in our land. VVAP is the name of an organization dedicated to decentralization. It subscribes to socialist ideology and is therefore committed to protecting the interests of the labouring classes. These slogans have been brandished in demonstrations protesting against the increasingly laissez-faire attitude of the state to the economy of vine cultivation, which has resulted in the opening up of the European wine market to international competitors, such as Spain and Portugal. The small growers have added '*et trabahar*' to the slogan underlining that they are involved in a struggle for livelihood in a regional context. In rural Languedoc, the deployment of the slogans in the Occitan language encapsulates the imperatives of making a living in the post-Fordist era, when territory and space have been conferred a new significance both economically and culturally. They also articulate the class interests of working people subjected to new forms of domination in this new phase of capitalism.

To return to an earlier point, studies of restructuring assume a correspondence between the rise of new social movements, such as European regionalism, and the changes in the organization of production that have accompanied the transition from one economic regime to another. The fragmentation of mass collective identities is associated with the fragmentation of economic and social patterns and work experiences. The decline of centralized production in mass factories located in metropolitan areas, the rise of geographically dispersed production, as well as the intensification of subcontracting, pluriactivity, homework and the informal economy, so it is argued, has been accompanied by the decline in the mass worker and class consciousness, and the rise of plural forms of collective solidarity. While these suggestions are provocative, our discussion of the shifting identities of Occitan rural working people suggest several limitations to these assumptions.

First, studies of rural southern Europe have demonstrated that making a living through multiple means has been a persistent feature of rural economies, at least from the mid-nineteenth century through to the present (G. Smith, 1991). My work on the viticultural areas of Languedoc also presents a striking example of this (Lem, 1994, 1995). Although monocrop vine cultivation ostensibly represents the principal way of making a living, the livelihood experiences of women and men have been more or less complex, heterogeneous and diverse for over a century, in many respects resembling the fully developed and extensive informal economies in Europe (Pahl, 1984; Redclift and Mingione, 1985).

In addition, class protest and consciousness was much in evidence in the rural scene in the early twentieth century to the 1930s and was taken up precisely by those rural smallholders who pursued multiple ways of making a living. Since multi-occupationality itself extends beyond the period of early post-war reconstruction through the period of the establishment of generalized Fordism and to the recent period of restructuring, the emergence of regionalism can in no direct and simple way reflect the forms of work that have purportedly arisen under post-Fordism. By the same token, class identities do not simply reflect participation in the labour process as a mass worker, since they persist amongst small peasants under late capitalism. The mechanistic approach to understanding how collective identities may be constructed through changing work experiences found in current approaches to the study of restructuring, reflects the fact that expressions of collective solidarities and the question of human agency are only discussed tangentially, or as an afterthought in a macro-analytical approach. As such, they are often located in a rarefied academic sphere, divorced from everyday people and their concerns. An ethnographically sensitive approach to the problem of regionalism and other forms of collective identity enables the complexity of working people's lives to be considered, precluding the treatment of human subjectivity and agency as an epiphenomenon of economic change.

CONCLUSION

In this paper, I have tried to explore the question of shifting forms of collective identity by drawing on suggestions made by theorists of restructuring. I have drawn upon these theories to determine the conditions under which class, regional and gender-based consciousness and identities find expression or become effaced. In doing this, I have tried to explore the relationship between restructuring, changing forms of work and identity. While it is a subject of much debate whether the changes under what is called post-Fordism are a new phase or simply the intensification of an 'older phase' of capitalist development, restructuring theory at least provokes us to question the assumptions of classic studies of the political economy of change, to determine whether they are relevant to changes in both industrial and agricultural forms of work and production under late capitalism. In focusing on a rural context, I have also attempted to extend the analysis of change in rural society beyond models of agrarian change which are based on assumptions about the nature of capitalism which may no longer hold. The puzzles of the emergence of different collective identities and new forms of solidarity may not have been unequivocally resolved through trying to extrapolate from perspectives that focus so tangentially on the question of human agency. Still, there is merit to employing a perspective that attempts to suggest ties between collective identities and material conditions. In this respect, the suggestions made by theorists of restructuring, that collective identity can be premised on the relationship and associations forged through work, remain provocative and serve as one point of departure in exploring at least one dimension of the processes which contribute toward defining group interests and solidarities, as well as the forces which mobilize people to defend their interests. Though I have argued that there are some limitations to understanding the emergence of regionalism in the light of current thinking on the nature of restructuring, the insights offered remain heuristically valuable, enabling us to move toward developing an understanding of the relationships between economy, regionalism and the much vexed concepts of regionalism and identity.

NOTES

1. Research upon which this chapter is based was generously supported by grants from the Wenner Gren Foundation for Anthropological Research and the Social Sciences and Humanities Council of Canada.

2. There are in existence three schools of thought on the nature of the this transformation, i.e. the institutionalist school (Piore and Sabel, 1984); the regulation school (Aglietta, 1979; Lipietz 1987); and the managerialist school. For a discussion on the similarities and differences between the schools, see Bagguley *et al.* (1990).

3. Occitan politics has been embraced by conservative and radical groups alike in Languedoc. For example, the contemporary heirs to the nineteenth-century Félibrige movement are essentially intellectual elites devoted toward the preservation of Occitan literature, poetry and language. Other groups such as Lutte Occitane espoused a radical politics which sought an end to 'internal colonialism' and the control of the state and regional bourgeoisie over regional economies and local proletariat (Touraine, et al., 1981). Regionalism in general can take on both conservative and radical forms, depending on its class basis. Heiberg, in a study of Basque regionalism, points out that to be Basque is in one sense to be conservative, to stress ethnic exclusiveness and frantic religiosity. In another sense, for the working class, it is to be socialist and revolutionary (Heiberg, 1985; Keating, 1986).

4. Loughlin (1985: 211, and personal communication, 1993) has pointed out that Occitan regionalism is often regarded as the domain of intellectuals and the elite largely preoccupied with the preservation of local culture. Touraine, after convening a conference of Occitan political groups, concluded that the creation of a coherent Occitan movement would be impossible since the interests of the groups were essentially irreconcilable. Le Roy Ladurie (1977) questions the accuracy of representations of history in texts written by Occitan historians.

5. Some observes have noted that as firms sought to decentralize production and to relocate, the re-emergence of regional economies with flexible systems of production has taken place. In France, according to Sabel (1989: 24–5), the area of Lyon contains industries that are organized along the same principles as those found in the Third Italy (Genoa, Turin and Milan).

6. For France, Lash and Urry discuss this uneven pattern of development in term of such indicators as the fact that after the Second World War, there were 35 per cent more men employed in agriculture forestry and fishing than in manufacturing. Before the Second World War, there were more women in agriculture than manufacturing. Until the war, spatially, widespread industrial development occurred mostly in and around Paris, Alsace and various parts of the Nord. Artisan production was highly localized in the provinces with the development of small workshops (Lash and Urry, 1987: 125–8).

7. For example, the multiplication of small shoe factories owned by multinational companies in small villages in Alicante, Spain, has accompanied the general decline of agriculture.

8. The thrust of agricultural policy in the post-Second World War era was to modernize French agriculture through structural reform and elimination of the weakest, for example, the Mansholt Plan of 1968 stated that 80 per cent of French farms were unviable and would be slated to disappear (Keeler, 1979: 9). With this knowledge, many small farmers speak of state aid as a 'double edged sword' and caution each other against accepting state support with the expression 'what the state gives you with one hand, it takes away with the other'.

9. For a discussion of this topic see Pech (1975).

PART II

CASE STUDIES

9
NAFTA: Regional Impacts

DAVID W. CONKLIN

THE FTA AND NAFTA

The Canada–US Free Trade Agreement (FTA) came into effect in 1989, reducing trade and investment barriers between the two countries (Doern and Tomlin, 1991). The North America Free Trade Agreement (NAFTA) came into effect in 1994, bringing Mexico into this special relationship (Hufbauer and Schott, 1993). Much of the content of the FTA was simply transferred to NAFTA and thus NAFTA did little to alter the Canada-US economic relations that had been established by the FTA. The bulk of NAFTA deals with the removal of trade and investment restrictions between Mexico and the other two partners.

With the FTA, tariffs between Canada and the US are to be reduced to zero over specified time schedules that vary from sector to sector, ranging from immediate elimination to gradual elimination over ten years. Unlike the European Union (EU), Canada and the US each maintains its own set of tariff rates for imports from other countries. Consequently, it has been necessary to establish 'rules of origin'. These rules determine whether a product has enough Canadian and US content in order for it to be permitted to cross the Canada-US border at the reduced FTA rates.

For many decades, the largest Canada–US flows of trade and investment have occurred in the automobile sector and, since the 1960s, Canada and the US have had a trade agreement that focused specifically on automotive goods. This 'Auto Pact' eliminated tariffs and it guaranteed that a certain portion of production would occur in Canada. The Auto Pact was entrenched in the FTA, thereby giving it a greater permanence. For automotive goods, the rules of origin are particularly important since many parts are imported from various countries and are built into larger components and assemblies which are then shipped across the border. Under the

FTA, a component or assembled vehicle has to have 50 per cent of its value originating in Canada and the US in order to be shipped across the border free of tariffs.

The FTA provided for special access to each government's procurement. Under GATT, purchases above $171,000 US were open for competition to foreign companies unless specifically reserved for small business or excluded for reasons of national security. The FTA lowered this threshold to $25,000 US, thereby opening much more of each country's government procurement to companies from the other country. However, as with other FTA provisions, provincial and state governments were not bound by this liberalization as they were not parties to the agreement, and they retain certain independent powers granted to them by the constitutions of Canada and the US.

In the period 1974–85, the Government of Canada operated a Foreign Investment Review Agency (FIRA) which screened applications by foreigners who wished to invest in Canada. This agency could refuse an application and it could negotiate terms and conditions, such as the requirement that the applicant purchase a certain percentage of its equipment, parts and components in Canada rather than import them. With the FTA, Canada and the US promised 'national treatment' for any new businesses owned and operated by citizens of the other country. The FTA significantly liberalized US investment rights in Canada but Canada did maintain a review for acquisitions with a value of $150 million or more.

The FTA schedules for elimination of Canada–US tariffs are included in the NAFTA Agreement with no changes. NAFTA provides different schedules for the reduction of Mexico–Canada tariffs and Mexico-US tariffs. The schedules provide for removal of tariffs over periods of five to 15 years, depending upon the extent of the adjustment difficulties faced by each sector. In this respect, NAFTA is a separate agreement for Mexico–Canada and for Mexico–US, although all tariffs will be eliminated by the end of 15 years.

As with the FTA, the three countries maintain different tariff rates for imports from other countries. Consequently, rules of origin are important for NAFTA as well, determining whether a particular product has enough North American content to qualify for cross-border shipping at the reduced NAFTA tariff rates. An exception is the computer industry where the three countries were able to agree upon a common external tariff, and where rules of origin will not be necessary when this common tariff is implemented.

Agriculture is unique in that NAFTA involves two separate bilateral agreements, one between the US and Mexico and the other between Mexico and Canada. For agricultural trade between the US and Canada, the provisions of the FTA continue in force. Of major significance with NAFTA will be the provisions that seek to establish uniform sanitary and phytosanitary standards in each country. This involves the establishment of working groups to study and agree upon standards for each agricultural product.

NAFTA will eliminate all quotas and tariffs on trade in textiles and apparel within North America. Rules of origin are extremely important for this sector because fibre and fabric could otherwise be imported from low-cost countries to make clothing that would be shipped throughout North America. NAFTA introduces a 'triple transformation test' which requires that apparel be cut and sewn from fabric spun from North American fibres in order for the apparel to be shipped tariff-free within North America. These rules of origin are more strict than the FTA rules. This threatens trade diversion through a reduction of imports from non-North American countries. Apparel and fabric from other countries may be replaced in North American production processes by fibre and fabric produced in North America, particularly in Mexico.

While Canada and the US had tariff-free trade in automotive products for many years, Mexico has had a highly protected market. NAFTA provides for the elimination of Mexico's tariff and non-tariff barriers in automotive products over a five- to ten-year period. NAFTA also changes the rules of origin, requiring that 62.5 per cent of the value of a product must be made in North America in order to cross the borders tariff free. These more strict rules of origin, as with textiles and apparel, will likely encourage trade diversion, with sourcing being done from plants within North America rather than from imports. With automotive products, Mexico is again likely to be the major beneficiary.

The FTA included several provisions that enabled Canadian and US banks to expand operations in each other's countries. Before NAFTA, Mexico had severe restrictions on foreign investment in its financial sector. However, NAFTA permits US and Canadian banks to operate in Mexico. This will be a gradual change, with specified limits on the total share of the Mexican financial market that can be owned by Canadian and US banks until the year 2007.

While NAFTA continues the FTA reductions in Canadian investment restrictions and opens many Mexican sectors to Canadian and US investment, Mexico retains a large number of exceptions. Furthermore, NAFTA provides for states and provinces to maintain their current restrictions on foreign investment if they have registered these before the end of 1995. Each federal government is actively involved in discussions with its provinces or states in an attempt to encourage investment liberalization within their constitutional jurisdictions.

For consumers in every region, NAFTA has lowered tariffs and so has reduced the price of imports, increasing consumer purchasing power and broadening product choice. However, the gains a region can receive from NAFTA depend to a greater degree upon the adjustment by businesses, as they shift out of activities where imports are cheaper than domestic production and as they expand into activities where domestic production is cheaper than foreign production. This means that some firms will be hurt by free trade, as will the employees of those firms. Government policies that maintain firms and employment in such sectors will reduce the gains from trade. This harsh reality has important implications for the appropriateness of alternative kinds of policies. In general, policies that support adjustment into the expanding sectors will have greater long-term benefits than policies that support the maintenance of sectors that are not competitive. From this perspective, the impacts of NAFTA will depend to some degree on the responses of governments at both national and sub-national levels.

DIFFERENCES IN IMPACTS AMONG REGIONS

Much of the literature about the FTA and NAFTA discusses the impacts on each of the three member countries as if each were a homogeneous unit. In reality, significant differences exist among the regions of each country and each region will experience its own unique adjustments. There are at least four kinds of differences that underlie the regional impacts of NAFTA.

First, each economic sector has experienced its own free trade impacts. For some kinds of products, tariffs were already very low and so for these sectors, the elimination of trade barriers will not have much impact. For some other sectors where trade barriers were high, adjustments have already been substantial. With regard to the regional impacts of NAFTA, a key point is that each geographical region has come to depend on its own unique set of business sectors. Consequently, the differential impact among sectors has meant that each region has been affected differently.

Before 1989, a vigorous debate occurred within Canada concerning whether it should in fact enter the FTA. This debate took on regional dimensions, with each of Canada's ten provincial governments representing the interests of its provincial region. The Ontario government strongly opposed the agreement. For many decades, Canada's tariffs have protected manufacturing, as opposed to agriculture and natural resources. Manufacturing has been concentrated in Ontario and so Ontario has benefited from the tariff. On the other hand, Canada's western and Atlantic provinces have had to pay prices for manufactured goods that have been raised by the tariffs to levels considerably above world prices. The differential costs and benefits of the tariff across regions means that the removal of tariffs will have differential regional impacts as well.

Second, some Canadian regions are geographically closer to certain US regions than they are to each other and this is likely to intensify the development of trade and investment clusters that cross national borders. Canadian public policies historically supported an east-west flow of trade. In order to unite the country, railroads and highways were built in the east-west direction, encouraging trade within Canada and public policies sought to reduce the natural north-south flows that would have tied Canada more closely to the US. The FTA marks a significant shift away from this emphasis.

Each cross-border region has its own industrial structure and growth dynamic. Some international groupings of regions have already achieved significant integration and NAFTA will intensify this development. This can be seen most dramatically with regard to the automobile industry, where a major portion of Canada–US trade and investment occurs among the US states of Ohio and Michigan and the Canadian province of Ontario. Similarly, there has been a growing integration among the north-east US, Canada's Maritime provinces and Quebec as a separate cluster. The southern part of Canada's province of British Columbia has also become increasingly integrated with the US states of Oregon and Washington, forming a third Canada–US regional cluster.

This phenomenon of cross-border groupings of regions is important along the Mexico–US border as well. The Mexican *maquiladora* region and the region around Monterrey have become increasingly integrated with the southern US states of California, Arizona, New Mexico and Texas. It is expected that NAFTA will intensify the development of these international regional clusters.

Third, geographical proximity creates the possibility of cross-border shopping by individuals, which strengthens the international regional clusters discussed above. For regions close to national borders, this can be significant, particularly depending upon the foreign exchange rates at any point in time. In the period immediately following the FTA, cross-border shopping by Canadians in the US became a significant political issue. However, in the early 1990s, the value of the Canadian dollar vis-à-vis the US dollar fell by nearly 25 per cent and so cross-border shopping changed, with increasing numbers of US residents shopping in Canada. Similarly, in the 1980s and 1990s, very extensive cross-border shopping by Mexicans occurred in the southern US but the sharp devaluation of the Mexican peso in the period following December 1994 abruptly reduced this.

Fourth, the various regions in North America have different capabilities in terms of attracting various kinds of investment. The regional impacts of NAFTA will depend very much upon these capabilities, for NAFTA has created a 'footloose' environment for business. With NAFTA, a business can now locate anywhere and serve the entire North American market. Various factors are increasingly facilitating this new aspect of investment, particularly modern telecommunications and transportation. It is important to note that while this greater mobility of capital may benefit corporate shareholders, it may simultaneously hurt the existing employees whose jobs may be shifted to a lower-cost region. This difference in impact between shareholders and employees adds another dimension to the political economy of each region. For each region, future employment and income will be affected by the decisions of businesses to locate in one region as opposed to another. In view of the importance of this subject, it is addressed more fully later in this chapter.

For some purposes, it is important to examine combinations of sub-national political units. In Canada, for example, the Atlantic provinces and the Prairie provinces form important regions. In the United States, many analyses focus on the north-east, the mid-west, the south and the west as regions based on combinations of states. Over the past few decades, most of Mexico's 32 states have experienced significant growth accompanied by changes in economic structure, a high degree of urbanization and an improvement in educational levels. However, the states surrounding Mexico City and those near the US border have grown more rapidly than have other regions. Apart from these regional groupings of provinces and states, it may also be useful, for some purposes, to examine smaller areas within the provincial or state boundaries. In particular, many metropolitan regions have developed unique economic features and a growth dynamic of their own. For example, in recent decades, Mexico City has stretched out to encompass an ever-increasing region with a population growth rate that has been among the most rapid in the world. Several previously independent urban areas are now a part of this huge metropolitan region. With this growth, problems of traffic congestion and pollution have become severe. In response, the government of Mexico has instituted many programmes to encourage investment in other regions, including a taxation system that imposes higher tax rates on businesses within the metropolitan city region and lower tax rates elsewhere.

CANADIAN PROVINCES: REGIONAL DIFFERENCES

Regional economic differences within Canada are well documented (Copithorne, 1979; Krasnick *et. al.*, 1986) and these may be further affected by NAFTA. For British Columbia, US tariffs on minerals, forest products and fish were non-existent or at very low levels before the FTA and as a result, market access through FTA tariff reduction has not been significant. NAFTA will eliminate Mexico's tariffs on these products and some increase in exports may therefore be anticipated. In terms of investment, NAFTA has opened new opportunities for British Columbian companies to create subsidiaries in Mexico's mining sector.

For Alberta, the oil and gas sector may be impacted by NAFTA provisions that guarantee energy supply to the US in time of energy shortage. Alberta corporations that are experienced in the oil and gas sector may also find new investment opportunities in Mexico. For the three prairie provinces of Alberta, Saskatchewan and

Manitoba, the predominant agricultural sector will experience new export opportunities in Mexico.

When considering the impact of NAFTA on each of Canada's ten provinces, a central focus is the economic structure of each province and how that particular set of activities may benefit from or be hurt by NAFTA. Impacts of NAFTA will vary from province to province depending upon the degree to which the various economic activities experience increased exports, increased competition from imports and the shift of jobs to the US south or to Mexico, because of their lower wage rates.

Perhaps the most significant restructuring will occur in Ontario and Quebec, as a result of their heavy dependence upon manufacturing. As indicated above, the government of Ontario firmly opposed the FTA because it believed that many Ontario businesses would be hurt by the liberalization of trade. The relatively low wage rates of Mexico and the US south may attract investment and jobs from these two provinces, particularly in the automobile sector. Yet, high-tech industries such as telecommunications are also concentrated in Ontario and Quebec, and these industries face new opportunities for exporting to Mexico. Similarly, Canada's financial sector is concentrated in Ontario and NAFTA opens new investment opportunities in both the US and Mexico. Ontario and Quebec may also experience new opportunities with exports of forest and mineral products.

For the Atlantic provinces – New Brunswick, Nova Scotia, Prince Edward Island and Newfoundland – the elimination of Mexican tariffs on fish and forest products creates new export potential.

Regional disparities have persisted for many decades, with the Atlantic provinces and northern Quebec consistently experiencing relatively high unemployment rates and relatively low per capita incomes compared with other Canadian regions. In response to these disparities, Canada has maintained an extensive set of subsidies to attract industry to the disadvantaged regions and to supplement personal incomes. As part of the FTA debate, these regions have been particularly concerned that Canada's subsidy programmes might be adversely affected. In the past, some US industries have argued that subsidies create unfair competition and consequently, the US has sometimes imposed countervailing duties against Canada's exports by businesses that have received subsidies. The FTA included provision for the negotiation, over a five- to seven-year period, of a subsidies pact that would clarify this situation but such a pact has not been negotiated. Under the GATT Uruguay Agreement, a subsidies code was established but it is not yet clear how its application might impact on Canada's programmes of assistance to disadvantaged regions.

For many years, some of Quebec's political leaders have worked towards the attainment of independent political sovereignty (see Martin's chapter in this volume). If this were to be achieved, an important set of issues would revolve around the role of Quebec within NAFTA.

THE UNITED STATES: REGIONAL DIFFERENCES

There have always been substantial differences among US regions in per capita incomes and economic growth (Miller, 1977; Cobb, 1982; Schmenner, 1982; Paul, 1984; Miller and Cote, 1987; Schulman, 1991). Each region has had a distinct set of economic activities and, to a major degree, the differences in regional economic performance have been linked to the differences in economic structure. Individual states have experienced periods of expansion and contraction as the basic business activities dominating their economy have expanded and contracted. These changes have led to significant economic adjustments among regions and to a gradual narrowing, since the 1930s, of regional disparities. The extent and pace of these previous adjustments indicate that change within many regions could be substantial and rapid as a result of NAFTA. As the recent decades have witnessed, many businesses are indeed prepared to shift their investments from one region to another in response to new economic circumstances.

The north-east was a particular focus of attention with regard to de-industrialization in the 1950s and 1960s. While New England was experiencing de-industrialization, it was also experiencing an expansion of white-collar office jobs in the business service sector and in the university-research sector. New high-tech industries, for example, chose to locate in the Boston area where they were often linked to universities. Consequently, the labour force became increasingly polarized, as did the urban landscape. Central business districts included new office complexes in the downtown areas. Yet these were surrounded with declining, often slum-conditions. At the same time, upper-income groups were moving to the expanding and attractive suburbs of the old cities. New manufacturing plants were also locating in the suburbs. As a result of these changes, the economic structure of this region changed dramatically within a period of 20 years.

In the period 1975–85, de-industrialization became particularly acute in the mid-west. States like Michigan, Ohio and Illinois lost millions of jobs as a result of cheap imports from low-wage foreign competitors and the shift of corporations to the US south. This massive de-industrialization occurred within a ten-year period. Meanwhile, the north-east was not hurt as severely over this decade as it was less dependent upon the automobile and steel industry, and to a major degree, had already adjusted to the earlier decrease in its industrial base.

Throughout the nineteenth century and until the 1970s, the south experienced relatively low average per capita incomes compared with the rest of the United States. Corporations viewed the low wage rates as a powerful incentive to locate there, particularly when faced with intense price competition from low-wage countries. Meanwhile, the federal government provided substantial assistance to the south to improve its attractiveness as an industrial location. In the 1930s, the Tennessee Valley Authority (TVA) began to provide inexpensive electric power and it facilitated productivity improvements in agriculture. During and after the Second World War, the federal government's huge and growing military expenditures also favoured southern jurisdictions. State and municipal governments in the south developed a wide array of subsidy programmes to attract corporations. They were also slow to introduce the generous welfare programmes and the expensive regulations that became a cause of higher production costs in the north. Hence, by the 1970s, the south had become a more attractive region for many business investments than was the north-east or the midwest.

Since the 1960s, the growth of new high-tech industries has been an important feature of the US economy. The south has been able to attract many of these expanding corporations to its urban areas. The newly expanding cities of the south have offered what many see as a superior quality of life. University research facilities have become the basis for 'clusters' of new high-tech industries whose labour force requirements are quite different from those of the traditional industries. These new businesses have provided a wide variety of high-paying professional jobs for the well-educated. Thus, in recent years, the south has been able to attract both low-wage businesses with their low-skill jobs, as well as high-income, high-tech businesses with their high-skill jobs.

Throughout the nineteenth and twentieth centuries, the west has experienced significant growth based upon its natural resources. In the 1950s and 1960s, agriculture and mining still provided a strong base for the region. In more recent decades, energy sources have added to the strength of the region. A noteworthy feature throughout the west has been the rapid urbanization, with the depopulation of rural areas and the growth of cities like Denver. Many of these urban areas have also been the location choice of new high-tech industries. This diversity has given the west a unique set of economic interests.

In general, each of the US regions has experienced a growth pattern which, to a major degree, has been determined by the growth pattern of those economic activities that have dominated the region. In this process, low-wage competition from foreign countries has been a powerful force in compelling change and adjustments. We can expect that with NAFTA, Mexico's low-wage competition will intensify these changes and adjustments. As part of this process, the role of governments has also been significant. The expensive government welfare programmes and higher taxation in the northern states created an incentive for many corporations to shift to the south. Government military expenditures in the south, together with a wide array of subsidy programmes – often by municipal governments – further stimulated investment in the region. Meanwhile, the new high-tech businesses have been able to choose locations in many cities where a skilled work-force and a university research atmosphere have provided a special attraction. For high-tech businesses in both services and manufacturing, NAFTA opens new export opportunities in Mexico, where Canadian and US businesses now have a preferential position vis-à-vis competitors from other countries.

MEXICO: REGIONAL DIFFERENCES

Regional disparities within Mexico have also been the subject of academic study (Baerresen, 1971; Brothers and Wick, 1990; Fernandez, 1989) and received new attention on 1 January 1994, when the state of Chiapas was torn by armed revolt. Rebels in Chiapas pointed to NAFTA as a serious threat to their livelihood.

Many residents are involved in agriculture, which had been protected in various ways from cheap imports. With NAFTA, this import protection will disappear *vis-à-vis* the US and Canada, who may increase their agricultural exports to Mexico. Furthermore, traditional Mexican subsidies to the farming sector will likely be reduced or even eliminated as a result of NAFTA. For residents of Chiapas, NAFTA brings a threat to their existing meagre livelihood, rather than the possibility of new economic opportunities.

Many commentators have seen the rebel movement as the result of extreme poverty in this region compared with other regions of Mexico. At the level of the individual, very low incomes have meant a standard of living significantly below that found in other regions and many claim that this relative deprivation is unfair. At the level of the region as a whole, the infrastructure of roads, educational facilities, water and power is also relatively poor compared with the rest of the country and hence, the possibility of future growth is also much less than the growth prospects of other regions. Consequently, such a region has little to gain from NAFTA in terms of attracting new investments.

In addition to these factors, Chiapas contains a large indigenous population and many of the rebels belong to this groups. To some degree, the revolt can be seen as the failure of Mexico to incorporate the aspirations of indigenous peoples into the national economy. This feature of distinct regions with unique ethnic or racial patterns has also been important in certain regions of Canada and the United States. The separation of aboriginal groups in Canada and the US has been exacerbated by the maintenance of 'reserves' where lifestyles, skills and opportunities have been severely limited. In each case, these regions will have their own unique futures in terms of economic prospects and NAFTA impacts.

The regional economic diversities within Mexico are influenced to some degree by Mexico's proximity to the US. Thousands of *maquiladoras* (foreign-owned plants) have been established along Mexico's border with the US. The increases in manufacturing activity and migration of labour associated with this influx of activity have resulted in tremendous growth within the region. Although the strong manufacturing sector in the border region is successfully enhancing its growth, the effects on the remainder of the country are often criticized as being negligible or even negative. In discussing NAFTA's impacts, the border region deserves special attention.

In 1965, the government of Mexico adopted the Border Industrialization Programme (BIP), as a concerted attempt to stimulate export-oriented manufacturing activities in its region bordering the US. By 1971, legislation in the US as well as Mexico supported this objective by giving US businesses locating plants in this region favourable tariff treatment. These businesses could export materials and components from the US to their Mexican operation, use low-wage Mexican labour to add value, then re-export the product to the US. Mexico did not impose any tariffs on these imports and the US imposed tariffs only on the value added in Mexico. This Maquiladora Programme resulted in the rapid creation of many US-owned plants in Mexico. By 1984, over 700 plants employed over 175,000 people and these generated a large portion of Mexico's foreign exchange. By 1992, the number of plants had reached about 2,000 with a work-force of nearly 500,000. 'Economically for Mexico, its northernmost territorial area, previously a largely uninhabited desert, has become a *pôle de croissance* (focal point of growth) which rivals the capital city in its capacity to attract labour migration and foreign investment' (Fernandez, 1989).

The essential aspect of the Maquiladora Programme was the limitation of US import duties to only the value added in the *maquiladora*, but a number of additional Mexican initiatives have also supported this growth pole concept, both at the national and local government levels. Mexico's extensive system of licences to limit imports was relaxed for this region. Various subsidies were offered to entice foreign investors. A further consideration has been the exemption of *maquiladora* plants from Mexican legislation requiring a certain percentage of domestic ownership. The rapid economic growth of the border region indicates the powerful impact that can be created by tariff reductions that alter business location decisions. NAFTA will carry these tariff reductions much further and thus the long-term impacts may be truly significant. Yet, while jobs have been created, these jobs have been largely low-wage, low-skill jobs. Following this pattern, the NAFTA impacts may result in new employment opportunities, with relatively little impact, for many years, on Mexican wage levels.

In spite of attempts to stimulate foreign investment throughout Mexico, more than 80 per cent of the foreign-owned plants created over the 1970–90 period were located in the border region. The success of the Maquiladora Programme has depended not solely on the special tariff provisions, but also on the provision of special financial incentives. Here, the political leaders in the border region have been skilful at creating incentive packages and in convincing US firms to move there. They have understood the need to deal honestly and efficiently with potential foreign investors. Political leaders in other regions have not been as quick to respond positively. The border municipalities have actively pursued US firms, encouraging them to locate in their particular municipality and often providing financial assistance geared to the corporation's particular needs. In addition, the border region has an advantage with regard to transportation costs and the time required for transportation. The border region offers easier travel by US executives for supervision purposes and it minimizes the danger of unforeseeable transportation and communication risks. The border region has developed a growth dynamic, for example, in attracting managerial and supervisory personnel, who are now an additional attractive feature for new investors.

While the *maquiladoras* have successfully created a strong manufacturing sector in the border region, this growth pole concept is open to severe criticisms. Many of these criticisms repeat the traditional literature concerning 'dual economies' in the Less Developed Countries (LDCs). While a limited number of regions enjoy rapid growth, the bulk of the country may be relatively unaffected. The national problems of unemployment and poverty may be reduced very little by the prosperity of the rapidly growing regions. Mexico's *maquiladoras* illustrate this dilemma. They also demonstrate how a region in one country may – for many purposes and from many perspectives – become economically a part of another country, as a result of tariff reductions.

MEXICO–US MIGRATION

The Mexico-US border region provides an interesting illustration of the tensions that may develop when regional disparities are substantial, particularly across a political boundary that limits migration (Seligson and Williams, 1981; Grindle, 1988). In general, the US south-western borderlands form a disadvantaged region within the US, with low wages and high unemployment. Consequently, Mexicans crossing the border look towards other areas as their final destination. Yet, per capita income in some areas of the US border, for example, the San Diego area, is more than five times that of Mexico and so the appeal of migration is ever-present. The attractiveness of migration to the United States may vary depending upon the US business cycle and the availability of jobs for unskilled workers. Immediately following the Second World War, when the United States faced shortages of labour, there were no objections to the influx of Mexican workers. In recent years however, the US has become increasingly concerned about this immigration. Certain labour groups fear that low-wage Mexican immigrants may endanger their jobs. Many Americans are concerned about the social difficulties and government obligations that arise with a growing number of unemployed, unskilled people congregating in slum areas of US cities. Sidney Weintraub has calculated that Mexicans account for over 90 per cent of the illegal aliens apprehended in the United States (Weintraub, 1990:185). This has become a special problem for certain regions such as California, where Mexican migrants have concentrated.

GOVERNMENT POLICIES AS A DETERMINANT OF INVESTMENT AND EMPLOYMENT

For many decades, North American governments at both the national and sub-national level have provided a wide array of grants and subsidies to attract investment, particularly investment directed toward disadvantaged regions and high-tech sectors (Bird, 1980, 1984; Reich, 1983; Courchene, 1984; Steed, 1987; Conklin, 1993; Schrecker and Dalgleish, 1994). With NAFTA, many businesses will be able to locate anywhere within North America and serve the entire North American market, and thus NAFTA will likely intensify the competition among governments to attract new investment. Existing corporations often argue that subsidies enable new competitors to reduce the prices of their products, thereby encouraging unfair competition. The US has taken a firm position that it should impose special countervailing duties if any of its corporations are being hurt by foreign subsidies. The FTA established bi-national dispute settlement panels to deal with conflicts such as this and NAFTA has extended the use of these panels to include Mexico. Subsidies will remain a contentious subject and NAFTA's regional impacts will depend to some degree upon the outcome of these disputes.

Apart from subsidies, many other government policies also impact business decisions concerning investment and employment. A region's ability to attract desirable types of high-tech investment and well-paying jobs will depend increasingly on the qualifications of the region's labour force. Rapid and significant changes in products and production technology mean that employee skills and education quickly become outmoded. Government-supported retraining programmes will become increasingly necessary if employees are to be able to shift into new occupations or to new products and processes. From this perspective, human resource development is an 'industrial development tool' and universities are a key attraction. Here, each sub-national government has a major role to play in determining the strength of its region.

Recent literature emphasizes that the mobility of capital as a result of trade agreements places new restrictions on tax design in each region. Tax differences between jurisdictions can be a cause of business mobility. The design of the tax structure will likely become a competition among jurisdictions for the pursuit of new investments.

Personal income tax provisions may encourage the individual taxpayer to invest in certain types of corporations and so may also play a role in business location decisions. In the 1980s, for example, several of Canada's provinces introduced provisions to increase 'private-sector equity capital. These provisions typically provided partial relief to the personal income tax liability of taxpayers who purchased the equity of designated corporations. However, the impact of such provisions on the aggregate capital stock within the province is unclear and depends, to some degree, on the 'openness' of the capital market. Potential impacts may be reduced to the degree that the provincial capital market is integrated with capital markets outside the province. Higher provincial personal savings may simply replace the capital that would otherwise have flowed into the province from other regions. This replacement of foreign by domestic capital may not reduce the local rate of interest and so may not stimulate aggregate investment within the province. The economics literature is inconclusive on the extent to which higher domestic savings simply alter international capital flows, leaving the amount of physical business assets unaffected.

Macroeconomic policies will also play a role in determining NAFTA's impacts. Closer economic linkages with the United States as a result of NAFTA will expose regions in Canada and Mexico to the likelihood that they will be susceptible to shocks emanating from the US economy. In some circumstances, these shocks may originate outside the United States and their impact may be felt by way of linkages with the US. The post-1989 recession demonstrated the degree to which Canada's various provincial economies can be affected by a Canadian recession that is linked closely to a US recession. Changes in exchange rates in the 1990s will likely be rapid, frequent and substantial and they too will alter the international competitiveness of many of the regions within North America. Agriculture and natural resource industries, for example, have long been affected by changes in exchange rates since they have generally faced 'world prices'. A higher Canadian dollar value has automatically reduced export receipts denominated in Canadian dollars, while a decrease in value of the Canadian dollar has increased them. The impact of fluctuating exchange-rates has become increasingly important for businesses in the manufacturing sector as well. Many manufactured products are now being sold at relatively uniform world prices. For manufacturers, exchange-rate fluctuations can alter the domestic prices of their exports and also the domestic prices of the imports against which they compete. As noted above, retailers are also impacted by exchange rate fluctuations, which can dramatically affect the extent of cross-border shopping.

In response to the insistence of the newly-elected President Bill Clinton, 'side agreements' to NAFTA were negotiated after the principal document was agreed upon. The side agreements cover the subjects of the environment and labour conditions and will also impact on many regions, depending on their economic structure. Furthermore, the individual provinces and states within North America have significant jurisdictional responsibility for these matters and each jurisdiction has been implementing unique regulations. A lack of harmony in legislation and its enforcement is creating differences in production costs, which threaten to alter trade and investment patterns. Some regions may appear to be corporate havens, attracting investors who wish to avoid the costs imposed by the more severe regulations of other regions. Of special concern are regions in Mexico, where legislation is poorly enforced and businesses may be attracted inappropriately. The NAFTA side agreements seek to limit these possibilities. While the costs related to labour regulations are well known, the costs associated with environmental regulations are not yet as certain, and so the latter may deserve special comment.

Financial analyses rely heavily on corporate accounting practices and the rapid changes in environmental laws are creating inter-jurisdictional differences in the reporting requirements for financial statements. Corporate obligations arising from new environmental laws are not being presented consistently among countries. Accounting standards in Canada and the United States have long required disclosure and in certain situations, expense recognition of contingencies. However, accounting standards are much less stringent in Mexico.

A number of significant differences have developed among jurisdictions in regard to various aspects of corporate liability. They include the size of fines, the administrative authority of public servants to negotiate with industry, the responsibilities of corporate boards of directors and the requirements in regard to environmental impact statements. In many North American jurisdictions, real estate carries with it a future legal obligation for clean-up and site restoration. Consequently, investors now have to consider potential future costs that may be connected with a specific piece of property because of environmental concerns. For mergers and acquisitions, these obligations now take a prominent position in the negotiation process. In the United States, New Jersey and California require that an environmental assessment be conducted for property before any purchase or sale. This is not yet a legal requirement in many other regions. Some provinces and states have also placed new responsibilities on lending institutions for the clean-up costs connected with their borrowers, in the event of loan default. The act of taking over a mortgaged property can make a bank responsible for the clean-up cost. Hence, both equity and debt elements of financial markets are being affected.

A variety of theories and location factors are most relevant today in explaining the relative attractiveness of each region as a site for future investment and job creation. A single theory cannot adequately explain location decisions concerning the diverse kinds of business activities. For established manufacturing in particular, cost minimization is most relevant, with differentials in wages being a key determinant. For many business services and for new high-tech products and production processes, behavioural theories are most relevant, with emphasis on the education and skills of the labour force, the quality of universities and the entrepreneurial culture of the area. With many business and consumer services, the emphasis may be on geographic proximity to customers and the projected demand will therefore vary among regions. From these perspectives, a wide range of government policies – including subsidies, taxation, macroeconomic and exchange rate policies, environmental and labour legislation – will influence future business decisions concerning investment and jobs. To a major degree, NAFTA's impacts will depend on these government policies.

CONCLUSION

NAFTA is not the only new trade and investment agreement that will impact regions within North America. The Uruguay Round of the GATT negotiations has also recently reduced international trade and investment restrictions, creating new export opportunities, new competition from imports and changes in employment opportunities and income levels as a result of new investments. Furthermore, it appears that more countries will join NAFTA, which will also impact future economic prospects of the regions within North America.

Within both the US and Canada, debate over NAFTA has strongly focused on the threat that jobs may be lost in regions heavily dependent upon manufacturing and that these jobs may be transferred to low-wage regions in Mexico. Some unions in the United States see the non-unionized Mexican workers as unfair competition, and as a way of avoiding US labour legislation and standards for occupational health and safety. Some argue that US production costs are higher than the Mexican costs because of the more stringent labour and environmental regulations in the United States. NAFTA has greatly intensified the competition to attract new investments, thereby influencing the role of government at the provincial or state level, as well as at the national level. These issues will be at the forefront of political debate in all three countries.

In discussing the impacts of NAFTA, it is necessary to consider the time profile of changes. As a result of a number of factors, the long-term impacts will be much more significant and also somewhat different than the short-term impacts. There is a lengthy phase-in process to the liberalization of restrictions, extending in the case of Mexico as long as 15 years. The NAFTA side agreements establish permanent offices with representatives from all three countries to deal with differences in environmental and labour legislation and enforcement, and the passage of time will be necessary before their impact can be felt. For several years at least, Mexico's growth will likely be concentrated in areas that already have appropriate infrastructure, such as the *maquiladoras*, Mexico City, and Monterrey. Furthermore, many businesses will take several years to examine the costs and benefits of relocating to a different region. The 1994–95 Mexican peso crisis will further slow the shift of investment and jobs to Mexico. NAFTA's regional impacts will be felt throughout the coming decades and, to some degree, the nature and extent of these impacts will be determined by the response of governments as each seeks to attract investments and jobs.

10

Competitive Regionalism in Australia:
Sub-metropolitan Case Study

LIZ FULOP

INTRODUCTION

In Australia, as elsewhere in the world, there has been a burgeoning of regional initiatives since the early 1990s. Historically, it has been the Australian Labor Party (ALP), at the federal level, that has championed regional policies, and after a 20-year break, the Keating Labor government announced a new policy in 1994. Key elements of competitive regionalism are to be found in a number of reports released by the federal government during 1993 and 1994, and later synthesized in the White Paper on national strategy, called *Working Nation*, also released in 1994. Unlike the previous eras of regional reform, this one has been dubbed by some as a 'report-led recovery' in which regional problems are seen as principally structural or economic in nature, as opposed to spatial or locational (Clare, 1993:15; Hurley, 1994a; Hurley, 1994b; Stilwell, 1994a; Stilwell, 1994b). It is an era in which low cost solutions (or competitive strategies) are being sought to deliver long-term sustainable national growth in the context of the internationalization and globalization of the Australian economy.

Regional development involves complex, overlapping responsibilities amongst the three tiers of government – local, state and federal (or Commonwealth). In the past, one of the major areas of conflict between the states and federal Labor governments has been the inclusion by the latter of metropolitan areas in their regional policies and programmes. In fact, a number of factors about the Australian system of government act to frustrate or subvert federal government initiatives in the area of regional policy-making.

The first of these is the historical tensions between the three layers of government in Australia, in which the States have constitutional power over urban and regional development, while the Commonwealth can use its residual and fiscal powers to intervene in the regional domain, in the name of national priorities. In New South Wales (NSW), which this chapter focuses on, the state Liberal Party does not even recognize sub-metropolitan regions such as Western Sydney – the oldest regional grouping in the state. Liberals often view Labor's regional forays as indicative of an anti-state agenda. Second, the Commonwealth has the fiscal capacity to influence and implement major regional policies and programmes on a scale not easily matched by state governments, and this has often led to claims of pork-barrelling on the part of Labor governments.   Third, regional policies also impact on local government who, in the case of Western Sydney, has been extremely aggressive in taking on the regional development role. In doing so, it risks opposition from state governments, particularly Liberal ones.

Local government in NSW has no constitutional recognition, and exists under Acts of Parliament. Nor is it recognised in the federal Constitution, although Labor has sought two referenda to alter this. Not all in local government welcome the federal government's involvement in regional affairs because whenever the latter enters the regional domain, regional boundaries and relationships have to be renegotiated creating new tensions and strains amongst regional stakeholders, and between state and local governments. In these struggles, local government is always the weakest party with the most to lose. There is no such thing as regional government in Australia.

The remainder of the chapter will identify the pressures that have given rise to competitive regionalism. A discussion follows on the emergence of sub-metropolitan regionalism in NSW and Western Sydney, in the context of the changing political climate of the 1970s and 1980s. This sets the scene for examining how competitive regionalism is impacting on the Western Sydney region, one of the oldest and most complex sub-metropolitan areas in Australia.

COMPETITIVE REGIONALISM

Competitive regionalism, and by extension regional policy in general, has become subordinated to a range of new economic, as well as political, necessities. Even though some would like to describe competitive regionalism as the third wave of conservative regional policies in Australia (Stilwell, 1994a), the fact remains that the 'economization' of regional policy had already begun in the 1980s at the federal level, and much earlier in some of the states such as NSW. The Hawke Labor government was responsible for deregulating the economy in favour of free market policies setting the scene for major changes to Labor's regional policies by the mid 1980s (e.g., Beilharz and Watts, 1986; Jaensch, 1989a; Jaensch, 1989b; Johnson, 1989; Maddox, 1989; Pusey, 1991). Much of the so-called economic rationalist trends of the 1980s are enjoying a resurgence in Australia through the competitive agendas of all spheres of government, aimed at creating competition in all areas of government activity, including regional policy (Hilmer, 1994; Hurley, 1994a; Industry Commission, 1995).

The new economic necessities of the 1990s relate to a growing acceptance amongst government, political parties of all persuasions, business, unions, the media and community groups that there is a new world order dominated by newly emerging trading blocs, and political realignments unthought of five years ago. At the federal level, regional agendas are inextricably linked to three major challenges posed by these changes. First, competitive regionalism has emerged partly in response to the burgeoning of new centres or blocs of political, social and economic influence that are beginning to transcend not only national and international boundaries, and raise questions about the relevance and importance of national identity and sovereignty, but also economic survival (Hurley, 1994b:7; Keating and Loughlin, 1993). The possibility of an Asia Pacific Economic Community (APEC) emerging by the year 2010 has hastened the pace, if not the demands, for micro and macro economic reforms in Australia in favour of market forces. Second, this is occurring at a time when Australia's overall market share in East Asia is declining (Evans, 1994:5). The 'level playing field' approach adopted by the Federal ALP, and the decline in tariff protection, especially to the manufacturing sector, have increased overseas competition and the level of imports. None of this has been helped by extremely poor balance of payment figures over the last five years (now at approximately $180 billion), and a drop in Australia's export ranking from 12th to 20th over a 25-year period (Evans, 1994:4).

Third, these changes have helped create serious structural imbalances across the nation, with a noticeable number of lagging regions with high levels of unemployment and low growth potential. These developments have proven vexing for the Labor government not only economically, but also politically. In the majority of cases, these lagging regions also contain a number of marginal seats, which are predominantly in country or rural areas of Australia where the Federal ALP has not generally enjoyed popular support. While the government denies pork-barrelling or trying to 'keep the bush quiet', the fact remains that the new regional programmes are being pushed in many of these marginal seats (Evans, 1994:2; Davies, 1995:34).

The recent injection of $150 million of federal funds (over 4 years) into regional projects, while being seen by many as mere tokenism (Sorensen, 1994; Stilwell, 1994b), is a means by which direct financial support will be given to new Regional Economic Development Organizations (REDOs) so that they can collaborate and implement a range of new strategies, as well as consolidate a plethora of ongoing regional programmes and initiatives funded by state and federal governments. The federal government sees these REDOs, and their leaders, as integral to creating more adaptive, dynamic, flexible and competitive institutional structures and processes in the regional context that will be better able to foster, *inter alia*, new forms of regional collaboration principally to assist business development and exporting. Under competitive regionalism, *all* key regional stakeholders, including business, industry groups and unions are to be represented on the REDOs. However, the REDOs have to be established in regions where, in some cases, there already exist several regional bodies (Fulop, 1995).

The new regional policy contained in *Working Nation* emanated from four commissioned reports by the federal government and from the pragmatic decisions it made to satisfy all key stakeholders, particularly business groups. The first of these was the Industry Commission's (IC's) Report *Impediments to Regional Industry Adjustment*, released in 1993, which was variously described by its critics as 'dry' in its analysis, and the IC itself labelled by many as the champion of economic rationalist prescriptions, or just plain 'out of touch' (Sorensen, 1993a:2; Stilwell, 1994b; Financial Review, 1993:10). Far from accepting any spatial dimension to public policy, the IC advocated that if the government was to get the 'big picture' right, through macro-economic adjustments, then regional problems would take care of themselves. The major recommendations of the IC report were: further deregulation of the labour market (including differential regional wages); deregulation of transport (in line with competitive regionalism); improving infrastructure, but not necessarily through government support or funding; minimising red-tape and bureaucracy (less and smaller government); and better co-ordination of regional programmes as well as rationalising them where possible. It also went on to recommend better assessment (costs vs. benefits), planning and pricing of regional infrastructure. A number of these recommendations were adopted in *Working Nation* (Sorensen, 1994). The IC stressed the importance of consulting with the states and devolving regional programmes to this level, thus, rejecting a role for the central government in programme delivery or implementation.

The IC recommended that regional self-help be the overriding approach the government should adopt to regional development. This was a view already articulated by one of the architects of competitive regionalism some months earlier when he said, '... the onus is on the region to want to pursue competitive regional development and take the lead role in it.' (Garlick, quoted in Hurley, 1994a:24). In a similar vein, Prime Minister Keating used a 'President Kennedy-style' approach to regions when he said, '...ask not what the Commonwealth government can do for your region, but what can a region do for itself.' (Keating, quoted in Haward, 1993:13; also Hurley, 1994a:24). In the new discourse of competitive regionalism, 'bottom up' initiatives have been translated into a self-help ethos, and the exercise of choice by regional stakeholders in the strategies they choose to implement. Sorensen, who was critical of the IC's neglect of the role played by regional stakeholders in reviving regional economies, cautioned against rejecting all it had to say simply on the basis that it was toeing an economic rationalist line (Sorensen, 1993b:21). He went on to reveal a number of 'beneficial' recommendations in the report that might stimulate regional economies and create regional flexibility and competitiveness. Sorensen was in many respects responding to the reality that neither the federal nor state governments were going to adopt an interventionist or big spending approach to regions.

The antidote to the IC report was the Kelty Report also released in 1993. As Stilwell (1994b:53) noted, the Kelty Taskforce adopted a more inductive approach to policy-making by taking a grand tour of 63 regions across Australia, covering both metropolitan and country areas, to get a grass-roots response to what should be done in the regions. The Kelty Report highlighted the importance of regional leadership in revitalising regional economies, and the need for partnerships and collaboration among all key regional stakeholders, including unions. It urged empowering regions and making them more autonomous and powerful within the Australian system of government – a position usually viewed as anti the states. The Kelty Taskforce did not reject elements of competitive regionalism, but rather favoured collaborative regionalism. In marked contrast to the three other reports, it lent support to increased subsidies and a more interventionist approach by the Commonwealth. In a path-breaking way, the report also attempted to link industry and regional policies – the latter being normally a state responsibility. The report also advocated interventions in the labour market (especially to address high youth unemployment), training, regional industrial relations and regional industry plans (for sectors such as arts and tourism).

The Kelty Report also recommended large investments (approximately $2 billion) by the Commonwealth on infrastructure such as rural roads, but concurred with the IC that only cost-effective developments should be funded. In an effort to attract private-sector investment, changes were also recommended, and adopted in *Working Nation*, to the ways in which Infrastructure Bonds and Regional Pooled Development Funds had been managed. Again in concurrence with the IC, it also recommended the privatization of ports and other facilities that the states were not managing on a commercially viable basis. Finally, the Kelty Report recommended that the Commonwealth, and not the states, should fund REDOs, but only to those representing all key regional stakeholders. This was accepted and endorsed in *Working Nation*.

For many, the Kelty Report represented a promise of a return to another golden age for regions (Cameron, 1993). The breadth of areas it sought to incorporate under the new regionalism, including indigenous people's role in regional development, was reminiscent of the Whitlam government's approach in the 1970s. The media described the Kelty Report as '...a dollop of 1970s-style tax-and-spend interventionism lightly spiced with a few new ideas from the economic rationalism of the 1980s' (Burnelly, 1993:2). In its defence, Labor ministers and senior public servants repeatedly asserted that managing regional diversity meant devising strategies and projects (hence the claim that what was now occurring was a strategic policy approach) that did not aim to identify 'winning' or 'losing' regions *per se*, but rather created strategic options for all regions to pursue in terms of national priorities (Evans, 1994; Hurley, 1994b).

The notion of managing diversity, which underscores a range of policy agendas in Australia (see Meekosha, 1993:174–8), was translated into regional policy by the Kelty Report. Hence considerable emphasis was placed on devising an integrated approach to regional development to include economic growth, social and environmental needs and quality-of-life issues, or what some term, 'a whole of Government' approach to sustainable development. In other words, the Kelty Report was not entirely dominated by economic rationalist considerations (Kelty, 1993; Evans, 1994:2; Howe, 1994; Stilwell, 1994b). Somewhat reminiscent of the 1970s, grass-roots involvement and ownership of regional plans and processes became a central theme of the Kelty Report. Managing regional diversity translated into the federal government limiting its role to facilitation, and hence the development of soft regional infrastructure such as integrated planning, strategic management, regional leadership, entrepreneurship, local culture, skills enhancement, diffusion of expertise and innovation, education, research and development (Murphy, quoted in Hurley, 1994a:26). Indeed, the government adopted the view that whatever happened in regions must be demand driven, in response to demands from within the regions, and not orchestrated by the central government (Evans, 1994).

The third report on regional development was prepared by management consultants, McKinsey & Co and had the most impact on policy making, and the 'marketization' and 'managerialization' of the regional discourse. The report was commissioned as an antidote to the Kelty Report which had come under harsh criticism from business groups who felt their views had been ignored by the Kelty Taskforce. McKinsey & Co used an earlier report on emerging exporters, and the micro level behaviour of firms, to develop a macro approach to regional economic development and revitalization (Davies, 1994:36). Released under the title *Compete Local Lead Global* (1994), the report created what some termed a 'new cargo cult of exporting' because it largely appropriated (or misappropriated) pragmatic management ideas and tools and applied them to solving complex regional economic development problems (Gordon, 1994).

The exporting, hence marketing, emphasis emerged from the linking of regional development to notions of competitive advantage, and ideas associated with mega-regions or clusters of excellence, made famous by Porter's book, *Competitive Advantage of Nations* (1990), and also reinforced in various OECD reports (for example OECD, 1992). Porter's ideas had gained wide acceptance in business and policy circles, creating pressures to redefine the role of regional policy making, especially in favour of supporting lead regions that might have the capacities to push export and globalization initiatives through supporting industries that were showing export promise such as the service sector, and elaborately transformed manufacturing (ETM). As a corollary of the marketization of regional policies and programmes, emphasis shifted to the strategic management of regional resources, opportunities and threats in order to create competitive advantages within regions. Thus, one of the principles of the new regional policy was to build '...a capacity to generate sustainable economic activity at the regional level relevant to national and international markets' (Evans, 1994:7; Howe, 1994; also Hurley, 1994b:5).

The managerialization of the regional discourse translated into a second principle: '...ensuring that this new capacity reflects 'best practice' approaches to regional development organizations, strategies, implementation plans, including best practices by local firms' (Evans, 1994:7). The competitive regionalism discourse, predominantly espoused through McKinsey & Co, appropriated ideas and practices associated with world class businesses, and included management concepts such as best practice, benchmarking, regional learning, strategic regional leadership and strategic vision. While the advocates of competitive regionalism had acknowledged the need for regional diversity (and flexibility) there remained an implicit assumption that lead regions would more easily embrace many of these ideas irrespective of their unique contexts. McKinsey & Co agreed with the Kelty Report on a number of points, such as the need for representative REDOs, the importance of regional leadership, and the need for some infrastructure developments. However, the McKinsey & Co recommendations were difficult to translate into the highly politicized regional context (Hurley, 1994a; Gordon, 1994; Stilwell,

1994b). While the role of leadership, for example, might be important at the level of the firm, a study testing this proposition found that there was no conclusive evidence to suggest that leadership was a critical factor in either local or regional economic development (Sorensen and Epps, 1994).

The final report in the so-called report-led recovery was prepared by the Bureau of Industry Economics (BIE), and released in 1994 under the title *Regional Development: Patterns and Policy Implications*. As Stilwell (1994b) again observed, the BIE took an open view of regional issues and adopted a liberal pluralist approach in dealing with all major sides of the regional debate (this replicated a similar report prepared in NSW in 1993 by the Standing Committee on State Development under the title *Regional Business Development in New South Wales*). The BIE report drew vague conclusions and had the least immediate influence on regional policy-making. In essence it sought to highlight the complexity of regional development strategies by examining in detail the arguments behind comparative versus competitive advantages.

Much of the BIE's study concentrated on testing Porter's theory of competitive advantage, despite the fact that few of the conditions exist in Australia that Porter cited as essential for competitive advantage of nations. Resource-based exporting has dominated the Australian economy, but this was not a sector Porter saw as having the potential to create competitive advantage. Porter also argued that to sustain competitive advantage, lower-order advantages (or comparative ones) such as labour, location, mass markets, cheap raw materials, and even economies of scale were no longer relevant. The BIE study concluded that there were no adequate explanations for differences in regional performance and argued that the government should assist growth by improving incentives for individuals and firms to develop local capacities, hence lending support to competitive advantage strategies. It also opposed inter-state and inter-regional competition in the use of incentives to attract businesses to locate to a region, that is, traditional comparative advantage strategies were not greatly supported (Stilwell, 1994b: 56).

METROPOLITAN REGIONALISM

The architects of competitive regionalism included sub-metropolitan areas in their regional strategies, thus continuing a controversial tradition started by the Whitlam Labor government in the 1970s. There are those who, even back then and still now, strongly believe that the paradigm of regional policy-making should be non-metropolitan or restricted to rural Australia (Cameron, 1993; Hurley, 1994b:7-8). The new federal initiatives did favour rural or provincial areas from whence emerged *the Regional Australia Now Campaign* – a major catalyst for the Keating government resurrecting a regional strategy (Cameron, 1993). At the height of the recession, a revolt by the Country Mayors' Association of NSW, helped bring regional Australia back onto the political agendas of both state and federal governments. The Country Mayors produced a manifesto of reform aimed at countering the neglect of the economic and social plight of country areas by all levels of government. This group sought to have balanced development, which is a euphemism for decentralization, brought back into regional development strategies, particularly of the Liberal state governments in NSW and Victoria (Collits, 1994:3).

From 1967 onwards the ALP had begun to transform its political agendas, and locational inequalities were made synonymous with, *inter alia*, the reform of urban and regional planning. Under Whitlam, both regionalism and decentralization became important strategies for realigning the powers of the Commonwealth *vis-a-vis* the states and local government. In this period, regionalism focused on democratization and devolutionary issues in suburbia (or Labor's heartland), while regionalization dealt with growth centre policies and economic development of country areas. The concept of regionalization had already gained currency in state politics where it was mainly associated with decentralization of government administration, and programmes that promoted competition among the States for industrial development. Labor's unprecedented and historical decision to intervene directly in urban affairs, and the planning of cities, raised the chagrin of both state and local governments. The states objected to this constitutional infringement while the local government associations in NSW, who had had little involvement in regional co-operation because of restrictions placed upon it by state legislation, developed a misguided belief that Whitlam's regional policies were motivated in part by Labor's desire to abolish local government.

Labor introduced the deprived area thesis into the urban debate and along with it, the ghetto metaphor, and its associated claims of political neglect and plundering of sub-metropolitan regions such as

Western Sydney and West Melbourne (Stretton, 1975). Both regions had high concentrations of welfare housing, unemployment, and social problems which were amplified by the media through reports of high rates of crime and violence in these urban slums. Declining manufacturing industries, poor transport, inadequate housing, human services and infrastructure added to the picture of 'gloom and doom' in the western suburbs. Regionalism became coterminous with social democratic reforms aimed at improving the quality of life and opportunities of citizens (notably Labor ones) in the suburbs. It also became a symbol of the democratization of society, and the commitment to encourage public participation through bottom-up reforms and grass roots involvement in politics and policy-making. The Whitlam years contributed immeasurably, and irrevocably, to the emergence of multiple sites of contestation and struggles over regional issues and policies in the suburbs.

Under special legislation introduced by the Whitlam government, Australia was carved into 76 regions with different types of regional organizations established in them. Western Sydney became the highest funded region in Australia because of its categorization as a disadvantaged area (Fulop and Sheppard, 1988). Whitlams's electorate was in Western Sydney. The Western Sydney Regional Organization of Councils (WSROC) was created under these initiatives, and came to be considered as one of the best models of regional co-operation in Australia (Wettenhall, 1987). However, there were no satisfactory or appropriate administrative or policy mechanisms to deal with ROCs, especially those established in areas such as Western Sydney, which was a diverse and complex region. At the time, the Liberal state government was reluctant to recognize WSROC, especially for planning and development purposes. In fact, WSROC was created by the forced amalgamation of two pre-existing regional groupings of councils. Its ten constituent members struggled for many years to establish a regional identity and programme. Half the members were drawn from the older, and more wealthy 'Inner West', while the others came from the newer, rapidly expanding, but poorer 'Outer West' areas. However, the intention of the Whitlam government was that ROCs should represent all key regional stakeholders, although business was not included. This never eventuated in Western Sydney, with local government dominating the organization to this day (Fulop, 1993).

After the dismissal of the Whitlam government, NSW came under Labor rule with the election of Neville Wran to office in 1976.

His government was the first to give recognition to sub-metropolitan regions in NSW. Wran's programs and policy initiatives directly buoyed a regional growth-at-all-cost ethos that contrasted with Whitlam's efforts to create a strong locational inequality regional agenda in Western Sydney. By the late 1970s WSROC had adopted employment, economic development and transport as its three major regional needs or priorities. The imperatives of rapid growth and expansion of the region became synonymous with regional development, and along with it, property enhancement and protection. Regional boosterism, and an essentially property-led regeneration of the region, became synonymous with the metaphor of the region as the 'powerhouse' of the State's economy (Anderson, 1990:473; Fulop, 1992).

Wran was the first Labor leader in Australia to win office on a political platform that had shunned the idealism and democratic socialist reform agendas of the Whitlam years and who instead had shown the efficacy of populism and pragmatism in achieving electoral success. He won office when the state, and the nation were in recession or economic crisis, which in turn he attributed in large part to Whitlam's economic mismanagement and anti-business policies. Wran's decision to commit large amounts of monies and resources to attract private-sector investment and industry to select regions of NSW, such as the coal-rich Hunter and the steel-dominated Illawarra, were justified by him as essential to creating jobs. He also embarked on a deliberate and vigorous campaign to improve Labor's standing with the business community and the media, by boosting private-sector investment in NSW and showing that Labor could manage the State's economy. In fact, the NSW branch of the Labor Party had always been strongly committed to the politics of development, placing a high premium on economic growth and development and job creation. Wran began Labor's transformation into a modern, catch-all political party (Carr, 1978:17; Frankel, 1992:156).

Under Wran's regional economic development programs, Western Sydney was allocated approximately $502 million over a ten-year period, but this paled in comparison with the injection of some $1000 million for infrastructure developments alone in the Hunter Region (Gardiner, 1987:240; Steketee and Cockburn, 1986:202-11). Wran's economic show piece was always the Hunter, where he believed NSW would be able to create an industrial conglomerate on the scale of the Ruhr Valley in Germany. Wran justified his investment and development policies by arguing that he was saving a generation of Australians from the unemployment scrap heap (Steketee and Cockburn, 1986:199-205).

Through a combination of pressures, including the release of the regional strategy funded under the Whitlam government, party factionalism and electoral strategies, the Wran government introduced the first State-funded disadvantaged area programme in Western Sydney, and for that matter, in the State (Fulop, Neosjirwan and Smith, 1988). The programme was introduced in 1980 and became so popular that it was extended to other regions in the State. Service provision was given high priority although only $1 million was allocated per annum for a three year period. The amount was increased in subsequent years, and mainstream departments had to pick up ongoing projects, substantially increasing the net value of the programme, and forcing these departments to rework their programmes to incorporate regional considerations. Wran also introduced a promotions programme and employment creation initiatives in Western Sydney, as well as a number of powerful committees at cabinet level to manage the region's special needs and problems (Fulop, 1992).

Yet under Wran regional policy-making had started to lose its status as a meta-policy used to enact reforms in other policy areas such as welfare, housing, education, environment, health, transport and employment (Stewart, 1983:211). Increasingly, regional policies either came to emphasize development and economic outcomes, as in the case of the Hunter Region, or were subordinated to policies and planning strategies designed to fine-tune the allocation and distribution of resources for capital accumulation (Stilwell, 1989:72).

By 1986, the year Wran retired as Premier, the first major amendment in 20 years was made to the ALP's urban and regional development and local government platforms. These amendments involved the addition of three new principles relating to efficiency and equity: facilitating economic growth in areas possessing natural development and comparative advantage; assisting the adjustment of urban and regional communities to structural change, and promoting equity and access to regional social facilities and services. Labor's new- found economic determinism was defended by some as part of an essentially evolutionary trend in which the focus had to shift to managing structural changes and economic reforms. Only the last amendment suggested any ongoing commitment to regional equalization that was a key to the Whitlam reforms.

The left wing of the Federal ALP had generally supported feminism, environmentalism, regionalism, and participatory democracy throughout the 1960s and 1970s. The left was a product of the British class struggle, unionism and a commitment to socialist objectives. Many British-born MPs were in the left faction. In sharp contrast, the right wing had embraced deregulation, internationalization and privatization during the 1980s. The right, especially in NSW, was influenced by the Democratic Party in the US; key unionists attended Harvard trade union courses and various prominent figures in the party joined select societies in the US such the Chester Alan Arthur Society. Many of them revered Roosevelt and the Kennedy dynasty, and derived their intense republican fervour from these connections. Nonetheless, by the 1990s the left and right were converging into a catch-all party, particularly as the economic models that divided them in earlier periods were being destroyed by the internationalization of the economy, and the need to manage cultural diversity, as opposed to class-based politics (Tanner, 1994:9). Both sides of politics seemed to identify and embrace a common set of necessary economic adjustments by the late 1980s (Stilwell, 1989:72-3).

Specifically, these economic adjustments referred to a package of measures described as an obsession with budget deficits, restoring profits, wage restraint or cutting of real wages, financial deregulation, the balance of payments, and encouraging market forces (Beilharz and Watts, 1986:101; Stilwell, 1989:86). Thus, in the 1980s regional economic policies were used selectively to address problems wrought by micro-economic reforms associated with industry restructuring strategies, and dismantling tariff protection. Various industry plans, such as the Motor Vehicle and Steel Industry Plans, were introduced in regions such as the Hunter and Illawarra – both bastions of Labor support. As a concession to the left, a special allocation of $30 million was made to assist inner-city areas of Sydney affected by industry restructuring in the clothing, footwear and textile industries. Western Sydney was not targeted for any special assistance under these regional interventions even though its manufacturing base was suffering from the deregulation policies of the Hawke government. The Commonwealth's decision to construct a major office complex in the region, and the controversial second airport at Badgery's Creek, were the only two forms of assistance given to the Western Sydney (Stilwell, 1989:87; Orchard and Sandercock, 1989:349-355).

REINVENTING SUB-METROPOLITAN REGIONALISM

However, Western Sydney benefited from the disadvantaged region's programme introduced in the early days of the Hawke government as a result of a deal with the left wing. WSROC, and its member councils, received approximately $1.5 million of federal funds under the Local Government Development Program (LGDP) to conduct various regional studies between 1984–87. With these funds WSROC was able to commission another major strategic plan or blueprint for regional development which was released as the West Sydney 2000 Study (WSROC, 1985). Later, the West Sydney 2000 Study became the basis for the first sub-metropolitan economic strategy to be introduced by a NSW state government. The Unsworth Labor government released The Western Sydney Economic Development Strategy in early 1988 with the promise that it would '...turn western Sydney into a national powerhouse.' The document represented what some in government thought marked Labor's return to a '...'back-to-basics' philosophy of economic development.' This philosophy was translated into a package of incentives for business that drew heavily on the recommendations of the West Sydney 2000 Study, and other related LGDP projects such as the Advanced Technology Development Strategy for Western Sydney (WSROC *et al.*, 1986).

Employment and economic development dominated the West Sydney 2000 Study and was used by WSROC to place renewed pressure on the state government to produce a separate regional economic development strategy for Western Sydney, and establish a Western Sydney Economic Development Unit. The employment and economic development strategies in the West Sydney 2000 Study reflected, in part, the commitment WSROC had made in its 1977 regional strategy to tackle the issues of industry restructuring and skills formation in the region. However, in typical post-Keynesian fashion, the study focused on government or state level interventions and planning, and excluded serious scrutiny, criticism or debate about the role of the private sector or international capital in creating unemployment or regional decline.

Unsworth's economic strategy for Western Sydney built on this legacy, and was predicably conservative in its recommendations: reducing regulations and charges for business, identifying growth opportunities, providing assistance to business to take these opportunities, and establishing the necessary infrastructures for business development. At best, Labor's new economic strategy acknowledged a commitment to social development programs, such as the disadvantaged area programme introduced by Wran, stating categorically that economic development depended upon improving the skills and opportunities of residents in the region, including social ones. However, it was argued that all future programmes had to demonstrate their relevance to economic development.

Unsworth lost the 1988 state elections and the victorious Liberal Party promptly shelved Labor's economic strategy for Western Sydney. In order to consolidate the Liberals' win in Labor's traditional heartlands, economic development taskforces were set up in both the Hunter and Illawarra Regions, but not in Western Sydney. The Greiner government advocated the introduction of enterprise zones and task forces based on approaches used by the Thatcher government to revitalize depressed industrial and inner-city areas in the UK (Stilwell, 1989:86-7; Anderson, 1990:468-489; Stewart, 1986). After the 1987 local government elections, the majority of WSROC's member councils were dominated by Liberals and Independents. This meant that the organization was also brought under the control of Liberal and Independent representatives. For next three years WSROC was stalemated by internal conflicts and struggles to redefine regional priorities and needs, and the role of the organization in general (Fulop and Sheppard, 1988:623).

At the time of his election, and despite a landslide of votes to the Liberals, the Premier made it clear that Western Sydney would not receive any special treatment, and would not be regarded as a separate regional entity. Nor did he accept that the residents of Western Sydney had a separate regional identity (Fulop, 1992:2). Yet within 12 months of its election, the Greiner government found itself having to introduce special programmes in Western Sydney, and even expand the disadvantaged area scheme which Wran had also attempted to scrap. The myriad of interest groups and 'problem-solving publics' (Boyte, 1992:350, 355), or multiple sites of contestation that Whitlam and Wran had unleashed in Western Sydney, were impossible to silence or control. There was an entrenched Western Sydney voice in all spheres of politics (Fulop, 1992).

Nonetheless, in the wake of the disastrous 1991 state election results, in which the Greiner government won by only a one-seat margin, the Liberals 'out-Labored Labor' by announcing that they would establish and fund a Greater Western Sydney Economic Development Committee (GWSEDC) that would '...develop a tourism and industry powerhouse', and a 'mini-multi-function polis' of commercial hubs or enterprise zones to hoist the region into international and global markets. The Greiner government made no apology for the fact that its economic development strategy had a business bias, and an overarching concern with private-sector investment, except that pollution in the region was now reluctantly conceded as an important social issue for businesses. Far from supporting an interventionist role for the government, the Greiner model fitted perfectly with the new right dogma and the economic rationalists' agendas that favoured a *laissez-faire* approach to markets and reduced government expenditure and interventions. 'Greinerism', and its euphemism 'NSW Incorporated', deliberately emulated Thatcherism, and along with it the corporatization and privatization of government enterprises. The Liberals never intended to promote a government-funded economic recovery in regions, let alone in Greater Western Sydney, but rather a private-sector-driven one. Business interests and local growth coalitions dominated the new GWSEDC, guaranteeing that the regional economic policy would be shaped by a corporate definition of economic recovery (Orchard and Sandercock, 1989:353).

The ill-fated GWSEDC was formed in 1992, and although it had strong regional representation, the committee was almost entirely dominated by business interests, and chaired by the failed ex-CEO of Westpac Bank, who claimed he knew little about the region. Even though WSROC had been the main force behind the creation of the WSEDC, it was allowed only one representative on the committee. More importantly, the definition of the 'region' was extended to cover non-WSROC local government areas. The Macarthur Development Board and the Macarthur Regional Organization of Councils (MACROC) were included in what became an expanded region called Greater Western Sydney. Much of the work that WSROC, and local government, had undertaken to politicize and economize regional issues was ignored, and diminished by the WSEDC who, with the help of consultants, began to re-write the economic (and political) agenda for Greater Western Sydney.

When in 1984 WSROC had prepared its submission to the LGDP, it had sought support for a regional development board. In doing so, it had already argued for a more representative structure to reflect the diversity of the region's labour market and to include the community sector – one of the largest growth areas in the region. By 1990 WSROC had also begun to include groups such as conservationists in their strategic planning processes and was developing a more integrated approach to regional development. However, given WSROC's political links to local government and the Labor Party, the Greiner government's funding of the WSEDC provided the best opportunity the Liberals had to capture the regional agenda in Western Sydney, and neutralize one of the most successful ROCs in the Country.

Although the GWSEDC conducted extensive consultations to develop a new blueprint for regional economic development, much of what they proposed in their final report was largely distilled from the masses of reports and data produced by WSROC and Western Sydney's Regional Information Service (WESTIR). The Greater Western Sydney Economic Development Statement (1993), already reflected the marketization of the regional discourse. It made extensive use of Porter's ideas by seeking to identify regional competitive advantages using a strategic planning model that talked of the region as the product. An international outlook, regional leadership and joint action were seen as important to economic growth in the region. Industry clustering was favoured as a major strategy as was the targeting of top exporting companies. The achievable image that the GWSEDC wanted for Greater Western Sydney was one of 'quality, diversity and connectivity' (Greater Western Sydney Economic Development Committee, 1993:48).

In 1994 the Greater Western Sydney Economic Development Board (GWSEDB), which had succeeded the GWSEDC, produced its Strategic Plan and The Economic Powerhouse of Australia investment prospectus. Neither document was original and, in many respects, replicated previous efforts by WSROC, including appropriating the powerhouse metaphor as a key marketing device – a metaphor that even WSROC had stopped using. The strategy reiterated the ideas in the earlier 1993 document and identified the following as important to developing the region's economy:

marketing, investment projects, business enhancement, tourism, transport and planning. Because of public criticisms and a growing environmental lobby in the region, some concessions were made in the Strategic Plan to include sustainable development and integrated planning. Regional cohesion and joint economic action were also mentioned as important to the implementation of the strategy, but the GWSEDB's own structure remained entirely dominated by private sector representatives. Although the Strategic Plan made mention of including all regional stakeholders and forging strategic alliances with regional organizations, no strategies were devised to improve or achieve this form of 'representation' – an essential component of an integrated approach to regional development.

In 1994 WSROC also released its strategic plan called Western Sydney – a Vision for the Next 20 Years (WSROC, 1994a). Unlike, the GWSEDB, the WSROC document was a manifesto for integrated regional development in which it envisaged establishing a regional planning committee that would incorporate the four major sub-metropolitan regions of Eastern Sydney, Greater Western Sydney, Hunter and Illawarra. One Sydney Metropolitan Strategy Taskforce would oversee the development of the economy, human services, environment, housing and infrastructure, and transport action plans. The proposal recommended joint planning committees in all these areas, except for economic development and transport. Under WSROC's proposal each sub-metropolitan region would have a separate REDO and transport board. The REDO was to include community, local government and ROC representation – a strategy supported by the federal fovernment's REDO policy and the Kelty Taskforce.

However, even WSROC's strategy faced challenge. There were marked differences amongst its ten constituent members with differing levels of commitment to the idea that local government should take a lead or even embrace the agendas set by the federal government. Some councils in Western Sydney had been aggressive in developing their local economic strategies within a competitive framework, while others lagged in this regard. For those favouring the competitive agendas, WSROC's vision lacked the marketization and managerialization that was so evident in the work of the GWSEDB. From about the early 1990s, WSROC became concerned about the high levels of pollution and environmental degradation. In this context, even the powerhouse metaphor appeared 'dirty' and 'out of touch', especially with WSROC. The unnatural grouping that the Whitlam government created in 1973 was straining under these competing pressures to redefine the nature and substance of regional development strategies.

The Kelty Taskforce had urged regions to rethink their regional boundaries, and create more fluid and relevant entities that could meet the new economic challenges facing the nation. The representation conditions placed on the funding of REDOs was meant to apply specifically to areas such as Western Sydney where the issue of regional groupings had been the most difficult to resolve. The Kelty Taskforce recognized the disruptive nature of the Liberal state government's initiatives in Western Sydney, and its efforts to diminish the influence of organizations such as WSROC. The most likely scenario was that there would be two REDOs in Greater Western Sydney constituted along the lines of WSROC and MACROC's groupings with a 'pan REDO' to oversee major developments such as Badgery's Creek Airport and Olympic facilities. WSROC still favoured one REDO for Greater Western Sydney, but acknowledged the difficulties of bring all the competing interests under the one 'umbrella' of an expanded regional entity (WSROC, 1994b). Three REDOs were finally created.

CONCLUSION

Given the federal government's re-entry into the regional policy arena, and its funding of REDOs, all regional groupings became unstable and contested entities. At the regional and local levels the complexity, sophistication and intellectual nuances of regional policy talk, and its associated agendas, were not so readily translated into policy and practice. Nor could it be assumed that competitive regionalism was necessarily understood or embraced in terms of the political, social and economic intentions or transformations intended by its architects in government. There is usually enormous confusion and slippage surrounding the implementation of any new policy, especially at the mundane, everyday level. Political trade-offs and compromises also become necessary as competing and contradictory discourses circulate across a range of differentially structured regional arenas. This point has been illustrated by the historical struggles to forge sub-metropolitan regions in NSW.

The discussion of competitive regionalism was used to set the scene for the case study and to contextualize the material in the global and international contexts, and the responses made by the central government to these challenges. Of importance to the discussion was the way in which competitive regionalism was and is reshaping federal–state relations. Underlying the federal government's new regional initiatives is a concerted effort to create a national grid of regional organizations that will be able to support the micro-economic reforms the Commonwealth sees as critical to Australia's long-term economic prosperity. Competitive regionalism does not mark a return to a golden age of regions, but rather a continuation of the economic rationalist agendas of the 1980s, except that pragmatism and low-cost solutions have become the keys to regional development.

Competitive regionalism has become the catalyst for reshaping territorial politics, and forging new political alignments between ROCs and REDOs as has happened in Greater Western Sydney. These new realignments will predictably entail different forms of co-operation, collaboration, co-determination, complementarity, convergence and competition in the sub-metropolitan context. Ultimately, the clash will be between the forces favouring integrated development and those supporting the wholesale marketization and managerialization of regional economic policies. In the process, it is likely that new forms of co-determination will have to emerge to create what the government has deemed to be a representative REDO. The degree to which regional stakeholders can find some complementarity in their respective approaches to regional development, and the extent to which they can create a collaborative context for regional action, will determine the place that regions such as Greater Western Sydney have in the new world order.

11

When Nationalism Meets Continentalism: The Politics of Free Trade in Quebec[1]

PIERRE MARTIN

In comparative and international political economy, the association of nationalism with protectionism is strong and enduring. But are the forces of nationalism and international economic integration, so dominant in the 1990s, necessarily pulling in opposite directions? 'Must we', as Robert Reich (1991: 311) recently asked, 'choose between zero-sum nationalism and impassive cosmopolitanism? Do these two positions describe the only alternative modes of future citizenship?' In short, is 'free-trade nationalism' a contradiction in terms?

For students of comparative politics or international political economy, support for free trade by nationalists can appear puzzling, given the conventional connection between nationalism and protectionism. In recent years, however, nationalist movements have flourished in the midst of increasing international economic integration. Moreover, some of these movements are not just sitting idly by to observe this process of economic integration; they are taking an active part in supporting continental trade liberalization initiatives. In Quebec and in other regions where strong nationalist or autonomist movements exist, such as Catalonia or Scotland (Clavera, 1990; Macartney, 1990), political leaders have justified their support for continental economic integration on the basis of appeals to nationalism. Is there a positive linkage between nationalism and free trade?

The politics of free trade in Quebec since the mid-1980s provides important clues to understand this linkage between nationalism and free-trade orientation. As a Canadian province, Quebec cannot negotiate international trade agreements or raise tariffs, but its support was instrumental in Canada's decision to move toward continental free trade. Two features of the Quebec case make it useful to address the more general issue of the relationship between nationalism and international economic integration. First, conventional theories of international political economy would lead one to predict that Quebec should have resisted free trade. Second, the political context in Quebec during the period of decision on free trade was dominated by nationalism. Indeed, during the debates over free trade, the parties that represented the two 'faces' of Quebec nationalism, the Parti Québécois (PQ) and the Liberal Party of Quebec, were strong supporters of continental trade integration.

This chapter examines the linkage between the revival of Quebec nationalism since the late 1980s and this support for North American free trade by Quebec's political parties and public opinion. The argument can be stated plainly: Quebec did not endorse free trade in spite of its nationalism; it endorsed free trade largely because of it. Because nationalism is the core issue of partisan competition in Quebec, parties define their position on secondary issues in terms of how outcomes can affect their nationalist goals. For the partisans of Quebec sovereignty, the expansion and institutionalization of continental trade relations can reduce the anticipated costs of transition to independence and help to ensure the economic viability of a sovereign state. For moderate nationalists, those seeking more autonomy within the Canadian federation, trade liberalization can be seen as a way of reducing the relative power of the central state compared to that of the provincial government, which was, during the period covered by the study, close to the Quebec-based business community. Thus, this chapter shows that the bipartisan consensus and the high level of support for free trade in Quebec was a consequence of the partisan pursuit of nationalist goals.

The demonstration of this argument proceeds in two stages. The initial step consists of confronting alternative hypotheses to the evidence available from the case. In the first section, theories of international political economy are surveyed to look for alternative explanations for the high level of support for free trade in Quebec.

This survey reveals a puzzle, since none of the well-established theories gives a satisfactory explanation for this phenomenon.

The second section develops an explanation by looking at the interaction between the politics of nationalism and the politics of free trade in Quebec. The plausibility of the argument that nationalism led to support for trade liberalization is evaluated on the basis of a case study of the politics of the Canada–US Free Trade Agreement (FTA) and the North American Free Trade Agreement (NAFTA). The conclusion summarizes elements of a theoretical framework for free-trade nationalism that can be identified from the Quebec case. In short, nationalist movements see trade integration as a way of reducing dependence upon a central state; first because market integration enhances the autonomy of the private sector and second, because the institutional structures that regulate trade relations tend to reduce the anticipated costs of the transition to independence.

THE POLITICAL ECONOMY OF CONTINENTAL FREE TRADE IN QUEBEC

Analysts of foreign economic policies generally rely on three main levels of analysis to explain trade and other international economic policies: a country's position in international structures; the relative strength of groups in society; or the actions of state officials evolving in an environment where ideas and institutions matter (Ikenberry, Lake and Mastanduno, 1988). Conventional theories of international political economy at these three levels fail to explain adequately Quebec's support for free trade, but this analysis reveals two crucial elements of the explanation: party politics and nationalism. First, the debate over free trade in Quebec is summarized.

The Support for Free Trade in Quebec

Although there were historical precedents to the debate on continental integration in Quebec, this issue only became prominent in the mid-1980s. A consensus on free trade between Quebec political parties has endured since 1988, but parties vacillated on the issue between 1984 and 1987 (Martin, 1994). When plans for the Canada–US FTA were initially announced, Liberal opposition leader Robert Bourassa was reluctant to endorse it. René Lévesque, in his last months as Premier and leader of the Parti Québécois, cautiously supported the FTA and his party remained favourable until its defeat in the December 1985 provincial election. In 1986, the two parties traded positions. In 1987, business endorsement of free trade reinforced the Liberals' support. Most importantly, the Meech Lake constitutional accord of June 1987 tied Robert Bourassa's destiny to that of his federal counterpart, Conservative Prime Minister Brian Mulroney. In the Parti Québécois, Lévesque's successor, Pierre Marc Johnson, who had expressed doubts about the FTA, resigned and was replaced by the former PQ Finance Minister, Jacques Parizeau, in March 1988. Parizeau, who became Premier of Quebec in September 1994 until his resignation in the aftermath of the October 1995 referendum defeat, pulled his party back into the pro-FTA camp as the debate over ratification came into full force in 1988.

In the November 1988 federal election, the question of free trade was put squarely before the Canadian electorate: a vote for the Conservatives was a vote for free trade. Quebec voters, who had traditionally supported the federal Liberals before their shift to the Tories in 1984, cast a majority (53 per cent) of their ballots for Brian Mulroney's party, far above the Canadian average of 43 per cent. The Conservatives swept 63 of the 75 ridings in Quebec. The Tory majority in the House of Commons ensured the passage of the FTA.

Public opinion has also been more favourable to free trade in Quebec, particularly amongst francophones, than in the rest of Canada. Figures 1 and 2 show that, while opinion on free trade in Quebec has fluctuated as it did in other regions, public approval has been consistently higher, notably since late 1987, when both Quebec provincial political parties made their support clear. Support for NAFTA has also been higher in Quebec. When the trilateral talks began, the balance of opinion about NAFTA was 58 per cent in favour to 35 per cent opposed in Quebec, compared to 46 to 50 per cent across Canada, and 36 to 60 per cent in Ontario (The Gazette, 26 Feb. 1991).

The Political Economy of Regionalism

TABLE 1

WOULD CANADA BE BETTER OFF WITH FREE TRADE? REGIONAL OPINION
DYNAMICS, 1985-1989

	Feb. '85	Nov. '86	Mar. '87	Oct. '87	Jan. '88	Jun. '88	Sep. '88	Oct. '88	Nov. '89
Quebec	72.0	46.2	55.8	60.3	78.3	69.1	68.7	65.4	68.8
Atlantic	58.7	57.8	60.0	52.4	64.3	64.0	60.7	63.0	29.9
Ontario	61.9	48.8	47.6	50.0	44.6	49.4	45.9	45.9	29.6
Prairies	63.6	58.4	58.1	59.5	60.8	59.0	60.3	55.8	40.6
BC	66.7	63.0	61.4	56.8	55.1	57.3	52.4	58.7	40.6

* Data from all available Gallup polls, as reported in the *Gallup Report*. The
percentages are based only on respondents expressing an opinion. The question was
worded as follows: 'Do you think Canada would be better off, or worse off, if US goods
were allowed in here without tariff or customs charges and Canadian goods were
allowed in the US free?'

TABLE 2

PUBLIC APPROVAL FOR THE CANADA-US FREE TRADE AGREEMENT AND
THE NORTH AMERICAN FREE TRADE AGREEMENT, 1988-1993

	Oct. '88	Nov. '88	Jan. '89	Oct. '89	Mar. '90	Jun. '90	Dec. '90	Nov. '91	Jul. '92	Apr. '93	Aug. '93	Dec. '93
Quebec	54.4	38.8	72.5	57.0	50.0	64.6	52.6	42.7	39.0	52.9	42.9	59.8
Atlantic	59.5	30.4	61.1	37.6	23.4	53.8	34.1	41.7	30.3	40.2	37.2	43.8
Ontario	34.2	29.4	51.9	38.7	36.9	31.4	29.5	30.0	28.1	33.7	25.0	43.4
Prairies	49.4	42.7	60.0	55.3	34.9	51.8	40.0	38.8	41.3	40.7	39.5	46.8
BC	40.0	29.5	59.2	48.9	43.0	44.0	33.3	45.3	24.7	37.0	32.6	49.4

* Data from all available Gallup polls as of January 1995, as reported in the *Gallup
Report* and *The Gallup Poll*. The percentages are based only on respondents expressing
an opinion. The questions were worded as follows. October 1988, November 1988,
January 1989: 'Are you in favour of the proposed Free Trade Agreement with the
United States or not?'; October 1989, March 1990, December 1990, November 1991:
'Are you in favour of the Free trade Agreement with the United States or not?'; June
1990: 'Are you in favour or opposed to the idea of setting up a free trade agreement
among Canada, the United States and Mexico?'; July 1992 to December 1993: 'Are you
in favour or opposed to a free trade agreement among Canada, the United States and
Mexico?'

Structural Conditions and Quebec's Support for Free Trade

The trade orientations of governments are conditioned by the structure of international trade and by their position within it, both of which define the opportunities and constraints facing policy-makers (Lake, 1988; Yarbrough and Yarbrough, 1992). When looking for structural sources of support for the FTA and NAFTA in Quebec, two basic facts stand out: the openness of Quebec's economy and the extent and concentration of its trade and investment links with the United States.

Quebec is highly dependent upon trade. In 1990, exports of goods outside Canada amounted to C$24 billion and imports totalled C$28 billion. With the United States, the balance was positive, with exports of C$18 billion and imports of C$13 billion. That year, exports represented 15 per cent of the province's gross domestic product (GDP), down from 21 per cent in 1980. In the same period, the share of exports to the United States increased from 60 to 75 per cent. In contrast, imports from the US amounted to only 50 per cent of total imports in 1990. In the 1980s, small and midsize firms gained in export markets, but Quebec's exports are still dominated by a few very large firms in newsprint, wood products, electronics, transport and communications equipment. Intra-firm trade accounts for 40 per cent of Quebec's exports, highlighting the role of foreign investment ties in the political economy of trade (Government of Quebec, 1991: 40-51; Langlois, 1990: 53).

In terms of trade openness (accounting for Quebec's trade with the rest of Canada), Quebec can be compared with small northern European states. As Peter Katzenstein (1985) argued, governments in small, trade-dependent countries tend to let markets determine economic adjustment while developing social policies to adjust to integration into the global economy. Small states with open economies have been steady supporters of a strongly institutionalized multilateral trade regime, but they have also supported the formation of regional trading blocs. Also, domestically, trade openness in small northern European democracies has been accompanied by institutions of concertation – an experience which has been followed, albeit to a limited extent, in Quebec (Jalbert, 1990).

Given such structural conditions, it may not be surprising to find some support for free trade in Quebec. If structural conditions were determinant in shaping support for free trade in Quebec, however, one would expect a comparable level of support in the neighbouring province of Ontario, whose southern region is even more closely linked with the industrial core of the United States (Krugman, 1991: 71). In fact, although parts of Toronto's business elite were supportive of the FTA and NAFTA, and although economists had predicted that Ontario would reap a large share of the benefits of free trade (Courchene, 1989), Ontario's governments and public opinion have remained opposed to the FTA and NAFTA.

Another structural dimension of the political economy of trade is the effect of economic conjuncture on the overall demand for protection or trade liberalization. Other things being equal, regions where declining industries are more prevalent tend to be more opposed to trade liberalization, particularly during economic downturns (Cassing, McKeown and Ochs, 1986). Also, high unemployment tends to be associated with demand for protection, while high inflation tends to be associated with demand for freer trade (Magee and Young, 1987). Again, the comparison with Ontario reveals a puzzle. First, compared to Ontario, Quebec has a much higher proportion of its work-force in declining industries, such as textiles, clothing and furniture. Second, throughout the free-trade debates, Quebec had higher unemployment than Ontario (about four percentage points more between 1986 and 1989; Noël, 1993). Still, Ontario's public opinion and governments have opposed free trade.

In sum, structural conditions do not explain Quebec's support for continental economic integration, as the comparison with Ontario clearly shows. We must therefore look at the domestic political dynamics of the free-trade debate to find explanations for Quebec's positions. At the level of society, there are three sources of pressures: class cleavages, sectoral cleavages and cultural resistance to economic integration.

The Central Tension: Labour, Business and Trade Politics

Besides the potential for overall benefits to consumers, trade expansion has two types of redistributive effects: between industries; and between factors of production, broadly defined as capital, labour and land (Rogowski, 1989). The FTA and NAFTA imply a dramatic increase in the international mobility of capital in North America, which has tended to polarize the debate along class lines. Free trade with the United States poses concrete challenges to labour and agriculture, because of their relative immobility compared to capital. For this reason, the core debates amongst class-based groups tend to take place at the level of the very principle of economic integration, while debates amongst sectorally defined interests tend to focus on the modalities of trade agreements. In Quebec as in Canada, labour and agriculture representatives have formed a vocal coalition in opposition to the FTA and NAFTA.

Evidence from the debates over the FTA and NAFTA in Quebec brings some support to class-based arguments, but also reveals their limitations. As in English Canada, the main cleavage in the free-trade debate in Quebec has been between labour unions and central employers' organizations. Opposition to free trade has been led by the Fédération des travailleurs du Québec (FTQ), the Confédération des syndicats nationaux (CSN), the Centrale de l'enseignement du Québec (CEQ) and the Union des producteurs agricoles (UPA). Other opponents have included environmentalists, artists, religious and women's groups.

On the other side, the leaders of the movement in favour of free trade have been business associations, led by the Conseil du Patronat du Québec (CPQ) and the Chambre de Commerce du Québec (CCQ). The chief executives of the largest francophone-controlled financial and manufacturing corporations, collectively known as 'Québec Inc.', were actively involved on behalf of the FTA and have generally been supportive of NAFTA as well. Of course, business does not speak with a single voice, as employers in import-sensitive sectors have also voiced their opposition (this dimension is addressed below).

The opposition between labour and business groups over free trade reveals three basic features of Quebec trade politics: the asymmetry of political resources between the two categories of groups; the absence of a political party to convey labour's opposition to continentalism; and the lack of co-ordination between Quebec opposition groups and their Canadian counterparts.

Business groups throughout Canada mobilized enormous resources to help the Conservative government sell the FTA to the public (Doern and Tomlin, 1991). For these groups, the government's decision to initiate free trade talks was in itself a victory, but they also needed to convince an electorate that had serious doubts. To overcome these doubts, they had a big advantage over opponents: money. When the real 'crunch' came, in the 1988 election campaign, pro-FTA groups spent millions of dollars in a frenetic advertising campaign for free trade, eschewing legal limits upon campaign spending (Fraser, 1989: 325-7). Quebec business also mobilized for the FTA. Only two weeks before election day, prominent francophone executives, including the presidents of Bombardier, Canam-Manac and Power Corporation, instantly raised C$300,000 for a pro-FTA advertising blitz (Walle, 1988). Facing this armada of business support, opponents were not without resources, as evidenced by the numerous protest marches held throughout the country. But it seems unclear whether activity by union leaders made much difference in mobilizing their own members.

A second characteristic of the free-trade debate in Quebec was the absence of a political party carrying the message of opponents. Since 1988, both the PQ and the Quebec Liberal Party have endorsed free trade. Elsewhere in Canada, anti-free-trade groups are typically linked with the New Democratic Party (NDP), but this party has never been effective in Quebec. The federal Liberals were partly neutralized in Quebec by the pro-free-trade position of the provincial Liberals, but they were successful in mobilizing opposition to free trade from their most solid constituencies in Quebec: anglophones and members of ethnic minorities. In both provincial parties, free-trade opponents were able to ensure that leaders demand accommodations for Quebec's troubled industries. They have not been able, however, to steer party leaders toward an opposition of principle comparable to that of the provincial Liberals and the NDP in Ontario.

The third striking feature of the free trade debate of 1988 was the lack of co-ordination between opponents in Quebec and in English Canada. Throughout the 1988 campaign, the strong Canadian nationalist accents of the opponents to the FTA chilled their communications with Quebec's sovereignist union leaders (La Presse, 13 Oct., 1988).

Seeking Accommodation: Sectoral Demands and Free Trade Politics

The sectoral dimension of the political economy of trade is often more important than class distinctions in shaping policy (Magee, Brock and Young, 1989: Ch.7; Wallerstein, 1987). At the industry level, determinants of the level and impact of demands for protection tend to relate to the nature and extent of an industry's involvement in international trade and investment and to the industry's capacity for political action. Export-dependent or import-vulnerable firms have clear trade interests but foreign investment ties are also a determinant of trade policy preferences (Milner, 1988). Studies of the political economy of trade often point to multinational corporations (MNCs) – locally owned or foreign subsidiaries – as the most active and efficient proponents of trade liberalization (Pugel and Walter, 1985; Milner, 1988).

Because of the massive presence of US investment in the Quebec economy and because most of Quebec's foreign exports are directed toward the United States, one would expect a core of business support for free trade among US-owned subsidiaries and domestically owned exporters to the US market. The large size of these industries is also a major asset in the contest for political influence. By contrast, import-vulnerable industries, such as textiles and clothing, are expected to oppose free trade. Inasmuch as they can use their labour force to exert political leverage, however, firms in such import-sensitive industries generally tend to hedge their bets by seeking special treatment within negotiated agreements or through administered protection (Aggarwal, Keohane and Yoffie, 1987).

In Quebec, the FTA and NAFTA debates have mostly taken place at the level of principles: whether or not to support the federal initiative. Generally, once the principle of free trade is agreed upon, the public is not overly concerned about the details of trade agreements. Industrialists, however, do read the fine print. Thus, the bulk of their political activity is directed at maximizing their share of the gains, or cutting their losses. This is why trade battles are mostly fought along sectoral lines. Can support for free trade in Quebec be explained by a particular convergence of sectoral demands?

In Quebec, peak business associations all supported the principle of a free trade agreement. At the sectoral level, industry reactions to the FTA and NAFTA followed the pattern of reactions across Canada, where export orientation and import vulnerability determined industry positions, along with foreign investment ties (Litvak, 1986). Three types of industry reactions prevailed in Quebec. A limited number of industries enthusiastically supported the projected FTA, including aluminium, led by the multinational Alcan which, in 1986, just before the free-trade talks, exported 64 per cent of its Quebec production to the United States (Alcan, 1987). Important supporters also included: Domtar (pulp and paper); Bombardier (transportation equipment); SNC and Lavalin (now merged, engineering services); Canam-Manac (metal products); and the Mouvement Desjardins (Quebec's provincially-regulated financial giant, built around grassroots credit unions). Other export-oriented industries with strong investment ties to the United States were favourable, including newsprint, electronics, business machines and telecommunications equipment (Litvak, 1986).

Strong opposition to the projected FTA came mostly from small-scale industries geared toward local markets or from Canadian-owned industries already subject to strong import pressures. Among these industries, textile manufacturers, brewers and consumer and household-product makers were typical. The opposition of cultural industries was also highly visible and they were successful in gaining special status in the negotiations.

A third type of reaction was one of cautious support from industries that primarily sought accommodations built into the modalities of the projected FTA. These included softwood lumber and, surprisingly, the furniture and clothing industries, which were facing heavy import competition but chose to seek accommodations within the FTA in the hope of restructuring their production (Cogesult, Inc.; Apparel Manufacturers Institute of Quebec, 1987).

With respect to NAFTA, Quebec industries anticipated only marginal effects and their representative associations were much less politically active than in the case of the FTA. Strong supporters of the FTA continued to advocate further liberalization, but many industries were concerned that NAFTA allowed the United States to renegotiate FTA clauses favourable to Canada. Industries that were initially reluctant toward NAFTA included plastic products, footwear, textiles, furniture and clothing (Québec, Ministère de Industrie, du Commerce et de la Technologie, 1990). The recession of the early 1990s eroded some industry support for the original FTA and made support for NAFTA more difficult to obtain.

Cultural Vulnerability and Resistance to Economic Integration

In addition to class and sectoral cleavages, the symbolic and cultural implications of a continental trade agreement are also an important societal factor. In English Canada, free trade with the United States has been perceived as a threat to national identity because of the increased penetration of American culture that it would bring about. For French-speaking Quebeckers, the language barrier and a more secure sense of cultural distinctiveness could be argued to counter the fear of cultural assimilation. There are two problems with this explanation of free-trade support in Quebec.

First, in the general public, it does not seem that Quebeckers are more or less anti-American than other Canadians. A second problem with the cultural explanation relates to the political activities of cultural elites. In English Canada, artists, publishers and broadcasters fought against free trade in the name of the survival of Canadian culture. In Quebec, cultural elites also saw free trade as a threat to Quebec's culture. The Mouvement Québec Français (MQF), a French-language defence group opposed the FTA in the name of the preservation of French (Association du disque et de l'industrie du spectacle et vidéo québécois, 1987; Mouvement Québec Français, 1987). Although cultural elites in English Canada and Quebec claim to defend cultural identity, they mostly represent the interests of the cultural industries, which managed to obtain exemptions in the FTA and NAFTA. As for the MQF, its links with unions made it a natural foe of free trade. In sum, although the relative cultural security of French Quebeckers might have contributed to their support for free trade, the evidence to this effect is inconclusive.

Institutions and Ideas: The Enduring Impact of the Quiet Revolution

A central theme in recent political science literature is the impact of state institutions and ideas on policy making (Goldstein, 1988; March and Olsen, 1989). Can the convergence of the two main Quebec provincial parties on support to the FTA and NAFTA be explained by reference to institutional factors? This bipartisan support may stem in part from the common roots of the two parties in the 'Quiet Revolution' of the 1960s, a period of rapid social and economic change in Quebec.

Although the Parti Québécois was formed after a schism in the Quebec Liberal Party over the national question, the PQ did not turn its back on the reforms instigated by the Liberals. Quebec institutions were radically transformed in the 1960s through what has come to be known as the Quiet Revolution, following a period of slow political progress during the reign of Maurice Duplessis'

Union Nationale (1936-39 and 1944-60). Before 1960, Quebec nationalism was mostly defensive and French-speaking Quebeckers controlled a very small portion of their own economy. The Quebec Liberal Party, in power from 1960 to 1966, gave itself the task of bringing Quebec up to par with other western industrial societies. The main catalyst of this rapid transformation was the provincial government. As the Quebec government took on an activist social and economic role, the emerging Quebec nationalism became linked to social progress and political modernization (McRoberts, 1988; Gagnon and Montcalm, 1990). After the disappearance of the conservative Union Nationale (in power from 1966 to 1970), Quebec's party system was primarily defined by two nationalist visions: the autonomist vision of the Liberals and the PQ's vision of Quebec sovereignty, associated with an economic association with Canada.

In addition to its impact on the party system, the Quiet Revolution redefined dominant norms and ideas about the role of the state in the economy and society. The new ideology, first implemented by the Liberals in the 1960s and early 1970s, combined nationalism and interventionism, but not *dirigisme*. A consensus emerged on the role of public enterprises and other forms of government intervention to allow francophones to gain control over the Quebec economy, after two centuries of anglophone domination. The dynamic role of the Quebec state and of the provincially-regulated financial sector encouraged francophones to become involved in business and, after 1970, francophone control of private enterprises grew rapidly (Vaillancourt and Carpentier, 1989). The Liberal Party was closer to these new entrepreneurs than the Parti Québécois in the 1970s, but the attitudes of the two parties toward the private sector tended to converge after 1980, partly because of their common origins.

In the mid-1980s, when free trade with the United States was proposed, the two parties at first wavered but then positioned themselves squarely in support of continental economic integration. This consensus was in part a reflection of the converging views of the two parties on the economic institutions inherited from the Quiet Revolution. Beyond institutions, however, a powerful idea played a role in defining both party competition and demand for free trade: nationalism.

NATIONALISM AND THE POLITICS OF FREE TRADE IN QUEBEC

The analysis of the political economy of free trade in the preceding section shows that conventional models of trade politics cannot fully explain support for free trade in Quebec. Two factors, however, were identified as key elements of this explanation: party competition and nationalism. Here, I analyse trade politics in Quebec by integrating within a coherent framework the three levels of analysis of international political economy.

The emphasis on party competition provides the core mechanism to explain the linkage between nationalism and free-trade orientation. The argument rests upon three propositions. First, trade policy is generally tied to other issues and thus, trade orientation often depends on coalitions forming around these core issues of partisan competition. Second, the nature of their nationalist demands, autonomy or sovereignty, is the fundamental difference between the two major political parties in Quebec and the incidence of trade policy on these options is therefore likely to influence coalition formation. Third, and most importantly, free trade can be a sensible strategy to further the cause of both autonomists and sovereignists. Thus, the politics of nationalism explains the bipartisan consensus behind free trade in Quebec.

Trade Policy and Coalition Politics

Given the wealth of models on the economics and political economy of trade, it is often tempting to isolate this issue when seeking to explain changes in trade orientation. Trade, however, is seldom the foremost issue on people's minds. Indeed, the dynamic of trade politics depends largely upon the coalitions that form around the core issues of partisan competition. Although one cannot deny the material interests involved in trade policy decisions, these decisions most often come in tandem with more politically sensitive issues. Examples from the political economy of trade in North America can illustrate this point.

In the United States, trade has often been politically important, but most often somehow subordinated to a more salient issue. In the nineteenth century, the regional and sectoral redistributive implications of the tariff linked it to the struggle between the industrial north and the rural south. In the 1930s, the policy of reciprocity was subordinated to the New Deal agenda and to foreign policy (Ferguson, 1984; Haggard, 1988). After the Second World War, multilateralism was a pillar of national-security policy (Nelson, 1989). In the 1980s, trade was often a pawn in partisan struggles over the Reagan economic agenda (Destler, 1992). In Mexico, the recent move away from protectionism cannot be isolated from the process of political and economic liberalization that is rocking the foundations of Mexico's one-party system (Vega-Canovas, 1994).

In Canada, there has been a long-standing, but mostly rhetorical (McDowall, 1994) opposition between Liberals and Conservatives on free trade. In 1988, free trade was at centre stage in a federal election, but for Quebeckers and many others, it was tied to the Meech Lake Accord, which was meant to bring Quebec back into the Canadian constitutional fold. In short, free trade shared the Quebec stage with the perennial issue of Quebec provincial politics: nationalism.

The Parti Québécois and the Liberal Party as Nationalist Coalitions

Although it has been pronounced dead on several occasions, nationalism, like the phoenix, keeps coming back as the central issue of Quebec politics. This ability of nationalism to rise periodically from its ashes says something about the durability of the phenomenon (Latouche, 1993: 43). Quebec nationalism is not limited to support for sovereignty. In a way, the distinct situation of Quebec in North America makes almost every francophone Quebecker, to some degree, a 'nationalist'. In a 1991 poll, a mere six per cent of French Quebeckers claimed a greater 'feeling of attachment' to Canada than they did to Quebec, while 68 per cent were more attached to Quebec (Canadian Facts, 4–15 April 1991). This feeling, however, is not unambiguous, as revealed by Quebec's support for the antinationalist Pierre Elliott Trudeau, from 1968 to 1980. Despite this ambiguity, one basic fact remains: no provincial party can ever hope to win an election in Quebec by demanding less power for the Quebec government.

Several scholars have noted a tendency toward convergence between the two main political parties in Quebec, although they remain somewhat differentiated (Tanguay, 1993). This, as discussed above, should not come as a surprise, since the two parties emerged from the same reformist experiences of the 1960s. Indeed, the preponderance of the national question has, over time, transformed the two parties into coalitions of strange economic bedfellows (Martin, 1994).

The Parti Québécois' central objective is to make Quebec a sovereign state, while the Quebec Liberals have sought more autonomy for Quebec within Canada. The two parties nevertheless share a common origin in the Quiet Revolution. René Lévesque, who led the PQ until 1985, was a Liberal cabinet minister between 1960 and 1966. Disenchanted by the prospects for social and economic reforms in Quebec under federalism, Lévesque tried to steer the Liberals toward his idea of 'sovereignty-association'. His failure forced him out of the Liberal Party in 1967 and he founded the PQ the next year, attracting many Liberals who had taken part in the construction of the new Quebec state. One fellow Liberal whom Lévesque failed to attract was Robert Bourassa, who later became Liberal Party leader and Premier of Quebec from 1970 to 1976. He returned at the helm of his party in 1983 and was premier again from 1985 to 1994.

The Parti Québécois was founded as a social-democratic party. When it first came to power in 1976, it had the support of public-sector workers, trade unions and the left (Blais and Nadeau, 1984). In government, however, the PQ's actions were more pragmatic than its programme. Partly because of apprehension generated by its sovereignist option in the business community (in Quebec and abroad), the PQ sought to shed its 'radical' image by adopting a conciliatory attitude toward business (McRoberts, 1988). Alain Gagnon and Mary Beth Montcalm sum up the transformation of the PQ: the defeat in the 1980 referendum 'shifted the focus from political nationalism to economic nationalism: failure to achieve political independence, in other words, stimulated efforts by the PQ to achieve economic independence' (Gagnon and Montcalm, 1990: 65). For Thomas Courchene, the PQ then became 'the most business-oriented or market-oriented government in Canada' (Courchene, 1986: 7). In the 1980s, a bipartisan consensus formed around market-led development strategies within a context defined by the economic institutions inherited from the Quiet Revolution.

The slump in support for sovereignty after the 1980 referendum caused profound dissensions in the Parti Québécois. The PQ lost the

December 1985 election after René Lévesque and his successor as leader, Pierre Marc Johnson, shelved the sovereignty option. In 1986 and 1987, the two parties wavered on free trade. In the PQ, some of the strongest proponents of free trade, including Bernard Landry, the minister responsible for international trade, were defeated in 1985 and the party's position was redefined by critics of the FTA from the party's left, who feared job losses in soft sectors. The PQ's lack of direction on sovereignty led to Johnson's resignation and to the election as leader of Jacques Parizeau, who had taken clear positions in favour of Quebec sovereignty and in favour of free trade.

In the Parti Québécois and in the sovereignist movement, free trade finds a receptive audience in parts of business and in public opinion. Although support for sovereignty is the exception among business elites, there have been significant expressions of support for sovereignty since the rejection of the Meech Lake Accord in 1990. For example, the Mouvement Desjardins has been associated with sovereignty and its president, Claude Béland, is one of the few top business executives to have taken a public stand for sovereignty[2]. Another prominent sovereignist is Jean Campeau, former president of the state-owned Caisse de dépôt et de placement, former Chief Executive Officer (CEO) of Domtar, and co-president of the 1990–91 Commission on the Constitutional Future of Quebec. In May 1992, he founded an association of sovereignist executives, the Regroupement Souveraineté-Québec Inc., to counter the federalist Regroupement Économie et Constitution. In contrast with the latter group, sovereignist business elites tend to be recruited from small- and medium-sized enterprises (Lessard, 1992).

Frustration with federal economic policies also led many small and midsize firms, through the Quebec Chamber of Commerce, to say they would back sovereignty if the process of constitutional reform did not lead to significant devolution of powers to Quebec. A poll of the Chamber's members published before the death of Meech Lake gave more than 60 per cent of support for sovereignty in that group if the accord was rejected (Chambre de Commerce du Québec, 1990: 2). This result shows that business aversion to sovereignty has receded since the 1980 referendum.

Support for free trade in the PQ and among sovereignists has not been unanimous. Many of the PQ's activists are social democrats and some of the most persistent supporters of sovereignty are found among labour unions, agricultural producers and other free-trade foes. The federal New Democratic Party (NDP) has always been marginal in Quebec, but the NDP's anti-free trade arguments are shared by the Quebec nationalist left. Also, despite the relative harmony between the PQ and organized labour on sovereignty, their relationship soured after the 1980 referendum, when the recession-strained PQ government rolled back salaries in the highly unionized public sector.

The Quebec Liberals, mainly because of their federalist option, tend to attract support from most business leaders. This is particularly true of top executives from some of the largest firms in Quebec, who formed the Regroupement Économie et Constitution in 1991 to stem the tide of public support for sovereignty. Members of this select group have also been at the forefront of support for free trade: Laurent Beaudoin, CEO of Bombardier, Raymond Cyr of Bell Canada Enterprises and Guy Saint-Pierre, president of SNC-Lavalin (Lejeune, 1991). Interestingly, these flagship firms of 'Québec Inc.' were beneficiaries of provincial government policies, notably the Quebec Stock Savings Plan instituted by the PQ when Jacques Parizeau was Minister of Finance. They might prefer the Liberals, but they can certainly do business with the Parti Québécois.

Despite their strong business support, the Liberals and, by extension, the federalist camp have two weak spots on free trade. First, Quebec Liberals have to take into account links with the Liberal Party of Canada. Although the two organizations formally split in 1964, they still share an important part of the Quebec electorate, notably among anglophones in and around Montréal, whose first allegiance is to the federal party, but also among francophone voters across the province. This mattered in the free-trade debate, when tensions between provincial and federal Liberals in Quebec surfaced in the midst of a federal election. Second, there are important electoral ties between the Liberals (at both the federal and provincial levels) and ethnic-minority workers in low-wage import-sensitive industries such as textiles and clothing.

In sum, the PQ and the Quebec Liberals, and the two 'faces' of Quebec nationalism which they represent, are internally divided on free trade. Divergences within parties rather than a rift between them are the main sources of friction in Quebec trade politics. If each party claims to offer the best recipe for the growth of export industries, their programmes and policies also keep a watchful eye on 'soft' industries. In practice, the two parties realize that there are bound to be winners and losers as Quebec becomes further integrated into the continental and global economies. Still, the two parties have remained committed to their endorsement of the FTA and NAFTA since 1988 and both have defended free trade on the basis of appeals to their own vision of nationalism.

Party Competition and Free-Trade Nationalism

Analysts of Quebec politics have discussed the linkage between free-trade orientation and nationalism, but few have developed an explicit theoretical model to explain it. François Rocher calls the support for free trade by Quebec nationalists a 'paradox'. He observes that the FTA should have a centralizing effect on Canadian federalism because it can potentially limit economic interventions by provincial governments (Rocher, 1993). Rocher has an instrumentalist explanation for free-trade nationalism: Quebec's francophone business class seeks to distance itself from the federal state because it can better control the Quebec state (Cox, 1990). This explanation is useful but somewhat incomplete, for it neglects the autonomous actions of political parties, as well as public opinion.

To elaborate an adequate model of free-trade nationalism, we must combine the three levels of analysis of foreign economic policies. First, the model relies on a representation of why individuals or economic agents might opt for sovereignty, or more autonomy, instead of the *status quo*. Although there are core supporters of the two extreme positions, autonomists might be inclined to move in either direction. The choice of Quebec nationalists between autonomy and sovereignty is influenced by what Hudson Meadwell calls 'enabling conditions' (the affective dimensions of individual choice and of a collective sense of identity) and 'constraining conditions' (the evaluation of the economic costs of sovereignty) (Meadwell, 1993b). The increasing irrelevance of socio-economic groups and the preponderance of these two dimensions – primary national identity and prospective evaluation of economic costs - as predictors of sovereignist attitude has been confirmed by empirical studies of opinion on sovereignty (Blais and Nadeau, 1992; Martin, 1994).

Nationalist identity formation varies with generation replacement (Nadeau, 1992) and with the state of the Canadian constitutional debate (Meadwell, 1993a). Prospective evaluation of the economic impact of sovereignty, however, is likely to be influenced by international-level factors such as the institutional context of international economic relations. Therefore, inasmuch as nationalist leaders can influence the consolidation of the supranational institutional context of trade, thus reducing dependence upon the Canadian market, it makes sense for them to be free traders. The logic behind the latter affirmation is similar to that which has led small, trade-dependent northern European countries to support the liberalization and institutionalization of trade.

Second, because parties compete primarily for the allegiance of voters whose nationalist preference may fluctuate between autonomy and sovereignty, they are most likely to advocate policies that can enhance their own nationalist goal. Support for continental free trade agreements can be used to enhance either of these goals. Indeed, the free-trade debate was affected by both the autonomist agenda of the Liberal Party and the sovereignist agenda of the Parti Québécois. But why would autonomists and sovereignists support continental free trade? Historically, English-Canadian nationalism has been associated with resistance to the forces of north-south economic integration. That Quebec nationalism defines itself in opposition to this historical tendency is thus not completely surprising. The logic of autonomists and sovereignists are similar in this respect, as free trade with the United States means a relative loosening of the political constraints associated with economic ties to the rest of Canada.

Free Trade and Demands for Quebec Autonomy

For autonomists, the part of the electorate most actively courted by the Liberals, the market consequences of trade integration are more important in consolidating their position against both the sovereignists and the proponents of centralized federalism. As mentioned above, the strengthening of Quebec's economic institutions and the development of an efficient local financial sector have loosened Quebec's dependence on Canadian economic ties. This greater economic independence enhances autonomy, since francophone-controlled businesses operate in a distinct provincial regulatory space. Although this dynamic can be seen as improving the prospects for a viable independent Quebec, it made sense for the

Liberal government after 1985 to continue the autonomist policies of the PQ. Indeed, as Thomas Courchene has noted, the Quebec Liberals could easily 'adhere to the position that a strong private sector controlled by Québécois can be a bulwark against independence'. From the autonomist's point of view, he concludes, 'Quebec is not so much "opting out" of the Canadian federation as it is "opting in" to the world economy' (Courchene, 1986: 11–12).

The politics of autonomy had a clear impact on Quebec's endorsement of the FTA in 1988. After the referendum defeat of 1980 and the exclusion of Quebec from the constitutional reform of 1982, both the PQ and the Quebec Liberals gave Brian Mulroney's Conservative government a chance to accommodate Quebec's autonomist demands. The Meech Lake Accord was central to the 1988 federal election campaign in Quebec. Indeed, many have argued that the highly 'English-Canadian nationalist' tone of the opposition to free trade outside Quebec led many Quebeckers to give a chance to Mulroney, Meech Lake and the FTA.

For nationalist Quebeckers, the arguments of the Ontario-centred Canadian-nationalist opposition to free trade sounded (as it did also, perhaps, for Westerners) like another power grab by Ontario. Lucien Bouchard, who was then one of the most popular Conservative ministers in Quebec, argued in speeches that 'opposition to free trade was basically a plot by the Ontario establishment to retain its wealth and privileges at the expense of the rest of the country, particularly Quebec' (Fraser, 1989: 367-8). This strategy of linking resistance to free trade with historical grievances toward Ontario seemed to strike a chord amongst Quebec nationalists, whether they be sovereignists or autonomists. From the point of view of Quebec nationalism, thus, the Meech Lake Accord and free trade were a package deal. The combination of the two gave Robert Bourassa and his Quebec business supporters exactly what they wanted by turning the PQ formula of sovereignty-association 'upside down'. Brian Mulroney 'never made the connection overtly', writes Graham Fraser 'but with the Free Trade Agreement, he was offering Quebec the ideal of economic independence; with Meech Lake, he was offering a political association with the rest of Canada' (ibid.: 354).

In sum, autonomists could justify their support for free trade by basing their electoral strategy on the ambiguity of Quebec nationalism. Free trade can give Quebec more economic autonomy while preserving the political security of federalism. If Quebec could reap the economic rewards of continental integration without incurring the political risks of secession, the Liberal reasoning went, why take the leap from decentralized federalism to sovereignty? With the continuation of the constitutional debate overlapping the NAFTA negotiations, the Liberals have continued to argue that in an environment where Quebec is becoming increasingly autonomous in the economic sphere, political independence is an outdated concept (The Gazette, 2 Feb. 1993). Sovereignists, however, see things differently.

Implications of Continental Trade Agreements for Quebec Sovereignty

In 1990, one major event tipped the balance toward sovereignty in Quebec public opinion as the free trade debate was about to start again over NAFTA: the failure of the Meech Lake constitutional accord. After the failure of Meech Lake, the feeling of rejection felt by Quebeckers pushed support for sovereignty to its highest levels ever, as it peaked around 65 per cent in some opinion polls (Cloutier et al., 1992). Again, the free trade issue was in the midst of the political debate over Quebec's national future.

For sovereignists, free trade can reduce Quebec's dependence upon the rest of Canada, thus reducing the economic risks of sovereignty. The key element from this perspective, however, is not that unfettered markets would provide a more secure environment for firms in a small sovereign state. For firms, the risk involved in taking the leap toward sovereignty is not so much economic as it is political. Indeed, firms in small states face the political uncertainty of predatory trade policies by larger states, which can only be contained by international institutions. Thus, what sovereignists seek in continental or global free trade agreements is the combination of open markets, which favour the natural north-south flow of economic transactions, and strengthened international institutions, which reduce the risks of open trade for a smaller political unit. This strategy can be called 'trading for independence' (Meadwell, 1993a; 1993b). Thus, in the debate between autonomists and sovereignists, it makes sense for sovereignists to emphasize that continental (and global) economic integration, in a tight institutional setting, can enhance the viability of Quebec after sovereignty (Meadwell and Martin, 1996).

Given the preoccupation of the sovereignists for the institutional structure of the trading environment of an independent Quebec, it is understandable that the FTA and NAFTA have become central parts of the debate over sovereignty. In debates between sovereignists and federalists, one question is omnipresent: 'Would an independent Quebec remain a part of the FTA or NAFTA?' In this rhetorical game, federalists (partisans of autonomy or the status quo) tend to emphasize the risk of losing the advantages conferred by present trade agreements. Sovereignists, for their part, seek to reassure the public that when the chips are down, everyone will be reasonable. US government officials, in the meantime, refuse to engage in hypothetical conjectures.

Interpretations differ on the issue of whether an independent Quebec could become party to Canada's commercial treaties, such as the FTA, NAFTA or the GATT, and it is beyond the scope of this chapter to make a definite judgement (Ritchie *et al.*, 1991; Québec, Assemblée nationale, 1992). A balanced analysis is provided by Ivan Bernier, who argues that a sovereign Quebec's insertion in the legal framework of international trade would 'cause some problems, but none that would be really insurmountable' (Bernier, 1992)[3]. Bernier adds that multilateral accords, such as the GATT, pose even less problems than bilateral or trilateral trade agreements, because their rules – including those for admitting new members – are defined more generally. However, from the point of view of 'free-trade nationalists', one thing is clear: the presence of credible international institutions to manage trade relations is a distinct advantage and to support their formation can be a politically sensible strategy.

CONCLUSION

This chapter leads to a few specific conclusions on the linkages between nationalism and free trade in Quebec. It has shown, first, that conventional international political economy models of trade-policy-making fail to explain adequately this level of support. This probe into the political economy of free trade in Quebec identifies the case as an anomaly that requires an explanation combining effectively the international forces and domestic mechanisms of trade-policy-making.

Second, I have presented a general proposition underlying the domestic mechanisms behind trade policy orientation. In short, the conditions bearing directly upon the issue of trade are often insufficient to explain trade policy decisions, especially when more salient issues dominate the political agenda. If trade has an incidence on a more politically salient issue (in this case, nationalism), trade policy orientation can be more readily explained as a function of the dynamic of coalition formation on the more salient issue. In Quebec, support for free trade was the product of the quest for power by political parties operating in a political space where parties compete over two nationalist visions. For each party, endorsement of free trade can be understood as part of a partisan strategy to attract nationalist support.

The third task of the chapter was therefore to indicate how such a strategy can make political sense. In line with a theoretical model of nationalist mobilization, I have argued that the pursuit of free trade by nationalists, to enhance the institutionalization of trade relations, can be a rational political strategy. In the Quebec case, continental free trade can be shown to make the environment more favourable to the nationalist objectives of the two dominant provincial political parties: autonomy or sovereignty. For each party, although for different reasons, endorsement of free trade was thus a politically rational strategy to attract support from their respective constituencies and to court nationalists uncommitted to either of the two options. Under these conditions, nationalism can be conducive to the mobilization of domestic support in favour of international economic liberalization.

This argument leads to specific hypotheses that should apply to some of the most important nationalist movements in the developed world. For example, in the last 20 years, nationalists in Scotland have reversed their position regarding integration in the European Union. With the further institutionalization of trade relations in Europe, Scots have increasingly seen the EU as a counterweight to the central state and as a way of reducing their dependence upon the British market. Since the late 1980s, and particularly since the Single European Act of 1987, however, Scottish nationalists have made 'Independence in Europe' their official policy and even their slogan, and public opinion data show that support for an independent Scotland increases markedly when it is specified that Scotland would be a member of the European Union (Levy, 1990; Macartney, 1990; McCrone, 1990; Keating, 1993a).

The same logic is also at work elsewhere in Western Europe, where regionalist movements have seen the process of European integration as a means of gaining more autonomy from their respective central states (Keating, 1992b). In Spain, surveys analysed in the late 1980s have shown that support for regionalist parties was closely related, at the individual level, with support for further integration within the European Union (Lancaster and Lewis-Beck, 1989). Catalan nationalists have also been key supporters of European economic integration. As has been the case in Quebec, this strategy of 'free-trade nationalism' in Catalonia has been espoused both by partisans of regional autonomy and by partisans of independence (Clavera, 1990).

Finally, although nationalist movements in Eastern Europe have been spurred primarily by the changes in the security environment, linked with the end of the Cold War, the prospect of integration within institutionalized networks of economic relations was used to mobilize support for independence in parts of the former Czechoslovakia and in republics of the former Soviet Union.

At a different level, the notion of free-trade nationalism provides an example of how, in an increasingly open world economy, nationalism can express itself through openness rather than isolationism. Free-trade nationalism suggests that it may not be necessary to choose between 'zero-sum nationalism and impassive cosmopolitanism'. The Quebec experience suggests that nationalists need not be protectionists. Indeed, the linkage between nationalism and free trade in this case may be a variant of what Robert Reich (1991) calls a 'positive economic nationalism', whereby integration in a global economy can be compatible with the maintenance of a distinctive sense of national identity and community. Thus, inasmuch as international institutions provide cover against some of the political uncertainties of economic interdependence, 'free-trade nationalism' may be a means of reconciling the nationalist goal of seizing control over one's own destiny with the goal of managing a successful insertion in the global economy. The two goals need not be incompatible. With increasing economic globalization, all countries, large and small, will have to find ways to reconcile them.

NOTES

1. An earlier version of this chapter was presented at the Biennial meeting of the Russian Association of Canadian Studies, in Moscow, July 7-10, 1993 and subsequently published in *Regional and Federal Studies: an*

International Journal, Vol. 5, no. 1. I am grateful to André Blais, Michael Keating, Antonia Maioni, Laurence McFalls, Hudson Meadwell, Alain Noël, Panayotis Soldatos and the anonymous reviewers of this journal for comments and suggestions. Thanks are also due to Benoît Leduc and Catherine Rioux for their research assistance. Part of the research for this chapter was funded by grants from the Fonds FCAR (Québec), the Social Science and Humanities Research Council of Canada, and the Université de Montréal.

2. An October 1990 survey of 20,000 managers and volunteers in Desjardins' network of credit unions found a two-thirds level of support for independence (Mouvement des Caisses Desjardins, 1990: 7).

3. The issue of whether Canada would agree to enter into an economic association with a sovereign Quebec is also, of course, a contentious one. The tone of the pre-referendum debate in Quebec has tended to leave a bleak picture of prospects for such an association, but support for association is far from non-existent in Canada outside Quebec (Martin, 1995).

12

Regional Economic Development and Political Mechanisms: Western Pennsylvania in Comparative Perspective

B. GUY PETERS

In the United States, the socio-economic changes that have occurred in the region of Western Pennsylvania, and especially within the city of Pittsburgh, are often considered one of the minor miracles of recent years. The region has undergone massive economic change, from being the centre of steel-making and other primary metals industries in the United States to having only a single full-size steel mill in operation.[1] Despite the massive loss of manufacturing jobs, Pittsburgh has an unemployment rate below the national average, with the majority of jobs now being in service industries such as education, health care and banking.

Likewise, when the architect Frank Lloyd Wright was asked what might be done to improve the appearance of 'Hell with the roof off', he replied that dynamite was perhaps the best option. Some 50 years later, Pittsburgh could be voted the 'most liveable city' in the United States, with more green space per capita than any other American city and cleaner air than most.[2] The deceptively simple question to be posed here then is: What happened to produce this massive urban change? The answers are not simple, however, and understanding the very complex interactions of a number of public and private actors is required.

Even more fundamentally, we might want to inquire whether all the political and economic changes that have occurred were really as positive as they first appear, especially when we consider their differential effects on the variety of possible target groups in the region. Those target groups should be differentiated by socio-economic as well as geographical categories, but these differences are important for understanding the continuing politics of socio-economic change for the region.

Any attempt to answer these simple questions will require the examination of a number of factors related to the economic, social and political systems of the area. It also can best be answered by looking at this one case in comparison with other declining, or actually declined, industrial areas around the world. Some of these areas could be argued to have prospered even more than Pittsburgh, while most do not appear to have done as well. What can explain the differences? Another interesting point of comparison will be with the rest of the Western Pennsylvania region that has not done as well as Pittsburgh itself and in which the scars of the steel-making days now remain and, indeed, have become much deeper socially, economically and environmentally.[3] Further, there are some important temporal differences, with the possibility that successes during the initial stages of the revitalization process may have sown the seeds for failures during the subsequent stages.

The success of the several 'renaissances' that have occurred in Pittsburgh itself have been driven largely through a top-down process and have been dependent upon the city government working effectively with the private sector. These successes also have been heavily dependent upon the benevolent role of state government to support the redevelopment efforts, financially and legally.[4] The challenges facing this region are now largely within the public sector itself rather than in the private sector, or are lodged in the interface between the public and private sectors. The challenge now is to create a regional taxing and expenditure system and, with it, some form of regional government. There is a county government (Allegheny County) but its powers (and political will) appear insufficient to either force significant revenue-sharing across local government boundaries or foster mechanisms for joint service provision.

Pittsburgh, like most other American cities, is surrounded by suburbs whose residents utilize many city services but pay little or nothing to support those services. Unlike most other countries included in our comparative study of regional government, there is little political support for regional co-operation in taxing, spending or economic redevelopment. Further, by concentrating attention almost entirely on its own problems during the 1950s, 1960s and 1970s, the city lost the opportunity to make an alliance with the surrounding area. Although perhaps somewhat diversionary at that time, co-operation, in the long run, had the potential to produce more positive economic and social changes for all parties involved.

The suburbs that surround the city now face their own set of governance problems. Many of the local governments are now too small and/or too poor to pay for their own principal local services such as police, fire and sanitation. Yet they lack the legal and political frameworks that would permit and encourage co-operation across local government boundaries on either taxes or services. They also have strong senses of local identity and pride that make co-operation difficult.[5]

It appears now that the problems facing this one region are as much governmental as they are ones of economic development, although the economic development issues will never go away entirely. For example, much of the Pittsburgh economy is now built on health care and the continuing reorganization of health care in the United States, with or without the Clinton plans for reforms, pose some potential threats to that economic sector once considered absolutely certain to continue to grow. Further, many of these suburbs are not the affluent dormitory communities typical of more recent suburbanization, but rather are former industrial towns now burdened with ageing and/or declining populations and a tax and employment base that has vanished.

The focus of this chapter will be on Western Pennsylvania but there will be several comparisons with other 'declining industrial regions'.[6]

We will be arguing that the political and social constructions (Rochefort and Cobb, 1994) that were placed on the problems of the region have been crucial for understanding what has happened to the region. While the problem certainly had a number of 'objective' socio-economic features, those features had to be interpreted through the political process. Given the governmental fragmentation of the region and the variability of the socio-economic fabric even of individual units within the region, the political process was able to produce some remarkable results. Ultimately, however, the process may have produced less positive changes for a large portion of the affected population. The changes have helped to solidify the hold of certain groups on the city and its politics, while seeming to exclude effectively other contending groups.

THE PITTSBURGH STORY

It is in many ways misleading or presumptuous to argue that there is a single story that could be written to describe the multiple changes that have occurred within this city. The stories actually differ very markedly by occupation, socio-economic class, race and a number of other characteristics of the individuals involved. A city that is now a comfortable home for middle-class professionals has for many former steel workers and their families lost its character entirely. To them, the glittering city has become a soulless collection of people with whom they feel little sense of common purpose or common culture. The good service jobs created in health care and computer services are mirrored by the minimum wage jobs on which the former industrial workers and their families must now subsist. Still, for most people, particularly outsider observers, there has been a remarkable transition in the city that has made it one of the outstanding success stories of American urban life.

The most fundamental mechanism employed for the socio-economic transformation in the city of Pittsburgh has been the partnership of the public and private sectors. This developed at first informally and later, more formally, with the title of 'Renaissance' being used to describe each of the three programmes of planned socio-economic change in the city. In the partnership, it was important that there were strong and relatively unified actors on both sides of the table. On the government side, there was first Mayor David Lawrence and then later Mayor Richard Caliguiri. Although not as successful as her successors in promoting redevelopment, Mayor Sophie Masloff continued the tradition of strong advocacy for economic and social revitalization from the centre.

Pittsburgh is an overwhelmingly Democratic city with local politics that sometimes still resemble the traditional 'machine' characterization of urban politics in the United States (but see Weber, 1988). This one-party dominance meant that the mayor would not face any significant internal opposition in the public sector and could bargain effectively on behalf of government with business interests. The current mayor, Tom Murphy, came to office as a strong advocate of partnerships between the public and private sectors. While no major deals have been struck in his 18 months in office, the general style of governance has been retained.

The business community in these several 'renaissances' was represented by the Allegheny Conference. This is an association of almost all major firms in the City of Pittsburgh and has been a model for similar business groups in other cities. The principal purpose of the Allegheny Conference has been to promote the economic development and redevelopment of the city and to promote 'good government'. This group was strong enough to extract financial resources from its members and could guarantee the commitment of the business community to the goals of economic change. Just as the public sector had its strong leaders, so too did the business community. Initially, the Allegheny Conference was promoted by Richard King Mellon who was later followed by a number of powerful, if not so famous business personalities.[7]

The successful economic partnerships in the city of Pittsburgh were followed by a variety of partnerships between the state government, county governments and private industry which have attempted to address the difficulties of the mill towns surrounding Pittsburgh. Despite some local improvements, many of these efforts must be considered to be failures and the socio-economic life of most mill towns remains at best bleak. Despite the availability of even greater public resources than those that had been available to the city government, these partnerships have not been able to generate the fundamental socio-economic change desired by their advocates.

CRITIQUE

The partnerships that were so crucial to the redevelopment of Pittsburgh, and substantially less successful in rejuvenating the mill towns in the Monongahela ('Mon') Valley, had one thing in common. This was that organized labour played a rather minor role in their formation and in their implementation (Hathaway, 1993). As two scholars (Pempel and Tsunekawa, 1979) once described policy-making in Japan, these programmes were 'corporatism without labour'. Given this political and organizational structuring, these partnerships tended to conceptualize the problems of generating economic change largely from the 'top-down' perspective (Peters, 1994). There tended to be an operating assumption that if the problem of generating investment and creating new jobs were solved, the problems of the former employees in the metals industries and their subsidiaries would also be solved. In this view, a job was a job, regardless of the level of education or training that it may require, and people were to some extent considered to be interchangeable in those jobs.

Another factor that tended to be underestimated in the planning for economic change was the importance of the locality and of 'localism' as a cognitive value for the people of the area. Although economically often very similar, Pittsburgh neighbourhoods and the mill towns in the Mon valley were socially very distinctive. One might be heavily Polish, while the next is Slovenian, and the next predominately German. These ethnic traditions have been maintained through churches that conduct services in the respective languages, media in languages other than English, and relatively low rates of intermarriage. Localism, in turn, has meant that labour was not as mobile as might have been assumed and jobs had to be brought to the people rather than people moving to the jobs. This localism often separated neighbourhoods and towns in the area and also meant that the out-migration of labour following from the mill closures was not as great as economists would have expected. Again, many people were willing to remain unemployed in McKeesport rather than take a new job in Clarion or California.

The above discussion of the importance of individual cities and neighbourhoods in Pittsburgh and its surrounding region points to the importance of social constructionism in this and other areas of political life (Hilgartner and Bosk, 1988; Best, 1989). The manner in which the character of the economic redevelopment problem came to be defined, and even the manner in which the region itself came to be defined, had a profound effect on the success of the reform project. We will be arguing, in fact, that the definition of the relevant geographical area and the policy goals produced success at one level (the city), but they were also crucial to subsequent failures at another (the region). Further, the definition that was successful at the city level initially may prove to be the undoing of the city at the later stages of its attempts to generate economic and political development. To some extent, these definitions were the received wisdom of development experts of the time, but they were also the product of a great deal of political bargaining among the principal participants – again, with labour largely excluded.

First, the development project initially was defined as a problem for the city and as involving (as noted above) primarily government and business interests. In this initial definition, the problem was conceptualized as being located almost entirely within the confines of the city. As much as dealing with a declining (or declined) metals industry, the initial formulation was to clean up the environmental effects of industry and to attract a more diverse array of economic actors into the city. Even at the stage of 'Renaissance I', steel had become a severely threatened industry in the Pittsburgh region and in the United States as a whole, but the rapid decline experienced during the 1960s and 1970s had not yet begun. Thus, the operating concept for economic change within Pittsburgh was to build on the economic power of what was assumed to be an existing strong economic base, to address some of the environmental side-effects from that industrial base and to promote even higher levels of economic and social growth.

This conceptualization of the nature of the problem, and of the appropriate geographical area to target, proved extremely successful at the inception of the economic revitalization efforts. It enabled a focus on the one political unit and could then mobilize political and economic pressures toward the relatively well-defined economic target. This strategy did not appear to require any trade-offs, either among economic groups or among different political units. Those trade-offs almost certainly existed from the inception of the revitalization effort, but they could easily be masked behind the euphoria over the early successes of the programmes. The complexity of the changes and the ability to export many of the costs to other governmental units made change appear costless.

Another problem in this historical scenario was that this constituted one case of 'lesson drawing' (Rose, 1993) in which government 'learned' an apparently successful strategy for addressing problems of economic and social change. Once that strategy was so successful in the one event, it became difficult for government to unlearn those lessons it thought it had learned. Again, however, it should be noted that the evidence being used to judge the success or failure of the efforts at economic change was drawn primarily from a subset of the region that was being affected by the changes.

These initial successes set the stage for two subsequent rounds of policy failure. First, by conceptualizing the appropriate locus of change as the central city, the strategy tended to ignore much of what would become the parts of the region most deeply affected by deindustrialization. The strategies of attracting high-technology and knowledge-based industries that could work in the city – with two AAU universities[8] and five other institutions of higher education – could not work in the rest of the region that had only minimal educational resources. If an industry of that sort were to be interested in the region at all, it would locate in the university area or in the area near the large international airport, not in the area that arguably needed it the most. The impoverished mill towns of the Mon Valley could neither provide the infrastructure nor, perhaps most importantly, the high-quality education for the children of workers in knowledge-based industries that would be necessary to attract those industries. Conventional mechanisms for intergovernmental competition, such as lowering taxes, may actually have had the effect of reducing the competitiveness of these poorer areas for the new industries that would be attracted by factors such as good education and good transportation.

Further, by ignoring organized labour in the first round of bargaining over the city's redevelopment efforts, the stage was set for the continuing neglect of labour in the redevelopment efforts. That failure to incorporate labour into the redevelopment process contributed to the emergence of more radical labour movements, making any subsequent inclusion of labour into the process all the more difficult.[9] The mill towns of the Monongahela Valley really needed an industrial policy strategy that would have used large volumes of semi-skilled or unskilled labour, but the prevailing conceptualization of positive economic change depended more upon the employment of substantially smaller numbers of much better educated people. The labour shed by the closing of the steel mills was of little or no use in this new high-tech world and the local tradition of men leaving high school to go directly into the mills made the task of preparing the next generation for the emerging economic environment all the more difficult.

The concentration on the city in the initial stages of economic restructuring also constituted a failure to establish a more regional conception of the focus of restructuring and ignored greater co-operation of surrounding territories with the city, required for a more comprehensive strategy. Again, this strategy performed well for a short time but was not able to carry the region on to the next stage, which is the creation of a stronger regional vision with means to share public revenues and policy responsibilities. The City of Pittsburgh now needs substantial assistance from non-residents (increasingly, commuters into the city during the daytime) in order to maintain its own services and to continue to serve as the magnet for economic growth within the region. It appears to be the case that the remainder of the region does not want to help maintain the city, citing revenue problems of its own, yet it may also be unable to prosper if the central city is encountering any severe financial problems.

There has been one slight move in the direction of greater co-operation among local governments in Allegheny County. This has been the creation of a Regional Assets District to help fund major cultural, sports and recreational assets in the area, most of which are located within the city. The creation of this district involved adding one cent to the sales tax levied in the county and establishing a broad-based committee to allocate the revenues among the many organizations and institutions competing for the funds. Although this has helped alleviate some of the financial drain on city government, it has also tended to diminish the already weak sense of community. The immediate result appears to be the loss of some residents and employers from the county in order to escape the impact of the new tax. Had a stronger sense of community been created earlier, there might have been greater willingness to pay.

The second impact of the failure to develop a clear regional focus for the redevelopment effort is that the numerous small cities and towns contained within the boundaries of Allegheny County have not developed mechanisms for needed co-operation among each other. Not only do these municipalities not co-operate effectively with the City of Pittsburgh, they also do not co-operate with themselves to provide common services. Almost all of these units are too small to constitute efficient catchment areas for services such as police, fire and garbage collection (Altenberger and Kearns, 1989). The traditions of local pride, ethnic differentiation and an inadequate state legal framework for intergovernmental co-operation have kept these municipalities from developing a co-ordinated strategy for dealing with their common problems.

COMPARISONS

As noted above, we have access to a number of studies of attempts to produce structural economic change in a number of industrialized regions around the world. Most of these regions had once enjoyed the same type of economic base dependent on heavy industry (especially primary metals) as had Pittsburgh. They were also faced with the same problems of adjusting to a rapidly changing international economy that encouraged a number of their pre-existing jobs to migrate to countries with areas of lower labour costs and/or lower regulatory costs. They also faced the need to attempt to revitalize their economies around service industries.

Although they faced very similar economic problems, they had to, or were able to, cope with the demands for action in very different ways. Several regions appear to have been more successful than the Pittsburgh region taken as a whole, while most appear to have been less successful than was the city itself during the early portions of the period of change. For example, although none of the individual cities within the Ruhrgebiet in Germany have restructured as successfully as has the city of Pittsburgh, the area as a whole appears to have coped with change somewhat better than has the Pittsburgh metropolitan region.

There are a number of sources of variation in the responses of these regions to demands for economic change. Perhaps the most important variable is the operational definition of the region and the ability of the political interests to act effectively and naturally on a regional basis. As noted above, the Ruhr area in Germany has been defined as a region for several policy purposes for a number of years. As such, it could respond in a less competitive and more co-ordinated fashion than could those areas that had previously lacked any clear regional authority and history. Further, the Ruhr area was defined on a rather clear social and economic basis while at least in the early days of their restructuring efforts, the French, Italian and Japanese regions were forced to function with regional definitions crafted more for political convenience than economic rationality. Even those regions, however, appeared to be better off than the American example which had localities that were more competitive than co-operative in their efforts to mobilize resources for economic change.

A second important variable influencing the effectiveness of government in promoting economic change is the level of policy autonomy available to the regional authority and to sub-national governments in general. In the case of Pittsburgh and its region, there was very little that the region (in particular, the county government) could do to force localities within it to co-operate. Its ability to manipulate incentives was almost as restrained as its power to command, given a rather limited tax base. The Commonwealth of Pennsylvania could provide some legal resources but found it difficult to do so without creating equal legal authority for other areas of the state that were already more prosperous. Thus, there was always the danger that any creation of authority for local restructuring efforts would only fuel the tendency toward intergovernmental competitiveness that often undermines regional and industrial policies within the United States (Peters, 1986).

These limitations on authority are further extended in the United States by the inadequacy of funding available from central sources for regeneration efforts, in comparison to that available in other industrialized democracies. For the United States, regional problems are just that and are of little concern to the federal government. One major exception to this generalization is the ability of individual Congressmen to direct funds toward their districts for any number of reasons, including the political necessity of generating support through 'pork barrel' legislation (Fiorina, 1988). Another source of aid is in the form of grants from federal agencies, for example, the Economic Development Administration in the Department of Commerce. Both of these tend to be ad hoc policies that may have much less benefit for regional needs than would a more systematic policy allocating resources to regions on some clear criteria.

Certain traditions of policy-making can also play an important role in the success or failure of attempts at regional restructuring. For example, the corporatist pattern of decision-making in most European democracies, even at the local level (Pierre, 1994), at once makes the initial adoption of policy more difficult, but can improve the possibilities of eventual programmatic implementation and success. By involving the major groups in society in policy-making over a period of years, habits of co-operation can be established that will pay important benefits when creating programmes of economic change. The German and Swedish cases mentioned above were perhaps the most effective in integrating a variety of socio-economic interests into the policy-making process.

CONCLUSION

This paper has been an examination of some of the political struggles surrounding economic restructuring in the city of Pittsburgh and its surrounding area. It has attempted to examine these changes in light of similar efforts in other countries that have had the same policy needs. In this preliminary examination, the experiences of the United States cannot be considered to have been especially positive, despite the positive publicity which they sometimes have received. Certainly, the policy initiatives adopted did help to restructure and 'save' the city, but there may have been a substantial price that was paid for this salvation. That price was paid initially by other parts of the region, but now may be being paid by the residents of the city themselves.

NOTES

1. There are a variety of other operations, such as small speciality steel firms, that do remain in business in the region, but these represent a tiny fraction of the former output of steel from the region. Likewise the headquarters of several major national steel and aluminium businesses remain in the area.

2. The city came in second in a similar poll two years later and has remained in the top five since, so this was apparently not a fluke.

3. The old steel-making towns in the Monongahela River valley, for example, have unemployment rates above the national average and even higher rates of underemployment. A service industry in towns like Rankin and Monessen is a McDonald's, not a high-tech computer or robotics firm.

4. From a political perspective it is especially interesting that all the mayors of Pittsburgh in recent memory have been Democratic while the most important governor in the redevelopment of the area was Richard Thornburgh, a Republican. It is not unimportant, however, that Thornburgh is originally from the Pittsburgh area.

5. Some of these differences represent patterns of settlement by different ethnic groups (Polish, Slovene, Irish, German, Ukrainian, etc.) and the desire to maintain their respective traditions.

6. The information for these comparisons come from a project co-ordinated by the University Centre for International Studies and the University Centre for Social and Urban Studies at the University of Pittsburgh. The title of this project was Regional Structural Change in International Perspective (RSCIP) and included data from the Ruhr area of Germany, Lille and the Pas de Calais in France, Gothenberg in Sweden, Glasgow in Scotland, Osaka in Japan and Wuhan in China. To

call what is available from this comparative study 'data' is perhaps somewhat over-generous, but there is a good deal of descriptive material about the policies and the relative successes of economic revitalization policies in these areas. The author gratefully acknowledges the access to the materials generated by this project provided by the two University Centres.

7. The role of the Mellon bank in financing many of the major industries in Pittsburgh gave R. K. Mellon a great deal of leverage (to say the least) in the city's business community.

8. The Association of American Universities (AAU) is an organization composed of the 50 top research universities in the country.

9. The Denominational Ministry Strategy was a coalition of radical labour leaders and equally or more radical religious leaders. They engaged in a variety of confrontational tactics, involving, among other things, dead fish and skunks.

13

Regions in the New Germany

ROLAND STURM

INTRODUCTION

In the 1980s, the paradigmatic change of the dominant economic philosophy from Keynesianism to a form of supply-side economics in Germany, together with growing financial problems and the imminent new challenges of a future European Single Market for regional economies, triggered for the first time a serious debate on alternatives to top-down economic development strategies in Germany. A bottom-up approach of regional self-help seemed to offer a lot of attractive possibilities: it could mobilize neglected local and regional economic potentials; it could perhaps be also more cost-efficient; and it could shoulder some of the responsibilities for regional development, especially if the European Single Market really were to reduce considerably the national competencies for regional development.

If regions are more than an administrative tool for central government, what strategies are appropriate for their economic development? The simple truth that regions want to be economically successful justifies both efforts to protect local and regional industries and to improve their capacities for innovation. Politically, the defence of declining industries is a major issue for state (*Land*) governments, although economically, the decline of outdated industries can at best be prolonged. The aim of every effort to support regional economic development is to identify productive capacities which guarantee a certain level of net exports of regional products and/or services. The competitiveness of a region cannot be defined by its ability to protect the status quo. Regional development is unthinkable without innovation. German unification added to these core problems both a regional development problem of new dimensions and with the *Treuhand* (national privatization agency for East German state-owned property) a new dimension of central government intervention (Fischer *et al.*, 1993).

The following argument concentrates on two aspects: the role of the German states in regional development policies and their industrial modernization policies. With regard to these aspects, there is a marked difference between East and West Germany for two reasons. East Germany's major problem is deindustrialization, West Germany's central problem is the defence of its position in the world market. West German states have greater autonomy than East German states over their regional development. Though the *Treuhand* finished its work by the end of 1994, federal intervention with regard to East Germany's economic development priorities has *de facto* not ended. The remaining *Treuhand* business was not transferred to the East German *Länder*, but was given to a number of quangos and central state agencies. They own, for example, still more than one third of the East German territory. From 1995, these estates are the sole responsibility of the *Treuhand* - *Liegenschaftsgesellschaft*. This company will try to sell the property, but it will not consult the East German states, which would need to control land use for industrial development. The income generated by the sales will fill the coffers of the federal finance minister and will not be given to the relatively impoverished East German states, where the estates sold are situated. In addition to the unusual degree of federal interventions in state affairs in East Germany, the East German states are disadvantaged with regard to the civil society structures which are needed to organize regional modernization. In particular, potential science and local finance institutions are in their infancy and cannot be expected to play the same role for the strengthening of regional autonomy that they play in West Germany. This situation makes the difficult search of the East German states for strategies to improve their regional competitiveness even more complicated.

INSTITUTIONAL RESTRICTIONS FOR A MODERNIZATION POLICY OF THE *LÄNDER*

In Germany, regional autonomy in economic policy on the state level is limited. Modernization policies are initiated and implemented today at all levels of government from that of the EU right down to local authorities. The *Länder* are in an intermediate position. They have their 'masters': the EU and the federal government; they enjoy some autonomy; and vis-à-vis local authorities they are also 'masters' themselves. The division of tasks among these levels of government is neither logical nor clear-cut, nor transparent to the general public. It is much less based on a separation of tasks between the federal and the state governments than is the case in the United States, for example, where this separation provides a potential for regional diversity with regard to modernization strategies and allows for a great deal of economic competition among the states (Van Horn, 1993). The present division of tasks in German federalism is the historical product of a process of muddling through, justified by the constitutional requirement of uniform living conditions everywhere in Germany. Efforts to institutionalize the notion of personal welfare rights have undermined the principle of territorial politics as the cornerstone of federalism and have culminated in interlocking federalism (*Politikverflechtung*), which defines the joint responsibilities of the federal government and the states.

The independent tax base of local government and states, and also of the federal government, is fairly insignificant. The bulk of the administration of major taxes – personal and corporate income taxes, wealth taxes and sales taxes - lies with the states, but the total of public income collected by the states is then divided among the states and federal government. Joint tax income of state and federal government makes up 75 per cent of the tax income both levels of government have together. The separation of financial responsibilities is further restricted by vertical and horizontal financial equalization mechanisms.

If German states want to modernize their industrial structures, they have to work within this framework of limited autonomy. They also have to accept that their present boundaries (including the boundaries of the new states in East Germany (Benz, 1993), were not defined by economic criteria. This means that core-periphery problems plague one group of the *Länder*, whereas the smaller ones complain about insufficient financial strength and a possible unfair advantage size gives to the bigger ones. In the context of economic modernization, co-operation of states among themselves, especially north Germany, and even their merger, in the proposals for Berlin and Brandenburg (rejected by Brandenburgers in the 1996 referendum), has become an important strategic option. Although co-operation may increase the economic viability of regions, it will not increase the *Länder* autonomy.

It is not only the competencies and capacities which German states have for their modernization policies that are limited. Restrictions also operate for policy instruments (Sturm, 1991a). Here, subsidy control on the EU level is the greatest obstacle. Its importance increases in fields where the EU has its own development programmes. This is especially true for regional policies, for which the EU has established its structural and cohesion funds. The German states would prefer to use their autonomy to initiate their own regional development policies in addition to, and outside, regional support provided by the constitutionally guaranteed joint effort of the federal government and the states. But if Brussels stops state subsidies, the states are in a no-win situation. There is no chance that help will be given to regions which are in need of help only from the state's viewpoint, nor can the state involved shoulder the responsibility for priority-setting in its regional policy because Brussels forbids the allocation of state funds. This restriction is a direct result of the conflict between a top-down approach to regional development and a bottom-up one. For the EU, a level playing-field in the Single Market as a whole is the aim. Regional aid only serves the purpose of correcting the excessive geographical inequalities produced by market mechanisms. From the perspective of the states, what counts is improved competitiveness for them as regions in the Single Market. Competitiveness can be improved through the states' financial support for regions or industries, although this might create unfair regional advantages if EU averages are taken as yardstick.

Until the mid-1980s, state governments had been very reluctant to oppose the traditional decision-making process. However, the logic of interlocking decision-making on both the federal and the European levels is a trap, at least from the point of view of the regions. It blocks out regional interests by three mechanisms. First, once elected, regional governments prefer an administrative approach to decision-making, that is, the finding of compromises between high-level bureaucrats and top politicians working through their party political networks. When they come back to their parliaments (if at all), they confront them with sophisticated formulae and compromises which cannot be altered, unless they want to restart negotiation processes from point zero. A regional voice is only one among many and is powerless against a political majority backing a broad and complicated compromise. Second, the transparency problem increases with the addition of the EU level of decision-making. A German region is only a national sub-unit, not necessarily consulted, and with very few administratively independent allies in a European Union, where federal states are the exception. The *Länder* overestimate their influence on the other European nation-states and underestimate how they can be used as transmission belts by bureaucrats in Brussels. Third, representation of the regions on the federal and national levels can only be assured at the price of an aggregation of regional preferences. In the bargaining process, there is only one voice for all regions and this is rarely representative of the needs and preferences of all German regions.

A NEW ROLE FOR THE *LÄNDER* IN EUROPE?

European integration seemed to erode rapidly national sovereignty. Maastricht was supposed to move Europe closer to a common foreign and defence policy and to a harmonization of economic policies not yet europeanized by the Single Market project, including a common European currency. With very few economic competencies left on the national level, the states expected a 'sandwich model' (Eser, 1991) of policy-making to emerge. The responsibility for economic integration was to lie in the hands of the EU, but the European level is too far detached from regional needs, which still can only be articulated efficiently through national channels, although the Committee of the Regions may be able to add a new voice. German citizens would no doubt expect from their state governments political and financial support for the economic competitiveness of their region. The state, as the elected regional entity closest to the people, looks like the ideal candidate for the defence of the relative economic position of regions in the Single Market.

The *Länder* also found an ideological tool to justify their new activism: the 'rediscovery' of the subsidiarity principle. Though constitutional lawyers doubt the legal quality of the principle (Blanke, 1991), it could be used as a battle-cry to rally the federal forces. The German *Länder* even organized European regional conferences to which the then President of the European

Commission, Jacques Delors, was invited and at which he paid lip-service to the subsidiarity principle. The *Länder* had hoped to establish the rule that regions should be entrusted with the tasks they are better qualified to deal with than the nation-state or Europe, and that they themselves should be able to make the binding judgement on their respective abilities. In addition, more regional financial autonomy, with regard to both spending and taxation policies, should accompany the clear division of policy responsibilities. However, even disregarding the utopian character of a general regionalization of Europe, within their own political system the German *Länder* are far from getting even approximately the kind of powers this model implies.

Regional room for manoeuvre for the *Länder* on the European level has, nevertheless, been secured without creating political hostilities because of two convincing arguments: it is needed for practical reasons, and it brings economic advantages. Because of a lack of an institutional regionalism in Europe (Bullmann and Eißel, 1993), this kind of co-operation necessarily had to progress piecemeal and it is weak in its institutional superstructure, but that does not mean it is inefficient. Cross-border co-operation is tried out in the border regions of all states. One better known example of a successful institutionalization of these forms of co-operation is the Saar-Lor-Lux initiative which integrates the Saarland, Lorraine, parts of Rhineland-Palatinate, Luxembourg and the Belgian province of Luxembourg (Raich, 1995). What unites this cross-border region is its dependency on declining industries (coal and steel) and its position outside Europe's major growth regions. In environmental research, Baden-Württemberg co-operates in the REKLIP project with Switzerland and Alsace and, in 1992, a Franco-German ecological research institute was founded, with branches in Karlsruhe and Strasbourg. The Dutch provinces of Drenthe, Friesland, Groningen and Overijssel co-operate with Lower Saxony and Bremen in the *Neue Hanse Interregio* project to strengthen their common regional identity and to develop a regional profile. Another local and regional cross-border initiative is the close co-operation of local government districts (*Landkreistag*) of the Saarland with the French *Département de la Moselle*.

A few states have even tried to develop initiatives for their own foreign economic policy. Baden-Württemberg, for example, founded an Association for International Economic Co-operation (*Gesellschaft für internationale wirtschaftliche Zusammenarbeit*). Within the framework of the 'Four Motors of Europe' concept, it is seeking to develop co-operation with regions once identified as high-growth areas (Catalonia, Rhône-Alpes, Lombardy and the associate partners, Wales and Ontario). Baden-Württemberg has not only tried to use its once comparative economic lead in Germany to leave behind German-centred regional economic development goals, it even thought it possible – the utopian character of such plans is now obvious – to take the lead, together with growth regions in other European nations, in the process of European integration. The tacit assumption of this strategy was that in the future Europe of the Regions, economic strength would be far more important than the constitutional and administrative powers of nation-states, and that the national and European ideas of social and economic cohesiveness would be no obstacle to a greater regional diversity.

NEW REGIONAL MODERNIZATION STRATEGIES

Economic modernization has been sought by the *Länder* more actively and earlier on the domestic than on the international level. The pioneering states were Baden-Württemberg, where the government started to support technological change in 1976, and North Rhine-Westphalia and Hamburg, which followed suit in 1978. Early instruments of regional modernization policies were subsidies and the credit-financing of research and information networks. A qualitatively new dimension of state activism was provoked by the internationalization of markets and the Japanese and South-East Asian challenge of the 1980s. The American example of successful innovation, especially the now legendary Silicon Valley 'model', was imitated in a wave of so-called new technology parks. The initiative for these centres came both from the *Länder* and from local government. There was a remarkable boom period for this kind of modernization policy between 1985 and 1986. Most of the technology centres were founded in Baden-Württemberg, Lower Saxony and North Rhine-Westphalia.

Soon, however, the competition of local governments for industries and innovators willing to come to their centres led to a problematic situation. Many centres were established which lacked the basic preconditions for innovation. They were neither in contact with outside research at a university, for example, nor were the firms situated in the centre interested in regional economic networks. In addition, the centres were not in full use. Even in the mid-1980s, when the centre idea was still young and there were fewer centres around, only little more than a third of the existing centres used all their capacity. The situation worsened with the economic crisis of the late 1980s and after unification, when East German local government began to imitate West German local government strategies and to some extent, to repeat their mistakes (Sturm, 1994). Whereas there are about a dozen business parks in West Germany which cover an area of about 50,000 square metres, East Germany already has more than 100 that are double that size. Too many local councils chase too few potential investors, which means that if a council finds one at all, it very often has to accept conditions which are costlier than the benefits a business park may yield, even in the long run.

A new type of co-operation between science and business was established in Ulm (Baden-Württemberg) in the late 1980s. The example of Japanese technology towns (technopolis) was taken here as a model for a science town. This model rests on four pillars: state-funded university research, industry-financed research, technology transfer institutions, and mixed state-business research institutes. In contrast to the traditional technology park, the science town is not primarily oriented towards the support of small and medium-sized industries and towards applied research. It is controlled and co-financed by big international firms, such as Daimler or Siemens, and has a great interest in basic research (Schmid et al., 1991).

The decision on the European level to prepare for a Single Market increased state activism. In particular, the economically more successful states saw the Single Market as a new economic opportunity for their industries. They started to organize their capacities for modernization policies more systematically. State administrative structures were streamlined and grouped around the purpose of economic modernization. Networks of information and advice on technology for regional industry in connection with a plethora of subsidy programmes were made available. State-owned banking institutions became actively involved in the credit-financing of innovations. Regional research capacities were to be developed in close connection with the needs of regional industries. To some degree, this was a voluntarist strategy. It ignored the possibility of an economic recession with its severe consequences for the ability of states to co-finance regional economic modernization. It also ignored the regional effects of the Single Market integration process, especially with regard to sharper imbalances between sub-state regions as a result of Euro-wide economic competition. To avoid interventions and subsidy controls of the EU, the new regional modernization strategy was mostly not defined as regional development policy, but either as regional technology policy or support for small and medium-sized industries.

For every successful regional modernization initiative, a number of minimal conditions have to be fulfilled:

- Regional identities have to be defined as a focus for initiatives and as a force for motivating co-operation. Such identities may be closely connected with common economic problems, but they are more convincing if some kind of traditional cohesion can be found for the economic region in question. Very often, historic ethnic roots or historic events are re-invented in order to justify the regional boundaries chosen for economic reasons. Public relations experts are given the task of creating a special regional image, both to produce support among those living in the region, and to make the region attractive to outside investors and recognizable as a new regional competitor (Sturm, 1991b).

- Regional support must be able to count on 'motivational resources', that is, support given freely or cost-efficiently by the local people, because not only do they identify with their region, they are also ready to do something for its economic future. This kind of support depends very much on the psychological factor: the individual sense of belonging has to be strong enough to create a feeling of responsibility in the individual, not only for him/herself and his/her family, but also his/her region. Motivational resources have to be goal-directed. They cannot stand too much frustration and should therefore be given a clear framework with regard to the tasks to be fulfilled and the time this is going to take. After successes are visible, it is easier to come back to originally mobilized regional support or to create new social coalitions.

- Such regional co-operation is formally organized as local corporatism (public/private partnerships, regional networks). Typically, local government, universities, chambers of commerce, local savings banks and, in some states with a social democratic tradition, also union representatives organize projects and support, or invent, regional initiatives.

Two 'models' of state modernization policies can be distinguished: regional centralism and regional decentralization. The regional centralism model has been identified with Baden-Württemberg. Here, the state government organizes the social coalition of regional modernizers and provides the administrative framework, the instruments and the aims of modernization policies. The cohesion of such a regional initiative is provided by incentives (financial, moral, careers etc.), but not by force or law. Of central importance is an integrated network, which in Baden-Württemberg is situated in the same building, the *Haus der Wirtschaft* (literally, 'the industry house'), in Stuttgart. In every region of the state, there are centres for technological advice and technology transfer. This network is based on independent state-funded research institutes, universities, polytechnics and regional centres specializing in different fields of technological advice under the auspices of the Steinbeis Foundation, which is responsible for the support of technology transfer. Although as a rule, small and medium-sized firms are the main targets of *Länder* technology policies, Baden-Württemberg is also strongly promoting close co-operation between big and successful companies and the state.

A variation of the centralist model is typical for East Germany. Here, social coalitions of modernizers are, in contrast to such coalitions in West German states, mostly without an independent resource base. They have to rely heavily on transfers from the West. In addition, modernization in the east has so far often meant the transformation of production from non-marketable to marketable products, without a dramatic input of new technology. One kind of initiative are employment firms (*Beschäftigungsgesellschaften*), which have the strategic purpose of keeping firms alive through outside financing provided by, above all, social security funds, *Treuhand* funds and sometimes state funds. The idea for such firms, which specialize in re-training and occasionally also try to secure new production by looking for marketable products, came from the trade unions, in particular, the metal workers' union (*IG Metall*). These firms also have the effect of helping regional economies to survive. However, to a great extent, they are doomed because they cannot reverse the fate of declining industries and because even after re-training, alternative employment in the same region is rarely available. In a way, they mirror a more general interest of the unions – to attract new membership in East Germany – and the state governments – to find a temporary solution for the unemployment problem – rather than represent genuine regional initiatives.

A direct transfer of the modernization experience of Baden-Württemberg has been tried in Jena (Thuringia), where the former Prime Minister of Baden-Württemberg, Lothar Späth, was made chairman of Jenoptik (the former Zeiss Jena firm). The firm is financed by the state of Thuringia and the *Treuhand*, and is supposed to work in a product niche provided by an agreement with its West German Zeiss Jena mother firm. So far, economic success for the region has not been achieved, though in theory many of the preconditions for successful regional economic initiatives (skilled personnel; a culture region to attract investments; Weimar is in close proximity to West Germany) are said to be available.

The decentralized model of regional modernization is a strategy first tried in North Rhine-Westphalia and now imitated above all by Lower Saxony (Krafft and Ulrich, 1993) and, to a lesser extent, Brandenburg. In North Rhine-Westphalia, sub-state regionalism is supposed to be the driving force behind regional modernization. Flexible *ad hoc* coalitions of modernizers in a context still small enough for face-to-face decision-making, and with a certain potential for personal trust, come together to suggest modernization strategies for their regions. The major resource sub-state regions have is their consensus, which is not only used to create boundaries of regional co-operation, but which is also the major argument for funding decisions by the *Land*. It is open to debate, however, whether consensus mechanisms produce synergy effects and new innovative ideas, or whether they are only a euphemism for local power structures. It is also still unclear how stable local coalitions are when certain group advantages resulting from regional modernization are reduced. For all participants, the exit option is always available (Heinze and Voelzkow, 1990).

In North Rhine-Westphalia, the regional initiatives are expected to present regional development plans at conferences of the regions. During these conferences, the different plans competing for limited funds to finance them should be ranked according to their relative merits. The state government which provides the funds is also the sole arbitrator and finally decides which regional initiative gets state aid. For the state government, this position is attractive because it does not have to discuss the fact that funds are limited, it does not have to develop by itself regional economic initiatives and it is not necessarily blamed for a lack of spending in certain regions. The government can always argue that it would have preferred expenditures there, but the project the region in question presented was not as well drawn up as other projects. It has been pointed out that today's practice of decentralized regionalism is in essence paradoxical. Decentralization is made possible only as a strategy of state centres unable to cope with current political challenges, but who intend to regain control over the policy process through the backdoor of sub-state regionalism (Forth and Wohlfahrt, 1992).

However, even in North Rhine-Westphalia, institutionalized regionalism remains fairly weak with regard to its 'constitutional' status. A lot of policy initiatives end up, or are planned from the outset, as symbolic politics for which a successful image campaign is already a great political success. Yet the fundamental problem to which regional initiatives have drawn attention remains of central importance to the political economy of regionalism in Germany, namely how to bridge the gap between existing and democratically-legitimized administrative structures, and viable regional economic co-operation. Answers to this question are crucial for future regional economic survival.

The problem of control of local and regional activism based on local and regional initiatives at the state level is also unresolved in the above-mentioned context of cross-border regional co-operation, although this kind of co-operation could be defined as falling into the competence of national foreign policy. But the regions involved are not content with being represented abroad by either their state or the national government. They want a direct say in such initiatives. The problem of state boundaries and sub-regional autonomy is even more obvious with regard to regional self-organization in Germany itself. Co-operation efforts on the sub-state level range from regular contacts for the exchange of information to technical co-operation of local governments, and even to institutionalized sub-regional economic development associations. State governments support such initiatives, which often involve regional co-operation across state borders to accommodate common regional economic interests in economic regions divided by state boundaries. The limits for this kind of regional self-organization are the existing constitutional arrangements. From the point of view of the regions involved, the very inflexibility of current arrangements is often blocking initiatives.

MODERNIZATION PROFILES OF THE *LÄNDER*

Although there is a strong incentive for mutual learning, and the states' room for manoeuvre with regard to modernization policies is restricted, it would be wrong to expect a completely uniform reaction of the German states to the modernization problem. The structure of regional economies is diverse and this diversity determines strategic action. Preferences for certain modernization strategies can also be explained by a number of strategic choices especially with regard to policy instruments.

There is now a broad consensus among the states that the co-operation of science and industry is essential for regional development strategies. Not all the states, however, stress this fact in the same way. One reason for the diversity of opinions is that this co-operation is so much the rule that it is not deemed necessary to underline it. States with social democratic governments may also have some ideological problems with acknowledging that political steering is severely restricted by a type of economic priority setting which allows for a strong independent role of the business sector. Technology transfer has without exception become a standard policy procedure. It is at the heart of the states' modernization efforts. Their role is to organize advice, infrastructure and contacts to improve the technological standards of local and regional firms, and even to help them find new products or improve the quality of existing ones. The states' role as provider of venture capital has lost importance. One reason may be that in the recession of the 1990s, capital is much cheaper than it was in the high-interest-rate decade of the 1980s. Another reason may be the severe pressures on regional budgets after unification, which the states are co-financing.

The shortage of funds and short-term goal-oriented support for technological modernization have reduced the states' interest in basic research. This does not mean that this disappears. It means, however, that the importance of applied research has grown in comparison. International and cross-border regional co-operation has made great progress. For regional decision-makers, the Single Market and the globalization of the economy have become influential as new factors shaping the economic environment of regional modernization policies.

The list of unresolved problems of regional modernization in Table 1 is certainly not complete. It documents more the incompetence of state administrators when it comes to long-term problem-solving than the full scale of the modernization challenge. The problems mentioned are, however, serious ones of central concern to regional governments. What is also striking is the almost complete absence of state efforts to improve programme evaluation and implementation. The states seem to be satisfied when the financial incentives their programmes offer are accepted by the business community. Research has shown that efficient support for regional industries is a highly complex matter. On the one hand, there is the problem of differentiated needs for state help. Industry is most interested in the state financing of dimensions of basic research which are beyond its means. In the case of applied research, the picture is less clear. Here, the probability that industry uses state funding for a free ride is high (Grande and Häusler, 1992). A second problem concerns incompatible expectations of the state on one side and industry on the other (Hofmann, 1993). Whereas state administrators have an abstract idea of modernization and technology transfer as social processes which can be activated with the help of incentives, the single firm involved has less global problems it wants to solve. State aid may in some cases be helpful either financially or with regard to cheaper scientific advice. But it has also been shown that for many firms, such advice may also be available elsewhere and financial help is not in every case essential.

TABLE 1

MODERNIZATION POLICIES OF THE STATES

State	CIS 88 93	TT 88 93	BR 88 93	ICBC 88 93	VC 88 93	Other unsolved problems 1988	Other unsolved problems 1993
Baden-Württ.	+ +	+ +	+ +	+ +	? +	?	?
Bavaria	+ +	+ +	+ +	? ?	+ ?	balanced regional development	balanced regional development
Berlin	+ ?	+ +	+ +	+ +	? ?	catch up on industrial research potential	solve unification problems
Branden.	- ?	- +	- ?	- +	- ?	-	?
Bremen	+ +	+ +	+ ?	? ?	? ?	catch up on scientific infrastructure	catch up on scientific infrastructure
Hamburg	+ ?	+ +	+ +	? +	? ?	more money	?

TABLE 1 (CONTINUED)
MODERNIZATION POLICIES OF THE STATES

State	CIS 88 93	TT 88 93	BR 88 93	ICBC 88 93	VC 88 93	Other unsolved problems 1988	Other unsolved problems 1993
Hesse	+ +	+ +	+ +	? ?	? ?	regional balance	?
Meckl.-West Pomer.	- ?	- +	- ?	- ?	- ?	-	overcome economic monostructure
Lower Sax.	+ +	+ +	+ ?	? +	? ?	?	?
North Rh.-Westph.	? ?	+ +	+ +	? +	? ?	economic + ecological renewal	economic + ecological renewal
Rhinel.-Palatin.	+ +	+ +	+ +	? +	? ?	?	?
Saarland	? ?	+ +	+ ?	+ +	+ ?	overcome economic monostructure	?
Saxony	- +	- +	- +	- ?	- ?	-	?
Saxony-Anhalt	- ?	- +	- +	- ?	- ?	-	?
Schleswig-Holstein	? +	+ +	+ ?	? +	? +	?	?
Thuringia	- +	- +	- +	- ?	- ?	-	solve unification problems

CIS = cooperation between industry and science; TT = technology transfer; BR = basic research; ICBC = international and cross-border cooperation; VC = venture capital.
- = no policy, because this state was not part of the Federal Republic at that time; + = policy exists and has high priority; ? = policy either does not exist or has low priority.

Sources: Bundesbericht Forschung 1988 and 1993 (BTDrs. 11/2049, p. 202ff. and 12/5550), p. 269ff.

In addition to the more general preferences of state modernization policies summarized in Table 1, individual states keep developing their own special institutions and programmes. In 1991, for example, Rhineland-Palatinate established a Foundation for Technological Innovation and in 1993, a new investment and structural development bank (ISB, *Investitions und Strukturbank Rheinland-Pfalz*). The general aim of this strategic decision is to co-ordinate the state's resources for technological modernization. In

1990, Schleswig-Holstein started the programme *Mittelstand, Technik und Innovation* (MiTI) for a similar purpose.

Baden-Württemberg has tried to secure its conceptual lead with regard to state industrial policy strategies by a major effort to mobilize experts from the fields of industry (both business and union representatives), science and public administration. The state's commission on the economy in the year 2000, *Zukunftskommission Wirtschaft 2000*, (Staatsministerium, 1993; Schmid, 1994) argued that the role of the state government should be to organize a dialogue and act as communicator between business and public administration. The new industrial policy should change the often negative public image of new technologies and help develop a certain number of decisive and competitive key industries. The aim is to bring together the key players in each industrial sector – leading firms, industry associations, unions, chambers of commerce, research institutes etc. – so as to design a commonly agreed sector strategy for the 1990s. Two joint initiatives have been launched, for autos and machine tools. Initiatives are planned for textiles and the small craft-based firms (*Handwerk*). The emphasis of the common initiatives varies with the problems and the nature of inter-firm relations in each sector. The Economics Ministry is offering financial incentives for the creation of strategic alliances between producers, their trading partners, their suppliers and the regional scientific community. The new strategy reminds the observer of Japanese efforts to restrict competition in favour of co-operation. Though the autonomy of firms is not questioned, a new balance between collaboration and competition in sectors of industry is sought. The broader aim is to tap the region's collective modernization potential and thereby to improve its competitiveness (Cooke *et al.*, 1993).

As organizational tools, the *Zukunftskommission* supports the establishment of an innovation council (*Innovationsbeirat*) on the state level. This council should be interdepartmental and half of its members should come from industry. On the federal level, the commission would like to see the establishment of a council of technology advisers. Infrastructure investments of the state should aim at transforming Baden-Württemberg into an information society, especially with regard to computer-guided traffic systems and communication networks which should be conceptualized as data 'highways'.

CONCLUSION

Economic regions, even if their territorial boundaries are identical with those of the present German states, lack a strong institutional backing. Still, the regional economies in Germany are better off than those in unitary states. Sub-state regional needs cannot be ignored by state governments who seek re-election. The states' powers and instruments for intervention may not be regarded as sufficient, but at least some room for manoeuvre can be secured for a better positioning of the regions in the context of national and international competition. The trend for a greater strategic autonomy of states and regions with regard to regional economic modernization seems to be unstoppable. Even the anti-industrial-policy credo of German market purists, who have a strong position in academia and a great influence on the media, have been unable to prevent a close co-operation of public and private initiatives on the regional and local level. We see forms of a re-regionalization of regional economic policies, but we also see a lot of short-termism and an on-going debate on strategies.

Regionalism as an essential part of the future European constitution has been praised for a number of reasons, of which the advantages of a functioning regional economy are only one. In this context, the question arises whether the Single Market can ever avoid producing regional disparities. These disparities may count for little politically, as long as they are passively accepted by the regions affected. The situation changes when they give rise to an economic and political reaction, expressing itself – as is now the case in Germany – in flexible local/regional societal partnerships. The EU, with its need for definitions of regional sub-units to channel its structural funds and to identify the candidates for a Committee of the Regions, may contribute to the political consolidation of regional entities Euro-wide. Will this top-down regionalism be compatible with the bottom-up regionalism created by Single Market pressures and 'invented by the German states'? And how will a Europe of nations coexist with a Europe of economic regions?

14

The Euro-region and the C-6 Network: The New Politics of Sub-national Cooperation in the West-Mediterranean Area

FRANCESC MORATA

INTRODUCTION

This chapter aims to shed light on the processes of co-operation among three regions – Catalonia, Languedoc-Roussillon and Midi-Pyrénées – and six cities – Barcelona, Montpellier, Palma de Mallorca, Toulouse, Valencia and Zaragoza – known respectively as the West Mediterranean Euro-region and the C-6 network. Despite the fact that the two groups are led by the Catalan government and the city of Barcelona respectively and seek to reach similar objectives by using complementary – or at least non contradictory – strategies, they are not only unco-ordinated but even competitive. This is not surprising, given the political and personal rivalries between the two main political institutions in Catalonia and their respective leaders. Nevertheless, both experiments are based not on partisan considerations, but on political pluralism. This is especially true in the case of C-6. It is interesting to note that, besides the increasing European orientation of Catalonia, Barcelona's international activism to a large extent results, paradoxically, from the abolition of its metropolitan government by the regional government in 1988.

Here we are concerned to retrace the genesis of both macro-regional projects analysing the organizational aspects as well as the objectives and the programmes enacted up to now. We will start with some theoretical assumptions and conclude by underlining both the potentialities and limitations that the Euro-region and the C-6 network must cope with.

THEORETICAL FRAMEWORK

Economic, political and ideological considerations account for the emerging and developing of new forms of inter-regional and inter-local co-operation at the transnational level in Europe, and especially between Spanish and French sub-national governments.

The phenomena of globalization and interdependence are significant factors which provide a new context for the activities of sub-national units. Increasing international interdependence fosters the emergence of sub-national governments as active players in the international arena. In ways similar to national governments, sub-national actors adjust their behaviour according to domestic and international challenges. Interdependence leads to the diversification of the international agenda and erodes the traditional division between foreign and domestic policy (Keohane and Nye, 1988). New issues, such as the environment, health, communications, social services, transport, urban and territorial planning and culture, which have in some countries been within the policy sphere of sub-national governments, are more and more affected by international constraints and opportunities (Cappellin, 1990).

The recent evolution of sub-national governments stresses the need to focus on the impact of developments within the EU on the redefinition of territorial units and, in particular, on emerging functional and territorial interdependencies (Goldsmith, 1993; Sharpe, 1993). The transfer of some areas of national sovereignty upwards to the EU and the progressive dismantling of boundaries have contributed to the transformation of established territorial boundaries and to the redefinition of the traditional functions of sub-national governments. These institutional changes, along with new technologies in communications and transport, are leading to three converging strategies at the local and the regional levels: competition for promoting new activities; the setting up of macro-regional networks based on common interests; and lobbying central government and EU institutions.

In the economic sphere, new technologies of production and changes in the market system have established the basis for a new international inter-regional division of labour. Competitiveness among states is shifting to competitiveness among territories, that is among institutionalized territorial units such as regions and cities. On the one hand, these are endowed with resources and competencies to perform essential economic and social functions (for example, transport, energy, water and solid waste management, communications, social services, education). On the other hand, they act as 'innovation centres' promoting social and cultural diversity. Strong regions and metropolitan cities compete in the international-European arena to attract private investment and especially the location of business decision-making centres.

Another relevant element relates to the increase in trans-border flows. Sub-national units must cope with common functional problems (the environment, infrastructure, the movement of people and goods) which force them to intervene in the international arena in search of additional resources and know-how. In addition, technological change in the field of communications is transforming the notions of space and time, reducing these to an extraordinary degree. The rapid circulation of information is enhancing new forms of co-operation among sub-national governments in terms of policy and administrative exchange and inter-organizational networks involving public and private interests (Borrás, 1992). It also encourages policy competitiveness and emulative initiatives.

In Europe, the combined effects of supranational integration and internal institutional transformations have also impacted on the international role of sub-national governments (Keating, 1993b). First, the crisis of the nation-state has led to the re-emergence of cultural and historical identities while sovereignty is pooled among a number of states on a wider number of issues (Loughlin, 1994). Although the strengthening of the 'meso' level may be viewed as the necessary adjustment of unitary states in order to accommodate new responsibilities (Sharpe, 1993), the processes of regional devolution have weakened the central state's ability to control some relevant policy areas, giving to sub-national governments a salient role as implementers of both domestic and European policies (Morata, 1993). It is worth noting the possibilities opened up by new ERDF regulations which provide for official regional participation in European regional policy. This will happen through partnership and the joint policy-making and implementation structures for border regions. In addition, the Committee of the Regions might prefigure a future European second chamber of nations and regions to replace the existing Council of Ministers (Mazey and Mitchell, 1993). Regional governments and local associations have set up offices of representation in Brussels bringing together representatives of public and private sector bodies with an interest in EU affairs and financial subsidies. However, some regions have not given up the goal of enjoying an official or, at least, a more influential status in the European arena according to their national or cultural identity.

The international dimension of sub-national politics is further enhanced by ideological arguments. According to the Catalan President, Jordi Pujol, the international presence of Catalonia is closely linked to the defence of national identity. Priority is thus given to the establishment of stable relations with other societies presenting characteristics similar to those of Catalonia (for example, Quebec, Wallonia, Flanders and Wales). In this scenario, with regard to European integration, the regions must not imitate states. On the contrary, they have to develop a new concept of power and collective action closely linked to the supranational-federal project represented by the European Union. Each level of government performs different and specific functions in the context of supranational integration and the regions are well adapted to provide incentives for closer relations among economic, social and scientific agents within their territories. They should also enhance co-operation with other regional governments since the process of political and economic union will inevitably lead to the reshaping of the European space on the basis of coherent and competitive macro-regions. The main idea is 'to counteract the isolation produced by boundaries by establishing strong relations of any kind with the other regions in order to shape wider geographic areas, which have to be more competitive at the European level' (Pujol, 1993).

CATALONIA AND BARCELONA IN THE EUROPEAN CONTEXT

Representing 20 per cent of the Spanish GNP and almost a quarter of Spanish external trade, Catalonia is the most industrialized region in Spain and the one with the highest concentration of foreign investment. During the last ten years, foreign, and especially European, investment in Catalonia amounted to around 35 per cent of the Spanish total. Its geographical position makes Catalonia a 'hinge-region' linking northern and southern Europe. This explains why it shares more common interests with the French Mediterranean and the regions of the Pyrenees regions than with other Spanish regions (Jouvenel and Roque, 1993). Strong national identity, combined with increasing institutional and financial resources and political activism, allow Catalonia to play a relevant role in the European regional and local context.

In addition, Barcelona is the most important metropolitan area of the Western Mediterranean arc. Although the central city has a population of 1.72 million inhabitants, the metropolitan region of Barcelona (3.5 million inhabitants) is the most populated and industrialized area in Spain. The organization of the Olympic Games was an opportunity to regenerate the city through the provision of new territorial infrastructure, advanced technology and business services. Indeed, public and private investment, linked directly or indirectly to the organization of the Olympic Games, amounted to nearly 6.5 MECU. Confronted with the challenge of exploiting its new urban environment, the city is redefining itself as a European metropolis by a twofold strategy based on competition and complementarity with other European cities (Borja, 1990). Moreover, alone or joining forces with other local partners, Barcelona is an active player in the EU funding and resource game.

As a consequence, both the President of Catalonia, Jordi Pujol, and the Mayor of Barcelona, Pasquall Maragall, are increasingly involved in European politics. While the former has been president of the Assembly of European Regions (ARE) since June 1992, the latter was appointed to chair the Council of Municipalities and Regions of Europe in January 1992. Both Catalan politicians were involved in negotiating the setting-up of the Committee of the Regions which was established by the Maastricht Treaty. The committee's political board reveals rather clearly the importance of the new European institution for both Catalan leaders. Although the president of Catalonia refrained from presenting himself as a candidate for the presidency of the committee, he strongly supported the candidacy of its first President, Jacques Blanc. Blanc is also President of Languedoc-Roussillon and is involved with Pujol in the trans-Pyrenean Euro-region project. In addition, Pasquall Maragall, the Mayor of Barcelona, was elected as first vice-President with the proviso that the regions will support him for the position of President of the Committee in 1996.

Catalan political activism in Europe is further reinforced by initiatives aimed at promoting transnational co-operation – that is, without geographical contiguity – and cross-border co-operation with other local and regional partners. The 'Four Motors of Europe' (FME) and 'Eurocities' groups both relate to the first type of functional co-operation. The FME is a mutual co-operation agreement established in 1988 among Baden-Württemberg, Catalonia, Lombardy and Rhône-Alpes, with Wales and Ontario involved as associate partners. The agreement covers such diverse matters as foreign economic relations, economic co-operation, technology transfer, promoting research and development, environment and culture policies. Besides regular presidential meetings, permanent working-groups and bilateral exchanges, co-operation among the four regions is mainly carried out on an informal basis, leaving more room for bottom-up initiatives promoted by companies, chambers of commerce, business associations, research centres and other public and private agents (Bacaria, 1992). Clearly, technological innovation has been chosen as the core of the co-operative experience (Borrás, 1993; Colletis, 1991).

Likewise, in the later 1980s, the city of Barcelona has been very active in creating a transnational network made up of major European cities, known as 'Eurocities' presently integrating more than 60 European cities. This network emphasizes the crucial role of the cities as a source of economic innovation and social and cultural integration. By increasing functional co-operation among its members, Eurocities would like to behave as one main axis of territorial cohesion within the EU. The organization, which has already set up an office in Brussels, demands more political attention and financial subsidies for urban problems from the European institutions.

The second approach may be seen in the trans-Pyrenean Euro-region, promoted by the government of Catalonia, and the C-6 Network, promoted by the city of Barcelona. Despite coincidences and complementarities, both in terms of territorial range and policy goals, the C-6 Network and the Euro-region are competitive projects which are based on different political strategies aimed at reshaping the European space: the Europe of the Cities and the Europe of the Regions.

THE C-6 NETWORK

The C-6 Network is the result of a co-operation agreement signed by six French and Spanish regional capitals, the main objective of which is to promote a macro-Mediterranean region within the framework of the EU. It was officially created in September 1990, following a proposal on co-operation, made in 1989 by the mayor of Barcelona to his counterparts in Montpellier, Palma de Mallorca, Zaragoza, Toulouse and Valencia. Previously, one technical committee had been set up to explore the main features of future co-operation among the six cities.

Two significant factors connected with political and economic developments in Barcelona provide an explanation for the creation of this network. First, there was the need to rethink the role of Barcelona after the abolition of its metropolitan government in 1988, after a bitter struggle between the city council and the regional government which feared the institutional power of the metropolitan government (Morata, 1992). Second, there was the need to take advantage of the economic opportunities generated by the Olympic Games in 1992. In 1988, the city government of Barcelona put forward a strategic economic and social plan, Barcelona 2000, which aimed at promoting the central city and its metropolitan area both in Spain and in Europe. The proposal placed special emphasis on the transformations which were likely to affect the city in the near future (PEES, 1990):

- the consequences of Spanish entry into the EC and the new perspectives linked to the implementation of the Single European Market;
- the configuration of a European macro-region within a radius of 350 km around Barcelona and the configuration of an urban system within this area;
- the transformations resulting from the Olympic Games in terms of urban renewal, technological innovation and economic prosperity.

Local government assumed the leadership of the process, giving priority to the involvement of the main public and private interests operating in the city and its metropolitan area. The executive committee of the plan consisted of ten public and private institutions (the city council, the Chamber of Commerce and Industry, the Barcelona Fair, the main business associations, trade unions, the Port and the University of Barcelona) which decided to discuss and establish common strategies. In addition, the General Council of the Plan reunited 190 members of the most representative public and private organizations operating in the city (city council, central government delegations, regional government, public companies, professional associations, political parties, banking and credit institutions, and multinationals, among others).

With regard to the implementation process, each one of the 19 measures which developed the strategic baselines of the plan were assigned to a group composed of members of the organizations involved in the formulation phase. The main task fulfilled by the groups was the elaboration of periodic reports stating the actions to be undertaken in order to carry out different measures. Monitoring functions were also carried out on the basis of periodic reports stating progress made in the implementation of the plan.

The C-6 project largely draws inspiration from Eurocities (Barcelona, 1990). This network emphasizes the role of the cities as a source of economic innovation, social and cultural integration. By increasing functional co-operation among its members, Eurocities would like to behave as one main axis of territorial cohesion within the EU.

However, compared with Eurocities, the C-6 network presents greater territorial homogeneity and seeks more specific goals. The capital cities constitute a macro-region of 16.5 million inhabitants – five per cent of the entire EU population – over an area of 180,623 sq km, eight per cent of the whole EU territory. One significant characteristic relates to the fact that the area is structured through a cities system in which Barcelona plays a central role. Moreover the six cities share three significant characteristics: a high economic and demographic presence at the regional level; the strong economic impact of each city on its respective hinterland; and the fact they are administrative capitals. With regard to the economic structure, the six regions have close similarities: the predominance of medium and small industries; the presence of multinational companies; a highly developed tourism sector; export-oriented productive structures; an insufficiently developed communications network; innovative policies of economic management and business promotion at the local level (Carreño, 1991). Finally, the six cities share a set of common values related to the Mediterranean culture.

The Declaration of Zaragoza, signed by the six mayors in 1991, underlined the existence of common interests among the respective cities and the common will to establish stable co-operation on the basis of four main considerations:

- Within the system of European cities, the C-6 Network presents specificities based on factors such as economic complementarities, territorial contiguity, interpenetration of the respective hinterlands, communication and transport flows, and the fact of belonging to the north-western Mediterranean axis.
- The urban dynamics of each of the six cities, as well as efforts aimed at improving the quality of life and accessibility, will generate synergies which should increase their economic attractiveness.
- The effective exchange of innovation among both the cities and the economic and social actors will improve the definition of a strategy for transforming and developing the whole Network.
- The network represents a potential contribution to strengthening the current processes of integration and territorial cohesion within the EU.

The central idea is that the effective circulation of public and private innovation among the six cities will lead to the definition of a common strategy for transforming and modernizing the whole network.

In addition to the lack of legal instruments to cope with this new kind of local transnational co-operation, the organizational framework reflects a clear option for functional decentralization. It has been decided to set up an executive committee chaired every six months by each of the cities in alphabetical order. The chairing city also assumes the network secretariat.

Tasks are performed through six technical committees of co-operation including tourism, universities, software, historical centres, environment and communications. The first of these, co-ordinated by Barcelona, is intended to foster both tourism exchanges among the six cities and the promotion of the whole area abroad. The second one, so-called 'University Europol', attempts to gather university-available resources with the aim of formulating joint projects in professional training on water and environmental resources, public health economy, foreign languages, software applied to small and medium-sized industries and transport regulation. Under the co-ordination of Montpellier, the project is carried out through a network involving universities, industries and local administrations. The software committee is responsible for elaborating both a database on tourism supply and software programmes on financial management for European local governments. Starting with the previous common experiences of urban renewal, the historical centres committee, which is located in Valencia, has set up a programme to co-ordinate the different policy areas dealing with the problem (economy, small trade, transport, urban planning). The environment committee, placed under the co-ordination of Zaragoza, is carrying out studies intended to improve the future implementation of the 1991 EU directive on sewage treatment. It is also developing a computerized system of industrial sewage control as well as a common database on the environment, integrated in the EU programme TECHWARE. Finally, Toulouse co-ordinates the communications committee, aimed at reducing the present infrastructure deficit with two priorities: developing the transport network among the five continental cities and improving the railway system.

THE EURO-REGION

The North-West Mediterranean Euroregion is a regional association of cross-border co-operation, established in October 1991 by the presidents of Catalonia, Languedoc-Roussillon and Midi-Pyrénées. Comprising 10.6 million inhabitants, the Euro-region covers an area of 105,000 sq km. This represents five per cent of the total EU area and is larger than the surface areas of Benelux, Ireland or Denmark. From 1989, the three presidents held annual conferences in preparation for the formal agreement. The Euroregion seeks to promote closer relations among the three regions which present common characteristics and share common concerns (Euroregion, 1993). The main objective is to create a consistent framework providing a coherent space for economic, scientific and cultural development through horizontal and sectoral programmes of co-operation including:

- cross-border co-operation both to overcome shortcomings linked to the fact of the border and to face socio-economic problems created by the implementation of the Single European Market;
- inter-regional co-operation in policy fields of their respective competences;
- the international promotion of the Euro-region.

Furthermore, the inter-regional agreement foresees the cross-border co-operation of local governments, universities, research centres, chambers of commerce, and industrial and professional associations. The three regions strongly supported the first Pyrenean INTERREG programme.

The organizational structure includes four bodies: the Conference of the Presidents, the tripartite Committee of Co-operation, the working groups and the Secretariat. The Presidents usually meet once a year to take stock of current developments regarding co-operation actions and to approve the programme for the following year. They can also meet at any moment to take a common position on some relevant issue. The Tripartite Committee, which is composed of regional officials, sets up the annual programme of co-operation submitted to the conference. In addition, it performs three main tasks: common actions monitoring; proposing new actions; and establishing the budget. It also reports annually on the effective implementation of programmes. The working-groups are made up of regional experts responsible for implementing the several projects included in the programmes. There are six working groups and each region co-ordinates two of them: 'communications and telecommunications', and 'culture, tourism, youth and sports' are coordinated by Catalonia; 'industries, economic environment and professional training', and 'environment and quality of life' are coordinated by Midi-Pyrénées; and 'research and development and technology transfer', and 'agriculture and fisheries' are coordinated by Languedoc-Roussillon. Finally, the secretariat rotates biannually among the three regions.

In recent years priority has been given by the Euroregion to the following issues:

- exchange of experiences concerning the EC programmes in which the three regions participate;
- setting up coordination structures aimed at harmonizing regional cross-border interventions;
- improving cross-border communications;
- supporting and promoting joint ventures;
- increasing commercial and professional exchanges;
- organization of conferences on Research and Development policy;
- university and cultural exchanges;
- setting up a common data base on coastal resources; increasing co-operation on cross-border nature areas protection;
- running a summer university on the environment.

TABLE 1
EURO-REGION AND C-6 POPULATION AND SURFACE AREA

Area	Surface Area (sqkm)	Population (m)
Catalonia	32,000	6.1
Languedoc-Roussillion	27,400	2.1
Midi-Pyrénées	45,350	2.4
Total Euro-region	104,750	10.6
Aragon	44,669	1.2
Balearic Islands	5,014	0.8
Valencia	23,305	3.9
Total C–6	177,738	16.5
EU–12*	23,614,000	344.9

* Source of EU–12 figures: Brettschneider *et al.*, 1994

FINAL REMARKS

Detailed analysis of the effective working of these experiences would at this point be somewhat premature. Empirical analysis will be necessary to fill the information gaps necessary to evaluate the real effectiveness of both projects in terms of political and institutional innovation. Whereas the attitudes of the various public actors involved seem to be quite positive, specific research regarding the implementation of the various programmes and the mobilization of social and private interests is still lacking, as is information on financial resources allocated to different activities. Therefore, it is preferable to conclude with some general remarks aimed at stressing some similarities and divergences between the Euro-region and the C-6 Network as well as potentialities and limitations affecting such a co-operation.

First, both experiments are clearly linked to the new dynamics of European integration. On the one hand, changes at the EU level are leading local and regional governments to form partnerships with their counterparts in order to lobby EU decision-making centres, by-passing national governments. On the other hand, the removal of the economic boundaries encourages the emergence of new patterns of interterritorial co-operation beyond traditional cross-border co-operation. It allows the configuration of new spaces of supraregional integration in southern Europe to enhance competitive capacities vis-à-vis northern Europe. Since it is provided with rather consistent political, economic and cultural cohesion, Catalonia potentially plays a leadership role in the West Mediterranean Arc.

Although Barcelona is the strongest Mediterranean metropolitan area, both in demographic and economic terms, it lacks a metropolitan government capable of taking more advantage of its new centrality. Hence, it is not surprising that the city is trying to strengthen its potentialities through the C-6 Network. Co-operation among the six cities should lead to substantial economies of scale, while lobbying activities should provide the network with internal cohesion and external visibility.

While the involvement of local governments is almost non-existent in the case of the Euro-region – leaving aside the small municipalities included in the Community INTERREG programme – the regions almost ignore the C-6 cities network. Capital cities increasingly tend to dominate their hinterlands, which creates conflicts with regional governments' attempts to shape territorial areas. Although in this first stage of co-operation, institutional sectarianism is supposed to increase competition, in the long term conflicts could dramatically weaken both structures since they are closely interdependent. It is unlikely that private interest groups would support such a mismatch. At least, financial resources should be allocated on a complementary basis to avoid inefficiencies and lobbying activities should be co-ordinated. Moreover, economic projects should be encompassed within cultural ones (that is, common values based on linguistic similarities, popular traditions, art initiatives and common environmental resources such as the Pyrénées and the Mediterranean coast).

Institutional and political aspects should be taken into consideration too. The Catalan government possesses a considerable amount of political and financial resources, while the two French regions are much more dependent on central and local authorities to decide and implement programmes. On the other hand, administrative and institutional disparities are less acute at the local level.

A more general problem relates to organizational shortcomings affecting co-operation structures. International co-operation among administrations is further affected by problems of communication and public management. There is a lack of resources and procedures allowing public actors to act efficiently. This explains why co-operation can be considered as a mutual learning process. Efficiency only appears in the medium and long terms when the structure is able to provide for the following four objectives: mutual adjustment and adaptation of each member in order to face its commitments; permanent monitoring of shared responsibilities; financial transparency; and evaluation of each project in cost-benefit terms.

Last but not least, the present lack of transparency and thus of democratic accountability on both projects will continue until a Euro-region provided with some kind of democratic representation is created.

15

Local Political Classes and Economic Development. The Cases of Abruzzo and Puglia in the 1970s and 1980s

SIMONA PIATTONI

STILL THE SOUTHERN QUESTION

Despite recent political changes and economic upheavals, the southern question still looms large in Italian political and economic affairs. Many problems today on top of the agenda are perceived as being directly or indirectly connected to the persistence of an economic, political and possibly a cultural gap between the north and the south of the country. The electoral success of the Lombard League in the north and the revival of the Movimento Sociale Italiano (MSI) in the south are arguably the political expression of this dualism. That these parties, which on many social and economic issues take opposite stands, had to accept an uneasy cohabitation in the Berlusconi government is a sign, at the same time, of the existence of the gap and of the difficulty of closing it.

While the southern question appears to be far from solved, the scholarly debate on it has somewhat subsided. This paradoxical situation is due more to a lack of new ideas, and to a widespread sense of disillusionment, than to a decreased intensity of the problem. The debate on the 'southern question' has revolved for many years around a few unchallenged propositions that, I believe, have pushed scholarly reflection into an intellectual cul-de-sac: that the economic gap is a reflection of a deeper socio-cultural gap, and that politics has been instrumental in preserving this gap despite state efforts to engineer an economic catch-up. Underlying these are the equally unchallenged assumptions that, despite its evident internal differentiation, the south can be treated as one relatively homogeneous area and that the north-south disparity is still more significant than any intra-south (or intra-north) inequality.

This chapter refutes the above assumptions and tries to push the scholarly debate forward by advancing a few contentious propositions. Intra-south differences are significant and, if studied in detail, may direct our attention to the factors that can explain the economic success of some southern regions and the disappointing performance of others. Insistence on the supposedly deep-seated social and cultural differences between north and south fossilizes the debate around the wrong conceptual categories and fosters a sense of false impotence. Politics, far from being irrelevant or altogether deleterious for southern development, has played a fundamental role in the development of the most successful southern regions.

By analysing the pattern of industrialization of four provinces in two southern regions, this chapter tries to capture the internal differentiation of the south and highlight the fundamental link between politics and economics. By changing the unit of analysis, we can not only put in due relief the independent and often positive role of politics for economic development, but also see successful cases next to disappointing or dismal ones.

The provincial level was selected as the most appropriate for studying the interconnection between politics and economics instead of the equally plausible regional and communal ones. Patterns of industrialization in Italy are a rather localized phenomenon, often involving areas smaller than the province. 'Industrial districts' and 'company towns' are obvious cases in point. However, also in these cases it is assumed that the province largely reflects the economic configuration of the district or town, so that the analysis can be safely carried out at this level of analysis. Moreover, as economic data are most commonly organized by province, sub-national economic analysis normally takes place at this level. Postwar politics, too, had a strong local component: most national-level political leaders had their strongholds in a given electoral district (which most frequently coincides with a group of provinces or a whole region). Despite the rise of regions in the

1970s, party structures retained their strong provincial articulation, so that the province is still the level at which political games and strategies are devised and implemented.

The selection of four provinces belonging to two southern regions (and two electoral districts) is thus aimed at allowing a double comparison. By keeping the pattern of industrialization (from the top or from the bottom) constant and varying politics, I will show that economic success is crucially determined by the behaviour of the local political leaders. By keeping politics (the region or electoral district) constant and varying the economic strategy, I will instead prove that, contrary to widespread belief, no single strategy works best in the south, but that development can tread many paths. This chapter will thus argue that the constellation of power at the local level explains why some southern provinces and regions managed to develop while others, which had also displayed a good economic performance in the 1970s, fell once again behind in the 1980s and early 1990s.

In what follows, I first review the existing literature on the southern question to underscore the common assumptions and contentions that characterize it, and to argue that only a change in focus and unit of analysis can allow us to account for the south's internal differentiation and explain successful as well as failed cases of development. I then propose a scheme for interpreting southern politics that moves beyond the worn-out category of clientelism to show how traditional clientelistic practices can be used to rather different ends and can produce rather different outcomes. Finally, I produce evidence from my four case studies to show how politics is responsible for the different degree of success with which similar strategies of industrialization have been pursued in the south in the postwar period. To conclude, I show how the incentives inherent in the political situation of Abruzzo and Puglia in the 1970s and 1980s induced the local leaders to adopt the strategies that generated the different clientelistic styles of government proposed in this paper.

POLITICAL INSTITUTIONS AND ECONOMIC DEVELOPMENT

The literature on the Italian Mezzogiorno is immense. Yet, little of it, geared as it is towards the explanation of southern overall underdevelopment, helps us understand the south's internal diversity and the successful development of some of its provinces, let alone the positive role that politics can play for economic development.

In the 1950s and early 1960s, economic studies of the south dominated the scholarly debate, reflecting the technical approach to the southern question adopted by the public authorities. On the basis of this scholarly production, the Italian state often adopted policies aimed at fostering a process of industrialization from the top. In the late 1960s and 1970s, it was the sociological and political science studies which became more prominent. Scholars had started to realize that the 'southern question' was not a purely technical question, to be handled according to the economic rulebook, but was complicated by social and cultural factors. They argued that development could not simply be engineered, but required the preliminary transformation of the underlying socio-cultural structure. This influenced policy-making and contributed to a partial modification of state policies in the south.

In the 1980s, the economic theories which had guided state action in the south were thoroughly challenged and an altogether new approach to southern underdevelopment was called for. The emergence of clusters of successful small firms in the Italian northeast and centre induced some scholars to suggest that the industrial district strategy could be usefully applied in the south as well. As the industrial district had sprung up in areas traditionally untouched by state intervention, proponents of this alternative strategy of industrialization from the bottom often premised it on the discontinuation of the old development policies. Opponents insinuated that the adoption of this strategy would simply mask the retrenchment of the state from the southern question, which had become too costly, both economically and politically. The debate that ensued produced little conclusive evidence, but rather a sense of general disillusionment and scepticism.

Despite differences in analysis and recommendations, the existing literature shares two common characteristics. First, it treats the south as one homogenous underdeveloped area with a single cultural, social and political profile. Second, it pays exclusive attention to the deep-structural causes of southern underdevelopment, thus conveying a false sense of immobility. The unquestionable economic development of some southern provinces and the independent and creative role of the local political classes are consequently overlooked. These common shortcomings are particularly evident in the political science literature which should put politics at the core of its analysis. Instead, this literature too sees politics, at best, as an intervening variable that cannot modify the impact of the deep-structural social and cultural factors.

Cultural explanations of southern underdevelopment have been proposed by Banfield (1958) and, more recently, by Putnam (1993). Banfield's work, although couched in anthropological terms, is in reality a theoretical treatise in the external and internal conditions for the existence of diffuse distrust in the south. External circumstances – the extreme uncertainty of the economic context – and mental attitudes – the generalized assumption that each individual will act to maximize the material, short-run advantage of the nuclear family – explain why the inhabitants of Montegrano, the town that Banfield selected as prototypical of the whole south, did not engage in collaborative enterprises. They thus forfeited the opportunity to learn the virtues of collective action and failed to develop that social capital of trust, on the basis of which more daring collaborative enterprises can be performed, in a self-reinforcing virtuous circle of shared values and economic progress.

The same amoral familist ethos that characterized Montegrano's peasants in their economic and social dealings also affected the way in which they saw politics and their political action. The Montegranesi, in fact, were politically passive, unstable in their partisan preferences and incapable of working through their representatives to improve their material lot. Their mistrust of public authorities and their belief in the corruptness of all public officials induced them to avoid involvement in politics as much as possible and, at most, use their vote as a token in exchange for personal favours. Thus it is explained how clientelism could grow even in the most politically barren environment of Montegrano.

More recently, Putnam has argued that the southerners' lack of trust in one another and their incapacity to engage in collective enterprises, and conversely the mutual trust of the northerners and their capacity to carry out collective action, can be traced back to the solutions that were devised in the twelfth century to the endemic problem of securing external borders and ensuring law and order within them. While in the south, the Norman kings took care of external and internal enemies, but also imposed their centralized control on all forms of social and economic enterprises, in the north, the citizens themselves provided for their external and internal security, and regulated their social and economic interactions. Consequently, while southerners learned the importance of tending to the solidity of their ties to power in order to secure their physical and economic survival, northerners cumulated collaborative enterprises and a stock of mutual trust that still characterizes the way in which they interact with power today. 'Clientelism' is thus contrasted to 'civicness' as the hallmarks of politics in the two halves of the country.

That distrust and cynicism inhibit collective action both in the economic and in the political spheres is a well-accepted contention. Healthy and dynamic societies are assumed to develop collective structures to regulate social and political interactions. The diffusion of collective structures of interaction, next to dyadic structures that prevail in the private sphere, ensures that in their public dealings, individuals learn to base their behaviour on deferred rewards and general principles rather than on immediate rewards. Graziano (1974) has developed this point further.

The legitimation of power, which transforms power in authority, and the emergence of an organized opposition are intrinsically collective processes which require the supersession of dyadic relationships. More generally, only the type of exchange mediated by common values makes the functioning of complex social structures possible and allows for that process of institutionalization – that is, the 'explication' of the norms that rule collective behaviour – which characterizes stable and efficient mass societies (Graziano, 1974: 43).

But how exactly do social and political structures of exchange influence economic development? The paradox of the market is that, in order to function, it needs something which it cannot generate. This something is trust. Market exchanges, says Graziano, are typically dyadic, for goods and services are exchanged immediately and personally. They contain in themselves all the incentives for their successful execution and do not need – nor do they tend to generate – more general and impersonal principles than the satisfaction of the actors' preferences. Yet, although each exchange taken in isolation may be so regulated, in the aggregate, the market needs structures and principles which it cannot generate and which it must borrow from the social and the political spheres. These structures and principles, according to transaction cost economists, are meant to avoid those opportunistic behaviours that would eventually jeopardize the functioning of the market.

The market borrows the solution of its capital problem from the political institutions which enforce property rights and contracts. The state, by socializing the costs of the credible enforcement of contracts, makes transactions among economic actors possible (North, 1990). While this is a primary requirement for the functioning of the market, it is often not enough. High levels of economic development can be reached only by those societies in which economic actors succeed in establishing trust relations among themselves and in engaging in collaborative enterprises, whose boundaries are flexible and subject to continuous renegotiation (Sabel, 1993). In this second task, political institutions are flanked by social and cultural institutions which facilitate communication among economic actors and often provide a first test-case for future economic interactions. Hence, political and social institutions 'square the market's circle' and allow it to bring about economic development.

The different nature of social and political institutions in the north and the south of Italy thus explains the different economic development of the two halves of the country. The cynicism and disaffection that characterize state-citizens relations in the south, and the clientelistic mode of interaction between voters and politicians, are traced back to the fragmented nature of the southern social structure. As Tarrow puts it:

> *Clientelismo* is a pattern of political integration that is linked directly to the inflexibility, disjunctiveness and fragmentation of the stratification system of the Mezzogiorno; it is characteristic of fragmented systems passing from a traditional to a modern organization of social roles. Hence politics is nonideological, broad functional interests cannot be expressed and access to authority can expand only through the further vertical extension of clientele links. One reaches the structure of authority not by merging one's demands with parallel demands of others, but by linking oneself to a hierarchical chain of personal acquaintance that reaches power holders at the higher level (Tarrow, 1967: 74-5).

Thus, for both Tarrow and Graziano, the incomplete transition of the south to capitalism is, at the same time, cause and consequence of the persistence of particularistic relationships in all spheres of social life. The incapacity of southerners to form categorical associations to further their common interests, and their cynical rejection of secondary associations as illegitimate and corrupt, resulted in what Graziano calls a 'totalitarian conception and practice of power' (Graziano, 1974: 358). This amounts to conceiving social conflict as a struggle amongst factions and demanding from the state private protection and selective access to the spoils of government. No-one in the south seems to know what the common good is. Rather, joining in a clientele remains the sole antidote to the exclusive and discriminatory use of authority. As the provision of collective goods is unproductive in gaining political influence, so the argument goes, all state functions – including justice, taxation and defence – are performed in a discriminatory way.

Clientelism is thus the way in which southerners are integrated into the political system. Even after the Second World War, when universal suffrage was introduced and veritable mass political parties could develop, clientelist politics did not give way to principled politics in the south. Rather, clientelism was reinterpreted and updated. As the new political leaders enjoyed no personal or social prestige independently from the party, they had to engage in mass patronage. 'Clientelism of the notables' thus became 'clientelism of the bureaucracy':

[As] political power shifts from prestigious individuals to party organizations without a corresponding rise in political ideology, patronage must take the place of personal loyalty as a basis of affiliation. But it is patronage channelled through an organization rather than through a chain of individuals. It is the mass patronage of the modern state and mass party, distributed within the framework of a progressive programme for economic development (Tarrow, 1967: 325-7).

For these authors, then, just as for Banfield and Putnam, social structures and cultural values determine politics. The socially fragmented and ideologically totalitarian environment of the south stifled southern economic development in the postwar period. Clientelism caused underdevelopment by preserving and strengthening vertical links at the expense of horizontal ones, by stifling the formation of an organized opposition to power and rather co-opting it through patronage, and by inhibiting the accumulation of trust and breeding cynicism and distrust (Gambetta, 1988). Moreover, clientelism also negatively affected policy-making. Decisions guided by clientelistic criteria normally failed to meet economic rationality standards and thus led to sub-optimal and wasteful results. Yet since the power base of the political leaders lay in their mediating role between the state and the citizenry, these policies served to reproduce the objective conditions for the mediating role of the politicians (Gribaudi, 1980).

At the heart of the non-economic literature on the Italian south, then, are two assumptions which render these studies unable to explain the recent economic success of some southern areas. The first is that, although the importance of political institutions for economic development is widely acknowledged, the performance of these institutions is explained by underlying structural and cultural factors. Thus, any independent effect of politics on development is ruled out. The second is that the structural and cultural features of a society perpetuate themselves by self-reinforcing processes that tend to push initially different societies onto increasingly divergent paths. Consequently, the possibility that social systems might start to converge again, or might simply tread different paths, is overlooked.

In the following sections, an alternative argument on the role of local political classes for economic development is proposed. By political class, I mean both the national representatives elected from the provinces under examination and the regional and local representatives. The next section will argue that, by looking at clientelism in its own terms, that is, as a political strategy for gaining and maintaining power, it becomes possible to identify a variety of styles of clientelistic government which, although superficially similar, nevertheless operate according to rather different logics and produce widely different results in terms of economic development. The last two sections argue that the different degrees of success with which the four provinces that are focus of this study managed to weather the crisis of the 1980s and early 1990s, and keep up the growth spurt of the 1970s, depended on the ability of the local political classes to help the local economies tackle the necessary restructuring.

DIFFERENT STYLES OF CLIENTELISTIC POLITICS

Patronage can be defined as an 'informal contractual relationship between persons of unequal status and power, which imposes reciprocal obligations of a different kind on each of the parties' (Silverman, 1965: 296). The contract is never formally drawn and the obligations never fully specified. Generally speaking, these relationships aim at a large and unspecified series of performances of mutual assistance. The patron-client relationship presupposes the availability of alternative, fully legitimate channels of access to desired resources, for example, markets. By entering patron-client relations, the clients give up access to markets except through the mediation of the patrons, because of the supposedly lower benefits or higher costs that direct access would entail.

> The client 'buys' protection against the exigencies of the markets or of nature or of the arbitrariness or weakness of the centre or against the demands of other powerful groups or individuals. The price he pays for it is not just a specific service, but the acceptance of the patron's control of the client's access to markets and public goods, as well as of his ability to convert fully some of his resources (Eisenstadt and Roniger, 1981: 281).

Historically, the clients have had little actual choice, as the patrons stood 'guard over the critical junctures or synapses of relationships which connect the system to the larger whole' (Wolf, 1956; quoted by Silverman, 1965: 294). Nowadays, this is less true. Today, insofar as they are willing to accept the mediation of the patrons to obtain resources which they could access through more legal and legitimate channels, the clients freely underwrite the clientelist contract.

The literature on clientelism claims that the main goal of the patrons (the local politicians) is to preserve their uneven power position vis-à-vis the clients (the citizens) by mediating between the centre and the periphery in such a way as to reproduce the dependence of the periphery on the centre and, therefore, perpetuate their mediating role (Gribaudi, 1980; Chubb, 1982). From this assumption derive a number of behavioural consequences. First, the patrons will seek to avoid any real economic integration of the areas under their control into the national and international economy, because the introduction of market channels of access to desired resources would challenge their power. Second, the patrons will seek to prevent the formation of secondary associations among clients, as these would represent a potential threat to the personalistic and vertical relationship that links each client to his patron. The vertical and atomizing way in which the clientele system integrates each citizen into the political system through a chain of personal relationships with powerful individuals should already prevent the aggregation of political demands, defuse conflicts and pre-empt the formation of an organized opposition. However, the patrons might also deploy additional tactics – most probably a mix of threat and persuasion, fear and affection – in order to keep their clients individually tied to them.

If, in order to retain their power, the patrons wilfully try to preserve the economic backwardness of the areas under their control, does not this constitute a breach of the patron-client contract? Or, in Chubb's formulation, 'Given the undisputed failure of [Palermo's] local government not only to provide essential public services but even to guarantee the functioning of normal administrative activities, how can the unbroken electoral success of the Christian Democrat Party (DC) in the past 30 years be explained?' (Chubb, 1982: 3). Scholars of clientelism believe that, far from being contradictory, clientelist politics and economic backwardness imply one another. Given the general scarcity of resources in a situation of economic backwardness, what clients ask from their patrons is not economic development – a public good that benefits all if it benefits some – but personal material advantages. However, material advantages are also in short supply and patrons may be unable at any given moment to satisfy all the clients' requests. Moreover, as limited resources are allocated according to clientelistic criteria – that is, criteria which do not command legitimacy and are, therefore, incapable of providing an accepted justification for the existing distribution of resources – there will be no self-enforced upper limit to the demands of the clients and inflation will ensue. As a consequence, clientelism should collapse under the weight of its own contradictions or, paraphrasing a famous expression, it will cause the 'fiscal crisis of the polity'. Refuting this conclusion, Chubb showed that clientelism entails not just the exchange of material favours for votes, but also the exchange of those products of the public administration (permits, licences, authorizations, etc.) that do not cost the patrons any money, but have a big economic impact on the clients. 'The essence of clientelism lies ... in the skilful manipulation of scarcity. ... The patron-client bond ... is dependent not on a continuous stream of benefits, but rather on sustaining the expectation of rewards in the maximum number of people with the minimum payoffs in concrete benefits' (Chubb, 1982: 5). In this way, patrons are able to preserve their power even in the face of systematic breaches of the patron-client contract.

Given this picture of clientelism, why should a patron bother to attract investment to the area under his control? Why should he use his power to provide collective goods rather than limit himself to satisfying the clients' individual demands or simply manipulate resources so as to create the expectation of rewards in the maximum number of people with the minimum of payoff? Why should he try to create a community where parochial interests once dominated? And, finally, why should he try to reinforce market mechanisms where clientelistic methods of distribution can be used? True enough, private and public investment, even of an apparent collective nature, can be used for clientelistic purposes. Thus, highways may not be built because of their potential effect on economic growth, but because their construction creates numerous occasions for clientelistic exchanges. Similarly, firms may be attracted to an area not because of their impact on the local economy, but because the jobs that they create can be distributed among loyal clients. When such investments are realized in clientelism-ridden areas, it is almost automatically assumed that their justification lies not so much in their effective utility, but in their political fallout. As a consequence, it is also expected that these investments will be scarcely profitable and will soon fail. Any actual economic progress that should result from these investments should then be considered as unexpected and uncalled-for, as it would have the undesired consequence of weakening the dependence of the clients from their patron.

Even more puzzling is the behaviour of those patrons who seem actually to care for the area and people that they control, and maintain relationships of personal acquaintanceship, if not affection, with their clients. Students of clientelism have argued that an affective component is inherent in the patron-client relationship and that the rituals through which this component is created and maintained (for example, godfatherhood) must be understood as largely symbolic. Attending a handful of weddings and baptisms is a small cost if it ensures faithful electoral support from scores of relatives and friends for years to come. Similarly, attendance at village fairs, inaugural events and local celebrations may be interpreted as skilful and inexpensive promotional activity. Again, the creation and strengthening of community ties that might derive from these activities should be considered unexpected and undesired consequences, as they could give rise to collective identities and sustain collective actions which might challenge the power position of the patron.

This interpretation of clientelism is clearly too restrictive and is incapable of explaining the observed variety of patrons' behaviours. The interpretation I propose here, on the other hand, makes sense of the above behaviours without resorting to the notion of unforeseen consequences, but rather fully integrating them into the range of strategies available to the patrons. Patron-clients networks are interpreted as 'strategies for the maintenance and aggrandizement of power on the part of patrons and of coping and survival on the part of the clients. They are probably never the sole strategies available. ... One may often find individuals employing a number of seemingly incompatible strategies simultaneously or seriatim' (Waterbury, 1977: 332-3).

Strategies imply choice. Borrowing from the game-theoretical vocabulary, we might say that patron and clients are engaged in a two-level game. At the first level, patron and clients bargain over the terms of the contract that binds them. At this level, the relative power of the players is skewed in the patron's favour: it is he who decides who will have access to the resources which he controls. The clients are weak and divided as they compete against one another over access to the desired resources. At the second level of the game, however, the patron competes with similarly positioned patrons over access to those centrally managed resources which determine his political status and which he then has to allocate among his clients. At this level, the relative power of the players is skewed in the opposite direction, as the clients decide with their vote the amount of resources that each patron will obtain, assuming, as is the case in Italy, that resources are allocated among patrons according to the size of their clientele. At this second level, the clients have the opportunity not just of choosing amongst different patrons, but of choosing between the patronage, or clientele, system and alternative systems of resource allocation. In order to choose alternative systems, however, the clients must be able to recognize their common situation, develop structures of horizontal interaction and overcome the reciprocal mistrust that derives from their competition at the first level of the game.

As already seen, the patrons will probably try to avoid the emergence of similar relations among clients and, insofar as they do emerge, they will consider them as unforeseen and undesired consequences. However, the patrons might also employ a different strategy and play the second level of the clientelistic game in an altogether different way. They might, that is, pursue the economic development of the area which they control, gauging that this might be the best way to preserve or increase their electoral support and, consequently, preserve or increase their power vis-à-vis the centre. As has been argued by Silverman (1977), it is possible that patrons, far from trying to prevent the formation of horizontal links among clients, may indeed foster the formation of a community in the name of which they can subsequently claim resources from the centre. 'Public patronage', that is patronage exerted with respect to groups or entire communities with the aim of providing public goods, rather than political nonsense, could in fact constitute a highly sophisticated political strategy. Similarly, it is also conceivable that the clients might create secondary associations not in order to oust the patrons and replace the clientelist system, but in order to tilt in their favour the patron-client relationship. Again Silverman (1977) suggests that clients may be interested in perpetuating the myth of patronage, irrespective of the real or symbolic nature of its content, as a way of drawing the potential new patrons into local commitment.

What factors determine the respective power of patrons and clients? The existence of few competing patrons will enhance the power of each one of them *vis-à-vis* the clients while also making their claim for centrally distributed resources more likely to succeed. On the other hand, the existence of a strong opposition will give the clients greater leverage in their power game with the patrons as well as enable them to choose among patrons. Four main situations can be thus singled out by plotting the cohesiveness/divisiveness of the ruling patrons against the strength/weakness of the opposition.

TABLE 1
TYPES OF CLIENTELISTIC GOVERNMENT

	Cohesiveness/Divisiveness of Patrons	
Strength / Weakness of Opposition	Cohesive Patrons	Divided Patrons
Strong Opposition	*Virtuous clientelism* Collective goods Growing legitimacy Economic Development (Abruzzo)	*Challenged clientelism* Symbolic output Eroded legitimacy Economic involution (Campania)
Weak Opposition	*Vicious clientelism* No output No legitimacy No economic development (Sicily)	*Ineffective clientelism* Individual goods Fading Legitimacy Economic Stagnation (Puglia)

To each situation correspond specific incentives that will induce the patrons to play one or another type of clientelistic game. So, for instance, the hegemonic patrons of the box 'vicious clientelism' will have no incentive to sustain economic development, nor to provide material goods to the individual clients, as they can count on the absence of available alternatives, and probably on the existence of fear, to keep clients' dissatisfaction in check. On the contrary, the patrons of the box 'virtuous clientelism' will probably be induced by the strong opposition to foster economic development and deliver actual goods in order to maintain their hegemonic position. While in both cases patrons are powerful because they are hegemonic, in the first case they can afford to disregard the clients' demands and resort to symbolic tactics. In the second case, on the other hand, they are induced by the opposition to use their power to attract resources from the centre and to allocate them effectively in the periphery. The patrons of the right half of the table, being weak and divided, will lack the power vis-à-vis the centre to attract resources and the power vis-à-vis the periphery to enforce any given distribution. Their actions, therefore, will most likely cross-check one another and will lead to insignificant or contradictory results. Therefore, they will either be engaged in petty squabbling among themselves when faced by a weak opposition – ineffective clientelism – or challenged and eventually overthrown, when faced by a strong opposition – challenged clientelism.

The incentives entailed by any given situation, however, are not all. External shocks may propel clientelist systems from box to box, just as patrons may adopt strategies and clients create pressures capable of moving them to a different box. The latest hegemonic patron of Abruzzo, the Christian Democrat Remo Gaspari, succeeded in eliminating competing patrons and achieved full leadership within the local party and control over the entire region, thus becoming hegemonic. Conversely, after an external shock deprived Puglia of its charismatic leader, the Christian Democrat Aldo Moro, the remaining patrons failed to recompose their internal quarrels and regain hegemony, thus allowing prospective patrons to gain some power and complicate the regional political landscape. Moreover, Abruzzo's leader used his hegemonic power to support the opposition – the Communist Party – against the would-be patrons – members of the Socialist Party – thus preventing, at the same time, the weakening of the opposition and the strengthening of potential competitors. He chose this strategy over the alternative strategy of weakening the opposition to the point at which he could dominate uncontested. The low-equilibrium point reached by Puglia's political system, on the other hand, induced local leaders to act in order to maintain the status quo. However, if one patron had gained hegemonic power over his competitors, or if the opposition had gained sudden strength, this region's politics would have conformed to a different type of clentelism.

Clientelist systems, then, are determined by the incentives inherent in each situation, by the creative choices of the patrons but also by the reactions of the clients. Abruzzo's citizens seemed uninterested in simply changing the identity of the patrons and, contrary to what has happened in other regions, kept voting either for the existing patrons or for the opposition, thus helping maintain the system of incentives associated with virtuous clientelism. Even when at the central level an alliance between the Christian

Democratic Party and the Socialist Party suggested an overture to competing patrons, Abruzzo's voters either reconfirmed their trust in the traditional patrons by voting representatives from the hegemonic faction of the DC or signalled their wish to change the system altogether by voting PCI. Puglia's voters, on the other hand, expressed their dissatisfaction with their traditional patrons by supporting competing patrons even before centrally agreed-upon formulas granted greater power to the PSI. Their behaviour thus resulted in governmental stalemate and decision-making gridlock, two typical elements of 'ineffective clientelism'. The economic consequences of these different political situations will be examined in the next section.

THE ECONOMIC DEVELOPMENT OF ABRUZZO AND PUGLIA IN THE 1970s AND 1980s

The existence of a north-south gap is well-known. Conventional accounts show that the south drew slightly closer to the north during the 1960s and part of the 1970s, but that it lost ground since then, so that the north-south gap is as wide today as it was in the fifties (Garofoli, 1986: 53). What is less well known is that, in the last 20 years, intra-south inequalities have grown more than north-south disparities (Table 2).[1] Moreover, looking at the data disaggregated by province, it becomes evident that some southern provinces, and even entire regions, have progressed so much as to deserve to shed the attributes of backward and underdeveloped which have denoted the Mezzogiorno for so long (Table 3).

The transformation occurred in the 1970s and 1980s. The first years of the 1970s witnessed the stepped-up effort of the Italian authorities to promote southern growth by inducing public and private companies to locate their new investments in the south, according to an industrialization strategy from above. The first oil shock, and the economic crisis that ensued, caused a reconsideration of policy priorities, which now assigned highest rank to the overhaul of the northern industries. The crisis, however, far from halting southern development, allowed some southern entrepreneurs to take advantage of the difficulties experienced by northern and foreign firms to insert themselves into particular market segments and begin a process of industrialization from below. Similarly, the restructuring that, at the beginning of the 1980s, public companies in the south were forced to undertake, while destroying the precarious equilibrium somehow reached between outside firms and local society, released human and financial resources which became available for re-employment by local entrepreneurs. The 1970s and 1980s, therefore, by upsetting the growth patterns and economic hierarchies established after the war, constitute a watershed in the history of the development of the Mezzogiorno.

Industrialization From Above

L'Aquila and Taranto constitute examples of the strategy of industrialization from above pursued by the Italian authorities in the 1960s. Both towns experienced, after the war, remarkable economic growth and wealth increase thanks to heavy investment by public companies. Even though the scale of industrial production differed noticeably in the two cases – at its peak, Taranto's steel-making company employed 22,000 workers while L'Aquila's telecommunications company never employed more than 6,000 – both towns shared the same alternation of heightened hopes and deep disillusionment with regard to the development of local entrepreneurship. While the objective of the strategy had been to stimulate the emergence of local firms through the presence of outside companies, the goal of the local people simply became obtaining a job in the big factory. The objective difficulty of finding a productive connection with the highly integrated processes of the public companies resulted in a dearth of local industrial enterprises. The opportunity for a turnaround came at the beginning of the 1980s, when the two public companies entered a deep crisis and were forced to restructure.

Italtel, the state telecommunications company of L'Aquila, had to change its production line from electromechanical to electromagnetic telephone switches, which required both a reduction and a requalification of the labour force. The 3,000 workers who became redundant were induced to join early retirement schemes or were simply laid off, but many were re-employed by other firms of the IRI group present in the area. At the same time, Italtel hired some 300 engineers, mostly from other parts of Italy or Europe. The restructuring of Italtel was successful, allowing the firm to become profitable and start investing again. However, the characteristics of the electronics industry are such that periodic shedding and requalification of the labour-force are permanent, rather than episodic, features of this company. This creates recurrent problems that the local authorities need to solve if they want the economy of L'Aquila to keep growing.

The vicissitudes of the state steel-making company, Italsider, are fundamentally similar. The construction of the plant, in the early 1960s, attracted many engineering construction companies from the north and induced the creation of a few local firms as well. When the construction of the plant was completed, these firms stayed on and survived by carrying out the numerous repair jobs that were continuously needed in the steel plant of Taranto. This survival strategy seemed to pay off when, in 1968, it was decided to double the productive capacity of the plant. Yet more firms were attracted to Taranto and those already present expanded their work force. The cosy, but costly, relationship that developed between state company and subcontracting firms bred a superpaid and protected work-force that eventually was to feel the consequences of the plant's restructuring.

The restructuring entailed a complete reformulation of work relations between state company and subcontracting firms, and the shedding of half of the work-force directly and indirectly employed by the state company. The increase in productivity, brought about by higher automation, work-force requalification and a gamut of management improvements, was momentous and the impact on the local economy was equally heavy. The restructuring process succeeded in restoring profitability, but only for a short time. Thus, also in this case, the problems that Taranto had to face required the active involvement of the local political class.

The economic crisis of the 1980s thus unveiled the limits of the strategy of industrialization from above. The expected upstream and downstream linkages with local enterprises had failed to materialize or had failed to launch local firms onto autonomous growth paths. Given the magnitude of the public companies and the repercussions of their restructuring on the local economy, the local authorities were asked to intervene. In particular, they were called to moderate often very harsh industrial conflicts, attract new investment from outside, and foster the creation of a stratum of local firms linked to the existing ones but also capable of independent growth. The superior capacity of the local political class of L'Aquila, in Abruzzo, as compared to that of Taranto, in Puglia, to perform the above tasks explains why the province of L'Aquila kept growing throughout the 1980s, while that of Taranto plunged into a deep recession.

The social conflict surrounding the restructuring of Italtel was one of the harshest of that period. Local authorities, however, intervened effectively: they convinced SIP, the public company that sells telephone services, and Alenia, another public company that produces civic and military satellite communication systems, to invest and hire in the area. In this way, 2,000 workers were hired back and only 500 were laid off, induced to retire before age or handed over to the employment redundancy fund. The University of L'Aquila created within the Department of Engineering a specialization in Electronic Engineering, so that in future, local companies could hire engineers from within the area. Scholarships for carrying out research in communication technology were created and joint research projects between the university and the existing companies were developed. New firms have also been attracted to the area: Texas Instruments and Optimes, in the electronic sector, and Dompé, in the chemical sector, are among the latest arrivals, thus further defining the economic profile of the area. Finally, the Abruzzo Region is creating a technology park centred in L'Aquila which will connect in a systematic way the many private and public research facilities already present in the region and promote the creation of local high-tech firms. Some results have already been achieved: a handful of local entrepreneurs have created small firms whose production is connected to that of the existing electronic companies.

Also in Taranto, social conflict was extremely harsh. The trade unions succeeded in postponing until the early 1980s the needed rationalization and even then this was accomplished only slowly and partially. No other public or private company was induced to invest in the area, and many of the existing companies had to reduce their presence in Taranto or leave altogether. Several prospective firms have been turned down for lack of industrial areas, that is, because of the incapacity of the local authorities to designate new industrial areas or to redefine the use of old abandoned ones. Alternative projects for the revitalization of the local economy, like that of the construction of a commercial port, also did not take off because of the planning incapacity of the local authorities. The University of Bari – the capital of the Puglia Region

– proposed to offer in Taranto, which lacks a university of its own, two programmes particularly suited to the local economy: Material Engineering and Marine Biology. The offer was rejected. Not a single local firm has been created in the area since the 1970s.

Industrialization From Below

Teramo and Lecce, on the other hand, pursued a strategy of industrialization from below. In the 1970s and 1980s, both provinces experienced a remarkable growth in industrial production and firm creation that led many commentators to conclude that the industrial districts typical of north-eastern and central Italy were beginning to emerge in the south as well. In reality, neither province owes its industrial growth entirely to the process of decentralization ignited by the crisis of the early 1970s. Nuclei of artisanal tradition and industrial production were already present in both provinces since the inter-war period. In the 1980s, while the manufacturing activities that rested on local artisanal traditions underwent a process of autonomous evolution and entered national and international markets, the foreign and northern firms sometimes present in the territory started to generate a steady flow of subcontracting traffic which induced local entrepreneurs to start up new activities.

Key to the success of these new enterprises mainly engaged in the production of traditional manufactures (clothes, leather goods, furniture) were the lower production costs that the client firms incurred by subcontracting part of the production to southern firms. Lower production costs derived from lower salaries and from the various forms of financial and fiscal incentive to which these firms were entitled. In some areas, like Lecce, southern entrepreneurs could initially afford to pay their workers lower wages than those established at the national level because, in such economically depressed areas, factory jobs were so cherished that no one dared run the risk of being laid off by asking for better labour conditions. In these areas, the trade unions were effectively ignored by both workers and entrepreneurs. In other areas, like Teramo, low wages were accepted because the local population could rely also on the revenues stemming from sharecropping and small farming.

In the second half of the 1980s, however, the international situation changed again and the young southern firms were called to face new challenges. The fashion content of traditional manufactures was increasingly unable to sell Italian products on the market and foreign buyers started to demand goods that appealed more to their national taste. Also, the price of the products acquired new relevance and promptness of delivery became a major competitive advantage. Small southern firms had to equip themselves to meet these new requests, which entailed buying new machinery, selecting the labour force and improving management techniques, and resulted in increased production costs. At the same time, the new wealth that ten years of industrial activity had distributed among the local population made the labour force less willing to work for low wages. Even when outright union activity did not emerge, labour shortage problems emerged in the guise of very high turnover rates. Competition from developing countries became tougher as firms there raised the quality of their products while keeping the cost of labour at unbeatable levels. The market for southern manufactures consequently became smaller and the competition among southern firms more intense. Many firms were driven out of the market; some tried to increase the work pace while subcontracting part of their production to smaller workshops; others tried to obtain a greater share of the overall profit margin by offering their northern and foreign counterparts better services.

It soon became clear to most southern entrepreneurs that the current difficulties were of a permanent nature and that, if they wanted to appropriate the entire profit margin and withstand the increasingly tougher market conditions, they would eventually have to make the jump to independent production. This goal could be achieved through two alternative routes. The first consisted in trying to make the leap individually: many entrepreneurs tried, most failed and only a small percentage succeeded. The second route, more difficult but potentially more rewarding, had already been successfully implemented in the north-eastern regions of Italy, but required mutual trust and willingness to co-operate – two allegedly rather scarce goods in the south.

The behaviour of the local authorities could make a difference and determine whether the small southern firms would move on to high-value-added, growing market segments, or would be confined to low-value-added, shrinking niches. Local political authorities were thus called on to support the attempts of the local entrepreneurs at upscaling the quality of their production, to ease the transition to a regular system of industrial relations, and provide incentives for the continued expansion of the local economy. Once again, Abruzzo's political class performed all these tasks better.

In both provinces there had been attempts in the early 1970s to create consortia among small firms for the marketing of products in distant markets, for the purchase of expensive machinery (laser cutting stations, CAD/CAM equipment), for the training of skilled workers and the acquisition of advanced managerial and accounting techniques. In Teramo, after the first few failures, public authorities stepped in: the Chamber of Commerce of Teramo, the Abruzzo Region and a local politician are sponsoring four such consortia and service centres for small local firms. A precondition for participating in these consortia is the regularization of the fiscal situation of the firm and its system of industrial relations. Cheap, often underpaid labour was the initial asset of these areas, but later became a liability, as it induced a high turnover and discouraged the accumulation of practical knowledge. Even though the individual entrepreneurs see the advantages that could stem from gradually reaching fully regular contractual relations, they have no incentive to do this unless all others do the same. By linking the acquisition of valuable services at convenient prices through participation in the consortia to the respect of fiscal and employment regulations, the province of Teramo is reaching fully regular contractual relations.

In the province of Lecce, on the other hand, local authorities failed to support the attempts of the local entrepreneurs to create consortia similar to those of Teramo. Instead, they supported individual entrepreneurs by giving them permits to build their factories outside infrastructured industrial areas, failing to enforce national contractual agreements and indeed helping them to break the nascent local trade unions. Of the many artisans and small entrepreneurs of the province of Lecce, now only few survive and only three or four really prosper, having forced the others to turn into semi-legal workshops, which produce parts for the bigger firms. Even though these companies are quite successful and export all over Italy and Europe, they achieved their hegemony at the expense of the diffused know-how which is at the basis of the success of this type of industrialization.

THE LOCAL POLITICAL CLASSES OF ABRUZZO AND PUGLIA

As argued earlier, clientelism may not necessarily inhibit economic development. While almost certainly harmful for the healthy and correct development of the political system, clientelism may indeed sustain the development of the economy. Abruzzo seems to be a case in point. Widely considered as a prototypically clientelistic region, Abruzzo has nevertheless experienced a remarkable development which is uneasily accommodated by the explanations reviewed in the second part of this chapter. In this section, I will produce some anecdotal evidence in support of the claim that some clientelist systems may be development-sustaining while others development-inhibiting. In line with the criticisms levelled earlier against the sociological literature on the south, I will not resort to structural or cultural explanations. Rather, I will emphasize the importance of the local constellation of power, as it comes to be constructed by contingent factors, the creative strategies of the local political leaders, and the choices of the voters.

Abruzzo

Throughout the postwar period, Abruzzo has been represented at the national level by first-rate political figures. Immediately after the war, Giuseppe Spataro, one of the founders of the Popular Party, represented the region in the Constitutional Assembly and in the republican parliament – between 1948 and 1963 as a deputy, and between 1963 and 1976 as a senator. Lorenzo Natali, a follower of Fanfani under whose secretaryship he made his career, was Abruzzo's main political figure from 1948 to 1968. Between 1968 and 1972, a fierce political competition developed between Natali and Gaspari, a *doroteo* of the Taviani faction who would become Abruzzo's peak political figure in the years to come. This competition, which produced a multiplication of roads, universities and Areas of Industrialization, benefited the region as a whole and afforded it an unusually even increase of standards of living in all of its sub-areas (Rea, 1973; Mutti, 1994). Although Remo Gaspari's parliamentary career had already started in 1953, his take-off as a regional representative coincided with the formation of the *dorotei* faction and its surge to hegemony within the Christian Democratic party in 1959. In 1968, Gaspari surpassed, for the first time, his colleague and antagonist Natali in numbers of preference votes and, even though he was overtaken once more in 1972, nevertheless managed to establish his power as boss of Abruzzo, forcing Natali to abandon the fight altogether in 1979.

Between 1972 and 1992, Gaspari occupied a central position in Abruzzo's constellation of political power. He firmly controlled the DC in Abruzzo which, in its turn, firmly controlled the regional government (Table 4). After the exit of their leader from the political scene, the *nataliani* constituted an opposing faction still for some time, especially in the historical strongholds of L'Aquila and Teramo. More recently, a syndicalist faction-based in the Marsica area under the leadership of the CISL – the Catholic trade union – secretary Franco Marini, claimed to represent DC's hope for renewal and a *forlaniani* faction, guided by the vice-secretary of the Minister of Agriculture Romeo Ricciuti, challenged Gaspari's leadership in Teramo and elsewhere. However, the *gaspariani* remained in control of the regional political situation.

Abruzzo's political landscape is also characterized by scattered, although important, pockets of Communist followers. Many communes of the province of Teramo, several towns in the Fucino basin, a few centres in Pescara's proto-industrial hinterland and even a few municipalities of the province of Chieti have at some time or another been ruled by a Communist government. Gaspari himself recalls with horror the fact that, after the war, Gissi, his native town, was in Communist hands, a testimony to the diffused presence of Communist support throughout the region. Finally, a consistent neo-Fascist minority limits the DC's hegemony on the right, sometimes forcing the DC to seek its support in order to retain its hegemony. The centrist parties, and to a certain degree also the Socialist Party, never gathered more than marginal support, thus leaving the local political landscape rather simple and uncomplicated.

This particular situation – the existence of well-rooted left and right oppositions, with specific geographical strongholds in the region – may explain why Gaspari's style of government was never outrageously biased in favour of his followers. Indeed, one might argue that Gaspari used the opposition to create and maintain the hegemonic position of the DC in Abruzzo. As conversations with privileged observers have suggested, Gaspari has occasionally shown magnanimity towards Communist sympathizers, granting them unexpected favours in order to demonstrate the impartiality of his methods and probably with the hope of winning them over to his party. More regularly, local DC branches helped elect opposition councillors in order to eliminate ideologically closer, but for this reason more threatening, candidates (Messina, 1992). In this way, Gaspari achieved two notable results: he controlled the likely escalation of requests for the spoils of the system from within the governing coalition, and he kept at bay both the smaller parties, whose co-operation he occasionally needed, and the Socialist Party, which, although numerically stronger, always found itself in the uneasy situation of being neither a credible opposition party nor a necessary government ally. In fact, one of the notable features of Abruzzo's vote in all 1968-92 national elections (Table 5) has been, next to the regularly bigger size of the DC's, PCI/PDS's and MSI's vote with respect to the national figures (Table 8), the regularly smaller size of the Socialist vote. The relative weakness of the Socialist Party, as we shall see, distinguishes Abruzzo particularly from Puglia, where the PSI came to play an increasingly important role.

A second element of Gaspari's peculiar style of government has been his capacity to outwork most of his colleagues. In his 30-year-long ministerial career, many have acknowledged his pragmatic and exacting work style. Neutral witnesses have testified to his great dedication to work and organizational ability. He is known for following up on every directive he gives and making sure that, whenever he promises that something will be done, it is really done. He is also notoriously available for people, in general, and for his fellow *abruzzesi* in particular. He knows virtually everybody in Abruzzo, attends hundreds of public and private ceremonies, no matter how small and unimportant they may seem. An indicator of this attachment to his region and its people is given by the fact that, so far, the only charges that have been pressed against him in the context of the *Tangentopoli* scandals concern the alleged use for private purposes – attending the inauguration of a local fair or the meeting of a local branch of the party – of the helicopters of the police. All of the above behavioural features certainly indicate a personalistic and clientelistic style of government. Indeed, Gaspari openly professes little faith in impersonal rules and bureaucratic structures: he often declares that the bureaucracy cannot work unless one makes it work by constantly keeping track of even the minutest details. Moreover, he sees democracy as being available for the people and satisfying their requests when possible.

Finally, the third aspect of Gaspari's style of government is his economic philosophy. In his policy choices, he was apparently guided by the belief that if Abruzzo had been rescued from its natural isolation, its people had been given higher education and the main infrastructures had been built, this region could not have failed to develop. Therefore, throughout his political career, he consistently aimed at achieving these objectives. And in fact, today, Abruzzo has the highest density of roads per inhabitant of the whole country and one of the highest levels of education of the south (Centro Studi Confindustria, 1991). His efforts have also aimed to attract to Abruzzo investment from outside. His ability in securing all the necessary permits and providing the requested infrastructures to important prospective investors is by now proverbial. That his control over the region and his determination and reliability have been determining factors inducing external firms to locate their new plants in Abruzzo has been confirmed in interviews with the directors of some of the main companies in the L'Aquila area. A complementary aspect of his power is his alleged capacity to overrule some of the regulations that would otherwise slow down or constrain private investors' freedom of manoeuvre. He recounted how he arranged that an entrepreneur, who needed a particularly qualified labour force, could select the future workers regardless of the priority expressed by the unemployment list. In return, he arranged that all workers be hired in Abruzzo. While one may question the methods, their effectiveness is beyond doubt.

To conclude on Gaspari, the strengths of his governmental style have been his reliability and effectiveness. Both derived from his unquestioned control over the region's political situation, which he achieved through clearly clientelistic practices. Reduced uncertainty and credible enforcement are, as we saw in the second section, the two fundamental requirements for economic development. While their satisfaction may entail, at the political level, sub-optimal arrangements, they certainly produce positive results at the economic level. Gaspari's clientelism, thus, seems to conform to the virtuous type identified earlier. His manipulation of the opposition to keep the demand for the spoils of the system under control indicates the pursuit of a power-maintaining strategy in accord with the incentives generated by virtuous clientelism. His constant efforts at attracting investment and building infrastructures suggest a genuine interest in the economic development of the region. Moreover, Gaspari's use of his hegemonic power to uphold and strengthen market mechanisms suggests that he is not afraid of losing his electorate by allowing it to access resources through alternative channels. This strategy would make little political sense if Gaspari's objective were to keep in check his clients' demands along the lines of vicious clientelism. In the context of virtuous clientelism, on the contrary, they represent a fulfilment of the patron-client contract that is likely to increase the legitimacy of the patron in the clients' eyes and, for this reason, perpetuate his power. Gaspari's clientelist system is bolstered also by his remarkable availability and cultivation of personal, almost affective, relationships with fellow abruzzesi. It may even be argued that Abruzzo – once called Abruzzi, as if to stress its internal division into three distinct socio-economic areas – has, under his entrepreneurial leadership, become one community.

Puglia

Puglia's political landscape has been, during the entire postwar period, more fractured than Abruzzo's. First of all, Puglia's territory and population are larger and, consequently, divided into two electoral districts, which complicates the power struggle among parties and factions. Second, although Puglia has also produced a number of first-rank politicians, they somehow were never identified with the region and never played the unifying role that Gaspari played in Abruzzo.

Until 1978, the leading political figure in Puglia was Aldo Moro. According to one author (Pirro, 1983), after the war the DC fought in Puglia one of its hardest political battles. Puglia thus became a sort of laboratory in which the political formulas that would be later applied to the entire country were initially experimented. In the 1946 and 1948 elections, the DC emerged as the first political party, especially thanks to the massive support of the Church and on the basis of ideological mobilization. In 1953, on the other hand, the DC experienced heavy losses, tumbling from 48.6 per cent to 38.5 per cent. The absentee landed classes resented the agrarian reform which, even in its diluted version, had redistributed the most poorly cultivated areas to the southern peasants, while the landed bourgeoisie, which had been untouched by the reform or had even benefited from it, did not appreciate the DC's failure to protect private property, in the name of which the DC had asked for its vote only few years earlier. The DC in Puglia thus found itself squeezed between a strong left, which had successfully organized the peasant struggles for the land, and an equally pugnacious right, which was appealing to the anti-republican sentiments of the southern population in order to carry home its conservative message. The task that the DC had to fulfil, after 1953, was to 'articulate, on the base of the state, a new and larger bloc of social consensus. The pursuit of this ambitious, and in the long run victorious, strategic programme implied a veritable reconstitution of the party, which was no longer equipped, from the organizational and ideological points of view, to manage the new phase of Italian politics' (Pirro, 1983: 11).

The strategic programme consisted in restructuring the party in the image of a mass party and in reconquering the south by pushing for its industrialization in a way which would not alienate northern industrial interests. The axis of economic and political development was therefore shifted from the countryside to the urban centres, and the protagonists of party renewal became the middle classes. In 1951-2, in fact, the DC had lost the government of all five Puglia's main cities to the opposition, governments which it was now determined to win back:

> The driving force behind this vigorous campaign of political and ideological reappropriation of the region would then be embodied in policies aimed at the accelerated growth of its productive structure, to be ignited by state intervention ... which would ensure higher levels of employment, more rapid increases of incomes and a wider diffusion of welfare (Pirro, 1983: 103).

The political figure which, at the regional as well as at the national level, became the symbol of this new policy course and the spokesman of the social bloc that sustained it was Aldo Moro. Under his premiership, the centre-left government formula was experimented at the local as well as at the central level and the big industrial projects of the state-holding companies in Taranto, Brindisi and Bari were completed. Moro's centre-left formula lasted from 1963 to 1968. After a period of rightwards oscillations, it was resuscitated in the second half of the 1970s under the label of 'historic compromise'. Although at the central level Moro's strategic programme experienced ups and downs, at the regional level his prestige remained untouched. Of the other main DC leaders – Lattanzio, Russo, Caroli and Leccisi – only Lattanzio represented a challenge, although a rather weak one, to his otherwise uncontested supremacy.

Moro's assassination in 1978 deprived Puglia of its main leader. According to Carrieri (1989), with Moro's death, the DC in Puglia becomes a polycentric party:

> The *morotei* faction breaks up after the death of its leader, but Lattanzio produces a weak leadership, incapable of unifying the party at the regional level. Internal competition within the majority party breaks out, anticipating the competition that will develop later with the PSI, which will determine the loss of Bari's prominence that the *morotei* had until then guaranteed. At the end of 1978, the incapacity of the *morotei* and *lattanziani* to reach an agreement brings Nicola Quarta at the head of the regional council, a new leader with a prefectorial past from the Salento area, who will mark the following 15 years. A spatial redistribution of regional power occurs, which brings in relief the emergence of a new leadership in areas of Puglia other than that of Bari (Carrieri, 1989: 986).

Carrieri writes specifically about the regional representatives, but his remarks are valid more generally for the whole regional political class. A host of partial conflicts for the representation of the new politically relevant social strata replaced the global conflict between DC and PCI of the immediate postwar period. Thus redefined, the space for political competition was increasingly occupied by the Socialist Party and by the other centrist parties (Table 6). Already at the beginning of the 1980s, the Socialists overtook the Communists as second biggest party in Bari's municipal elections, a result which anticipates the 1992 national electoral results in Puglia (Tables 7a, 7b). It thus became possible for political figures like Michele Di Giesi (PSDI), Minister for the South between 1979 and 1980, Claudio Signorile (PSI), also Minister for the South between 1983 and 1986, and Rino Formica (PSI), several times Finance Minister since 1989, to surge to regional leadership at least for a while. This fluid and fragmented political situation did not allow the re-establishment of those solid channels between centre and periphery that had characterized Puglia's relationship to the state in the 1960s and early 1970s, leading many to fear a general worsening of Puglia's economic conditions.

In the 1980s, the regional DC failed to fulfil its mediating role between the more stratified and fluid clients and the centre, and became prey of a host of different pressure groups and social strata. The Socialist Party, on the other hand, revealed itself capable of interpreting the aspirations of these new social groups and to compete with the DC for their representation. As Carrieri has observed:

> The PSI in Puglia manages to juxtapose to the residuals of its mass-party organization an extremely personalistic command structure, connected to the centre through the person of the Minister Formica, and to be highly permeable to the new strata in search of social promotion and self-fulfilment, attracted to the PSI because of its pivotal governmental role and its capacity to obtain political returns superior to its electoral weight (Carrieri, 1989: 994).

The policy-making that resulted was highly fluid, based on shifting coalitions of interests. This made the formation of a stable leadership, capable of interacting in a lasting way with the public agencies in the decision-making process, difficult. Consequently, in the 1980s, innovative policies got interwoven with clientelistic degeneration and conditioned by the inertia of the public administration:

> While up until the end of the 1970s, Puglia could command comparatively more resources than the other regions... [in the 1980s], no new grand strategy has been conceived and implemented. Today, every active political faction contributes innovative pieces and microregulations, with which it satisfies the interests of its own area. The numerous hints of change have been translated into a diffuse but superficial modernization without any authentic development (Carrieri, 1989: 1000).

CONCLUSIONS

Political institutions play a crucial role for economic development. Their task is not just to create a context conducive to exchange and accumulation, but also to intervene actively in support of the economic actors in times of crisis and transition. The literature on the Italian Mezzogiorno acknowledges the importance of political institutions, but underscores solely their negative impact on the development of the southern economy and polity. The fragmented social structure, distrustful mental attitudes and atomizing political patterns prevalent in the south translate into social and political behaviours that perpetuate and reinforce southern economic backwardness. Clientelism – the southern mode of political integration – is thus identified as the direct and indirect cause of southern underdevelopment.

This chapter has tried to challenge the above view, by asking some provocative questions. Does clientelism necessarily entail economic backwardness? Is it possible that a development-sustaining type of clientelism might exist side by side to a development-inhibiting one? If so, what determines what type of clientelism will prevail in a given locality? In the light of the economic and political records of Abruzzo and Puglia, this paper suggests that clientelism does not necessarily entail economic backwardness, but rather can be instrumental to economic progress. Local political classes which are stable and cohesive and which also face a compact and sizeable opposition can support economic development while local political classes which are unstable and fragmented and face a fissured and negligible opposition, inhibit it.

More generally, the performance of political institutions is not dictated by the structural context in which they are embedded, but is rather the result of the strategic and creative choices of the political actors who mould structural and contingent circumstances to their ends and, in so doing, redefine the context in which they operate. As for the southern question, the conclusion of this paper is that southern economic development is indeed possible if only the local political classes could find the internal cohesion and the external incentives to operate for its promotion.

TABLE 2

STANDARD DEVIATIONS OF NORTH-CENTRE, SOUTH AND ITALY[1]

Degree of industrialization by province.(1)

	1971	1981	1990
North-Centre	47.95	44.79	41.35
South	12.85	19.45	18.51
Italy	56.36	54.58	47.70

Per capita income by province.

	1970	1980	1989
North-Centre	19.30	11.10	12.60
South	19.60	10.10	10.00
Italy	29.00	23.50	25.20

Notes: (1) employed in industry every 1,000 inhabitants.

Sources: Centro Studi Confindustria, 1991; Istat, 1991; Istituto Tagliacarne, 1989; Svimez,1985.

TABLE 3
PER CAPITA INCOME AND DEGREE OF INDUSTRIALIZATION

	Per capita income			Degree of industrialization (1)		
	1970	1980	1989	1971	1981	1990
L'Aquila	73.2	92.0	98.0	39.0	59.6	72.6
Teramo	66.4	88.7	87.8	62.0	101.1	107.0
Abruzzo	71.5	86.2	86.3	52.0	74.2	89.5
Taranto	91.7	82.6	76.2	60.2	78.5	67.2
Lecce	55.8	64.1	62.2	30.7	41.3	71.2
Puglia	69.7	72.5	70.6	43.2	49.9	66.3
North-Centre	118.2	117.0	118.9	133.7	132.4	123.4
South	67.0	69.0	67.3	37.1	41.0	59.5
Italy	100.0	100.0	100.0	100.0	100.0	100.0

(1) Employed in industry per 1,000 inhabitants.

Sources: Centro Studi Confindustria, 1991; Istat , 1991; Istituto Tagliacarne, 1970, 1989; Svimez, 1985.

TABLE 4
REGIONAL ELECTIONS (1970-90), ABRUZZO

Party	1970 %	N	1975 %	N	1980 %	N	1985 %	N	1990 %	N
DC	48.2	20	42.5	18	45.8	20	44.3	19	46.7	20
PCI/ PDS	22.8	10	30.3	13	27.5	12	26.9	11	20.5	8
PSI	9.0	3	10.2	4	10.8	4	11.8	5	14.7	6
MSI	5.8	2	6.4	2	5.9	2	6.2	2	3.8	1
PSU/ PSDI	5.4	2	6.2	2	4.6	1	3.8	1	2.8	1
PRI	2.5	1	2.6	1	2.4	1	2.8	1	3.4	1
PLI	2.9	1	1.8	0	1.5	0	1.6	1	2.3	1
PDIUP/ DP	3.2	1	0	0	1.3	0	0.8	0	0.7	0
Others	0.2	0	0	0	0.2	0	1.8	0	5.9	2
Total	100	40	100	40	100	40	100	40	100	40

N = number of seats.

Sources: Istat,1990; Ministero dell'Interno.

TABLE 5
NATIONAL ELECTIONS (1968-92), ABRUZZO

Party	1968 %	1972 %	1976 %	1979 %	1983 %	1987 %	1992 %
DC	48.7	48.2	44.2	45.7	42.1	42.4	40.4
PCI/PDS	25.4	26.9	34.9	31.1	29.5	27.4	17.5
Rif. Com.							5.2
PSI/PSU	11.5	6.9	7.8	7.6	9.7	12.0	13.1
MSI	5.0	7.6	6.3	5.8	6.7	5.8	6.5
PSIUP							3.4
PSDI		3.9	2.5	2.6	3.6	3.7	4.1
PRI	1.8	1.6	1.7	1.8	2.5	2.1	3.2
PLI	3.1	2.1	0.7	0.8	1.7	1.1	3.1
PR					2.3	1.5	2.1
Verdi							2.8
Lega Nord							0.8
Others	1.0	2.8	2.1	2.3	2.7	1.7	3.3
Total	100.0	100.0	100.0	100.0	100.0	100.0	100.0

Sources: Istat, 1991; Corriere della Sera, 8 April 1992.

TABLE 6
REGIONAL ELECTIONS (1970-90), PUGLIA

Party	1970 %	1970 N	1975 %	1975 N	1980 %	1980 N	1985 %	1985 N	1990 %	1990 N
DC	41.3	22	39.2	21	42.1	22	38.4	20	40.7	22
PCI/ PDS	26.3	14	28.5	15	24.6	13	24.4	13	18.7	10
PSI	10.6	5	11.9	5	13.3	6	15.0	8	19.7	10
MSI	8.7	4	10.8	5	9.3	4	10.3	5	6.2	3
PSDI/ PSU	4.1	2	4.7	2	5.2	4	4.4	2	4.3	2
PRI	2.4	1	2.3	1	2.5	2	3.2	1	3.0	1
PLI	3.0	1	1.7	1	1.6	1	1.8	1	2.2	1
PDIUP/ DP	2.4	1	0	0	1.3	1	0.8	0	0.8	0
Others	1.2	0	0.9	0	0.1	0	1.7	0	4.3	0
Total	100	50	100	50	100	50	100	50	100	50

N = number of seats.

Sources: Istat, 1991; Ministero dell'Interno.

TABLE 7A
NATIONAL ELECTIONS (1968-92),
PUGLIA, DISTRICT XXIV (BARI – FOGGIA)

Party	1968 %	1972 %	1976 %	1979 %	1983 %	1987 %	1992 %
DC	43.8	40.0	40.6	42.2	34.4	37.8	36.8
PCI/PDS	29.5	27.7	32.6	27.1	25.7	23.0	12.3
Rif. Com.							5.8
PSI/PSU	13.0	10.3	9.0	10.2	15.0	15.3	19.3
MSI	5.3	12.2	9.8	8.3	10.5	7.8	9.0
PSIUP							2.8
PSDI		4.1	3.4	4.2	5.7	4.6	3.7
PRI	1.0	1.4	1.8	1.9	3.0	3.9	3.5
PLI	2.9	2.2	1.1	1.5	2.2	2.6	3.3
PR					2.5	1.2	2.0
Verdi						1.6	2.3
Lega Nord							0.2
La Rete							1.0
Others	2.8	2.8	2.0	2.1	2.2	1.4	2.8
Total	100.0	100.0	100.0	100.0	100.0	100.0	100.0

Sources: Istat, 1991; Corriere della Sera, 8 April 1992.

TABLE 7B
POLITICAL ELECTIONS (1968-92), PUGLIA

Party	1968 %	1972 %	1976 %	1979 %	1983 %	1987 %	1992 %
DC	44.7	43.6	43.0	43.6	38.6	38.9	34.5
PCI/PDS	24.5	23.2	30.6	26.3	25.2	23.7	15.6
Rif. Com							4.5
PSI/PSU	12.8	9.8	9.3	10.2	13.5	15.2	16.1
MSI	8.3	12.9	9.6	9.0	9.7	8.8	9.5
PSIUP							3.0
PSDI		3.1	2.8	3.5	4.3	3.4	4.7
PRI	1.9	2.5	2.1	2.0	3.4	4.3	4.5
PLI	3.4	2.1	0.6	1.1	1.9	2.0	1.8
PR					1.8	1.0	1.5
Verdi						1.7	1.9
Lega Nord							0.2
La Rete							1.2
Others	1.5	2.1	1.8	2.5	2.4	1.3	5.5
Total	100.0	100.0	100.0	100.0	100.0	100.0	100.0

Sources: Istat, 1991; Corriere della Sera, 8 April 1992.

TABLE 8
NATIONAL ELECTIONS (1968-92), ITALY

Party	1968 %	1972 %	1976 %	1979 %	1983 %	1987 %	1992 %
DC	39.1	38.7	38.7	38.3	32.9	34.3	29.7
PCI/PDS	26.9	27.1	34.4	30.4	29.9	26.6	16.1
Rif. Com.							5.6
PSI/PSU	14.5	9.6	9.6	9.8	11.4	14.3	13.6
MSI	4.4	8.7	6.1	5.3	6.8	5.9	5.4
PSIUP							4.4
PSDI		5.1	3.4	3.8	4.1	2.9	2.7
PRI	2.0	2.9	3.1	3.0	5.1	3.7	4.4
PLI	5.8	3.9	1.3	1.9	2.9	2.1	2.8
PR					3.4	2.2	2.6
DP						1.7	1.7
Verdi						2.5	2.8
Lega Nord							8.7
La Rete							1.9
Others	2.8	4.0	3.4	4.0	3.2	3.4	6.3
Total	100.0	100.0	100.0	100.0	100.0	100.0	100.0

Sources: Istat, 1991; Corriere della Sera, 8 April 1992.

NOTES

1. Table 2 shows that the standard deviation of the rates of industrialization by province, computed over the totality of the 92 Italian provinces, decreased betwee, 1971 and 1981, suggesting that a process of homogenization took place in the 1970s. However, when the same index is computed separately for the northern and central provinces, on the one hand, and the southern ones on the other, it appears that the increased similarity among northern provinces more than compensated for the increased dissimilarity among the southern provinces. Between 1981 and 1991, the standard deviation further decreased both in the country as a whole and in the two geographical partitions, but less in the south than in the north. Despite the slight reversal of the 1980s, therefore, over the course of the last 20 years the southern provinces have grown further apart at the same time as the northern and central provinces have become more similar.

   The standard deviation of provincial per capita income tells a slightly different story. The index computed over the entire population of Italian provinces decreased between 1970 and 1979 and increased again between 1980 and 1989. That relative to the north and centre followed the same pattern, while that relative to the south decreased in the 1970s and remained constant in the 1980s. It would thus appear that, in terms of per capita income, provincial differences within the south decreased more than those within the north and centre. The growing homogenization of the south in terms of per capita income, however, does not contradict the claim made above that, during the 1970s and 1980s, the south became increasingly differentiated. This claim, in fact, refers to the productive profile of the south and not to its purchasing power, which depends not only on its productive capacity but also on public and private transfers of money.

16

France: From the Regionalized State to the Emergence of Regional Governance?

BERNARD JOUVE

INTRODUCTION

In France, since the nineteenth century, regionalization has been on the political agenda and has been part of the high political stakes concerning decentralization and the deconcentration of state powers. This process refers, of course, to the exercise of power and coalition games between social groups operating at different levels of government. The transfer of executive powers of the regional prefects to the regional councils in 1982 only ratified a slowly emerging process. This slowness has been caused, for the most part, by ideological, political and administrative resistance to regionalization. It is true that regionalization puts into question the organization of public power by the creation of new decision-making centres, new elites and a loss of state centrality. In the French napoleonic state, projects of decentralization and regionalization have their origins in traditions of the right as well as the left (Rosanvallon, 1993). These strands converged in the early 1980s and enabled the decentralization laws, the '*grand chantier*' of François Mitterrand's first term, to be adopted without any major problems and led to legal acknowledgement of the region as a fully-fledged local authority.

The arrival of the regional councils within the political arena during the 1980s took place during a period which was also marked by structural changes of the political and economic environments. Among these changes were: the weakening of national territorial development policy that had been carried out by the state since the 1960s; internationalization of the economy; rediscovery of the virtues of the 'marshallian district'; promises of a post-Fordist production model which raised the question of the necessity of an 'intermediate' level of government; and the increase of European Community programmes notably through its regional policy. For certain scholars, the combination of these different processes has considerably reinforced the position of the regional councils in the French politico-administrative system (Palard, 1993) and, by building an institutional binomial European Union, regional councils would go against 'narrow, central or peripheral nationalisms' (Olivesi, 1994).

Here, we would like to nuance this hypothesis by developing the following idea: the weight of the regional councils, as a meso-level of government, has proved to be marginal for the moment with respect to their ability to develop their own public policies, to establish an autonomous political system and to weigh strongly on intergovernmental relations (Keating, 1988a). However, certain elements could, in the medium term, allow these institutions to reinforce their position in a politico-administrative system which no longer appears as exclusively French, but rather European. The regional question thus continues to be a topical issue: it constitutes one element of a whole in which exist different methods of exercising public power. This can be translated in terms of political and administrative innovations through the production of new policy networks supported by a regional political class which is in the process of constituting itself and through a very progressive redefinition of the territorial structure of public and private interests.

First, the long emergence of the region in the French politico-administrative system will be retraced. The fundamental ambiguity on which this movement is based will be brought out. Second, we will analyse the resistance, at the level of state administrations as well as at the level of local authorities (*départements* and *communes*), which has constrained the actions of regional councils elected for the first time by direct vote in 1986. The third part will show that, by emphasizing the European dimension, the regional councils have partially succeeded in extricating themselves from these constraints.

REGIONALIZATION OF THE PUBLIC SECTOR: BETWEEN DECONCENTRATION AND DECENTRALIZATION

In France, the regionalization of the public sector is based on ambiguity since it refers to the modernization of the state's bureaucracy, through the deconcentration of administrative tasks, as well as to the creation, by political decentralization, of a level of government between the local and national level. Overall, the regional question oscillates between 'regionalization-deconcentration' and 'regionalization-decentralization'. Modernization of the state goes back to the beginning of the twentieth century, while the creation of a regional government with executive power, exercised by elected persons and producing its own public policies, is much more recent.

The Constitution of a Regional Administrative Echelon

It was not until the 1940s and especially the 1950s that the regionalization of state powers took place. This process was based upon a series of structural changes which affected the French economy and society, as well as all other industrialized countries (Savy, 1993). This produced differentiated spatial effects leading to highly unequal levels of development among the regions. Those in favour of the deconcentration of the state to the regional level pointed to the excessive centralization of the state's administrative bodies and the gap between the new spatial forms of production and the *communes* and *départements*. The establishment of a new territorial framework, situated between the central state and local authorities, sought to change administrative and political practices through planning by associating the *'forces vives de la nation'* with economic development. The region was, therefore, designed as an innovative administrative area.

The 22 regions, as new administrative bodies of the state, were created in 1964 but did not lead to political decentralization. The statist approach of Gaullist ideology, congruent with the position at that time of the Socialist and Communist Parties, limited any attempt to reform in this direction (Mény, 1974; Mazey, 1993). The new regional institutional framework proved itself to be rudimentary. The prefect of the principal *département* making up the region also became the regional prefect. Administrative co-ordination was carried out within the *Conférence Administrative Régionale* (CAR) which grouped together all the departmental and regional prefects as well as the deconcentrated services of certain ministries (Agriculture, Public Works, etc.). In order to represent the *'forces vives de la région'*, the *Commission de Développement Economique Régional* (CODER), a consultative body, was instituted.

The regional administration quickly 'drifted' from the aims of the initial project. The region was more a grouping of *départements* than a truly autonomous administrative body. First, the function of the region was not so much to mobilize civil society as to 'regionalize' the orientations of National Plans developed at a central echelon by the *Commissariat Général du Plan*. Second, the participation of the 'civil society' in the CODERs turned out to be marginal. The regional prefects were the only ones to have at their disposal technical and administrative services who prepare meetings. This technical and administrative expertise was coupled with a mastery of procedures. They remained in charge of meeting agendas and, consequently, of a large part of the political agenda.

Following the decrees of 1964, the building of a regional administrative level led to a regionalization of the National Plan. There was no question of 'building' a new politico-administrative mediation unit which would be between the centre and the periphery as well as between public and private interests. In this context, the emergence of a relatively autonomous regional administrative echelon called into question the *département* and the mediation monopoly between the prefects and local *notables*. Among other factors, such as the events of May 1968, the opposition of local and central elites to any project of politico-administrative reform along regional lines was one of the reasons for the failure of the 1969 referendum, which notably aimed to reinforce regional powers, proposed by General de Gaulle.

After the failure of this referendum, the projects for regional reform during the 1970s were timid. In 1972, the legal status of the region changed. It became an *établissement public* with its own legal personality and a regional council indirectly elected and made up of regional senators and deputies, as well as members elected by departmental and municipal councils. The CODERs were replaced by the *Conseil Economique et Social Régional* (CESR) which remained a consultative body. These two institutions played a role of economic stimulation. However, their personnel and budgetary resources were very limited. In spite of the 1972 reform, the departmental and regional prefectures remained the essential links of public power at the local or regional level.

Creating a Regional Governmental Echelon

The 1970s, however, were marked by an 'irresistible progression of the region' (Rémond and Blanc, 1989). Ideological, institutional, political, economic and financial factors contributed to this process.

The protest movements of the 1970s included cultural regionalism to varying degrees. The regions most strongly affected by this phenomenon were Brittany, the French Basque Country and Corsica. The *'révolution régionale'* (Laffont, 1967) was notably based upon severe criticism of the state, criticism partially shared by militant supporters of leftist political parties who questioned the Taylorist production model and who proposed an alternative model based on self-management (*autogestion*).

With regard to institutions, there was a call for clarification of the relationships among the various regional bodies. The dialogue between the prefect, the regional council and the CESR was not very effective and lengthened the decision-making process. Moreover, tensions arose among the prefect, the different parts of the administration, the regional council and the CESR concerning who controlled access to the state and its budget.

After its unsuccessful bid in the 1974 presidential elections, the Socialist Party tried to profit from its position of strength in several regional councils in order to transform them into institutions capable of challenging the National Assembly.

The recession which began in the 1970s led the regional political players to demand more powers and freedom of manoeuvre. In fact, although the budgets of the regional councils were limited, their importance continued to increase during the 1970s, especially because of the pressure put on the Ministry of Finance by the regional political staff[1]. The budgetary increases for the regional authorities were used mainly for transport infrastructure, cultural policies and direct or indirect aids to companies.

These different elements contributed to produce a gap between the illegality of many decisions of the regional councils and their political legitimacy. Indeed, the councils based their legitimacy upon their ability to build a level of government with a good hold on major economic changes at the end of the 1970s. It is undeniable that this operational and managerial *raison d'être* of the region has been observed since the 1950s.

The 1982 decentralization laws have allowed regional councillors to become more involved in the domain of economic development.

The region has become a fully-fledged territorial authority, endowed since 1986 with an executive body elected by direct vote and proportional representation.[2] It also has its own budget, financed through various local taxes, as well as a portion of local taxes collected at the municipal and departmental levels. Like other local authorities, it benefits from financial transfers from the state. Its competences in planning and economic development have been confirmed. However, it does not have a monopoly in this domain. Indeed, the decentralization laws have largely contributed to promoting a new type of public policy based on contractual relationships between the different levels of government and systematic joint financing. Therefore, in economic development, four tiers of government (state, region, *département, commune*) are involved. Nevertheless, thanks to highly efficient public relations policies, the regions quickly established themselves in public opinion as key institutions for local development. The results of opinion polls carried out between 1986 and 1991 were eloquent in this sense. Beginning in 1986, the year of the first elections of the regional councils by universal suffrage, public opinion viewed the region as being the political and administrative unit of the future, and not the *département* which has been its historical 'rival'.

TABLE 1

RESULTS OF OPINION POLL ON THE QUESTION : "WHAT IS, IN YOUR OPINION, THE ADMINISTRATIVE AND POLITICAL UNIT OF THE FUTURE" (IN %)

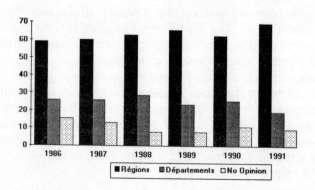

Source: Percheron, 1991.

Through the 1982 decentralization laws, and even more so after the 1986 elections, the regions have apparently become 'adult'. In a context of increasing economic difficulties and internationalization of productive activities, creating a level of regional government answered a desire to set up a meso-level of economic regulation. However, although the regional echelon is sometimes seen as a bastion against 'Jacobin centralism and political conservatism' (Ribaud, 1986), its future remains very uncertain. The German *Länder* are often cited in comparison to emphasize the weaknesses of French regional councils. The region must still prove its ability to occupy its new position within the French politico-administrative system.

THE REGIONAL COUNCILS BETWEEN THE ADMINISTRATION OF THE STATE AND THE ELECTED 'MANAGERS'

After the decentralization laws were passed, a certain number of factors prevented the regional councils from imposing themselves as a meso-level of government in the French politico-administrative system as they might have wished. Two of the most important factors were the recomposition of state intervention through the constitution of a strong regional administrative level and the emergence of new local elites.

The Modernization of the Regional State and Contract-Based Public Policies

Within the framework of decentralization laws which give more autonomy to local authorities, the co-ordination of public policies carried out by the different levels of government is carried out on a contractual basis. Thus, the *Contrats de Plan Etat-Région* (CPER), which establish major regional economic development axes, are drawn up for a five-year period and should, theoretically, allow a harmonization of the strategies of the state and regional councils. However, as Charles Millon, President of the Rhône-Alpes Regional Council, has pointed out, in drawing conclusions on the first generation of CPERs signed after decentralization (1989-1993), 'the state imposes its choices which are financed in large measure by the regions' (Millon, 1992). Contracting public policies, and notably national territorial development policy, was an answer to the state's fear of losing the greater part of its prerogatives following decentralization. By 'contractualizing the crisis' (Greffe, 1984) and by redefining the state's intervention, part of the administrative elite undermined the emergence of the regional councils.

The Plan-Contracts did not lead to an increase in the political weight of the regional councils in the development and implementation of public policies based on the 'partnership' principle. Several factors can explain this situation: the inability of the regional councils to translate the state's sectoral strategies into territorial policy (Balme and Bonnet, 1995); the electoral system of the regional council which favours a sprinkling of economic interventions; the absence of a regional identity. Here, we would like to stress another factor: the modernization of the state through the constitution of a strong administrative echelon.

The effort to deconcentrate the state administrative machine at the regional level is an answer to the demands of certain central elites, such as the prefectoral corps, in reaction to decentralization laws which reduced their powers. For these corps, decentralization threatened to break up the state, which, for them, embodied national unity and solidarity. Decentralization also favoured the birth of 'local fiefdoms' held by a certain number of *notables*, monopolizing the decentralization laws for their own benefit. On the other hand, in a context of economic difficulties and the necessity of reducing public deficits, the administration had to develop public management techniques based on methods used in private companies (Crozier, 1987). According to the well-known formula of F. Bloch-Lainé (1990), an exemplary member of the French senior civil service, the state had to have 'more muscle, less fat'.

Thus, the 1980s were marked by the setting up of a powerful regional administration which was no longer simply a collection of deconcentrated services of the state on a departmental level. While the state's numerous but loosely structured regional field services were previously competent in issues such as research and co-ordination, they now also became centres of control and management. The principal beneficiaries of this movement were the regional prefects who received certain financial instruments, such as the agricultural orientation premium and industrial policy credits, and who found themselves in the middle of important institutional frameworks such as the regional committees on industrial restructuring. The 'Joxe-Baylet law' on the Territorial Administration of the Republic, enacted in 1992, whose objective was to relaunch the decentralization process, has reinforced this trend of concentrating administrative powers at the regional prefecture level in order 'to take into account the demands of modern management and the development of the importance of the regional level in the European space'. The recent 'Pasqua law' on National Territorial Development, enacted in 1994, goes in the same direction, notably by letting regional prefectures put into practice a new solidarity principle: fiscal equalization between local authorities.

Since the 1980s, subsidiarity has been applied to public administration without there being a measure of how far it should go. There are many consequences of going from 'a procedural administration to an administration of responsibility by entrusting the periphery with everything that is not necessarily a matter of the centre', to reiterate the words of the former Prime Minister, Michel Rocard. Certain new administrative functions have been created, such as that of 'prefect in charge of economic development' in employment basins particularly affected by the recession or that of 'sub-prefect to the city' whose mission is to co-ordinate the actions of different ministries in troubled neighbourhoods. This recomposition does not only concern the prefectoral corps. The coming of a new generation of local civil servants, who base their legitimacy on a managerial ability and which has been expressed in a project logic, has been observed.

The Emergence of New Local and Departmental Elites

Parallel to the constitution of a powerful regional administrative echelon, the emancipation of the regional councils has equally been undermined by the emergence of new local political elites. It would be an exaggeration to claim that this process is due to the 1982 decentralization laws. The evolution of the general profile and legitimation of local elected officials began in the 1970s and accelerated in 1977 after the municipal elections, when a large portion of the local political class was changed (Mabileau and Sorbets, 1989).

In spite of certain analyses which tended to show that the decentralization laws were the opportunity to 'crown the notables' (Rondin, 1985), the 1980s were characterized by a structural modification of the 'periphery' which notably resulted in an increased professionalism of politics. There was also access to local power for middle-class politicians. This had developed during the economic expansion period (1950-1975) when this group built their political careers on local policy networks (Garraud, 1989), as well as by a new cultural model based on models of public management. This movement, particularly observable in cities, also affected rural areas (Faure, 1992).

These local elected officials considerably modified the municipal 'frame of reference'. The *commune*, the basic unit of democracy in France, has gradually become the privileged field of mediation between social groups and has been transformed into a central political target. The new generation of local councillors have notably relied on efficient advertising campaigns leading to total symbiosis between the identity of their municipality and themselves[3]. It has based its legitimacy on its ability to occupy a central position in all public policies and, thanks to a technocracy which resembles a government, to become the privileged mediators between state administrations, local associations and powerful private groups, such as the Lyonnaise des Eaux, the Bouygues group and the SARI taking part in managing local public services or in promoting and developing real estate (Lorrain, 1991).

This process has generated a profound recomposition of the local level which has notably resulted in fierce competition between urban areas in order to attract companies and favoured social groups (Le Galès, 1994). Helped in this respect by certain state administrations such as the DATAR, the large French cities have established 'entrepreneurial' strategies and have discovered a 'European' destiny. The locality has ceased to be considered as a field of conservatism embodied by the mythical image of the *notable*, managing his *commune* as a 'good father figure' and protecting it from excessive intrusion from the state, thanks to the close relationship he has with the prefect. On the contrary, the local level has been glorified and, it is true, often mythified. In a context characterized by acute of economic and social troubles, it has appeared as the laboratory of innovation and forms of non-marketing regulation between public power and private companies which make up the fundamental elements in the success of economic development policies (Benko and Lipietz, 1992).

The ambiguity surrounding these new 'managers' comes from the fact that they too have used certain governmental approaches which had been extensively tested by their predecessors. This is notably the case of clientelistic practices and the *cumul des mandats* which enhances their power by allowing them to participate in several decision-making centres (Mabileau, 1991). From this point of view, a mandate in the regional council is not considered as absolutely necessary for the elected 'managers'. The consequences of the vote on the 1985 law, which reduced the *cumul des mandats*, are significant. They show the minor importance attributed to the regional council by the elected 'managers'. Concerning the choices that certain councillors are led to make, the responsibilities of a mayor, a general council member and national mandates (deputy or senator) are clearly more important. In all, out of 84 elected politicians opting either for a seat on a regional council or for a seat on a departmental council, 64 chose the second.

Overall, the emergence of the regional councils in the political arena has been greatly affected by the modernization of the state administrative machine and the rise in power of new local political elites. The years immediately after the 1986 regional council elections were characterized by strong competition not only between the different local authorities but also between the deconcentrated services of the state and the regional councils. This competition was notably shown in the domain of European Community regional policy which should have 'transformed' the regional councils into fully-fledged political partners of the European Commission. From 1989, the European Structural Funds reform, on which Community regional policy is based, showed this desire on the part of the Commission to contribute to reinforcing local authorities, especially the regions (Balme, 1995). If the elements presented here have considerably limited the ambitions of the Commission, certain current trends still remain which suggest a readjustment, in the medium term, of the weight regional councils have in negotiations not only with Brussels and Paris but also with other local authorities.

FRENCH REGIONS AND EUROPE: TOWARDS A REGIONAL GOVERNANCE?

The 1988 Structural Funds reform presented itself partly as an innovative institutional policy aiming at lessening the extremely powerful relationships that the member states had developed with Brussels since the signing of the Treaty of Rome (Lequesne, 1993) by introducing a new player: the regions. This perspective therefore implied a restructuring of policy networks within which EU policies are formulated and implemented. However, the Commission's attempts to include the French regional councils in these policy networks came up against the obstacles described above. The state, through its deconcentrated administration at the departmental and especially at the regional levels, as well as the new generation of local and departmental 'elected managers', appeared to be the principal 'beneficiaries' of the 1988 reform (Balme and Jouve, 1996).

Nevertheless, if the modest attempts of the European Commission to reinforce the position of regional councils have not been crowned with success, the latter have succeeded in positioning themselves on the fringes of the policy networks by acting on the location of Commission interventions. Moreover, in spite of their absence from negotiation procedures dealing with the formulation and implementation of programmes eligible under EU objectives, they focused on some Community Initiative Programmes by inciting certain public and private interests to structure themselves regionally. They have thus initiated innovative public policies resulting in policy networks which express themselves both on a regional territorial and on a European basis.

(i) The Regional Councils and EU Programmes

The spatial distribution of EU programmes has been an important issue for the regional councils. While in 1992, the total budget for local authorities was 606 billion francs, the budget of all the French regions only represented 27.3 billion francs, in other words 8.2 per cent. They are clearly put at a disadvantage compared to the *départements* (28.8 per cent) and especially to the *communes* (63 per cent) – see Table 2. This situation is not without problems. Neoliberal approaches to macro-economic policy have caused a reduction in budget deficits and a stagnation of budgetary transfers

TABLE 2

FINANCIAL RESOURCES OF LOCAL AUTHORITIES IN 1992 (IN BILLIONS OF FRANCS)

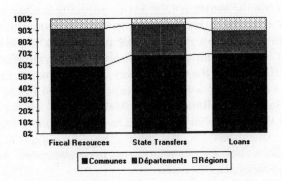

Source: Ministère de l'Intérieur, 1994.

from the state to local authorities. EU programmes from the Structural Funds were, therefore, an opportunity for the regional councils to compensate for the stagnant situation with regard to state budgetary transfers and to increase their capacity for action in development policies. This became all the more important after the 1988 reform which doubled the EU budget devoted to Structural Funds.

Community interventions have given rise to direct negotiations between the Commission and DATAR. The predominant position of DATAR was illustrative of the French state's desire to confine all negotiations with the Commission to the national level, while, on the other hand, the Commission tried to make the regional institutions responsible. DATAR took control of part of the Community regional policy in France, at least at the level of formulation, notably by transferring a portion of the credits initially destined for certain regions to other regions. While this measure was justified in terms of fairness and solidarity among the French regions, it was also a way for DATAR to point out to Brussels that the priorities in matters of territorial development remained a matter for the central French state.

Mastering the budgetary framework has not only been the monopoly of the central state. This has also been shown by the setting up, in accordance with the wishes of the Commission, of computer monitoring systems in certain regional prefectures such as Aquitaine or Languedoc-Roussillon. By such computer tools, these regional prefectures have been the only institutions to have at their disposal all the information relevant to public financing granted to all private operators. Instrumentalization of requests from the Commission conferred a monopoly of the information at the heart of Brussels bureaucratic activity. Among the evaluation criteria applied to EU policies, the Commission attaches great importance to the effective speed and level of consumption of the funds. In terms of policy networks (Rhodes and Marsh, 1992), these regional prefectures therefore occupy a position of 'gatekeeper' concerning budgetary questions with both the Brussels and Paris administrations, but also in relation to deconcentrated services of the state and to local authorities.

Nevertheless, if the regional councillors did not formally intervene in the initial negotiations, local councillors have often referred to them in order to claim the eligibility of certain zones for Structural Funds. By intervening at the fringes of general decisions, they have thus succeeded in having their voices heard in the process of programming EU interventions and, especially, in reinforcing their legitimacy vis-à-vis local councillors. In a dynamic perspective, the lobbying of the regional councils on the zoning of EU programmes has increased between 1989 and 1993. In this regard, the regional councils have notably relied on their representation offices (currently 17) in Brussels. Although initially the exact function of these offices was rather vague and was essentially limited to collecting information, it seems that it is turning more and more towards an actual negotiating activity with the Commission.

While this evolution goes against the 'Jacobin instincts' of certain French politicians such as Philippe Séguin[4], it goes in the direction favoured by the powerful DG XVI and notably of the new European Commissioner in charge of the Community regional policy, Monika Wulf-Mathies.[5] The change in the function of the 'Brussels branch' of the regional councils can be partly explained by a better knowledge of how the EU institutions operate and through recruiting administrative agents specialized in these questions. Next to the Brussels implantation strategy, the regional councils have also relied on more 'traditional' negotiation practices which are based on direct access of certain elected officials to the central Parisian administrations because of their 'weight' on the national political scene.

Concerning the place of regional councils in programming and implementing Community programmes, a distinction must undoubtedly be made between, on the one hand, negotiations dealing with allocating Structural Funds within the framework of the five objectives of the European Community and, on the other hand, the Community Initiative Programmes (CIPs) which are based on much more flexible and less restrictive procedures. Effectively, while in the first case, the regional councils have been relatively absent from discussions, the situation has been completely different in the case of certain CIPs such as the research and development programmes.

(ii) The Regional Councils Confronted with the Rigidity of the Community Support Framework

The 1988 Structural Funds reform was based notably on two types of procedures (the Community Support Framework – CSF – and Operational Programmes – OP) concerning respectively the formulation phase of Community regional policy and its implementation phase. The development of the CSFs and the implementation of the OPs have brought together principally the central and deconcentrated administrations of the state, the departmental councils, the councillors of large cities and certain socio-economic groups which are represented by corporatist bodies such as the Chamber of Agriculture. The 1988 Structural Funds reform reinforced a process of integration inside the state administration. This process had been started during the negotiations on the first generation of CPERs after the 1982 decentralization laws. The state administrations have also profited from the relations they had developed with the Commission from the mid-1970s, after the creation of the ERDF. The regional and departmental prefectures have therefore mobilized the policy networks that they had.

At the level of the central administration, this process has essentially benefited the DATAR, whose existence was called into question during the 1980s after the national territorial development policy was modified (François-Poncet, 1994). Thanks to negotiations with the Commission in Brussels, DATAR and the 'European Social Funds mission' of the Ministry of Labour gained expertise in managing European affairs; expertise that other central administrations lacked. At the local level, programming Structural Funds was an opportunity for the regional and departmental prefectures to assert both their ability to co-ordinate the deconcentrated administrative services and also to mediate vis-à-vis their environment. The prefectoral corps had been the principal 'victim' of decentralization laws because of the transfer of powers to local authorities. European integration and EU regional policy were the opportunity for them to counteract this process and to reinforce the legitimacy and expertise obtained during negotiations relative to the first CPERs.

The implementation phase of regional policy, through the OPs, brought out a different logic. A territorial integration of different central departments under the authority of the regional, and principally departmental, prefectures was observed. These two institutions have been at the heart of a policy network made up of deconcentrated state administrations, local authorities (*départements* and *communes*) and organizations representing sectorial socio-economic interests. In that, EU regional policy, associated with contractual policies initiated by the state in the domain of national territorial development, reactivated its administrative structure at the departmental and regional level.

Complementarity between the assistance given by the Commission, the state and local authorities has been made possible by co-financing. None of the various institutions had sufficient budgetary resources to finance large projects by themselves. Moreover, for departmental and regional prefectures, the partnership with local authorities enabled them to reposition themselves on the local political scene whereas certain 'elected managers' had tended, thanks to decentralization, to deny them access in this domain. We can now see certain cross-legitimization mechanisms between local elected officials and the deconcentrated state administrations; mechanisms which appear to be recurrent in the French local politico-administrative system (Worms, 1966). However, it should be noted that the content of the transactions and the composition of the policy networks of civil servants and local elected officials have changed. While, during the 1960s and 1970s, the negotiations dealt primarily with local adaptation of standards developed at the central level, today's dialogue deals with the definition and implementation of public policies through contractual procedures which no longer only bring together the prefect and a few 'notables'.

(iii) Towards a Beginning of Regional Structuring of Private and Public Interests?

Even if they only represent ten per cent of the total amount of structural programmes of the European Union, certain CIPs, such as the Research and Development programmes, have been opportunities for the regional councils to integrate EU regional policy in a comprehensive and continual fashion. Several elements can explain this situation.

First, the CIPs are based on negotiation procedures which are much more flexible than those in which Community programmes on the five objectives of the Commission are developed and implemented. In fact, the CIPs are generally managed in the form of public calls for tender where the Commission often occupies the position of arbitrator. The state field services, on both the local and central levels, do not participate in the selection of shortlisted tenders.

Nevertheless, distinctions must be made between the different CIPs. These differences have their origins, to a large extent, in the territorial structure of public and private interests. In fact, certain CIPs are aimed more specifically at public and private interests whose territorial logic in France has long been local and departmental. This is notably the case of LEADER and INTERREG. The LEADER programme supports local initiatives which diversify activities in zones highly sensitive to changes in the Community Agricultural Policy. INTERREG benefits border regions whose economic activity has been affected by the single market. Existing territorial structures of public and private interests have given rise to an appropriation of these programmes by the local and departmental echelons.

This situation illustrates the organization of local power in France. This has taken concrete form through extremely close ties which have been developed historically between the local and departmental levels and certain private interests represented by corporatist bodies. The regional councils lack such private partners who speak in an organized form through representative structures. This is partly due to the delicate relationships that they have with CESRs who, having been the privileged partners of the regional prefectures before the decentralization laws, are very often perceived by the regional political staff as 'avatars' of history and as direct competitors. In the case of the Regional Chambers of Commerce and Industry, the problem arises essentially from a lack of legitimacy. Only 20 per cent of eligible voters voted in the 1991 elections to the Chambers of Commerce and Industry.

Moreover, programmes such as LEADER and INTERREG are concerned with small geographical areas, whereas regional councillors are elected by proportional representation on a departmental basis. This type of election does not encourage a strong local base. On the other hand, the departmental council is made up of politicians elected on a cantonal basis. Because of this, departmental councillors and mayors are more likely to take into account social demands coming from a strictly local framework. This is notably the case of farmers. The activism of agricultural unions, also relayed towards state administrations and local elected officials through the corporatist *Chambres d'Agriculture*, has been a major advantage for 'rural society'. The experience of EU administrative procedures, specifically the Common Agricultural Policy (CAP), as well as the action of agricultural lobbies within the Commission has reinforced the capacities of agricultural interests.

While the regional councils, because of the manner in which their political personnel are elected and because of their recent formation, have not been able to go against this logic in the framework of LEADER and INTERREG, such is not the case for the CIPs consecrated to increasing research activities and promoting technological innovations (RACE, SPRINT, STAR). Indeed, these programmes do not address themselves to 'traditional' activity sectors based on interests registered on a local or departmental basis. Following the decentralization laws, the regional councils have made great budgetary efforts in this domain. The portion of regional budget consecrated to research has tripled between 1990 and 1994. This increase has been largely made possible by the structure of regional budgets where the volume of investments is much higher than overhead expenses, notably because of low payroll expenses[6] – see Table 3. This extremely strong position in

TABLE 3:
BREAKDOWN ON LOCAL AUTHORITIES BUDGETS BY BUDGETARY ITEM IN
1992 (IN BILLIONS OF FRANCS)

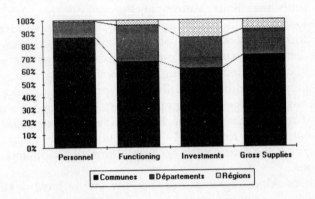

Source: Ministère de l'Intérieur, 1994.

the research domain can also be explained by the sociological make-up of regional councils (Dupoirier, 1995). A large proportion of regional councillors have completed university studies and are therefore more sensitive to the theme of technological and scientific innovation. In certain cases, this 'sensitivity' has been reinforced by the fact that regional councillors and certain company heads or heads of research laboratories knew each other during their period of higher education. These informal relationships, which refer to the socialization of the regional political elite, have sometimes played an important role in developing relations within an institutional framework.

Regional council policies in the domain of research are based on the setting up of intra- and inter-regional partnerships. For many research centres located in the provinces, the regional councils appear as an opportunity in the sense that the credits and subsidies granted by the Parisian administrations are often managed according to a corporatist, even a clientelist, logic favouring some large institutions and laboratories, but 'forgetting' many younger and less prominent teams. The Rhône-Alpes situation is illustrative.

Here there is a desire to structure the public and private research potential around the regional institution. While trying to establish genuine synergies between public and private research centres and industrialists in a sector of activity which appears to be at the heart of economic development, the regional council bases its strategy on a dual logic of co-operation with other European regions grouped together with the 'Four Motors of Europe' (Borras, 1993) and intensive lobbying with the Commission in order to defend research projects filed by researchers and regional industrialists. This intensive lobbying results in Community calls for tender and in attempts to obtain direct financing from the Commission for certain research projects without following these procedures, which have the major disadvantage of being rather long. Therefore, for a certain number of research projects, the Rhône-Alpes regional council has decided not to wait for official authorization by the Commission and, by giving the latter a fait accompli, partially to finance these applications.

The Rhône-Alpes region is not the only one to have developed what is looking more and more like regional 'diplomacy' in Brussels as well as towards its foreign counterparts. This is equally the case with the Nord-Pas de Calais region. In certain cases, several regional councils have decided to unite their efforts in associations operating at the European level. This is the case of the *Grand Est* that groups together Alsace, Bourgogne, Champagne-Ardennes and Franche Comté, or the *Grand Sud* which unites Midi-Pyrénées, Aquitaine and Languedoc-Roussillon. Sometimes, the association with other foreign regions has been carried out based on a stronger political project such as in the case of the 'Atlantic Arc' which groups together regions from Scotland to Portugal. This involves instituting a Community policy which would allow regions to plead their cause within national and Community administrations. The position of these regions in the European Union is at risk because of the opening-up of the central European countries and the movement of the centre of economic gravity from Europe to the East.

CONCLUSION

We have tried to provide a balanced interpretation of the political debate on the effectiveness of the regional councils as fully-fledged meso-levels of government. For certain people, the reality of this process leads, in the short term, to a 'Europe of the Regions' whose arrival is expressed through the creation, by the Maastricht Treaty, of the Committee of the Regions. However, contrary to the wishes of certain reformers, the regional councils are not really key institutions in the political and administrative landscape. This situation seems to be due, on the one hand, to the rapid reassertion of the central state, notably through the building of a powerful regional administration during the 1980s and, on the other hand, to the emergence of new local and departmental elites. In this context, the place of the regional councils in national as well as in Community public policies appears to be limited, for the time being.

In spite of this observation, the regional councils have succeeded in influencing from the margins certain aspects of European Union policies, for example the zoning of structural programmes or on research and development policies. This marginal position is not in itself a handicap. It has been shown that innovations, especially institutional ones that have accompanied the building of Europe, have initially established themselves on the fringes of policy networks (Majone, 1994). Therefore, thanks to all the marketing campaigns and the symbolic actions that they have carried out over the last few years, notably the opening of permanent representation in Brussels and their co-operation with foreign regions, the regional councils have gradually begun to impose themselves. The consecration of these institutions as a meso-level of government is partly taking place through the progressive introduction of this new type of political entity into civil society (Balme, Brouard and Burbaud, 1995). In this sense, while they still occupy a marginal position in the French political and administrative field, their progressive emergence contributes to reformulating the cognitive, instrumental and normative frameworks of public action. They do this notably by transforming the structures of European and French public space on new territorial bases and according to new rules.

A hypothesis can be put forward that, in the future, the emergence of the regional councils as a meso-level of government will be largely influenced by their ability to 'regionalize' public and private interests and to build institutions around which 'political regimes' (Stone, 1989), founded upon the alliances between certain social groups situated outside and inside the regional executive body, will develop. It can be said that this perspective will meet with quite a lot of resistance from the state as well as from the *communes* and the *départements*. As we have seen, the history of regionalization in France is largely based on a series of struggles between the centre and the periphery where the monopoly of mediation between public and private interests is at stake. Moreover, while regional emergence is an answer to a theoretical need for territorial regulation between the national and local echelon in advanced capitalist economies, it is uncertain that individual company orientations will go in this direction (Trigilia, 1991).

In spite of these reservations, it would seem that this regional structuring has begun to happen, first in the domain of research activities and promoting technological innovation. To the extent that it represents an investment in terms of legitimization, this structuring has been orchestrated by a regional political elite which is in the process of constituting itself. By choosing to build their political careers on the regional institution, they have set themselves apart little by little from the local political elite. In that respect, the emergence of a regional political system, which would tend to make the region a little more autonomous in the French politico-administrative field, can be anticipated in the medium term.

This recomposition will not take place without raising questions both among researchers and the general public. First, one of the research priorities for the coming years will certainly be to analyse the inter-regional differences that have already begun to appear. The institutional evolution of Europe has brought the same opportunities for all of the regional councils but their responses and their strategies diverge. This situation fully justifies a 'renewing' of the study of regionalism in a comparative perspective which would focus on an endogenous approach to regional governance. Second, the existence of such inter-regional differences brings into question the regulatory function of the state and the European Union. Beyond the thorny question of the sharing of this function, these two levels of government will have to avoid widening the gap between, on the one hand, regional governments which will be dynamic and at the heart of policy networks and, on the other, regional institutions isolated from their economic environment. If such were the case, it would be the construction of Europe and the existence of the state itself, through risks of radical regionalism as can notably be seen in Italy, that would be called into question.

NOTES

1. The fiscal ceiling, as specified in the law of 1972 which instituted the *Etablissements Publics Régionaux* has been progressively raised. Although it was 25 francs per inhabitant per year in 1972, it was 79 francs just before the 1982 decentralization laws were passed.

2. However, it should be noted that the electoral district is not the region, but rather the *département*.

3. This is the case with Georges Frêche in Montpellier, Dominique Baudis in Toulouse, Catherine Trautman in Strasbourg, Alain Carignon in Grenoble or Michel Noir in Lyon.

4. Philippe Séguin, president of the National Assembly and sworn enemy of the Maastricht treaty because of the 'risk' of losing national sovereignty, declared: 'In no way must subsidiarity be the pretext for establishing direct relations between local communities and the European Union' (*Le Figaro*, 7 December 1994).

5. During the sixth plenary session of the Committee of Regions, 1-2 February 1995, Monika Wulf-Mathies hoped that a stronger involvement of local and regional elected officials in negotiations with the EU could 'help to avoid the errors committed by the decision-makers cut off from local reality and ... to improve the efficiency and financial control of European programmes'.

6. The regional councils effectively employ 6,099 people compared with 94,689 in the departmental councils, 70,883 in the inter-municipality organizations and 749,594 in the *communes*.

17

Regional Reform in the Netherlands: Reorganizing the Viscous State[1]

FRANK HENDRIKS

INTRODUCTION: TRANSFORMATIONS IN AN OPEN ECONOMY

'In the Netherlands everything happens 50 years later,' the famous German poet Heine once said. If we look at the sub-national state structure, this statement seems to contain some truth. If we look at the Dutch economy, however, there appears to be little support nowadays for Heine's bold statement. Having an open economy, the Netherlands is very much influenced by the changes that have swept the international marketplace since the end of the 1970s (Harvey, 1989; Lipietz, 1992; Amin, 1994).

The most important developments in this respect are: the growth of international transport, communication and trade; the shift from a Fordist to a post-Fordist economy and the related arrival of 'just in time' principles for production and distribution; the intensification of competition between European cities and regions; and the growth of polycentric 'urban fields' and the blurring of the traditional town/country distinction. These developments – supported by technological innovation in the fields of communication and transportation and facilitated by the removal of institutional barriers in business and public administration – are highly relevant to cities and regions in the Netherlands (Cortie, 1991; Jobse and Musterd, 1994).

The growth of international trade and transportation has clearly created opportunities and threats for Dutch city-regions[2] –

especially for the conurbations around Amsterdam and Rotterdam, which contain the two mainports of the country. Amsterdam Airport and the Port of Rotterdam (Europort) are important gateways to Europe, and as such are the cornerstones of what is sometimes called 'Holland Distribution Country'. The two mainports are, of course, highly dependent upon infrastructural provisions for the distribution of goods. Thus, plans have been made to enlarge the capacity of Amsterdam Airport and the Port of Rotterdam and to improve the road and rail links between the two gateways and the European hinterland.

Developments towards a post-Fordist, or post-industrial, economy can be discerned around the two mainports, but also around some of the other urban centres (Jobse and Musterd, 1994). Energy-intensive industries are gradually moving out of the urbanized regions, whereas information-intensive industries are moving in. Dutch city-regions, which must compete with other city-regions in Western Europe for footloose companies, have shown an increasing interest in various factors of attraction of post-industrial investment, such as recreational and residential facilities as well as physical infrastructures and so-called 'knowledge centres' – science parks, museums, colleges, etc.

The development of polycentric urban fields can be discerned, first of all in the western part of the country where the *Randstad* – the urbanized ring that connects Rotterdam, The Hague, Amsterdam, Utrecht and some smaller cities – has come to resemble the megalopolis model that Peter Hall sketched in the 1970s (Hall, 1977). The Netherlands has also witnessed the rise of a network of middle-sized cities and towns in the centre and the south of the country. The result is a polycentric urban network extending from Amsterdam and the Hague in the west, to Breda and Eindhoven near the Belgium border and to Arnhem and Nijmegen near the German border.

It is often argued that transformations in the economic environment demand fast and decisive responses. Many commentators have come to doubt whether the sub-national system of the Netherlands offers an adequate framework for meeting this challenge. After discussing some of the rigidities in the Dutch system, this chapter will sketch the context of contemporary calls for regional reform. The following three sections will discuss the recent reform efforts at regional level and the institutional opposition that they have met. The concluding section will contain some remarks about the specific nature of the Dutch regionalization debate in a European perspective.

CONTINUITIES IN THE SUB-NATIONAL POLITICAL SYSTEM

While transformations in the world economy have led to marked social, cultural and spatial changes, the administrative structure of the Netherlands has remained rather static. In the 1980s, various countries reformed their sub-national state structures in the face of the economic and political transformations on the European continent (Sharpe, 1993). Regional governments were strengthened in France and Italy. In Belgium and Spain, regional governments even became the vital elements of federalized state structures. Compared to these countries, the sub-national structure of provinces and municipalities in the Netherlands appeared to be extremely stable. In the middle of the 1980s, the role and position of provinces and municipalities still conformed to the basic constitutional structure that was laid down by Thorbecke in 1848-1851 (1848 Constitution; 1850 Provincial Government Act; 1851 Local Government Act).

According to the Thorbeckean constitution, local and provincial governments have a general competence to regulate their own affairs. This regulatory competence is only constrained negatively. As long as municipalities and provinces do not diverge from the regulations of higher-ranking authorities, they are free to do whatever their councils deem necessary. The hierarchical ordering of municipal, provincial and national regulations underscores the unitary character of the Dutch state. The unitary state structure does not, however, necessarily go together with a centralized hierarchical system. The decentralized tradition, which had characterized the old Republic of Seven United Provinces in the seventeenth and eighteenth centuries, was kept alive in the newly constituted kingdom (Breunese, 1982). For this reason, textbooks usually describe the Netherlands as a 'decentralized unitary state' (Toonen, 1990; Hesse and Kleinfeld, 1990). The unity in this type of state is not based on control from above, but on agreement between the three levels of government of the state. The continuous search for agreement leads to an intensive pattern of interaction, in which all three layers have relative advantages and disadvantages. Municipalities can rely on local knowledge and operational experience. Provinces can benefit from their intermediary 'linch-pin' position. National government is in a position to resolve conflicts in the last instance, but will usually seek agreement with provinces and municipalities rather than impose central choices (Rieken and Baaijens, 1986).

Regional government in the Netherlands is typically a matter of 'co-government'. The value attached to consensus gives considerable blocking power to the various partners in co-governmental arrangements. This may stimulate the search for sophisticated solutions that are satisfying to all parties concerned, but it can also lead to frustrating stalemates. Consensual intergovernmental systems run the risk of falling into the 'joint decision trap' – as Scharpf rightly noticed (1988). The problematic aspects of joint decision-making already came to the fore in the 1920s, when the effects of the industrial revolution (which hit the Netherlands later than neighbouring countries) spilled over municipal boundaries and caused problems that could not easily be solved in a voluntary and consensual way (Van der Meer and Raadschelders, 1988). The first proposal for institutional change in regional government, made in 1929, has been followed by a stream of suggestions and proposals that bear one common characteristic: they did not cause lasting changes in the constitutional structure of sub-national government.

The debate about regional reform in the Netherlands has gone around in circles, always returning in the end to the constitutional starting-point. Radical proposals have always been defeated or withdrawn and followed by moderate proposals that confirmed, rather than reversed, the voluntary and consensual nature of intergovernmental relations. Instead of creating large two-tier city regions with special competencies – as In 't Veld suggested in 1929 – a moderate reform of interlocal co-operative arrangements was accepted in 1931. Instead of adding a fourth tier of government between the provincial and the municipal tiers – as the Koelma Committee suggested in 1947 – a bill was passed in order to strengthen the voluntary co-operation between sub-national governments. However, the resulting Joint Provisions Act of 1950 did not eliminate the need for regional reform (Hendriks, Raadschelders and Toonen, 1994).

In 1964, the Rijnmond Authority, covering Rotterdam and its neighbouring municipalities, was installed as an experimental form of regional government. This experiment did not last (Hendriks and

Toonen, 1995). Ten years later, however, serious changes seemed about to occur. In 1974, the Minister of Home Affairs proposed the creation of five large regions (*landsdelen*), which would cover 44 'socio-economic regions'. A year later, after a change in the government coalition, a brand new proposal figured on the reform agenda. The Netherlands was going to get 37 'provinces new style', which would fill the so-called regional gap. Over the years the number of new provinces would, however, drop from the initial 37 to 26, 24 and even 17; the envisaged competencies were curtailed as well. The idea was finally dropped altogether and replaced by a new Joint Provisions Act, authorized by Parliament in 1985. Thus, the process of territorial 'reorganization' came full circle again. In the middle of the 1980s, the Netherlands could still be typified as a decentralized unitary state, in which municipalities, provinces and national departments typically shared responsibility for issues of regional concern. The institutions for intergovernmental management have been tidied up – not changed – since the start of the regionalization debate in the 1920s (Toonen, 1993).

Institutional continuity is characteristic of the Dutch polity in general. The Netherlands has been described as the prototype of institutional conservatism (Andeweg, 1989) and the resistance to change has frustrated reformers of various kinds. The frustrations are related not only to the attempts at regional reform, but also to the efforts to reorganize the structure of central government, to transform the traditional party-political landscape, and to bridge the gap between government and society and between coalition politics and election results (Gladdish, 1991). In the course of the 1980s, the various frustrations provoked a rather vocal movement in favour of institutional renewal in general and regional reform in particular.

THE CONTEXT OF CONTEMPORARY CALLS FOR REGIONAL REFORM

Evaluations of the Dutch polity are influenced by two rivalling schools of political thought in the Netherlands – the Leiden school and the Amsterdam school. The dispute between these two schools, which started in the 1960s, has continued to the present day. The first school, led by well-known authors like Daalder and Lijphart, is characterized by a basically benevolent evaluation of the pluralistic and consensual patterns in the Dutch political system. Lijphart especially presented a strong case for the notion that the traditional rules for decision-making in the Netherlands were not less democratic, but simply 'democratic in a different way' (Lijphart, 1975; see also Daalder, 1981; 1990). The Amsterdam school, on the other hand, embraced what the Leiden school eventually rejected – the idea that Westminster democracies, characterized by clear-cut majoritarian decision-making structures and hierarchical intergovernmental relations, are essentially superior to consensual democracies of the Dutch kind.

While the ideas of the Leiden school may be well-known in academic circles abroad, they have not been very popular in elite circles in the Netherlands in recent times. Contemporary evaluations here are closer to the Amsterdam school. Public debate is nowadays in the hands of those who criticize the *stroperige staat*: the sluggish, complex, overorganized, viscous state (Chavannes, 1994). Those who value complex decision-making structures and cautious policy processes have been forced on the defensive. The critics of the viscous state point to the wide distribution of blocking powers in the political system and the complexity of interorganizational networks. The constitutional structure contains many checks and balances, which are supposedly leading to indecisiveness in the real world of policy-making (WRR, 1994). Many commentators fear that the Netherlands will get out of step in Europe when the institutions for public policy-making keep hindering, rather than facilitating, an adequate response to the external challenges. They usually have no difficulty in finding examples of projects that proceed slowly: the slowness in renewing river-dikes in the Dutch polderland; the failing construction of a relief road outside The Hague; the tedious planning of economically crucial rail links between Rotterdam and Germany (*de Betuweroute*), and between Amsterdam and Brussels (*TGV*).

The critique of the viscous state comes from different directions. Lobbyists for the pressure group called 'Netherlands Distribution Country' wish to improve the procedures that slow down the improvement of rail– road links between the ports and the European hinterland. This pressure group has coined the word Jutlandization, hinting at the risk of becoming a peripheral nation in Europe. The mayors of Amsterdam and Rotterdam echoed this complaint and connected it to other problems of governance in their regions, caused by the fact that single authorities can veto projects that are not directly beneficial to them, but which might be beneficial to the conurbation as a whole. A common reproach of these mayors is that the Dutch provinces are not able to break through the stalemates that often plague metropolitan decision-making (Van Thijn, 1991). Some would argue that the provinces rarely solve and often aggravate the problems (Van Schendelen, 1987; Klein, 1992). It is remarkable that quite a few provincial representatives agree with the complaints about the feeble role and position of the provinces in the sub-national state structure. The complaints of lobbyists and politicians have been amplified by high-ranking officials and by public opinion-leaders, who regularly express their concerns in the quality press.

Thus, a broad 'advocacy coalition' (Sabatier, 1987) in favour of administrative reform has become prominent in political debate. Proposals for regional reform can rely directly or indirectly on the support of this coalition. Some commentators have interpreted these developments in terms of a counter-cultural movement (Van Schendelen, 1995). In contrast to the counter-cultural movement of the 1960s, however, the counter-cultural movement of the early 1990s is an elite movement. The initiators are public and private entrepreneurs. And, unlike the counter-culture of the 1960s, they are not against authority but very much in favour of it.

RECENT DEVELOPMENTS AT THE REGIONAL LEVEL:
1988 - 1995

Those who thought that the regionalization debate had come to an end with the renewal of the Joint Provisions Act in 1985 were mistaken. In the second half of the 1980s and the first half of the 1990s, the window of opportunity for regional reform was opened by the accumulation of developments described above: economic, social, cultural and spatial changes in city-regions; growing frustration with institutional conservatism in general; and the emerging consensus that something must be done very soon about the inertia and viscosity of the Dutch political system. The renewed academic interest in the institutional factor in political life was also important, adding to the growing conviction that political institutions constrain and guide policy-making processes. However, the warnings in the literature on neo-institutionalism about the risks of reform were not always noted.

The first hint of change may be seen in the Fourth Document on Physical Planning, issued by the Government in 1988. The Cabinet acknowledged here the economic value of the major metropolitan regions and suggested that these regions be given more room to manoeuvre. A year later, this idea was taken up by the Montijn Committee, which suggested creating large-scale metropolitan authorities around the major cities of the country. The Montijn Committee also advised keeping the four economic 'trump cards' – Amsterdam, Rotterdam, The Hague and Utrecht – 'in one hand'. Some interpreted this as a clear signal to create a *'Randstad* Region'. Shortly after the Montijn Committee submitted its report, two national advisory councils – the RBB (the Advisory Council for Home Administration, 1989) and the WRR (Scientific Council for Government Policy, 1990) – presented critical analyses of the problems and opportunities for regional governance in the Netherlands. The Cabinet was more or less forced to react with its own policy statement.

The cabinet response took the form of a triple jump. It produced three successive documents under the heading *Bestuur op Niveau* (the level of government). This has a double meaning: it refers to the scale of government, which should fit the tasks at hand, but it also refers to the quality of governance, which should be high. The *Bestuur op Niveau* trilogy is usually discussed in terms of BON-1 (1990), BON-2 (1991) and BON-3 (1993). The Ministry of Home Affairs, well aware of its poor reform record, did not want to make the same mistakes as before (Koppenjan, 1993). It started off with the conviction that comprehensive blueprints for regional reform could not succeed in the Netherlands. Thus, the Ministry for Home Affairs developed a highly pragmatic reform policy which called for tailor-made solutions for the most pressing regional problems. The new reform policy called for a combination of bottom-up initiatives and top-down constraints for change. Blueprint rationality was exchanged for process rationality (Salet, 1994).

In the first part of the BON trilogy, the cabinet acknowledged that the problems of metropolitan regions were not easily resolved within the institutional framework of the day. The ministry encouraged those conurbations with the most pressing administrative problems to develop their own reform proposals, tailored to their specific situation. The bottom-up initiatives were constrained by a number of procedural and substantial criteria, which were quite general and self-evident. With the policy document BON-2, released in 1991, the ministry took the process a bit further. First, the document proposed to sharpen the rules for intergovernmental co-operation for the country at large. Second, and most importantly, the document defined seven metropolitan regions where new administrative structures were to be formed. The ministry gave explicit priority to the built-up areas around the 'big four' – Amsterdam, Rotterdam, The Hague, Utrecht – and to three additional areas built around the cities of Eindhoven, Arnhem/Nijmegen and Enschede/Hengelo. One year later, the BON-2 document was translated into framework legislation (*Ontwerp Kaderwet Bestuur in Verandering*, passed in July 1994) which further defined the procedure that the selected areas were to follow. Three steps were defined as follows: from intergovernmental 'joint provisions' (along the lines of the old Joint Provisions Act) towards 'regional corporations' (which would take care of a minimum package of steering tasks, adhering to sharpened rules for co-operation and co-ordination); from 'regional corporations' towards 'regional authorities' (which would be coupled only loosely to the participating urban districts); and from 'regional authorities' towards 'regional governments' (which would get a directly elected council and a more or less autonomous competence to define strategic policies at city-regional level).

In the ideal situation step two would be skipped – the conurbation would move directly from the regional corporation model to the regional government model. Knowing that administrative reform processes are rarely ideal in the Netherlands, the Ministry of Home Affairs opened the possibility of taking a bit more time to make the final jump. All seven areas were to make this jump before the year 2001. By that time, 158 municipalities, representing one third of the Dutch population, should be covered by seven regional governments. The municipalities concerned should surrender fiscal privileges and functional competencies. The consequences for the traditional meso-layer, the provinces, were not specified.

Not all parties were satisfied with this cautious approach. Reformers in the Rotterdam conurbation, in particular, wanted to move faster and go further than the official reform policy demanded. In 1991 and 1992, the Consultation Council for the Rijnmond Region (OOR) produced its own reform documents (*De Inzet-1* and *De Inzet-2*) which set out a policy that was both creative and explosive. The documents proposed creating a new regional government, which would cover almost the same territory as the old Rijnmond Authority had covered. It would also address the same sorts of issues: physical planning, economic development, traffic and transportation, environmental protection, housing, recreation and other tasks that surpassed the scale of the single districts. Apart from that, the Consultation Council proposed to diverge from the old Rijnmond model in three important ways. First, the new regional government should not only be a strategic planning authority, but should get important executive responsibilities as well. Second, the new regional government should replace the province of South Holland and deal directly with national government. Because the constitution demands that all Dutch territory be covered by provinces, the new region would be called a 'province new style'. Third, Rotterdam was persuaded to divide itself into units that would match the scale of the surrounding districts. The region should in the end cover about 26 'municipalities new style', which would take care of the small-scale living environment and the general well-being of citizens. The city-province would concentrate on the strategic challenges and large-scale facilities (Hendriks, 1993).

The proposals of the OOR created a momentum in the reform process. They were generally interpreted as a massive attack on the Dutch sub-national constitution. The framers of the proposals made no secret of the fact that the 'OOR model' could be translated to the country at large (Flierman, 1993). This would mean that the 12 Dutch provinces would be replaced by at least twice as many 'provinces new style'. Important members of Parliament – most notably, the Christian Democratic spokesman for home affairs - adopted this idea, which soon came to be known as the '25 regions scheme'. For a moment it seemed that the Ministry of Home Affairs was going along too. The ministry produced a 'province memorandum', which suggested replacing the provinces by a larger number of regions of a different kind - the *Randstad* Region alone would be subdivided in six or seven regions new style. This rather drastic departure from the usual cautious reform policy did not, however, receive the necessary Cabinet support. The Ministry of Home Affairs was urged to recapture the line set out in BON-1 and BON-2, concentrating on seven urban areas and touching upon the provincial layer only incrementally and incidentally. This was laid down in the third part of the BON trilogy, released in 1993.

Although the reform document BON-3 paid lip service to the incremental approach, many observers felt that comprehensive reorganization of meso-government was still in the air. When the

Ministry of Home Affairs proposed concentrating the patchwork of functional regions into a standardized framework of about 25 to 28 co-operation areas, this was generally seen as a revival of the '25 regions scheme', which was still the favourite plan of the Christian Democrats. The latter secretly hoped to deal with this issue during the formation of a new cabinet. However, for the first time since the Second World War, the Christian Democrats were not involved in the formation of a new cabinet. The new left-liberal cabinet, installed in mid-1994, has not yet shown much interest in sweeping regional reforms. Neither has the newly assembled parliament. Following the advice of the RBB (the Advisory Council for Home Affairs), parliament passed a motion that gives priority to regionalization around Amsterdam, Rotterdam and The Hague but it has come to doubt whether the other four urban areas should evolve towards the city-province model.

Looking back at the most recent reform efforts, one could say that reform thinking peaked in 1993. Regional reformers flew high for a moment, but came back to the ground rather soon. They had to transform the incremental reform logic into down-to-earth legislation for the urban regions. This has not been easy thus far. At the moment of finishing this chapter (winter 1995) only one region – the Rotterdam Region – has reached substantial agreement with the Ministry of Home Affairs on the special legislation that is meant to constitute a new city-province in 1997. There is still substantial disagreement about the *Lex Specialis* that should regulate the installation of regional governments in the Amsterdam area and the area around The Hague. The districts in the Eindhoven region have not even managed to reach agreement about the installation of a 'regional corporation' (the first step in the BON-process). The institutionalized resistance to change has again been stronger than the reformers estimated.

INSTITUTIONALIZED RESISTANCE TO CHANGE

The proposals for regional reform received warm support from those who criticized the sluggishness and viscosity of public administration in the Netherlands. However, many actors involved in public administration (in the broadest sense) resisted drastic changes in the sub-national political system. The combination of active opposition and passive non-co-operation has resulted in the dilution of regional reform. Active and passive resistance came from various directions. It came from representatives of provinces and municipalities, from advisory councils, from politicians with active experience in European politics, from citizens in the selected conurbations, from municipalities in these conurbations, and eventually from some of the organizations which had initiated regional reform in the first place.

First and foremost, resistance came from the provinces and their national association (abbreviated 'IPO' in Dutch). In the same period as the Ministry of Home Affairs started the BON-process and the Council for Administrative Reform in the Rotterdam Region recommended its regional government model for the whole country, the provinces tried to work out their own alternative. In 1992, an IPO committee suggested installing three or four *landsdelen*, relatively large-scale regional bodies between national government and the current provinces (Committee Hendrikx, 1992). In line with this suggestion, provinces in the northern, southern and western parts of the country intensified their co-operation, implying that this might in the end lead to provincial amalgamation. Although no one really thought that the provinces would regain their grandeur of the past, many saw the provincial moves as proof of regained self-confidence. The growing assertiveness of the provinces was further illustrated by their rather successful lobbying campaign against the 'province memorandum' of 1993.

The provincial opposition against division of the Netherlands into about 25 regions of the Rijnmond type was supported from different ends of the administrative scale. Although many local actors disliked supervision by the old provinces, they could not see how 'hands-on' regions, with ambitious governance tasks, would improve their position. The national association of local authorities (VNG) regularly expressed its concern about the envisaged regional reforms. In the Netherlands, the Ministry of Home Affairs is well advised to listen to the concerns of this association, which is generally seen as one of the most powerful lobbies in the country. The '25 regions scheme' was further criticized by the former Dutch EC Commissioner, Andriessen, who quite correctly remarked that the 'regions' in this concept did not resemble the sort of units that the European Commission envisaged in its 'Europe of the Regions' scheme. Fearing that the Netherlands would get out of step in Europe, he urged regional reformers in this country to think in terms of relatively large-scale *landsdelen*, just like the Hendrikx Committee advised in 1992.

Advisory councils, consultation committees and research institutes have always played an important role in the Dutch policy-making system, which is geared to downplaying potentially divisive conflicts and 'pacifying' rivals in a rational, pragmatic and consensual way (Van Schendelen, 1984; Van Putten, 1982). A standard response to difficult problems is to entrust them to more or less independent boards that explore the options that are both effective and acceptable all around. Even when government has already chosen a line of action, the reactions of professional advisers, consultants and other experts are usually taken very seriously. Continuous criticism coming from the state's intellectual guardians can kill constitutional reform in the Netherlands. The recent attempts at regional reform received intellectual opposition coming from basically two perspectives: physical planning and constitutional law.

Observers taking the physical planning perspective have argued that the tendency towards administrative down-scaling at meso-level makes no sense considering the processes of scale-enlargement in general and the growth of polycentric urban fields in particular. Geographers have made it very clear that the seven urban areas selected for reform are functionally embedded in remarkably larger urban fields (Cortie, 1991). It is generally acknowledged that Rotterdam and The Hague, two cities that would fall under separate regional governments, are functionally highly interdependent and actually part of an urban conglomeration covering The Hague, Rotterdam, Dordrecht and the urbanized area around these cities (Salet, 1994). The importance of this urban field has been confirmed by representatives of the three cities, who recently called for stronger co-operation across the conglomeration. Many experts would add that the urban area around Rotterdam is also inextricably bound up with the area around Amsterdam, thus forming the *Randstad* megalopolis, which should be approached as one coherent planning region (Van Rossem, 1995). The national physical planning department has recently produced a paper with the telling title 'Room for Regions', which assumes the existence of one economic core area covering the *Randstad* and large parts of the east and south (RPD, 1995).

The second type of expert criticism has followed a legal-constitutional line. It started with a report of three constitutional experts, who had been asked by the national association of provinces to react to the BON procedure (see the steps outlined above). The three strongly criticized the temporary constructions that would take over local and provincial responsibilities in the period preceding the installation of new city-provinces. The Parliamentary Commission for Home Affairs, apparently alarmed by the critical notes, asked for a second opinion from another group of legal experts, whose evaluations appeared to be rather negative as well. Things were getting worse when the critical emphasis shifted from the preceding stages to the final step in the reform process: the installation of regional governments in the form of provinces new style. The latter model came under serious attack when the *Raad van State* – the highest advisory council in the Netherlands, with roots going back to the old Republic of United Provinces – reacted negatively on the bill designed to install a city-province in the Rotterdam region.

The *Raad van State* criticized the city-province model for the Rotterdam region because this model would be at odds with the Thorbeckean constitution. The new city province would not become a real meso-government but rather an upper-tier local unit. The *Raad van State* asked: why not install a consolidated municipality in the Rotterdam region when it is urban management, and not intermediary government, that all parties want to improve? The *Lex Specialis* for the Rotterdam region would create an upper-tier unit that would not be really provincial, and it would create lower-tier units that would not be really municipal (in the Thorbecke sense). The lower-tier units would get curtailed competencies which would be at odds with the constitutional rights of local government. Apart from that, the local government system would suffer from the division of Rotterdam into ten 'midget-municipalities'. On the basis of this analysis, two members of the *Raad van State* totally rejected the city-province model. The other members expressed serious doubts and advised government to reconsider the model of consolidated local government.

The criticisms did not pass by unnoticed at national level. When administrative reforms take a long time, as they usually do in the Netherlands, it is almost inevitable that political leadership will change during the process. In 1994, the architect of the BON process, minister of state De Graaff-Nauta, was replaced by a new one, Van De Vondervoort, who has proved to be more reluctant with regard to comprehensive regional reform than was her predecessor. The new minister of state emphasized quite soon that she intended to use, rather than attack, the Dutch provinces. She distanced herself from the idea of synchronizing joint provisions into 25 or 29 co-operation regions, arguing that the provinces are better equipped to perform that task. Echoing the *Raad van State*, Van de Vondervoort criticized Rotterdam and Amsterdam for creating far too many midget-municipalities that would lack the necessary power to fend for themselves. She will probably not stop the BON process in the two or three major cities, but she is likely to stimulate the creation of strong consolidated municipalities for the other cities. Thus far, the new minister of state has strongly supported the new political consensus, holding that the provinces new style will be the exception, rather than the rule, for the Dutch system of home administration.

THE EXCEPTION REGIONS AND THEIR DIFFICULTIES

The developments described above contributed to the dilution of reform ambitions and to the concentration of the reforms into three urban areas. The resistance in these areas should not be underestimated, however. In the area around The Hague, many municipalities are reluctant to merge with the core city into a new regional government. The Hague is generally seen as the least attractive bride of the large cities. The city brings a rather negative dowry into the marriage – it has a huge financial deficit for which the other districts do not want to pay. Besides that, The Hague has not been willing to divide itself into smaller parts that would be perceived as less threatening by the other municipalities. Some representatives of the Hague have actually increased their neighbours' suspicions by threatening to annex the surrounding districts if they do not hurry to fall into line. This threat is tactless, although understandable – the region contains a few notorious municipal obstructionists.

Schiphol Airport is the greatest divisive issue in the Amsterdam region. The city of Amsterdam is opting for the so-called 'mainport model', which implies that the new city-province gets complete control of the airport. The problem for Amsterdam is that the airport is located outside its city boundaries. The district of Haarlemmermeer, the local home base of Schiphol Airport, is not willing to transfer all responsibilities to the city-province, and is supported by most other municipalities that would be covered by the new regional government. This has created a serious stalemate, since representatives of Amsterdam have always stated that they are not going to divide the city and transfer authority to a regional government that is not even capable of controlling the most important economic factor in the conurbation. The airport is not the only complication in the reform process. The province of North Holland excluded four districts from regionalization, thereby weakening the viability of the future city-province. The new minister of state suggested dividing Amsterdam not in 16 parts but in four or five parts, thereby arousing suspicion on the part of the surrounding districts. Finally, a group of citizens very much opposed to the fragmentation of Amsterdam are canvassing for a petition which should open the way to a corrective referendum. Opinion polls indicate that the division of Amsterdam into smaller units will not get a majority in a referendum.

The Rotterdam region is surely ahead of the other two main conurbations but the new city-province is certainly not yet assured. The chorus of popular opposition to fragmentation of Rotterdam has grown more vocal recently – the local new politics party and some affiliated groups have already demanded a corrective referendum on the issue. The suburban districts still fear the coming of a top-heavy city-province that will be dominated by former personnel of the core city. Municipalities like Schiedam and Vlaardingen prefer the creation of a 'lean and mean' city-province, which leaves plenty of room to the lower-tier municipalities, while Rotterdam prefers the coming of a robust and decisive upper-tier government. The stance of Rotterdam is understandable, considering the way in which some city wards foresee their future status as new-style municipalities. Against this background, and also considering the practical complications of a major reorganization, insiders have estimated that the city-province will not be operational before the year 2005.

One could say that the current situation is not very different from the situation some 20 years ago. Large-scale reforms were in the air, but they were successively toned down and focused on a few territories. The Rotterdam region is – again – far ahead of the rest of the country, but the viability of the new Rijnmond experiment has yet to be proved. The Rijnmond area witnessed the rise and fall of regional government before; this could happen again, considering the Dutch history of administrative reform in general and the recent resistance to reform in particular.

CLOSING REMARKS ON DUTCH PARTICULARISM

From a European point of view, the regionalization debate in the Netherlands appears to be quite peculiar. There are two sides to Dutch particularism. Few other countries in Europe have been preoccupied by regional reform for so long, yet have been able to achieve so little in terms of lasting constitutional changes. No other country, to my knowledge, has been so persistent in its focus on a rather narrow definition of regional government; the regional question has, almost without exception, been defined as a question of upper-local urban management.

This is not to say that nothing has changed at all. The recent calls for reform of the viscous structures of government have not been without effect. Parliament has accepted legislation that is designed to streamline procedures for infrastructural projects (the so-called *Tracé-wet*) and for other projects that tend to get bogged down in seemingly endless circles of non-decision-making (the so-called *Nimby-wet*). These pieces of legislation might not change the basic rights of authorities and groups in the decision-making process, but they do introduce some changes in synchronization and timetabling. Many critics of the viscous state hoped that government would proceed in this direction and create regional governments that would be powerful enough to 'set things right' at the sub-national level. In this respect, not much has happened yet. There appears to be strong institutionalized resistance to reforms that would concentrate steering power at regional level and break through the evolved structure characterized by power-sharing and power-diffusion. As a result, the actual changes at sub-national level are far less impressive than some hoped they would be. They are certainly rather modest in comparison to the changes achieved in countries like Belgium, Spain, France and Italy.

In the countries mentioned above, the regional question is traditionally defined much more broadly than it usually is in the Netherlands. What comes to mind in these countries, when talking about regions, are areas like Flanders, Catalonia, Rhône-Alpes and Lombardy. The regional debate in the Netherlands has, in contrast, been concentrated on urban areas like the ones around Amsterdam, Rotterdam and The Hague. The long-time 'regional' debate in the Netherlands is actually a metropolitan debate. The main issue has never really been meso-government in a true sense, but rather upper-tier urban government – at a level comparable to that of the

German '*Stadtkreis*' or the British 'Metropolitan County'. The history of regional reform in the Netherlands reveals a strong 'mobilization of bias' (Schattschneider, 1960): an institutionalized preoccupation with supralocal urban government and, at the same time, an institutionalized blind spot for the potential of the traditional meso, the Dutch province.

This is very odd, since the Dutch province, having an open household, a co-ordinating and supervisory role with respect to municipalities, and a strategic intermediary position, is formally a match for any meso-government in Europe (Toonen, 1993). Reformers in other countries, who had to invent institutions at the meso-level in order to anticipate societal and administrative changes, must be astonished when they find out that the Dutch tend to neglect a form of meso-government that needs only a few adaptations in order to play its part in a Europe of the Regions.

NOTES

1. The author would like to thank Willeke van Brouwershaven-Hoeke and Jos Raadschelders, both working at the Department of Public Administration of Leiden University, for their valuable comments on earlier drafts of this chapter.

2. In the Netherlands, the term 'region' usually refers to a level of governance situated between the *gemeente* (municipality) and the *provincie* (county). Its scale is equivalent to the old Metropolitian Counties in the UK or the metropolitan regions in the US.

18

Wales: A Developing Political Economy

BARRY JONES

INTRODUCTION

The need to restructure parts of the policy-making institutions of the British state was recognized as early as the mid-1950s when the problem of uneven economic activity between the various economic regions was first acknowleged. The problem was compounded because not all the economic regions were simply lines drawn on a map for administrative or economic purposes. Some, particularly Scotland and Wales, possessed significant political dimensions which would have to be accommodated in any new institutional arrangements. In the case of Wales, there were additional difficulties. Both economically and constitutionally, Wales is more closely integrated with England than is Scotland. For 500 years it has formed part of that constitutional hybrid 'England and Wales'. Despite this, Wales possesses a distinctive culture epitomized by a significant number of Welsh speakers. Thus, Wales is both an economic region and a nation, possessing both economic and political dimensions.

The modernization and the politicization of Welsh society took place in the last 30 years of the nineteenth century and proceeded along two distinct but connected lines. First, the uprising of Welsh-speaking and religious non-conformist tenant farmers who led a campaign to disestablish the Church of England in Wales, which attained its objective in 1922. Second, the growth of a Welsh working class linked to the chapels which found expression in trade union organization and, eventually, in the Labour Party. Both these developments were strongly imbued with Welsh cultural values and tended to assume an anti-English character. The established, yet alien, Anglican Church, the intransigent landlord and the exploitative capitalist classes were all capable of being identified with the English interest. While this did not lead to political nationalism in the form of a separatist party, it lent a nationalist tinge to political activity and debate in Wales.

In the last two decades of the nineteenth century, Wales became a more significant factor in British politics largely because of the rapidly developing economy in south Wales; specifically the creation of a vast coal mining industry based on the rich seams of steam coal and anthracite and the associated iron, steel and tinplate industries. Wales went from being an economically marginal region to one that was central to the British economy. Furthermore, the mixture of traditional Welsh radicalism and smoke-stack industries produced a dynamic trade union movement with aspirations and objectives which became increasingly political.

THE DEVELOPMENT OF WELSH INSTITUTIONS

It is against this background that the initial phase of Welsh institutional developments in the period 1889 to 1920 should be viewed (Jones, 1988). They reflected the pressing concerns of the Welsh radical political tradition for which Lloyd George was such an eloquent spokesman: education, public health provisions, agriculture and disestablishment of the Church of England. The second phase coincided with the immediate post-war years, 1945-51, when the Labour Party held office with a large majority, a radical programme of state intervention and a strong sense of obligation to Wales. The recognition that education in Wales should be treated differently was reiterated with the creation of a Welsh Joint Education Committee consisting of representatives of all the Welsh local education authorities and with responsibilities for curriculum development and public examinations. The establishment in 1948 of a Council for Wales and Monmouthshire to advise the government on the impact of government policies on Wales gave two quite contradictory messages; on the one hand, a recognition that Wales possessed interests distinct from England and that it was prudent to take note of such differences. However, the fact that the Council members were nominated confirmed the Labour government's reluctance to concede real political powers to Wales. This was the beginning of a pattern of administrative decentralization, balanced by opposition to political devolution, which has remained the norm for all subsequent British governments.

The third phase began in 1964 with the creation of the Welsh Office and the appointment of a Secretary of State for Wales with a seat in the cabinet. Initially, the Welsh Office powers were very limited and included administrative responsibilities for town and country planning, housing, water, sewage, some economic planning duties, some responsibilities for roads, plus 'oversight functions' (unspecified and unclear) with reference to the ministries of agriculture, education, health, transport, labour and the Board of Trade in so far as their activities were carried out in Wales. Subsequently, the Welsh Office has grown under both Labour and Conservative governments and it now has responsibility for local authorities, the health service, forestry and agriculture, tourism, primary and secondary education, further education and universities, child care, industrial location and inward investment. Since 1979, the Welsh Office has also been responsible for negotiating the Rate Support Grant (now the Revenue Support Grant) with the Treasury. With the exception of the Home Office, the Foreign Office and the Ministry of Defence, the Welsh Office is for most purposes the expression and means of government in Wales (Jones, 1990).

PARLIAMENTARY PROVISIONS FOR WALES

Unlike Scotland, Wales cannot be regarded as 'a state within a state'. In terms of parliamentary legislation, Wales is part of England. However, in certain key areas of Welsh culture and language, special legislation relating to Wales alone has been passed by parliament. The justification for these departures from the legislative norm is that these Acts provide for the protection of the 'Welsh way of life'. Thus, Welsh district councils have the power of initiative every seven years to hold a referendum to decide whether or not to open public houses on Sunday. Since 1967, the Welsh language has 'equal validity' with English; most government and public utility forms are now bilingual; in certain circumstances, evidence may be given in court in Welsh and courts are expected to have translation facilities available. These language rights have been extended by the 1993 Welsh Language Act.[1]

Special parliamentary provision is also made for Wales. The House of Commons (Redistribution of Seats) Act 1949 created a separate Welsh Boundary Commission and guaranteed a minimum of 35 seats for Wales regardless of shifts in population within the United Kingdom. Because of this, Wales (which presently has 40 seats) is, on a crude population measure, over-represented, deserving no more than 33 seats. Logically, any significant shift to Welsh political devolution would lead to Wales (and Labour) losing seats in the House of Commons. There are also two parliamentary committees designed to safeguard the Welsh interest; the Welsh Grand Committee, established in 1960, which meets three times a session and debates matters relating to Wales, and a Select Committee on Welsh Affairs set up in 1979 to provide better parliamentary supervision of the Welsh Office. Its remit extends to all aspects of public policy in Wales, but the breadth of its responsibilities inhibits the development of expertise, and the Conservative majority on the committee (contrary to Wales) tends to undermine its credibility and political legitimacy (Drewry, 1985).

THE POST-1979 REFERENDUM PERIOD

In the aftermath of the 1979 referendum, in which the Welsh electorate rejected political devolution by a 4:1 majority, there were profound economic and political changes.

In 1979 the Welsh economy was dominated by a public sector which employed 43 per cent of the working population. The Thatcherite policy of reducing state funding and promoting privatization consequently had a disproportionate impact on Wales and, during the decade of the 1980s, the Welsh steel industry contracted from almost 70,000 to 18,000 steel workers. The coal industry, upon which modern Welsh political identity had been built, was virtually eliminated; 43,000 had been employed in the industry in 1979. By 1995, there were fewer than 2,000 employed in deep mines (Balsom and Jones, 1984). There is no doubt that some of these changes were unavoidable. The decline of traditional industries is always difficult but the concentration of such industries in the Welsh economy made the exercise particularly painful and stoked up resentments in a declining working class.

The post-1979 political innovations introduced by Mrs Thatcher's Conservative government also produced significant changes. It soon became evident after the Conservatives came to power that they intended to treat Wales differently from England. The so-called 'culling of the quangos', which Mrs Thatcher regarded as crucial to rolling back the 'frontiers of the state', hardly applied to Wales at all. On the contrary, the 1980s witnessed a dramatic expansion of Welsh quangos created by a Conservative government with members nominated by a Conservative Secretary of State. With the Conservatives consistently polling between one quarter and one third of the vote for a handful of seats, it is difficult to avoid the conclusion that the Conservatives are the natural minority party in Wales. This raises a difficult question which became more pressing during the 1980s and into the 1990s; namely how a party, winning power because of its majority in the House of Commons, should exercise that power in Wales where it has no majority and a dubious mandate? It is not an easy question because Britain's constitution is undoubtedly unitary; sovereign power, such as is left after obligations to the European Union have been discharged, resides in Parliament. The territorial offices of Northern Ireland, Scotland and Wales are constitutional aberrations which do not fit easily with British conventions or parliamentary procedures. Thus, there are no absolute guiding principles which a Welsh Secretary of State can follow in making appointments, and such precedents as can be cited are rooted in a two-party system and a swinging electoral pendulum. Neither was a dominant characteristic of the 1980s.

The problem is compounded because Wales now possesses a cornucopia of quangos which in no small degree has contributed to the emergence of a Welsh political and administrative identity. After the creation of the Welsh Office in 1964, new quangos came into existence covering most aspects of Welsh life: the arts, sport, health and the countryside; tourism, inward investment, land, housing and economic development; and most recently, higher and further education. The Welsh quangos taken together are responsible for £1.5 billion expenditure a year. Two of the quangos – the Welsh Development Agency (WDA), authorizing £149 million a year, and Housing for Wales/Tai Cymru, £116 million a year – are among the top 40 quangos in the United Kingdom. Even the smaller quangos spend significant amounts; the Welsh Arts Council authorizes over £12 million of public expenditure each year. Nor is the process of 'quangoization' complete. The new hospital trusts and opting-out schools will bring further quangos in their wake (Morgan and Roberts, 1993).

There are concerns, not confined to party political spokesmen, that the growth of Welsh quangos and the amount of expenditure which they authorize has now reached a critical point. The first concern regards the power of appointment exercised by the Secretary of State for Wales: is this form of government patronage a good or bad thing in itself and is it being operated in an appropriate manner? The Welsh Labour Party has accused the government of 'stuffing public bodies in Wales with Tory placemen' and condemned the practice of Conservative representatives, both former MEPs and MPs, rejected by their respective electorates, subsequently being appointed by the Welsh Secretary to chair quangos (Labour Party, 1993). The clear implication behind these criticisms is that the Welsh Secretary of State should appoint more representative persons to the quangos – more Labour people, more women and fewer Conservatives. In short, people more typical and representative of Welsh interests.

The second major concern is that Welsh quangos are not properly accountable to the electorate but are lodged in the semi-secret world of the executive branch of government. The Welsh Development Agency (WDA) was subjected to the ordeal of examination by the respected and feared Public Accounts Committee in 1992. Various 'skeletons' were discovered and warnings were issued. But it is rare for public bodies in Wales to be subject to the attentions of the Public Accounts Committee; there are bigger, more expensive fish to fry in London. The Welsh Affairs Committee might undertake regular investigations of Welsh quangos but the committee is a flawed instrument; it is not specialist, nor could it be given its wide remit. It is too small to permit an effective sub-committee to operate and it lacks the kind of specialist professional secretariat which would be absolutely necessary if the supervision of Welsh public bodies were to be detailed and rigorous (Jones and Wilford, 1986).

Despite their limitations, the quangos are nonetheless Welsh and have helped construct a distinctive and largely separate Welsh administrative system which has provided additional evidence in the continuing debate on political devolution, linking the argument for an elected Welsh Assembly with increased democratic accountability.

POLITICAL MOBILIZATION AND THE EUROPEAN UNION

The economic reverses of the 1980s, and the continuity of a Conservative government lacking a majority in Wales and pursuing an ideological agenda at variance with the prevailing Welsh political values, have had a profound impact on Welsh political life. The political legitimacy of Conservative government initiatives has been called into question while successive Conservative administrations have reiterated their determination to 'preserve the union' and yet have found it prudent to treat Wales differently by, in effect, marginalizing it from the mainstream of British (that is, English) politics. This was a high-risk strategy dependent upon the appointment of moderate or centrist Conservative Secretaries of State and giving them a relatively free hand. The first three Secretaries, Nicholas Edwards, Peter Walker and David Hunt, fall into this category. However, the appointment of John Redwood from the hard right wing of the party produced additional problems for the Conservatives in Wales, alienated public opinion and provided Labour with a more favourable environment within which they could promote their new devolution policy for Wales.

In this situation, political activists have not been demoralized nor have they waited for Labour to win office – the traditional attitude. Instead they have reacted in a positive manner, seeking to exploit alternative avenues for political lobbying. The possibilities provided by British membership of the European Community (now Union) have been crucial in the development of this strategy. This is all the more remarkable given Wales' early scepticism about the 'Common Market' (Welsh Economic Council, 1971).

The Welsh Labour Party was hostile; first, on ideological grounds, to what it saw as a rich man's capitalist club and, secondly, because of the economic dangers for Wales located, as it was on the geographic periphery and far from Europe's economic hub, the 'Golden Triangle' (Welsh Council of Labour, 1978). Plaid Cymru's opposition echoed that of the Labour Party, but was reinforced by a deep distrust of such a large politico-economic organization in which minority national interests would be marginalized and disregarded (Plaid Cymru, 1984). Only the Conservatives and the Liberals could be regarded as pro-European.

In the wake of the UK-wide referendum on EEC membership in 1975, the attitudes of the major political forces in Wales underwent a substantial change. Plaid Cymru began to see the European Community (as it was then) as a community of communities in which the Welsh community might even thrive. The Wales TUC remained deeply sceptical but pragmatically decided to take advantage of the opportunities and benefits provided by the EC.

The Labour Party's opposition was total, favouring withdrawal until the 1983 election, following which it adopted a pro-European stance with the unqualified enthusiasm of the convert. In short, the parties in Wales have learned to love the European Community and now the European Union.

It is against this historical background that the evolution of the complex network of consultative relationships between Wales and the European Union must be judged. Within the network, the role of the Welsh Office is central, but of equal and sometimes greater significance are other UK government departments such as the Department of Employment, Department of Industry and the Ministry of Agriculture. In addition, various government agencies in Wales, such as the WDA and Mid Wales Development, play critical roles as do the two local authority associations, the Assembly of Welsh Counties and the Council of Welsh Districts. Not least there is the continual input of a wide variety of organized interest groups, covering all aspects of social, economic and political life in Wales. On the European side of the network, there is the European Commission Office in Wales, Welsh Members of the European Parliament (including its party groupings and committees), and the European Commission (including those key directorates with an input to regional support in all its guises). In addition, there are the European-wide territorial interest groups which aim to promote peripheral and regional concerns, such as the Conference of Peripheral Maritime Regions, the Assembly of European Regions and the Atlantic Arc. This is by no means a comprehensive list, nor does a listing of a particular group or organization imply that it is influential. But the list does give an indication of the range and complexity of the Welsh/EU consultative network.

The explanation of why such a network has come into being reflects both political and administrative factors. The notion of a territorial interest distinct from and possibly opposed to the United Kingdom interest was slow to develop in Wales. The late revival of Welsh nationalism as a political force in the 1960s made only limited progress in the business, industrial and trade union sectors. However, the creation of the Welsh Office and the subsequent delegation of a wide range of administrative functions brought with it an inexorable logic to which both governmental and interest groups were obliged to respond. A variety of organizations which did business with government, particularly in those areas where functions had been devolved to the Welsh Office, prudently established a Welsh institutional identity within their organizations. As the Welsh Office acquired more functional responsibilities, so the tendency for the organization of Welsh interests became more pronounced, a process accelerated after 1979 when the Select Committee on Welsh Affairs was set up, further encouraging various sets of interests to focus their activities at the Welsh level.

Organized interests in Wales, including political parties, have been equally active in seeking to influence the European Union, an exercise seen as complementary and – in some circumstances – as an alternative to lobbying the British government. Throughout the 1980s, the Thatcher government was unsympathetic to demands for government intervention and public investment and, consistent with its anti-corporatist stance, hostile to large-scale socio-economic groups, particularly the trade unions. Although the Welsh Office was to some degree insulated from the excesses of Thatcherite economic policies, its discretionary powers were restricted. Welsh trade unions soon realized that concessions to Wales were more likely to be extracted from London by confidential ministerial discussions and that public lobbying could, as likely as not, be counter-productive. By contrast, the institutions of the European Union were eager to be lobbied. Even though the EU benefits are small, the lobbying exercise publicized and reinforced the Welsh interest and publicity gained by one Welsh pressure group encouraged others to follow the Brussels road. The process has not displeased the Welsh Office whose ability to argue the 'Welsh case' with the Treasury is conditional upon evidence of a clear articulation of Welsh interests.

Lobbying the EU has produced curious relationships between Welsh interest groups. In 1981, the rapid decline of the Welsh steel industry, as required by the Davignon Plan, brought into existence the South Wales Standing Conference which encompassed south Wales MPs and MEPs, local authorities, the Wales TUC, CBI Wales and other community organizations in the area, to focus on the industrial and social problems and to lobby the European Commission. After a slight altercation, the Wales TUC established its right to give evidence to European Parliamentary Committees independent of the British TUC. The CBI Wales has adopted a similar role and frequently acts jointly with the Wales TUC in what is seen as a common Welsh interest (Jones, 1985).

The Welsh Office occupies a central position in the consultative network. Its European Affairs Division was set up in 1973 with a Principal and one Assistant Principal. But much of the implementation of policy relating to the EU is now the responsibility of the Economic and Regional Policy Division, whose section ERPII is almost exclusively concerned with EU matters as they relate to the coal and steel industries and the social aspects of their decline. ERPIII is broadly concerned with tourism, environmental and conservation matters, working with and through the Welsh Tourist Board and Mid-Wales Development. The European Affairs Division was reformed in 1989 to take account of the changes in the EU regional and structural funds, and the larger unit within the division is concerned with applying the structural funds in Wales, consulting with and advising local authorities, promoting development programmes which can attract EU support, and generally trying to anticipate future trends in funding policy, thus ensuring that Wales gains a fair share of the funding allocations. The smaller unit with only three persons is essentially a co-ordinating body acting as a conduit of EU information with various European sections of Whitehall departments. But of far greater importance is its role within the Welsh Office, ensuring that all its sections and divisions are aware of EU policies as they affect Wales. It is now the case that EU directives impact on virtually all divisions and departments within the Welsh Office, requiring several intra-departmental liaison committees. Inevitably, the Office has developed an increasingly well-defined Welsh interest and, as in other policy areas, the Welsh Office is doing what any good government department does; it is protecting and promoting the interests of Wales in the European Union.

However, the consultative network is not autonomous. Various parties within the network can consult one with another and even offer advice, but the consultations can be disregarded and the advice ignored because the power to make political decisions does not reside within the consultative network. There is a constitutional reality which cannot be ignored; ultimate political power is located in the Westminster parliament and effectively exercised by the cabinet.

Three consequences flow from this constitutional reality. Welsh local authorities through their associations are inhibited from entering into agreements with European regional/local authority organizations because of their limited legal and financial powers;

the Welsh Office is inhibited from pushing the Welsh case by the realization that it is a British government department which must necessarily balance a specific Welsh interest with a more general British interest; and the European Commission, although eager to establish contacts with British regions (that is, Scotland, Wales and Northern Ireland), negotiatiates exclusively with the UK government.

It is because of a perceived sense of weakness that attempts have been made in Wales during the last few years to create a more tangible framework for the consultative network. These attempts have taken three forms. First, there has been a deliberate attempt to emphasize the Welsh regional dimension by associating Welsh local authority associations, particularly the Assembly of Welsh Counties, with European regional organizations such as the Conference of Peripheral Maritime Regions, the Assembly of European Regions, the Council of Regional and Local Authorities and the Atlantic Arc. In effect, the Assembly of Welsh Counties seems to be acquiring a form of regionalization by association.

Second, there has been a sustained campaign to create a bureau dedicated to co-ordinating the lobbying activities of a variety of Welsh organizations. Welsh local authorities had been pushing for this development since the early 1980s, but the Welsh Office withstood the pressure, arguing that the Welsh interest could best be served by the inter-departmental discussions between the Welsh Office and the various 'lead' departments in Whitehall. Despite this, the WDA took the initiative in April 1991 and announced it was to set up a Welsh European Centre to add to the WDA's voice in Europe and that of other Welsh bodies. The centre was opened in February 1992 with the aim of putting Wales in the hearts and minds of the decision-makers in Europe. It is clear that the centre will be a central element in the WDA's operations, particularly in supporting Welsh Development International's promotion of inward investment from the member states of the European Union.

Thirdly, the Welsh Office has taken the initiative to link Wales with the regions of Baden-Württemberg, Rhône-Alpes, Lombardy and Catalonia (the so-called 'Four Motor' regions of the EU) to promote technological collaboration, research and development, and economic and cultural exchanges. The agreement with Baden-Württemberg was signed in March 1990 and in October, the five principals of the University of Wales flew out to Baden-Württemberg and set up a series of student exchange schemes and joint research projects with the Universities of Mannheim, Heidelberg and Tübingen. During 1991, up to 30 Welsh companies were engaged in negotiations with Baden-Württemberg companies to facilitate technology transfers. In June 1991, a meeting with Baden-Württemberg and Welsh Office civil servants agreed a series of joint projects and surveys covering industrial training, traffic congestion and land reclamation projects. In October 1991, an agreement was signed with Catalonia in Barcelona and a similar set of joint projects to those agreed in Baden-Württemberg have been set up with Lombardy.

Although all three developments are distinct, they are linked partly by a growing sense of regionalism in Europe and partly by increased regional competition within the European Union. So, for example, the Welsh Office justified ending its opposition to setting up a Welsh European Centre in Brussels by referring to the developing links with Baden-Württemberg while the WDA, in its press release, specifically linked the centre with the four motor regions, noting that each one had its own office in Brussels.

The Maastricht Treaty confirmed a regional element within the European Union with the provision, in Article 198-A, for the establishment of the Committee of the Regions. Although the original Commission proposals were somewhat emasculated, the new committee could develop into an influential body which will have to be consulted on education, economic and social cohesion, on administering the structural funds, and on public health and culture. However, the Committee will not have an easy path. The governments of member states will jealously guard their functions, while the regionalists in Europe will push to make the committee more significant. The Bavarian European Affairs minister welcomed the new committee with the demand that what was now needed was a European regional parliament. Doubtless that is some way in the future. But what will the committee of the Regions mean for Wales? Of the 24 members allocated to the UK, Wales has been given three representatives selected by the Conservative government (after consultations); hardly a powerful base to launch a defence of Welsh interests. Furthermore, many of the European regions represented in the Committee operate within quasi-federal structures of government; in particular, the Spanish Autonomous Communities and the German *Länder*. Representatives of these regions on the Committee have a powerful democratic mandate, and significant financial resources, backed up by expertise in government and administration. It is more than likely that those regions with the most developed institutional base will be able to argue their regional case most effectively and to exercise the most effective political clout. In these circumstances, Wales, lacking such an institutional base, could discover that European regionalism, far from being an unqualified benefit, would provide Wales with an opportunity for which it was not properly equipped to take advantage.

THE GLOBAL ECONOMY

The changes in the Welsh economy and in Welsh political attitudes cannot be fully explained with reference only to British politics or to British government economic policies. The changed international environment, with relatively free movement of capital and the increased competition of third world countries, have all contributed to these changes.

During the 1980s, Welsh industrialists and trade unions found common cause in promoting Wales and encouraging inward investment. The institutional focus of this activity has been the Welsh Development Agency (WDA), set up in 1975 by a Labour government and tolerated throughout the 1980s and 1990s by successive Conservative governments. There is a clear consensus across Welsh politics that the WDA, despite financial scandals, has made a success of promoting Wales.

The Welsh Development Agency's inward investment arm, Welsh Development International (WDI) has established offices around the world and constructed a package to help deal with everything from site location and planning procedures to labour training and employee housing. This 'one-stop-shop' service has encouraged major investments. Between 1979 and 1994 over 300 overseas companies relocated in Wales, helping to create a new industrial culture largely based on manufacturing high-value product industries. Wales now has the largest concentration of Japanese manufacturing investment in Europe and over 130 firms from mainland Europe (primarily France and Germany) have been attracted by the benefits of affordable land for development, proximity to markets and good labour relations. Foreign companies now employ over 70,000 people, 30 per cent of the Welsh manufacturing workforce. It has been argued that locating in Wales merely reflected the fact that average pay rates in Wales are below the UK average, but recent research has shown that in the manufacturing sector, where inward investment is most pronounced, Welsh wage rates are equal to and frequently above the UK figure, which suggests that Wales is close to, if it has not already attained, a momentum sufficient to sustain industrial growth (Hill and Keegan, 1993).

The evidence also suggests that the development of the global economy has had a disproportionate impact upon Wales (Osmond, 1994). This is particularly the case in manufacturing which during the 1980s grew from 24.8 per cent to 27.3 per cent of the Welsh GDP while the manufacturing share of the UK gross domestic product fell by almost 2 per cent. By 1991 more people in Wales were employed in the electronics industries (25,000) than in mining and steel (20,000), while still more (70,000) were engaged in the financial services sector. In 1993-94 inward investment to Wales both from overseas and from the rest of the UK totalled £765 million, thus safeguarding 5,800 existing jobs and creating more than 8,000 new jobs (Welsh Office, 1994). It is this pattern of investment in support of manufacturing industries with high levels of productivity that has led the Cardiff Business School to talk of a 'Welsh manufacturing renaissance' (Hill and Keegan, 1993).

The impact of inward investment on the Welsh economy should not be measured simply in quantitative terms; there has also been a qualitative change to the nature of the employment in Wales. During the period 1978-90 a trend towards occupation upgrading has been identified, involving the key category of professional engineers, scientists and technologists which increased by 1157 per cent in Wales compared with 115 per cent in the UK (Lawson and Morgan, 1991). Much remains to be done in order to translate the gains made from inward investment and the establishment of a wide range of foreign firms in Wales. Inward investment is a necessary but insufficient basis for reconstructing the Welsh economy. A more integrated approach to regional, technology and training policies is required (Cooke and Morgan, 1991). The adoption of an innovation strategy, with a well-developed research strategy, an effective system of vocational education, and a deeper commitment to public-private sector collaboration is necessary if Welsh economic renewal is to be attained (Morgan, 1994).

Thus the successful attraction of inward investment does not of itself guarantee success but it does provide the launch-pad for success, providing the basis for cross-national and cross-regional collaboration and technology transfers. To some extent this is already happening through Wales' association with the four motor regions of the EU. If succesful such an economic renewal would have a profound effect upon Wales' economic and social systems.

A CHANGING POLITICAL CULTURE

Although superficially in the British mould, Welsh politics continues to exhibit a distinct identity. A strong working-class electorate, a radical tradition allied to the Liberal Party and a deep suspicion of the Conservatives as the 'English' Party have invested Welsh politics with a distinctive agenda. The impact of Plaid Cymru, invariably disproportionate to the electoral support it attracts, has meant that such issues as the legal status of the Welsh language, the provision of Welsh language broadcasting facilities and the impact of (English-owned) second homes in Wales upon Welsh-speaking communities have occupied a unique position in the Welsh political debate. Other issues unique to Wales have emerged since 1979; political devolution and the case for an elected Welsh Assembly reverberates across several issues, and is now focused on the broader debate about quangos and the question of democratic accountability. But it is not only political issues which are different. The Welsh party system is quite distinct from that in England; electoral battles in Wales are fought between different antagonists on different fronts. In the Welsh heartland, the electoral battle is polarized between Labour and Plaid Cymru whereas in the industrial valleys, the Conservatives and Plaid Cymru pose a twin threat to Labour Party hegemony. In rural Wales, the Liberal and radical tradition is still strong, and must be respected by any party seeking electoral success. Wales has a multi-party system where the concept of swings as applied by the London media has little relevance. The idea that some parties have unofficial understandings or implicit alliances is not as alien to Welsh political thinking. Thus, although Welsh politicians might not fully understand the multi-party system in Holland, language politics in Belgium, or Basque politics in the Spanish state, they would be able to identify with these rather more easily than their English counterparts.

Developments in Welsh politics since 1979 have also had constitutional implications. The loss of a fourth successive general election in 1992 persuaded the Welsh Labour parliamentary group to question whether a government whose majority was based upon votes in the south east of England could legitimately claim a mandate in Wales. Similar doubts as to the legitimacy of Conservative authority in Wales are also promoted by Plaid Cymru; and the Liberal Democrats, with their strong federalist position on both Welsh devolution and the European Union, are sympathetic to the notion of divided sovereignty which disinclines them to regard the British parliament as an absolute authority. More recently, this view has found surprising support among Welsh local authorities who, while dominated by Labour councillors, have felt the full impact of a centralist and centralizing government exploiting the constitutional principle of parliamentary supremacy to undermine and down-grade these same local authorities. Thus, across the political spectrum in Wales, the twin principles of British sovereignty and parliamentary supremacy are now subject to sceptical appraisal.

The European connection has acted as a catalyst for some of the developments described above merely by changing some of the rules of the political game and offering an alternative avenue for lobbyists, both functional and territorial. The European Union has also made a direct impact upon Wales. The Commission has played a vital role in providing encouragement and financial resources, through Article 10 of the ERDF Regulations. Although Wales possesses no formal regional political machinery, the senior local authority association, the Assembly of Welsh Counties (AWC) has interacted with the regional authorities of other member states, discovering in the process the political clout which they carry and the financial resources at their disposal. In particular, Welsh representatives have been impressed by those regional political leaders (from Germany and Spain) who have been prepared to give of their time, energy and resources to strengthen the cross-national regional organizations (Owen, 1990). The AWC has been keen to play a full role; the European Centre for Traditional and Regional Cultures (ECTARC) was established in 1987 and is based in Llangollen in North Wales. Although it is funded largely by a Welsh county (Clwyd), its remit is regional, promoting inter-regional projects with cultural and tourism connotations. The AWC is also active in the Assembly of European Regions and has, in effect, presumed for itself a regional responsibility and confidently expects the Secretary of State for Wales to nominate Welsh members to the

Committee of the Regions from among its membership. The AWC has also taken the lead in responding to the WDA's invitation to help fund the Welsh European Centre in Brussels. Thus, the absence of a democratic regional level of government in Wales has not prevented Welsh organizations from involvement in EU regional institutions. On the contrary, it has encouraged Labour councillors, many of whom were opposed to devolution in 1979, to adopt an increasingly pro-regionalist position and to argue the case for Welsh devolution, not simply in the British context, but as a means of ensuring that the Welsh interest is more effectively safeguarded and promoted in Brussels. Gradually, Welsh political culture is changing and is no longer oriented exclusively towards London. The presence in Wales of foreign businessmen and managers, many of whom are from mainland Europe, has encouraged Welsh politicians, both parliamentary and local, to take greater account of the European dimension. The perceived importance of Europe to Welsh economic prospects is emphasized by the joint lobbying of the Wales TUC and CBI Wales to bring forward the completion date for the second Severn Bridge and for the early development of rail links between Wales and the Channel Tunnel. New outward-looking industrialists, a manufacturing base locked into the world economy and politicians less certain of the benefits of London government are indicative of the nature of a new emerging political economy.

CONCLUSIONS

Since the Second World War, but particularly since 1964, the position of Wales within the British state has changed significantly. In part, this merely reflects changes in British politics, in particular the asymmetrical party system, and Britain's changed status in the world. But it is also the product of fundamental economic changes: the decline, and in some cases, the death of traditional industries and the social structures which evolved from them. Against this decline, there has also been a renewal of Welsh economic life, facilitated in part by membership of the European Union and partly by the changed world economic order. Welsh entrepreneurs now have different perspectives and Welsh political activists different objectives. Westminster is still the most significant political arena for making decisions but it is no longer the only arena. A wider, more complex and inter-active world penetrates increasingly into

Welsh economic life. In consequence, the Welsh interests, while retaining their distinctive character, are also discovering similar interests and concerns in other regions across Europe.

NOTES

1. Welsh Language Act, chapter 38, 21 October 1993. This has extended the legal rights of the Welsh language without giving it official status in Wales. The Act set up a Welsh Language Board (yet another quango) to supervise and promote the use of the language to be chaired by Lord Elis-Thomas (past president of Plaid Cymru).

19

Scotland, the Union State and the International Environment

JAMES MITCHELL

INTRODUCTION: CHANGING CONTEXTS

For some areas of the world, 'globalization', and its attendant opportunities and dangers, is no new phenomenon. The Scottish economy has long been tied into economic structures well beyond the rest of the state of which it is a part and has been affected by international movements of population, capital and trade. At the beginning of this century, Scotland was a leading producer in steel, shipbuilding and related metals industries. Its strengths in law and accountancy made it possible in the years of the British empire to develop international financial services and investment funds which remain important to this day.

As part of the Atlantic economy, trade proved crucial to the Scottish economy. Scotland could not isolate itself from American economic fortunes, and demographic trends were affected as well as trade. Encouraging emigration from Scotland was official policy for much of the twentieth century. Isobel Lindsay has noted the long-established attitudes in Scotland regarding migration: 'an acceptance that it is a constant fact of Scottish life about which little can be done, a recognition that there is a qualitative loss and that explanations cannot be provided on the basis of socio-economic trends within Scotland' (Lindsay, 1992: 155). With one brief exception in 1932-3, Scotland suffered a net loss of population due to migration during the twentieth century until 1989-90. Since then, a net increase in population has resulted, largely due to movement within the UK as people from the south of England moved north.

Another feature of twentieth-century Scotland has been the

branch factory. The proportion of workers employed by companies with headquarters outside Scotland has been high. Areas dominated by branch plants were highly vulnerable during recessions (Hood and Young, 1982). Nonetheless, these factories often provided employment over many decades. Attracting inward investment came to be seen as a means of providing jobs, but these were unlikely to be senior posts or in research and development. During the late 1970s and throughout the 1980s, Scotland suffered a number of major job losses through the closure or retraction of branch factories and the decline of traditional manufacturing. In part, this reflected changes in production types and the rise of new economies in the Far East. Government fiscal and monetary policy had a devastating effect on manufacturing industry (Maynard, 1988). Structural economic changes combined with public policy to create a largely new environment in the Scottish economy in the 1980s.

Other changes were important. The traditional response of government from the 1930s to areas such as Scotland had been regional policy. The rise of urban policy marked a shift towards what was claimed to be a more targeted approach. In the 1960s, this change of emphasis was within the context of the 'rediscovery of poverty' following various official and non-official reports, and the increasing salience of race in English politics. During the 1980s, a different shift occurred when the role of the private sector was given greater prominence. The decline of domestic regional policy occurred at the same time as the regional policy of the European Community became more important. While fairly marginal in the overall scheme of things, EU regional policy has nonetheless helped Scotland.

The United Kingdom is often mistakenly assumed to be a unitary state. Unitary states are 'built up around one unambiguous political centre' enjoying economic dominance and pursuing a 'more or less undeviating policy of administrative standardization' (Rokkan and Urwin, 1982: 11). It is more accurate to describe the UK as a union state. Scotland and England united by treaty but the integration of the two countries was imperfect (Rokkan and Urwin, 1982: 11). The union state allowed Scotland to maintain some degree of distinctiveness, which was renewed periodically through the creation of new institutions or the extension of existing ones. There was no 'missionary nation-building ideology' in Britain (Keating, 1988c: 71), no attempt to eradicate Scottish identity.

In the twentieth century, the changing functions of the state have affected Scotland's distinct status within the UK. In the union state, new functions could be performed by the state at the centre, giving it a more unitary nature. On the other hand, the state's new functions could take account of the Scottish dimension. In practice, a mixed response in the territorial management of the changing functions of the state has been evident. In some cases, Scottish distinctiveness was catered for and in others it was not. Scottish education was administered centrally through the Scottish Office, a territorial department of state set up in 1885, which permitted some degree of autonomy. While Scots law had been a central pillar of Scottish distinctiveness, new bodies of law – labour and company law – developed which were British in nature.

By 1982, Richard Rose noted that the Scottish Office had jurisdiction paralleling the functions of approximately 11 Whitehall departments (Rose, 1982: 118). During the 1980s, there were changes in the functions and thereby the organization of British central government, including the Scottish Office. Mrs Thatcher's 'statecraft' involved off-loading problems and strengthening power at the centre (Bulpitt, 1986). The interventionist ethos which had dominated Scottish Office thinking in the post-war period was challenged.

Another feature of twentieth-century Scotland has been the issue of Scotland's constitutional status. Pressure for some measure of home rule played its part on the organization of the state. Though no Scottish legislature has been established, the 'national question' has been a persistent theme in twentieth-century politics. The interplay of the external environment, the national movement and the development of the union state have ensured that territorial politics have been dynamic and often unpredictable.

ECONOMIC MANAGEMENT IN THE UNION STATE

The union state is not a federal state and a considerable degree of central control is maintained. This is achieved through the existence of a single UK parliament. In the fields of industry and the economy, the central objectives and directions in public policy come from the centre in London. Monetary and fiscal policies were centrally determined in conformity with Keynesian economic reasoning. One aspect of the central control has been in the field of economic and industrial policy. Regional policy lay somewhere between central control and decentralized economic management: after 1945, public policy affecting infrastructure and planning came under the Scottish Office's remit. A degree of autonomy in these areas has been devolved to Scotland. Various groups – trade unions, business interests, local authorities, occasionally acting as one – operate in Scotland to put pressure on the government to protect their interests. The Scottish Office lies at the centre of this institutional nexus. It acts as mediator, adjusting UK policy to the special Scottish context, and represents Scottish interests in Whitehall. The degree of influence it has depends on the issue, its political salience, the strength of argument mustered and the relative power of its ministers in government (Moore and Booth, 1989: 39).

In 1975, the Scottish Development Agency, a regional development agency, was set up. Its origins lay partly in 30 years of regional planning (Wannop, 1984). It was also a response by the Labour government, elected in 1974, to the threat posed by the Scottish National Party (SNP). The SDA came to play a significant part in urban regeneration, in particular physical regeneration, reflecting the rise of urban policy and the decline of regional policy. In 1981, the SDA and the Scottish Office established Locate in Scotland, to provide a 'one door' approach for inward investment to Scotland through the provision of a package of assistance measures. By 1989, it claimed to have attracted 397 projects to Scotland with 54,000 jobs as a result of planned investment of £2,600m, but a National Audit Office (NAO) study of its activities concluded that these claims had not been adjusted to take account of actual results. Locate in Scotland had succeeded in converting one in five visits or enquiries by potential investors into decisions to set up in Scotland, a record the NAO felt compared favourably with many of its European competitors (NAO, 1989). The case of the hospital and health care facilities established in Clydebank, on the outskirts of Glasgow, by Health Care International (HCI) proved a massive financial disaster for the government and raised questions about assistance for inward investment. However, those involved argued that such matters had to be placed in context. Locate in Scotland's former director maintained that Scotland was a 'world leader' in winning international investment and HCI had been an atypical set back (Crawford, 1994).

Margaret Thatcher's announcement on the steps of Conservative Party central office on the morning following her third election success in 1987 that there was 'a big job to do in those inner cities' suggested that urban initiatives would be prioritized. What emerged was certainly a shift in rhetoric, but the dominant model in urban regeneration had been undergoing change for some time. The Glasgow East Area Renewal (GEAR) project had been the SDA's flagship policy from the agency's inception and was a public-public partnership of local authorities and central government agencies (Wannop, 1990). During the 1980s, the new model which had emerged was a public-private partnership with the private sector playing an increasingly important part (Boyle, 1993). The launch of 'Action for Cities' in England involved 'the triumph of packaging over substance' (Deakin and Edwards, 1993: 4). There was little that was new in the package and the priority attached to the private sector was made clear. The equivalent Scottish document, *New Life for Urban Scotland,* was different, at least in detail. It was 'less hostile to the local authorities' and displayed 'more flexibility regarding social investment and placed a great deal of emphasis on the role of the community in regeneration' (Atkinson and Moon, 1994: 158).

The urban policy of the Thatcher government, the most centralist government in Britain since the war, can only be understood in terms of the union state. The abandonment of an active regional policy and its replacement with a more focused urban policy occurred with Scotland playing little or no part in the decision. British urban policy has become the main territorial policy of British government. The main principles, its financing and ideological underpinning were informed by the government at the centre but in some important respects it was different. A degree of autonomy, within strict parameters, was permitted to the Scottish Office in the inception and implementation of urban policy, as in other areas.

This was evident in another major change which occurred in 1991 when Scottish Enterprise was established, replacing the SDA and Training Agency (the latter having formerly been the Manpower Service Commission). The source of change was Bill Hughes, chairman of the Confederation of British Industry in Scotland and later vice-chairman of the Scottish Conservatives. Hughes envisaged the merger of the SDA, Training Agency and the Highlands and Islands Development Board (HIDB), a regeneration agency for the Scottish Highlands and Islands set up by Harold Wilson's Labour government in 1965. He wanted a new body, Scottish Enterprise, with a network of about 60 local agencies headed by local business people. He was critical of the SDA's role in the regeneration of deprived urban areas and believed that the SDA was somehow seen as apart from government by the public and that its successes were not credited to the government. The new name proposed for the new agency, Scottish Enterprise, was as much an attempt to link its achievements to the 'party of enterprise' and caused anxiety within the SDA where it was felt that the SDA's 'familiar brand name' should not be abandoned. The suspicion was that Scottish Enterprise was more an attempt to 'address the political problems which the government faces in Scotland than it is to find genuine ways of improving the effectiveness of local economic development and training efforts' (Danson, *et al.*, 1989).

One remarkable feature of the change was its speed. Another was the extent to which the Scottish Office and its agencies were sidelined in the process. Hughes spoke directly to Prime Minister Thatcher in September 1988, having first proposed the idea that summer. A White Paper was produced in December. Scottish Enterprise came into operation in April 1991. A separate Highlands and Islands Enterprise was set up covering the territory of the HIDB. The late 1980s saw considerable institutional change and a weakening of the public sector throughout Britain but all within the context of the union state. Broad ideological coherence was maintained but Scottish distinctiveness was permitted.

THE NATIONAL MOVEMENT, THE INTERNATIONAL ENVIRONMENT AND THE UNION STATE

The cause of Scottish self-government was initially stimulated in the late nineteenth century by events in Ireland. Scots became irritated by the amount of parliamentary time devoted to the Irish Question at the expense, as Scottish MPs saw it, of Scottish business. Gladstone's conversion to the Home Rule cause further stimulated Scottish demands, in part, because the Scots did not want to lose out and in part, because 'Home Rule all round' appeared to many Scottish Liberals to make more sense than devolution to only one part of the UK. In its origins then, the Home Rule movement was greatly influenced by developments beyond Scotland. External influences have continued to be important.

After the First World War, Scottish Home Rulers petitioned the leaders of the powers meeting at Versailles, requesting Scottish participation and recognition of the Scots' right to self-determination. Founders of the SNP in the 1930s wanted Scottish self-government within the British commonwealth. In recent times, the European Union has provided the modern equivalent of the commonwealth for contemporary nationalists. Having opposed European Community membership from the 1960s, the SNP position changed radically in the 1980s, when the party argued for 'independence in Europe', especially after the 1987 general election. Support in Scotland for the EC and the SNP grew. Launching its revised position at the same time as Jacques Delors was leading the 'relaunch of Europe' with the '1992' project gave the SNP a modern, relevant appearance.

Other home rule forces in Scotland were forced to re-assess their position in light of European developments. Devolutionists in the Labour and Liberal Democrat parties attempted to add a European dimension to their home rule schemes. Their plans now include establishing an office of the prospective Scottish parliament in Brussels and the possibility of having ministers from the Scottish parliament attending Council of Ministers' meetings alongside British government ministers.

An important backdrop against which the national movement has developed has been the organization of the state itself. As Keating has observed, the central state itself may stimulate regional identity by organizing administration on a regional basis and 'effectively inviting people to articulate their demands in a regional framework'. Furthermore, modernization need not entail state integration but the 'politicization of regional identity' (Keating, 1988b: 17). This occurred with Scotland in the UK. While other factors were important, for example the existence of separate Scottish media, the state's part in keeping alive a sense that Scotland was politically different cannot be ignored.

There was little demand for a Scottish parliament in the second half of the nineteenth century. The national movement campaigned around the issue of establishing a ministry within the UK government responsible for representing Scottish interests. The concession of the Scottish Office and its developing range of responsibilities may be seen to have helped foster political nationalism. The language surrounding the state's management of territorial politics shows the links between the organization of the state and the demands made by Scots for some measure of self-government. From the 1930s, the Scottish Office has been described as 'administrative devolution', implying some degree of autonomy. Each wave of support for constitutional reform has been met by an extension of administrative devolution. It would be wrong, however, to suggest that nationalist agitation has been the only pressure which has brought about the extension of administrative devolution. Administrative efficacy has played its part too. It has often made more sense to administer matters at the Scottish rather than UK level.

Indeed, a phenomenon not dissimilar to European integration, as understood by neo-functionalist theorists, has taken place within the UK. Neo-functionalists have maintained that the process of integration occurred when 'loyalties, expectations and political activities' shifted towards the 'new, larger centre, whose institutions possess or demand jurisdiction over the pre-existing national states' (Haas, 1958: 16). Crucial to this process was the 'bureaucratic political leadership' of supranational institutions and the process of 'spillover'. The existence of a bureaucracy provided the drive towards increased integration. As European integration occurred in one area there was the prospect that it would spill over into related areas. Something similar can be seen to have occurred in the opposite direction. The existence of the Scottish Office ensured that a focus for further administrative devolution existed and the spillover into related matters occurred. Even during the 1980s, a period of centralization, the Scottish Office and its attendant quangos gained responsibilities in housing, nature conservation, higher education and training and enterprise (Hogwood, 1994). These changes have facilitated the prospect of a more comprehensive and distinctly Scottish response to current problems including those presented by globalization. Given the importance attached to higher education and training and enterprise in the European arena, where resources are available for economic development focusing on such matters, this is potentially important.

EUROPE AND THE UNION STATE

The growing importance of European integration has had its impact on territorial politics. The territorial organization of the union state was affected by these developments as much as Parliament and Whitehall were. Decisions taken in Brussels would impinge on the activities of the Scottish Office, Scottish local authorities and a variety of other public bodies. The Scottish Office had been presented to Scots as giving them a representative at the highest level of government. If Europe was a new locus of power, then the Scots might ask who was representing them there. The answer was determined by which institution of the EU one was referring to. Scotland's eight Members of the European Parliament might claim to represent Scotland there as well as any sub-state unit was represented. In the Court of Justice, the Scottish dimension has been fairly well represented. The UK's first member of the Court of Justice, and later its president, was the Scottish Judge Lord Mackenzie Stuart. The current UK nominee to the Court is another Scottish judge, David Edward.

Far more important than these supranational institutions is the Council of Ministers, an intergovernmentalist institution. The Council of Ministers is, of course, a misnomer implying the existence of an entity with a fixed membership. In fact, its membership is dependent on the issue being discussed and the responsible minister in each member state will attend meetings. In the UK, this gives rise to some potential problems, especially as the state is a union state. The existence of territorial departments - Scottish, Welsh and Northern Ireland Offices - in addition to other functional departments means that more than one minister will have responsibility for any function under discussion. This raises questions of precedence in cabinet government and of the likelihood of any of the territorial departments representing the UK in meetings of the Council of Ministers.

The wide remit of the Scottish Office places it potentially in the position of being able to represent the UK on a wide range of matters, but its junior status in government ensures that this rarely occurs. The one issue on which the Scottish Office has most often taken this leading role is fisheries policy. This reflects the relative importance of the fishing industry in Scotland compared to the rest of the UK. In 1993, the government announced that Scottish ministers and Scottish Office officials would 'take part in an increasing number of meetings of the Council of Ministers' in its 'taking stock' package of proposals (Scottish Office, 1993: 21). In the second half of 1994, the Scottish Office represented the UK government at three of the 46 Council of Ministers' meetings, each concerned with fisheries.

This applies equally to meetings of the Committee of Permanent Representatives (COREPER), which shadows the Council of Ministers and consists of diplomats and civil servants drawn from the permanent representation of each member state. The United Kingdom's Permanent Representation (UKREP) in Brussels has always contained a number of civil servants seconded from ministries affected by EU matters. Since the UK's accession to EC, UKREP has included at least one and sometimes three Scottish Office officials, thus ensuring some measure of Scottish input: usually from agriculture and fisheries or industry departments. The problem with this form of Scottish representation is that the individuals concerned will have a specialist background and will not be well versed in all aspects of Scottish public policy affected by the EU.

The growing importance of the European dimension is another example of how the changing international context presents difficulties for the UK. Sub-state units are rarely recognized in European affairs and international relations. Even federal states have problems in this respect. The debates leading up to the ratification of the Maastricht Treaty on European Union in Germany involved the contentious issue of the position of individual German *Länder*. In the case of the UK, an ad hoc arrangement has emerged. Criticisms have been made down the years that Whitehall is insensitive to the needs of the Scottish legal system if not wider matters of Scottish concern in public policy-making. The absence of a strong Scottish presence in Brussels might mean that those matters for which the union state caters through the Scottish Office are ignored.

The growing significance of the European dimension forced the Scottish Office and Scottish Development Agency to reconsider their operations in the late 1980s. A report was commissioned by the SDA, soon to become Scottish Enterprise, and produced by ECOTEC, a research and consultancy business with offices in Edinburgh, Birmingham and Brussels. It was published in 1991 and examined Scotland's performance in attracting EC funding and identified the key policies affecting Scotland. The EC structural funds and research and development funds were described as the 'most important to Scotland' (Scottish Development Agency, 1991). Between 1985 and 1989, Scotland's share of structural funds had fallen from 3.0 per cent to 1.5 per cent and funds per capita fell from 164 per cent to 98 per cent of the EC average, though the total amount had risen. In research and technological development (RTD) funding, Scotland's share was about one-third of the EC average and amongst these awards, higher educational institutions rather than industry were the main beneficiaries.

A number of issues were highlighted. The contentious matter of additionality was addressed – whether EC funds would supplement or simply replace central government funding. It was noted that Scottish Enterprise's budget assumed an EC element to its funding and failure to receive it would reduce the SE expenditure. In that sense, additionality was real but beyond that, EC funds were non-additional as the Treasury would deduct such sums from the annual award made to SE. From the point of view of Scottish local authorities, EC funds offered advantages in terms of cash flows, but in effect, European Regional Development Fund (ERDF) assistance was for the most part non-additional. Other types of funding were additional – for example, European Social Fund (ESF) money was additional but bids were less likely to be successful. The new European challenges required a change of approach focusing on both policy formulation and implementation. A 'strong strategic link' between the Brussels operation and SE was necessary while simultaneously, Scottish interests had to be made more aware of the existence and benefits of EC funds. In essence, SE would have to revise its operations both in Brussels and in Scotland.

In the late 1980s, the SDA/SE and the Scottish Office had been considering setting up a lobbying office in Brussels and the SDA commissioned a report on the options available. The existence of lobbying/information offices in Brussels from around the Community offered a variety of models. By May 1991, when SE produced a briefing document on the subject, there were 35 regional offices based in Brussels. The key issues for the Scottish Office in terms of an office in Brussels were how it would be funded, the extent of public-sector involvement and who would be represented in the office. The preference within the Scottish Office was for a privately funded body, which would consist of a range of Scottish interests. Discussions among ministers and senior civil servants in the Scottish Office became public knowledge when papers leaked to the press highlighted the different views held. While it was generally believed that a Brussels office would provide a powerful lobby, raise Scotland's profile there and improve the flow of information between Scotland and Europe, it was also recognized that there were potential dangers. In particular, there was a fear that it might cut across the UK government's position on any matter and be opposed by UKREP, the Treasury and Foreign and Commonwealth Office (Mitchell, 1995).

A fear expressed within the Scottish Office, reflecting the resurgence of interest in Scotland's constitutional status at that time, was that the Brussels office might be used by certain Scottish groups to undermine government policy. In particular, the role of local authorities and trade unions was of concern to Scottish Office ministers. In the event, it was decided that SE would set up a private company, Scotland Europa, funded through membership, which would have four main areas of activity: ensuring a Scottish input in EC policy development; intelligence gathering; facilitating Scottish access to EC funds; and developing networks with other regional offices (Scottish Enterprise, 1991). Suspicions within Scotland's predominantly Labour-controlled local authorities of the new body meant that, initially, there were difficulties in attracting local authority interest in Scotland Europa, but this was eventually resolved.

Scotland Europa was approved by the government in 1992. Its membership includes six organizations which have resident status in the Brussels office, plus others for whom Scotland Europa gathers information and acts as facilitator for lobbying purposes. Its work is divided into the two main areas, financial and (de)regulatory policies, with Scottish public bodies such as the local authorities primarily concerned with the former. A monthly report is sent to all members providing detailed information on a range of matters.

TABLE 1

EU FUNDING IN SCOTLAND, 1994

	£million	% of total spent
Agriculture and fisheries	282	54.0
European Regional Development Fund – ERDF	170	32.0
European Social Fund – ESF	50	9.6
Internal policies – research and development, innovation, educational exchanges, etc.	20	4.0
Consultancy and external aid contracts	2	0.4
TOTAL	524	100

Source: Scotland Europa, Monthly Report, February 1995.

Much of the publicity surrounding the establishment of Scotland Europa and the European dimension in Scottish politics generally focuses on Scotland's prospects of securing funding. The local authorities as much as central government have pursued this vigorously though the extent to which they can succeed is limited. In 1994, over £0.5 billion was received from the European Union budget, but this constitutes a small part of the total resources available to Scottish public and private sectors. Far more important are European policies and regulations and their effect on Scottish life and society. The Single Market project, fiscal policy, environmental policy, transport policy and a variety of other areas of EU concern will have a differential territorial impact and may affect Scotland differently from other parts of the UK. There is no direct way in which Scottish views can affect these matters.

The weakness of the model of territorial representation which Scotland Europa expresses lies in its limited definition of Scottish interests. Within Scotland Europa, Scottish interests are defined only by those organizations which have a financial stake within it. It has no aggregative functions. Wider Scottish interests not represented by those bodies which are members will not be voiced. It is also unlikely to perform a pro-active role. In essence, the weakness of Scotland Europa and the existing means by which Scottish interests are represented in the institutions of the European Union reflects Scotland's weak constitutional status.

THE COMPETITIVE ADVANTAGE OF SCOTLAND

In considering how to develop the Scottish economy in an increasingly competitive international environment, Scottish Enterprise in recent years has adopted an approach associated with Michael Porter of Harvard Business School. Porter's five year analysis of ten leading trading nations was described in his *The Competitive Advantage of Nations* (1990), in which he maintained that regions could still maintain and develop their competitiveness despite globalization. Notably, the size of the region is not important. He noted the existence of 'clusters' of related industries in which expertise had been built up over many years. These clusters, which may be geographically concentrated, include not only private businesses but also public institutions. Porter's notion of a diamond of competitiveness in developing successful clusters provides clues for regions hoping to compete internationally. He listed four elements to the diamond (Porter, 1990a: 71):

1 *Factor conditions.* The nation's position in factors of production, such as skilled labour or infrastructure, necessary to compete in a given industry.

2 *Demand conditions.* The nature of home demand for the industry's product or service.

3 *Related and supporting industries.* The presence or absence in the nation of supplier industries and related industries that are internally competitive.

4 *Firm strategy, structure and rivalry.* The conditions in the nation governing how companies are created, organized and managed, and the nature of domestic rivalry.

While the private sector is central to this model of economic development, the public sector too has a role. He noted the temptation to make the government the fifth determinant but argued that the government's role in national competitive advantage lay in influencing the four determinants and this could be done in a range of ways. Public policies may adversely affect each of the components of the diamond of competitiveness. Education policy, transport and infrastructure are all important: 'a nation does not inherit but instead creates the most important factors of production – such as skilled human resources or a scientific base' (Porter, 1990b: 78). Some 'simple, basic principles' need to be embraced by governments, according to Porter. They should 'encourage change, promote domestic rivalry, stimulate innovation' (Porter, 1990b: 87).

Porter's work has had more than academic interest in Scotland. His company, Monitor, was commissioned by Scottish Enterprise to analyse and advise on Scotland's competitive advantage. This concluded that Scotland had 17 industrial clusters in which actual or potential competitive advantage existed. While the Scottish economy was well diversified, specific areas of international competitiveness were few and highly concentrated. A number of clusters were analysed in detail and it was noted that the advantage accruing to Scotland in some cases rested on resource endowment and low wages rather than innovation, knowledge and higher value added activities (Scottish Enterprise, 1993).

It was noted that Scotland's financial services sector was the fastest growing cluster in the economy with great opportunity in employment and wealth creation. Fund management, insurance and retail banking were particularly strong and Scotland was the fourth largest European centre for equity management, ahead of Paris and Frankfurt. However, value-added engineering was 'severely threatened'. This cluster had weakened over the previous 20 years and continued to decline. Other clusters were commented upon, noting both their strengths and weaknesses: food, tourism, chemicals, educational services, beverages, textiles, forest products, and media/multi-media. A number of specific points were raised regarding government policy. It was noted that research in Scottish universities was 'neither closely related to Scottish industry nor focused on commercial applications'. Scotland had been 'extremely successful' since 1945 in attracting foreign direct investment especially in chemicals and electronics. However, the need to attract higher value-added jobs and corporate control was once more reiterated. As had been argued throughout the post-war period, Scotland needed to attract research and development and divisional headquarters. It was also noted that Scotland had become less competitive in attracting and retaining foreign direct investment and packages of incentives were required to improve the situation.

Scotland's geographical location, on the periphery of Europe, required transport and infrastructure to meet the needs of a trading nation. 'World-class road, rail, sea and air links and the upgrading of the telecommunications system' were necessary if Scotland was to be successful in attracting and keeping global companies. It was also noted that public sector demand was important. As a customer of businesses, the government could use its position to encourage firms to improve their products. Specific proposals were made regarding the oil and gas cluster in and around Aberdeen in particular to make recommendations enabeling the industry to survive beyond North Sea oil. The importance of Scotland developing expertise in order to maintain business contracts with global contractors was stressed, though the difficulties in doing this was noted. The danger of the demise of the North Sea inspired oil and gas industries going the same way and with similar repercussions as had the demise of heavy industry and shipbuilding earlier this century was evidently seen as a real prospect.

CONCLUSION

Throughout the twentieth century, there has been an interplay between Scotland, the global economy and the national movement. Changing contexts have not affected the main themes in Scotland's economic situation. Reliance on inward investment, population movements and opportunities for trade have been outside Scotland's immediate control. Indeed, these have also been largely outside the control of UK governments. Government responses both to the changes in the international political economy and the demands of the national movement have affected how they have acted to aid the Scottish economy. While it is tempting to portray Scotland as being at the mercy of influences beyond its borders, this would be wrong on two counts. First, the international links have proved invaluable in many instances. The strength of Scotland's financial services sector is in part due to the international links forged generations ago and maintained to this day. Second, in its limited way, state action has proved that a distinct Scottish response is possible. The limitations placed by the union state on Scottish autonomy have whetted appetites. The increasingly important European dimension may demonstrate the weakness of Scotland's present constitutional status but it also offers opportunities in the future.

20

The North of England and the Europe of the Regions, Or, When Is a Region Not a Region?[1]

HOWARD ELCOCK

INTRODUCTION: THE ISSUES

The accelerating dynamic of European integration has increased the role and influence of regions in the European Union (EU) at the expense of the primacy of the national governments of the member states. An American commentator, William Drozniak (1994) has declared that 'a resurrection of "city states" and regions is quietly transforming Europe's political and economic landscape, diminishing the influence of national governments and redrawing the continental map of power for the 21st century'.

However, because England (in contrast to Northern Ireland, Scotland and Wales) has no structure of regional government or representation, her regions are not in the best position to take part in, or benefit fully from, this emerging 'Europe of the Regions'. The reasons for this have to do not only with the highly centralized nature of the British state but also with the weak articulation of regional identities and interests in England. Such identities are stronger in Scotland and Wales but are not incontestable even there, as the failure of the devolution referenda in 1979 demonstrated.

THE EUROPE OF THE REGIONS

European Community (EC) regional policy was almost non-existent until 1975, when the European Regional Development Fund (ERDF) was established (Lodge, 1993). It was initially developed along the lines of British regional policies – ironically, near the beginning of a period during which the importance of regional policy has been greatly reduced in Britain itself (Hudson, 1989). Initially, the Commission funded mainly projects in areas which were designated by member states as assisted areas. The member state governments determined which regions were eligible to receive assistance. In the north-east of England, EC funds supported the regeneration of many derelict sites following the decline of heavy industry in the area. The ERDF also supported the electrification of the East Coast main railway line from London to Edinburgh via Newcastle, as part of its policy of supporting the improvement of the links between peripheral regions and the central areas of the Community.

The Community's regional policy was revised and strengthened in 1989, following upon the acceptance of the Single European Act in 1986 and the consequent development of the Single European Market (SEM). This was to be in full operation by 1 January 1993 and was thought to bring with it the danger that peripheral or under-developed regions would be even more at a disadvantage, once barriers to trade and the movement of people were removed and the 'Four Freedoms' of the SEM came into full existence. In order to prevent this, the EC's structural funds (the European Regional Development Fund, the European Social Fund and the Guidance Section of the European Agricultural Guarantees and Guidance Fund) needed to be deployed to hasten the development of such regions.

The 1989 reforms agreed by the Council of Ministers defined the objectives of the Community's regional policies, for which the structural funds are to be used. Three objectives are of direct relevance to this paper:

Objective 1:   To assist the development of underdeveloped, mainly rural regions. Their problems are likely to be low wages and under-employment although they may not necessarily have a high level of unemployment.

Objective 2:   To assist the regeneration of regions which are being adversely affected by the decline of traditional industries, producing high unemployment.

Objective 5b: To promote the development of rural areas.

Most of the grants received by the UK are awarded under Objective 2.

The development of stronger regional policies at the Union level has been accompanied by increasingly sophisticated lobbying of the Commission by the governmental authorities of the regions of Europe, most notably the German *Länder*, which now maintain sizeable representative offices in Brussels.

All this indicates the growing importance of regions in representing the interests of populations with common problems and interests at the increasingly important EU level. Under chapter four of the Treaty on European Union (TEU)(Maastricht), this has now been formalized by the creation of the Committee of the Regions (COR). However, the number of representatives from each region must be very small, given for example that the UK, like the other large member states, is allotted only 24 places (Lodge, 1993).

The importance of regional and local governments is also likely to be increased by the acceptance of the principle of subsidiarity under the TEU, because they must both respond to European Union policies and proposals and lobby for the interests of the regions' inhabitants. Hence, the increasing development of 'top-down' and 'bottom-up' channels of policy-making within the EU, as illustrated in Table 1:

TABLE 1

SUGGESTED FRAME WORK FOR THE ANALYSIS OF THE NORTH-EAST OF ENGLAND AS A EUROPEAN REGION

Level	Top-down	Bottom-up
European Union	Commission DGXVI Council of Ministers European Court Council of Europe (esp.ECHR) Signpost Europe	European Parliament ECOSOC COR
Nation-state	National government Parliament Courts	Local authority Associations Courts

TABLE 1 (CONTINUED)

SUGGESTED FRAME WORK FOR THE ANALYSIS OF THE NORTH-EAST OF
ENGLAND AS A EUROPEAN REGION

Level	Top-down	Bottom-up
Regional	Regional offices of govt. departments Regional directors Regional administration Regional agencies Local authority etc. e.g. N. Assembly of local authorities	Regional offices Regional agencies Consortia Regional identities Regional interests
Localities	Local authorities Local interests Local issues	Local identities

Note: the linkages among these various factors are many and complex. Some
organizations appear on both sides of the table because they may play both top-down
and bottom-up roles, alternately or concurrently.

THE ENGLISH CONUNDRUM

The UK is in a weak position to take advantage of these
developments because it has no regional structures of government.
It does possess important institutions of regional administration,
including the regional offices of several central government
departments, such as the Department of the Environment, the
Department of Trade and Industry and the Department of
Employment (Hogwood and Keating, 1982). The senior officials of
these offices sometimes become advocates for their regions in
Whitehall, although others see their roles as being chiefly to secure
the implementation of central government policies there (Young,
1982). There may be a particularly strong tendency for such regional
officers in the north-east to become advocates for the region rather
than Whitehall's consuls there (Elcock, Fenwick and Harrop, 1988).
These structures of regional administration will be strengthened by
the unification of the central departments' regional organizations
under new Directors of Integrated Regional Offices – already

dubbed 'regional commissars' by some people. In addition, the creation of unified regional regeneration funds under the control of these officers will replace the previous numerous government grant programmes available in England's depressed regions (Tinnion, interview[2]). Regional administration in the National Health Service (NHS), however, will be weakened by the abolition of the Regional Health Authorities (RHAs) in 1996, although regional offices will be retained within the NHS management structure.

Another relatively new form of regional administration has developed through the establishment of executive agencies under the programme initiated by the Next Steps Report (Cabinet Office, 1988), as the regional or national headquarters of these agencies are often based outside London. Thus the national headquarters of the Department of Social Security's Contributions Agency is based in Longbenton, Newcastle upon Tyne, along with the Northern Territorial Directorate of the Benefits Agency. However, these are executive rather than policy-making organizations, although the Longbenton complex is one of the biggest employers in the north-east and hence of considerable importance to the region's economy.

Local government has never held secure powers and functions under the UK's unwritten constitution and it has been systematically weakened since 1979 (Elcock, 1994). In particular, the abolition of the Greater London Council and the six metropolitan county councils in 1986 means that some of the areas most in need of regeneration funds no longer even have a subregional (county) authority to represent their interests in London and Brussels. The former metropolitan county councils had been important and fairly effective lobbyists for Union development funds. Lodge (1993: 35) identifies the weakness of British local government as a reason for the British central government being allowed to nominate those whom it wished to represent the English regions on the Committee of the Regions (COR), rather than appointing elected councillors as other member states have done. Thus the government would have the power to appoint those who are unlikely to constitute an alternative source of decisions, as well as those who will not criticize its own policies, even from those regions like the north-east of England which have massively rejected the Conservative Party in successive elections. However, in the end, 22 of the 24 members of the British delegation are councillors, the remaining two being government appointees (*The Times*, 9 March 1994).

The absence of regional governments weakens the ability of the

English regions to articulate their needs and demands in the 'bottom-up' side of the processes of interaction between the EU and regions outlined in Table 1. It also hampers them in competing against regions in other member states for attention and resources. The latter have regional governments which are well able to articulate their regions' interests. Significantly, the result has been an effort to increase the English regions' ability to articulate their interests and demands both from the bottom up and from the top down. As Richard Williams has put it, 'The British response to this competition has been for voluntary groupings of local authorities to set up representative offices in Brussels, as their "eyes and ears" and as a lobby' (R. Williams, 1993: 355). The regions of Britain, or at least some of them, have thus demonstrated that they are aware of the dangers of not being able to state their cases effectively in Brussels.

From the bottom up, some regions have formed voluntary consortia of local authorities, industrial and labour organizations and others to represent the regions' interests to Brussels. Among the English regions, the northern region is the furthest advanced in developing such consortia. They include the Northern Development Company, which brings together local authorities, industry, trade unions and others to develop an agency to lobby for the region's interests in Brussels (Burch, 1993). However, the fragmentation of local and regional administrations presents a major problem in securing agreement on a common regional strategy in the absence of a regional governmental agency which could bring them together (Burge, 1993: 65).

Of considerably increasing importance has been the Northern Regional Councils Association, which has now re-named itself the Northern Assembly of Local Authorities. Its External Relations Committee, advised by a powerful committee made up of the local authorities' European development officers, now plays an important role in scrutinizing and prioritizing the bids for European development funds prepared by the individual local authorities in the region. Its effectiveness is demonstrated because the Department of the Environment has entrusted the assembly and its committees with the allocation of European regional development funds in the region. The department has recognized that the External Affairs Committee and its officer committee are better aware of the ability of the individual councils to use the funds fully, than the Department of the Environment can hope to be. As a result, funds are allocated to those who can make the best use of them and in consequence, the north has a better record than any other region in spending its European allocations fully. In January 1992, local authorities in the north-west region formed the North-West Regional Association in an attempt to bring together the local authorities of that more politically diverse region for similar purposes (Ellman, 1993; Burch and Holliday, 1993).

From the top down, the Commission, especially DG XVI, has found it useful to encourage the development of such consortia and other agencies to ensure that people in the English regions are fully aware of the opportunities and funds the Union can offer them. Thus the European Union's Northern Office, 'Signpost Europe', is an important agency for disseminating information about EU policies and funding in the northern region. It reports to, and represents, the Commission's national office in London. More informally, officials from DG XVI have encouraged industry, trade unions, local authorities and others to form consortia. This has been particularly successful in Northern Ireland and the north of England, because otherwise there are no governmental structures with which DG XVI can relate (Interviews). A former Commission civil servant has suggested that 'the mere existence of resources in Brussels can be a catalyst which changes the way in which a region regards its future' (McIldoon, 1993). Furthermore, he argues that a region must first decide 'where it wants to go before considering how the European Community can help' (*Ibid: 9*). However, we may compare the slow progress in the development of English regional institutions with the implementation of Integrated Mediterranean Programmes in Greece, where Stephen George tells us that 'the Commission effectively forced the [Greek] central government to create a regional tier of administration in order to participate in the programmes at all' (1994: 145). Such strong-arm tactics have not yet been tried on the United Kingdom government!

However, the consortia established in the northern region are highly valued by leading figures in local authorities in the north of England, as indicated in Table 2.

Thus almost all the council leaders and a large majority of the chief executives attached considerable importance to regional consortia and similar organizations, while the national local authority associations, which are regarded by the same people as being of great significance in local authorities' dealings with the central government in Whitehall, are not regarded as having any great importance in the authorities' European Community liaison activities.

TABLE 2

RESPONSES OF LOCAL AUTHORITY CHIEF EXECUTIVE OFFICERS AND COUNCIL LEADERS IN THE NORTH-EAST OF ENGLAND TO THE QUESTION: 'WHICH CHANNELS OF COMMUNICATION ARE OF MOST IMPORTANCE IN YOUR DEALINGS WITH THE EUROPEAN COMMUNITY?'

	CEOs	Leaders
Letters	10	6
Telephone calls	6	3
MEPs	14	6
Local or regional organizations	13	6
National associations	5	2
N =	17	7

Respondents were allowed more than one response.
Source: NNPP, 1992

BUT WHAT IS A REGION ANYWAY?

The non-existence of regional governments in England is not simply the consequence of an arrogant assumption that no intermediate level of government is needed in the United Kingdom between Whitehall and subordinate local authorities. It also reflects the difficulty of clearly identifying the regional identities and civil societies that make up England. Scotland and Wales are easy to delineate geographically and they both have national identities which are represented by significant nationalist movements. No similar movement exists in any English region, with the possible exception of Cornwall. The lack of such a regional identity has been well described by Richard Williams (1993: 355-6) in discussing the development of the network of European Motor Regions: 'An English region such as the south-east or East Anglia was sought but there was no-one with the political authority to speak for them, so Wales became a British participant because it did have its own political authority.' However, that political authority is the Secretary of State for Wales, a member of the national cabinet. Nonetheless, this is a telling example of the weakness of the regional representation of the English regions in the EU.

Even the definition of the English regions is difficult. The eight standard regions have been developed for administrative convenience rather than as geographical entities representing popular communities (Hogwood and Keating, 1982). Some of these regions include areas whose interests fundamentally conflict, such as Greater Bristol and the 'Far South-West', both of which are included in the south-west region but which are in competition for industrial and other types of development. The northern region is arguably the most coherent of the standard regions but even here, there is the issue of how much Cumbria has in common with the four counties which make up the 'industrial north-east' (Johnston, Pattie and Allsopp, 1988). However, improved transport links and common problems of industrial decline in west Cumbria in particular constitute bonds of common economic interest. The need to secure assistance from the government and the EU in countering industrial decline has encouraged a number of Cumbrian local authorities to join the Northern Assembly of Local Authorities. At another level, it is significant to note that when the BBC transferred its Cumbrian activities from BBC North, based in Newcastle, to BBC Lancashire, popular pressure forced a reversal of the decision, indicating that the allegiance of Cumbrians lies with the north-east rather than Lancashire (Elcock *et al.*, 1993; Tinnion, interview).

Nonetheless, the question of whether or not the northern region constitutes an identifiable civil society is hard to answer at all conclusively. It is not altogether easy even in the more restricted context of the 'industrial north-east'. Its people speak with a very distinctive accent and use words and phrases which come close to constituting a regional dialect. It has a distinctive social structure which has been vividly been portrayed in the novels of Catherine Cookson, as well as in several television drama series. It has a distinctive folk culture, including the Northumbrian bagpipes, but none of this constitutes academically respectable evidence for the existence of a north-eastern civil society! (See Robinson, 1993, for a similar account of the problem and the means to its partial solution). More substantial evidence of a coherent identity is the north-east region's political solidarity, with 19 of its 26 local authorities being controlled by Labour; the Conservatives control none of them. In consequence, these local authorities have frequently come into conflict with central government, especially since 1979, but there is a 'lack of political conflict within the region' (Robinson, 1993). Thus, six out of 17 local authority chief executives responding to a questionnaire in 1992 stated that their authorities' ability to raise local taxation had been limited under the government's 'rate-capping' and subsequent legislation (NNPP, 1992). Also, the Labour Party holds all but six of the region's 30 parliamentary constituencies. One of the others is held by the Liberal Democrats, leaving only five held by the Conservatives (Fenwick, Harrop and Elcock, 1990). All the region's MEPs are Labour and they are regarded by leading local government figures as an important channel of communication between the region's local authorities and the Union (see Table 2 above).

Accompanying this Labour hegemony is a strong but moderate trade union movement, which traditionally has been spearheaded by the National Union of Mineworkers, the Amalgamated Engineering and Electrical Trades Union, the General and Municipal Workers' Union and, to a somewhat lesser extent, the Transport and General Workers' Union. These are, of course, the unions which organize workers mainly in what were until recent times the region's staple industries – coal mining, engineering and shipbuilding. The region's fourth traditional industry, steel-making, was largely concentrated in the town of Consett, where the steelworkers' union was therefore powerful. All these are large industrial or general unions which drew much of their membership from basic, traditional, heavy industries (Pelling, 1963). They were also stalwart supporters of the Labour Party's leadership until the splits of the late 1950s and the 1960s.

Both the Labour Party's dominance of the politics of the north-east, and the region's strong trade union movement stem in large part from the region's industrial history and structure, which constitutes further evidence in support of there being a coherent regional identity in the north-east. The north-east was for many years mainly dependent for industrial employment on four basic industries: coal-mining, shipbuilding, engineering and steel-making.

All four are quintessentially 'Fordist' industries, requiring large units of production, large labour forces and mass-production methods. The dominance of these industries retarded the development of smaller, light and high technology industries in the region. Their development was further inhibited after the Second World War by a government policy of discouraging new industries from establishing themselves in the north-east, because the national interest was deemed to require that nothing should be done that might encourage the region's workers to leave the coal mines. Equally, the rapid decline, and in most cases the eventual virtual disappearance, of these basic industries since the 1960s has resulted in a rapid rise in unemployment and consequent poverty which, during the 1980s, reached a scale comparable with the depression of the inter-war years (Chapman, 1985; Hudson, 1989). The north-east therefore has 'a shared experience of decline' (Robinson, 1993: 59). The problems of over-dependence on basic industries and the effects of their decline also dominate the western part of Cumbria, giving that area interests in common with the industrial north-east.

Another indication of regional identity and loyalty is a long-standing suspicion, even antagonism, towards the seat of government in London: 'Most of us who live in the north-east find the south fairly loathsome.' (Robinson, 1993: 61). Even regional civil servants declare that 'policies are south-eastern policies' (Elcock, Fenwick and Harrop, 1988). The Bishop of Durham's denunciation of the chairman of British Coal as an 'elderly, imported American' during the miners' strike of 1984-5 was another expression of a sense that the north-east was suffering from the hostility of a Conservative government whose power-base lay in the south-east of England.

One result of this sense of alienation from the national government has been that the trade unions have often collaborated with local authority employers and others in recent years, to reduce the impact on the region's workers of unwelcome national policies, such as compulsory competitive tendering in local government. They have reached agreements on management changes and the abolition of restrictive trade practices in order to maximize the chance of the 'in-house' tender winning in the competitive tendering process (Elcock, Fenwick and Harrop, 1988; Fenwick, Shaw and Foreman, 1992; Hudson, 1989). The north-east's solidaristic labour movement has also, however, led to some famous confrontations with private-sector and other employers, including the coal strikes of 1973-4 and 1984-5.

More generally, Hudson (1989) argues that central government has damaged the interests of the north-east through three successive phases of its policies towards the region since the Second World War. The first was the prevention of new industries from establishing themselves in order to preserve the coal industry's workforce after the end of the Second World War. This left the region ill-equipped to adapt to the rapid changes in national and international markets that have occurred since the late 1960s. Second, Lord Hailsham's appointment as Minister for the north-east notwithstanding, development assistance has never been sufficient to counter the decline of the region's basic industries. Lastly, such assistance as had been available was largely withdrawn in the 1980s. Hence, no effort was made by central government to ameliorate the region's increasingly desperate plight as the basic industries disappeared, and as branch plants in the north-east were closed in the early 1980s by multinational corporations, making these decisions often from far away headquarters in the United States and elsewhere (Hudson, 1989).

In consequence of these policies too, the north-east became a classic candidate for assistance from the EC under Objective 2, but even the impact of EC development aid was blunted by the Treasury's reluctance to regard EC assistance as being additional to, rather than a substitute for, government development funds. This dispute has still by no means been resolved despite pressure from the Commission, especially from Bruce Millan as the Regional Affairs Commissioner, to make the British government accept the principle of the additionality of EC development funds (Tinnion, interview).

The foregoing arguments for the regional coherence of the northern region are weakened, however, by two factors. The first is the distinctiveness of largely rural Cumbria, except for its western coastal area. The second is the wide diversities of interests that exist between the urban industrial areas in Tyne and Wear and around the Tees Estuary on the one hand, and the sparsely populated rural areas of Northumberland, County Durham and Cleveland on the other. The arguments that the northern region can claim cultural, economic and social coherence are strong but they cannot be offered without serious qualification.

THE FUTURE

We have seen that the local authorities and other interests in this region, more than in other English regions, have been able to establish stronger mechanisms to promote their collective interests in Brussels. Also, there have been periodic attempts to lobby for the creation of a regional assembly in the north. The Northern Regional Labour Party produced such proposals in 1984 (*A Voice for the North*) and again in 1991 (*A Regional Council for the North*). Another blueprint was produced by the then Northern Regional Councils Association in May 1991 (*Government in the Northern Region: The Next Steps*). Shortly before the 1992 General Election, Richard Caborn, MP, produced a set of proposals for the implementation of English regional government which could be executed within a single parliament by a Labour government (Caborn, 1991). With the Conservative victory in that election, the issue of regional government, along with devolution to Scotland and Wales, was off the political agenda. As the next General Election draws closer, however, it is being revived by the opposition parties, all of whom were committed to introduce devolution and regional government in their 1992 election manifestoes (see Burch, 1993).

The problem is that although such proposals command widespread support among political activists and political leaders in the north of England which has been strengthened by a widely shared suspicion of government from the south-east corner of England (Elcock, Fenwick and Harrop, 1988), it is much more difficult to perceive any support for them from the mass of the region's citizenry. In part, this is because the concept of regional identity is so nebulous in England. Some argue that the opposition parties lost the 1992 General Election partly because they concentrated their campaigns too much on esoteric issues of constitutional reform, including devolution and regionalism, which had little salience for the general public. Thus the Deputy Leader of the Labour Party, Roy Hattersley, had little regard for Charter 88, the organization devoted to pressing for the reform of the British constitution, including the implementation of devolution and regional government. He dismissed its largely intellectual and middle class members as 'the chartering classes'. The interests of his working-class constituents were different and more pressing. Furthermore, public support for the Conservatives may have been increased during the last days of the campaign by John Major's spirited defence of the Union (Butler and Kavanagh, 1993: 128).

Nonetheless, the issue is back on the political agenda as the next General Election approaches, although it may not be pressed so vigorously during the election campaign as it was in 1992 because the party leaders will not see it as a major vote-winner for them. However, the momentum of European integration, the threat posed to peripheral regions by the four freedoms of the Single European Market, as well as European Monetary Union, together with the increasing importance of competing effectively for attention and funds with other European regions, provide an additional and powerful argument for the introduction of regional assemblies and governments in England sooner or later.

NOTES

1. I am greatly indebted to my colleagues Dr. Ken Harrop and Dr. John Fenwick of the University of Northumbria at Newcastle for their collaboration in much of the research that is reported here. I am also indebted to Mr. Austin McCarthy of Northumbria University Library for information relating to the Committee of the Regions.

2. *Interviews*
   a) With officials of Directorate-General XVI of the European Commission, February 1991.
   b) With Councillor Paul Tinnion, of Gateshead Metropolitan Borough Council, January 1994.
   c) Also some further information collected from senior regional Civil Servants under Chatham House Rules.

References

Advisory Commission on Intergovernmental Relations, 1982, *State and Local Roles in the Federal System*, A-88 (Washington, DC: US Government Printing Office).

Aggarwal, V., R. O. Keohane and D. B. Yoffie, 1987, 'The Dynamics of Negotiated Protectionism', *American Political Science Review* Vol.81, No 2 (June), pp.345–66.

Aglietta, M., 1979, *A Theory of Capitalist Regulation*, London: Verso.

Agnew, J., 1987, Place and Politics: The Geographical Mediation of State and Society (London: Allen and Unwin).

Agnew, J. A. and S. Corbridge, 1995, *Mastering Space* (London: Routledge).

Agulhon, M., 1982, The Republic in the Village: the People of the Var from the French Revolution to the Second Republic, trans. J. Lloyd. (New York: Cambridge University Press).

Alcan, 1987, *Le libre-échange Canada-États-Unis: la position d'Alcan.* (Brief to the Quebec Parliamentary Commission on Canada–US Free Trade, September).

Alger, C. F., 1988, 'Perceiving, Analysing and Coping with the Local–global Nexus', *International Social Science Journal*, Vol.117.

Altenberger, C. and K. Kearns, 1989, *Restructuring the Pittsburgh Metropolitan Region* (Pittsburgh: Graduate School of Public and International Affairs, University of Pittsburgh).

Amin, A., 1994, 'Post-Fordism: Models, Fantasies and Phantoms of Transition', in Amin, A. (ed.), *Post-Fordism: A Reader*, (Oxford: Blackwell).

Amin, A. and J. Tomaney, 1995, 'The Regional Dilemma in a Neo-liberal Europe', *European Urban and Regional Studies*, Vol.2, No.2.

Anderson, B., 1991, Imagined Communities: reflections on the origin and spread of nationalism (London: Verso).

Anderson, J. 1990, 'The "New Right", Enterprise Zones and Urban Development Corporations', *International Journal of Urban and Regional Research*, Vol. 14, No. 3, pp. 468–489.

Anderson, J., 1992, The Territorial Imperative: Pluralism, Corporatism and Economic Crisis (Cambridge: Cambridge University Press).

Anderson, J. , 1990, 'Sceptical Reflections on a Europe of Regions: Britain, Germany and the ERDF, *Journal of Public Policy*, Vol.10, No.4, pp.417–47.

Andeweg, R., 1989, 'Institutional Conservatism in the Netherlands: Proposals for and Resistance to Change', in H. Daalder and G. A. Irwin, *Politics in the Netherlands: how much change?* (London: Frank Cass).

Apparel Manufacturers Institute of Quebec/Institut des Manufacturiers du Vêtement du Québec, 1987, *Mémoire de l'IMVQ sur la libéralisation des échanges commerciaux entre le Canada et les États-Unis* (Brief to the Quebec

Parliamentary Commission on Canada-US Free Trade, mimeograph, 25 August).

ARL/DATAR, 1992, Perspectives of Regional Development Policy in Europe (Hannover: Akadamie für Raumforschung und Landesplanung).

Armstrong, H., 1993, 'Community Regional Policy', in J. Lodge (ed.), pp.131–51.

Ashford, D. E., 1986, *The Emergence of Welfare States* (Oxford: Basil Blackwell).

Association du disque et de l'industrie du spectacle et vidéo québécois (ADISQ), 1987, *Libre-échange: en avons-nous les moyens?* Brief presented to the Parliamentary Commission on Canada US Free Trade, (September.)

Atkinson, Rob and Graham Moon, 1994, *Urban Policy in Britain* (Houndmills: Macmillan).

Aucoin, P., 1988, 'Contraction, managerialism and decentralization in Canadian government', *Governance*, Vol.1, pp.144–61.

Bacaria, J., 1992, Quatre Motors Per a Europa: análisi d'un experiment de cooperació científica i tecnológica entre les regions de Catalunya, Baden-Württemberg, Lombardia i Rhône-Alpes (Informe de l'Estudi: Análisi de la Cooperació, Universitat Autónoma de Barcelona (unpublished)).

Bachtler, J., 1990, 'North versus south in European regional policy', European Access,No. 6, pp.9–11.

Bachtler, J., 1992, 'The reshaping of regional policy in Western Europe', in G. Gorzelak and A. Kuklinski (eds.), *Dilemmas of Regional Policies in Eastern and Central Europe* (University of Warsaw).

Bachtler, J., 1995a, 'Regional policy and cohesion in the European Union', in R. Vickerman and H. Armstrong (eds.), *Convergence and Divergence Among European Regions* (European Research in Regional Science, Vol.5, Pion).

Bachtler, J., 1995b, 'Regional development planning in Objective 1 regions', *European Urban and Regional Studies*, Vol.2, No.4, pp.339–71.

Bachtler, J. and R. Michie, 1993, 'The restructuring of regional policy in the European Community', *Regional Studies*, Vol.27, No.8, pp.719–25.

Bachtler, J. and R. Michie, 1994, 'Strengthening economic and social cohesion? The revision of the Structural Funds', *Regional Studies*, Vol.28, No.8, pp.789–96.

Bachtler, J. and R. Michie, 1995, 'A new era in regional policy evaluation? The appraisal of the Structural Funds', *Regional Studies*, Vol.29, No.8.

Bachtler, J., R. Downes and D. Yuill, 1993, *The Devolution of Economic Development: Lessons from Germany* (Glasgow: Scottish Foundation for Economic Research, Glasgow Caledonian University).

Bachtler, J., R. Waniek and R. Michie, 1995, *Regional and Industrial Policy Research Papers*, No.16 (Glasgow: European Policies Research Centre, University of Strathclyde).

Baerssen, D.W., 1971, *The Border Industrialization Program of Mexico* (Lexington, MA: Lexington Books).

Bagguley, P., J. Mark-Lawson, D. Shapiro, J. Urry, S. Walby, and A. Warde, 1990, *Restructuring: Place, Class and Gender* (London: Sage).

Ballingand, J-P. and D. Maquart, 1990, 'Aménagement du territoire: la mosaïque dislocquée', *Revue Politique et Parlementaire*, No.946, pp.54–67.

Balme, R., 1995, 'La politique régionale communautaire comme construction institutionnelle' in Y. Mény, P. Muller and J.-L. Quermonne (eds.), *Les politiques publiques en Europe* (Paris: L'Harmattan).

Balme, R. and L. Bonnet, 1995, 'From regional to sectoral policies: the contractual relations between the state and the regions in France', in J. Loughlin and S. Mazey (eds.), *The End of the French Unitary State: Ten Years of Regionalization in France (1982-1992)* (London: Frank Cass).

Balme, R. and B. Jouve, 1996, 'Building the regional state: French territorial organization and the implementation of Structural Funds', in L. Hooghe (ed.), *EC Cohesion Policy and National Networks* (Oxford: Oxford University Press).

Balme, R. and P. Le Galès, 1993, *Stars and Black Holes: French cities and regions in the wake of European integration*, communication at the Eurolog Conference, Twente University, The Netherlands.

Balme, R. et al., 1994, *Le Territoire pour Politiques: variations Européennes* (Paris: L'Harmattan).

Balme, R., S. Brouard and F. Burbaud, 1995, 'La coopération inter-régionale et la genèse de l'espace public européen: le cas de la façade atlantique', *Sciences de la société*, Vol.34.

Balsom, D. and B. Jones, 1984, 'The faces of Wales', in I. McAllister and R. Rose, *The Nationwide Competition for Votes* (Frances Pinter), pp.98–121.

Banfield, E., 1958, The Moral Basis of A Backward Society (New York: The Free Press).

Barcelona, 1990, 'Barcelona y el Sistema Urbano Europeo', Barcelona EUROCIUDAD, No.1.

Bartlett, W., 1991, 'Quasi-markets and contracts: a markets and hierarchies perspective on NHS reform', *Public Money and Management*, Vol.11, No.3, pp.53-61.

Barzelay, M., 1992, *Breaking through Bureaucracy* (Berkeley: University of California Press).

Beauchesne, L., 1991, 'Canadian Opinion Split on trilateral Free Trade', *The Gazette* (Montreal), 26 February, p.D3.

Beilharz, P. and Watts, R., 1986, 'The Discourse of Labourism', *Arena*, No. 77, pp. 96–109.

Bellah, R. N., 1986, *Habits of the Heart* (Berkeley: University of California Press).

Bellin, W., 1989, 'Ethnicity and Welsh bilingual education', *Contemporary Wales*, Vol.3, pp.77–97.

Benda, P. M. and C. H. Levine, 1988, 'Reagan and the Bureaucracy: the bequest, the promise, the legacy' in C. O. Jones, (ed.), *The Reagan Legacy* (Chatham, NJ: Chatham House).

Bendix, R., 1964, *Nation-building and Citizenship* (New York: John Wiley).

Benko, G. and A. Lipietz (eds.), 1992, *Les régions qui gagnent* (Paris: PUF).

Bennett, R. J. (ed.), 1989, *Local Government in the New Europe* (London: Belhaven Press).

Bennington, J., 1994, Local Democracy and the European Union: the impact of Europeanization on local governance (Commission for Local Democracy, October).

Benton, L., 1990, *Invisible Factories: The Informal Economy and Industrial Development in Spain*, (Albany: State University of New York Press).

Benz, A., 1993, 'Redrawing the Map? The Question of Territorial Reform in the Federal Republic', in C. Jeffery and R. Sturm (eds.), *Federalism, Unification, and European Integration* (London: Frank Cass), pp.38–57.

Berg, M. and M. Schaafsma, 1991, 'Cities endangered, chances for urban regions', *Dokumente und Informationen zur Schweizerischen ORTS-, Regional- und Landsplanung*, DISP No. 105 (April), ETH Zurich.

Bernard, P., 1983, *L'etat et la decentralization: du prefet au commissionare de la Republique* (Paris: La documentation française).

Bernier, I., 1973, International Legal Aspects of Federalism (London: Longman).

Bernier, I., 1992, 'La dimension juridique des relations commerciales d'un Québec souverain', in Les Implications de la mise en oeuvre de la souveraineté.

Best, J., 1989, *Images of Issues* (Berlin: de Gruyter).

Best, J., 1991, *Images of Issues*. (New York: Aldine de Gruyter).

Biarez, S., 1989, *Le Pouvoir Local* (Paris: Economica).

Bird, R. M. (ed.), 1980, Fiscal Dimensions of Canadian Federalism (Toronto: Canadian Tax Foundation).

Bird, R. M., 1984, 'Tax harmonization and federal finance: a perspective on recent Canadian discussions' *Canadian Public Policy*, No.10.

Blais, A. and R. Nadeau, 1984, 'L'appui au Parti québécois: évolution de la clientèle de 1970 à 1981'; and 'La clientèle du OUI', in J. Crête (ed.), *Comportement électoral au Québec* (Chicoutimi: Gaètan Morin éditeur), pp.279–318 and pp.321–34.

Blais, A. and R. Nadeau, 1992, 'To be or not to be a sovereignist? Quebeckers' perennial dilemma' *Canadian Public Policy* Vol.18, No.1 (March), pp.89–103.

Blanke, H.-J., 1991, 'Das Subsidiaritätsprinzip als Schranke des Europäischen Gemeinschaftsrechts?' *Zeitschrift für Gesetzgebung*, Vol.6, No.2, pp.133–48.

Bloch-Lainé, F., 1990, 'Plus de muscle, moins de graisse', *Pouvoirs locaux*, Vol.5.

Borras, S., 1992, The New Dimension of Region's Policies on Innovation: guidelines and conceptual framework for a future analysis of four regions (European University Institute, June (unpublished)).

Borras, S., 1993, 'The "Four Motors for Europe" and its promotion of R&D linkages: Beyond geographical contiguity in interregional agreements', *Regional Politics and Policy* Vol.3, No.3, Autumn.

Bours, A., 1993, 'Management, tiers, size and amalgamation of local government' in R. J. Bennett (ed.).

Bowie, F., 1993, 'Wales from within: conflicting interpretations of Welsh identity', in S. Macdonald (ed.), *Inside European Identities* (Providence and Oxford: Berg), pp.167–93.

Boyle, R., 1993, 'Changing Partners: The experience of urban economic policy in west central Scotland, 1980–90', *Urban Studies*, Vol.30, No.2, pp.309–24.

Boyte, H.C, 1992, 'The Pragmatic Ends of Popular Politics', in C. Calhoun (ed.), *Habermas and the Public Sphere*, (Cambridge, MA: The MIT Press).

Braunthal, G., 1990, Political Loyalty and Public Service in West Germany: the 1972 Decree against radicals and its consequences (Amherst, MA: University of Massachusetts Press).

Brettschneider, F., *et al.*, 1994, 'Materialien zu Gesellschaft, Wirtschaft und Politik in den Mitgliedsstaaten der Europäischen Gemeinschaft', in: O.W. Gabriel and F. Brettschneider (eds.), *Die EU–Staaten im Vergleich* (Bonn: Bundeszentrale für Politische Bildung).

Breunese, J. N., 1982, 'Twee Nederlandse eeuwen provincie', Bestuur: Maandblad voor Overheidskunde, Vol.7, pp.14–19.

Brothers, D.W. and A. E. Wick (eds.), *Mexico's Search for a New Development Strategy* (Boulder, CO: Westview Press).

Brown, S., 1988, *New Forces, Old Forces and the Future of World Politics* (Glenview, ILL.: Scott Foresman).

Brunet, R., 1989, *Les Villes Européennes* (Paris: La Documentation Française).

Brunn, S. and T. R. Leinbach (eds.), 1991, *Collapsing Space and Time: geographic aspects of communication and information* (London: Harper Collins Academic).

Bryson, J., 1989, 'Strategic management: big wins and small wins', *Public Money and Management*, Vol.8, No.3, pp.11–15.

Bullmann, U. and D. Eissel, 1993, ' "Europa der Regionen". Entwicklung und Perspektiven', *Aus Politik und Zeitgeschichte* Vol.20–21, pp.3–15.

Bulpitt, J., 1986, 'The Discipline of the New Democracy: Mrs Thatcher's domestic statecraft', *Political Studies*, Vol.34, pp.19–39.

Burch M. and I. Holliday, 1993, 'Institutional Emergence: the case of the North West Region of England', *Regional Politics and Policy*, Vol. 3, No.2, pp.29–50.

Burch, M. and M. Rhodes (eds.), *The North-West Region and Europe: development of a regional strategy* (Manchester Papers in Politics, No. 6, 1993, University of Manchester).

Burch, M., 1993, 'The political dimension: the scope for a regional initiative?', in M. Burch and M. Rhodes (eds.), pp.46–51.

Bureau of Industry Economics (BIE) (1994), *Regional Development: Patterns and Policy Implications, Research Report* No. 56, Canberra.

Burge, K., 1993, 'The experience of setting up a Development Agency', in M. Burch and M. Rhodes (eds.), pp.62–5.

Burgess, M. (ed.), 1986, *Federalism and Federation in Western Europe* (London: Croom Helm).

Burnelly, S., 1993, 'It's a grab bag, and quite peculiar', *Financial Review*, 21 December, 1993.

Butler, D. E. and D. Kavanagh, 1993, *The British General Election of 1992* (London: Macmillan).

Cabinet Office, Prime Minister's Efficiency Unit, 1988, *Improving Management in Government: The Next Steps*, (London: Her Majesty's Stationery Office).

Caborn, R., 1991, *Regional Government for England: Labour's programme* (Richard Caborn, MP, June).

Caiden, G., 1990, *Administrative Reform Comes of Age* (Berlin: Aldine De Gruyter).

Cameron, N., 1993, 'Advancing regional futures' – the "Regional Australia Now" Campaign', 17th Australia New Zealand Regional Science Association Conference, 6–8 December, Armidale, N.S.W.

Camilleri, J. and J. Falk, 1991, *End of Sovereignty? The Politics of a Shrinking and Fragmenting World* (London: Edward Elgar).

Campbell, C. and J. Halligan, 1992, *Political Leadership in an Age of Constraint* (Pittsburgh: University of Pittsburgh Press).

Canadian Facts, 1991, *CBC/Globe and Mail Public Opinion Poll* (Toronto: Canadian Facts, 4–15 April), computerized dataset.

Cappellin, R., 1990, *The International Role of Regional Economies: the scope of inter-regional cooperation in Europe*, paper presented at the Symposium on Inter-regional Co-operation, European University Institute, Florence, 29–30 June.

Carr, B., 1978, 'An Australian Replies', *Quadrant*, Vol. XXII, No. 4, 1978, pp. 16–18.

Carr, R., 1992, *Explaining 'enterprise': an examination of the impact of Welsh language and culture upon economic and business activities in Wales* (Newport: School of Sociology and Social Policy, UCNW).

Carreño, L., 1991, *La Red de las 6 Ciudades (C6)*, paper presented at the Colloquium Bilan et Projets de la Société de l'Arc Méditerranéen, Nîmes, 9 November.

Carrieri, M., 1989, 'Le innovazioni imperfette del ceto politico regionale', in *La Storia d'Italia da ll' unita   ad oggi. Le regioni: la Puglia* (Torino: Einaudi).

Cassing, J., T. J. McKeown and J. Ochs, 1986, 'The Political Economy of the Tariff Cycle', *American Political Science Review* Vol.80, No. 3 (September), pp.843–62.

Casson, M., 1993, 'Cultural determinants of economic performance', *Journal of Comparative Economics*, Vol.17, pp.418-42.

Castles, S., H. Booth and T. Wallace, 1984, *Here for Good: Western Europe's new ethnic minorities* (London: Pluto Press).

Celimene, F. L., 1991, 'La réforme des fonds structurels européens: éléments d'une théorie du développement régional communautaire, *Revue d'Economie Régionale et Urbaine*, Vol.2, pp.183–219.

Centro Studi Confindustria, 1991, *Indicatori Economici Provinciali* (Roma: SIPI).

Chambre de Commerce du Québec, 1990, *L'avenir politique et constitutionnel du Québec: sa dimension économique* (Brief presented to the Commission on the Constitutional Future of Quebec, 1 November).

Chapman, N.D.H., *et al.*, 1990, *Dadansoddiad o gyfrifiad 1981 ar Weithgarredd economaidd a'r iaith Gymareg, Adran Economey ac Economey Amaethyddol* (Aberysthwyth: Coleg Prifysgol Cymru).

Chapman, R. (ed.), 1985, *Public Policy Studies: The North-East of England* (University of Edinburgh Press for the University of Durham).

Charpentier, J. and C. Engel (eds.), 1992, *Les Régions de l'Espace communautaire* (Nancy: Presses Universitaires de Nancy).

Chavannes, M., 1994, *De stroperige staat: Kanttekeningen bij de liefste democratie op aarde* (Amsterdam: Contact).

Chubb, J., 1982, *Patronage, Power and Poverty in Southern Italy. A Tale of Two Cities* (Cambridge: Cambridge University Press).

Clare, R. (1993), 'The new growth industry: Regional and urban policy', *Directions in Government*, November, pp. 14–15, 19.

Clark, R. P., 1979, *The Basques: the Franco years and beyond* (Reno: The University of Nevada Press).

Clark, R. P., 1984, *The Basque Insurgents: ETA, 1952-1980* (Madison: The University of Wisconsin Press).

Clavera, J., 1990, 'Le débat sur le libre-échange: le cas de la Catalogne face à l'intégration dans la Communauté', in G. Tremblay and M. Parès i Maicas (eds.), *Autonomie et Mondialisation: le Québec et la Catalogne à l'heure du libre-échange et de la Communauté européenne* (Sillery: Presses de l'Université du Québec), pp.55–65.

Clout, H., 1975, *Regional development in Western Europe* (London: John Wiley).

Cloutier, É, J.-H. Guay and D. Latouche, 1992, *Le virage: l'évolution de l'opinion publique au Québec depuis 1960, ou comment le Québec est devenu souverainiste* (Montréal: Éditions Québec/Amérique).

Cobb, J., 1982, *The Selling of the South* (Baton Rouge: Louisiana State University Press).

Cogesult, Inc., 1985, *Étude des conséquences économiques du libre-échange entre le Canada et les États-Unis sur l'industrie de la fabrication des meubles au Québec et au Canada* (mimeograph).

Cohen, S. B., 1994, 'Geopolitics in the new world era: a new perspective on an old discipline', in J. D. George and W. B. Wood (eds.), *Reordering the World: Geopolitical Perspectives on the Twenty-first Century* (Boulder, CO: Westview).

Coleman, W. and H. Jacek, 1989, 'Capitalists, collective action and regionalism', in W. Coleman and H. Jacek (eds.), *Regionalism, Business Interests and Public Policy*, (London: Sage).

Colletis, G., 1991, *Les Quatre Moteurs pour l'Europe: la coopération scientifique et technologique* (CERAT-Institut d'Etudes Politiques de Grenoble (unpublished)).

Collits, P., 1994, 'Business Costs in Non-Metropolitan Regions: Research Findings and Policy Issues', 18th Australia New Zealand Regional Science Association Conference, 12–14 December, Perth, Western Australia.

Commission Des Communautés Européennes, 1991, *Les Régions dans les Années 1990, Quatrième rapport sur la situation et l'évolution socio-économiques des régions de la Communauté* (Brussels).

Commission Des Communautés Européennes, 1993, *Fonds Structurels communautaires 1994-1999, textes réglementaires et commentaires* (Brussels).

Commission of the European Communities, 1992, *Communication from the Commission – Assessment and Outlook*, COM(92) Final, 11 February (Brussels).

Commission of the European Communities, 1995, *Communication from the Commission – The New Regional Programmes under Objectives 1 and 2 of Community Structural Policies*, COM(95) 111 Final, 29 March (Brussels).

Committee Montijn (Externe Commissie Grote Stedenbeleid), 1989, *Grote steden, grote kansen* (Den Haag: SDU).

Committee Hendrikx (IPO Commissie Provinciale Samenwerking), 1992, *Provinciale samenwerking op subnationaal niveau: Kwaliteitsverbetering door samenwerking* (rapport van het Interprovinciaal Overleg).

Commonwealth Government, 1994, *Working Nation: Politics and Programs*, Australian Government Printing Service, 4 May, Canberra.

Conklin, D.W., 1993, *Government and Business Location Decisions*, Government and Competitiveness series, 25 (Kingston: School of Policy Studies, Queen's University).

Cooke, Philip, 1987, 'Class Practices as Regional Markers: A Contribution to Labour Geography' in D. Gregory and J. Urry (ed.), *Spatial Relations and Social Structures* (London: Macmillan).

Cooke, P., 1989, 'Ethnicity, economy and civil society: three theories of political regionalism', in C. H. Williams and E. Kofman (eds.), *Community Conflict, Partition and Nationalism* (London: Routledge).

Cooke, P. and K. Morgan, 1991, 'The intelligent region: industrial and institutional innovation in Emilia-Romagna', *Regional and Industrial Research Report* No.8 (Cardiff: Department of City and Regional Planning, University of Wales).

Cooke, P., K. Morgan, and A. Price, 1993, *The Future of the Mittelstand. Collaboration versus Competition* (Cardiff: The University of Wales Regional Industrial Research Report No. 13).

Cooper, A. F., 1986, 'Subnational activity and foreign economic policy-making in Canada and the United States: perspectives on agriculture' *International Journal* Vol.41, No.3.

Copithorne, L., 1979, 'Natural resources and regional disparites: a skeptical view', *Canadian Public Policy*, Vol.5, No.2.

Cortie, C., 1991, *De dynamiek van stedelijke systemen: Veranderingen in de functies van steden in de Verenigde Staten en de Europese Gemeenschap* (Assen: Van Gorcum).

Council of Europe, 1991, *Assisting the regions: a new structural policy*, (Strasbourg: Council of Europe Press).

Council of Europe, 1992, *European Charter for Regional or Minority Languages* (Strasbourg: Council of Europe).

Courchene, T., 1984, *Equalization Payments: past, present and future* (Ontario Economic Council, Special Research Report, Federal-Provincial Relations Series).

Courchene, T. 1995, 'Celebrating Flexibility: an Interpretive Essay on the Evolution of Canadian Federalism', *Benefactors Lecture* (Montreal: C.D. Howe Institute).

Courchene, T. J., 1986, 'Market Nationalism', *Policy Options* No.7 (October).

Courchene, T. J., 1989, *What Does Ontario Want?* (Toronto: Robarts Centre for Canadian Studies, York University).

Cox, R., 1990, 'Dialectique de l'économie-monde en fin de siècle' *Études internationales* Vol.21, No.4 (December), pp.693–703.

Crawford, R., 1994, 'Inward investment is at the heart of a healthy economy', *Scotsman*, 15 November.

Credit Suisse First Boston Bank, 1992, 'Europe: core vs periphery', *CSFB Economics*, December.

Crozier, M., 1987, *Etat modeste, Etat moderne* (Paris: Fayard).

Daalder, H., 1981, 'Consociationalism: centre and periphery structures and nation-building' in *Mobilization, Centre and Periphery Structures and Nation-Building: A Volume in Commemoration of Stein Rokkan* (Olso/Bergen: Universitetsforlaget).

Daalder, H., 1990, *Politiek en Historie: Opstellen over Nederlandse politiek en vergelijkende politieke wetenschap* (Amsterdam: Bakker).

Danson, M., G. Lloyd and D. Newlands, 1989, ' "Scottish Enterprise": the creation of a more effective development agency or the pursuit of ideology?', *Quarterly Economic Commentary* (Glasgow: Fraser of Allander Institute, University of Strathclyde), Vol.14, No.3, pp.70–75.

Davies, A., 1994, 'Fine tuning policy for regional development', *Sydney Morning Herald*, 12 March, p. 36.

Davies, A., 1995, 'Regions given a steady diet of politics but little funding', *The Sydney Morning Herald*, 28 January, p. 34

Davis, M., 1990, *City of Quartz* (London: Vintage).

Deakin, N. and J. Edwards, 1993, *The Enterprise Culture and the Inner City* (London: Routledge).

DeGrove, J. M., 1991, *Regional Agencies as Partners in State Growth Management Systems* (Oxford: Joint ACSP and AESOP International Congress, July).

Delfaux, P., 1989, 'La perception des disparités régionales dans la Communauté Economique Européenne, *Revue d'Economie Régionale et Urbaine*, No.1, pp.41–70.

Destler, I. M., 1992, *American Trade Politics*, 2nd edition (Washington: Institute for International Economics).

Deutsch, K., 1966, *Nationalism and Social Communication. An Inquiry into the Foundations of Nationality* (Cambridge, MA: MIT Press).

DiIulio, J., 1994, *Deregulating the Public Service: can government be improved?* (Washington, DC: The Brookings Institution).

Doern, G. B. and B. W. Tomlin, 1991, *Faith and Fear: The Free Trade Story* (Toronto: Stoddart).

Doern, G. B. and G. Toner, 1985, *The Politics of Energy: The Development and Implementation of the NEP* (Toronto: Methuen).

Doran, C. F. and G. P. Marchildon (eds.), 1994, *The NAFTA Puzzle: political parties and trade in North America* (Boulder: Westview Press).

Doutriaux, Y., 1991, *La Politique Régionale de la CEE* (Paris: Presses Universitaires de France).

Drewry, G. (ed.), 1985, *The New Select Committees: a Study of the 1979 Reforms* (Oxford: Clarendon Press).

Drozniak, W., 1994, 'Rise of the Eurostate: regions within borders drive a new economic machine' *The Washington Post Weekly Edition*, 4–10 April, p.25.

Duby, G., 1976, *Histoire de la France Rurale*, tome 4 (Paris: Seuil).

Duchacek, I. D., D. Latouche and G. Stevenson, 1988, *Perforated Sovereignties and International Relations: Trans-Sovereign Contacts of Subnational Governments* (New York: Greenwood).

Dunford, M. and G. Kafkakis, 1992, *Cities and Regions in the New Europe* (London: Belhaven).

Dupoirier, E., 1995, 'The first regional political elites in France (1986-1992): a profile', in J. Loughlin and S. Mazey (eds.), *The End of the French Unitary State: Ten Years of Regionalization in France (1982-1992)* (London: Frank Cass).

Dusevic, T., 1994, 'Nation on the Move', *The Australian*, 26 December, p.11.

Dyson, K. H. F., 1980, *The State Tradition in Western Europe* (Oxford: Martin Robertson).

Easton, D., 1965, *A Systems Analysis of Political Life* (New York: Wiley).

Eisenstadt, S. and L. Roniger, 1981, 'The study of patron-client relations and recent developments in sociological theory', in S. N. Eisenstadt and R. Lemarchand (eds.), *Political Clientelism, Patronage and Development* (Beverly Hills: Sage).

Elazar, D. J., 1986, 'Federalism, intergovernmental relations and changing models of the polity', in L. A. Picard and R. Zeriski (eds.), *Subnational Politics in the 1980s* (New York: Praegar).

Elcock, H., 1991, *Change and Decay? Public Administration in the 1990s* (London: Longman).

Elcock, H., 1994, *Local Government*, third revised edition (London: Routledge).

Elcock, H., J. Fenwick and K. Harrop, 1988, *Partnerships for Public Service* (Local Authority Management Unit, Newcastle-upon-Tyne Polytechnic).

Elcock, H., J. Fenwick and K. Harrop, 1993, *Region, State and Europe* (paper read to the British Politics Work Group Conference, Hertford College, Oxford, September 1990, and to a Conference on Regional Government at the University of Western Ontario, Canada, November 1993).

Ellman, L., 1993, 'The North-West Regional Association', in Burch and Rhodes (eds.), pp.11–13.

Eser, T. W., 1991, *Europäische Einigung, Föderalismus und Regionalpolitik* (Trier: Zentrum für Europäische Studien).

European Commission, 1991, *Europe 2000* (Brussels: EEC, Directorate of Regional Policy).

Euroregió-Euro-région, 1993 (Barcelona: Direcció General de Planificació i d'Acció Territorial de la Generalitat de Catalunya).

Evans, A., 1994, 'Speech to the Australia New Zealand Regional Science Association Conference', 12–14 December, Perth, Western Australia (First Assistant Secretary Regional Economic Development Group, Commonwealth Department of Housing and Regional Development).

Evans, P., D. Rueschemeyer and T. Skocpol (eds.), 1985, *Bringing the State Back In* (Cambridge: Cambridge University Press).

Faludi, A., 1994, 'The Randstadt concept' *Urban Studies* Vol.31, No.3.

Faure, A., 1992, *Le village et la politique* (Paris: L'Harmattan).

Feigenbaum, H. B., 1994, 'The Political Underpinnings of Privatization: a typology', *World Politics*, Vol.46, pp.185–208.

Fenwick, J., K. Harrop and H. Elcock, 1990, *The Public Domain in an English Region: aspects of adaptation and change in Public Authorities* (Studies in Public Policy No.175, Centre for the Study of Public Policy, University of Strathclyde).

Fenwick, J., K. Shaw and A. Foreman, 1992, *Compulsory Competitive Tendering in Local Government: a study of the response of authorities in the North of England* (Department of Economics and Government, University of Northumbria at Newcastle).

Ferguson, T., 1984, 'From normalcy to New Deal: industrial structure, party competition and American public policy in the Great Depression' *International Organization* Vol.38, No.1 (Winter), pp.41–94.

Fernandez, R. A., 1989, *The Mexican-American Border Region: issues and trends* (Notre Dame: University of Notre Dame Press).

Financial Review, 1993, Editorial 'Kelty's Hollow Wish List', 21 December, p. 10.

Financial Times, 1991, 'Basle and the Upper Rhine', Financial Times Survey, 21 November.

Fiorina, M. P., 1988, *Congress: Keystone of the Washington Establishment* (New Haven: Yale University Press).

Fischer, W., H. Hax, and H.-K. Schneider (eds.), 1993, *Die Treuhandanstalt von 1990-1993* (Berlin: Akademieverlag).

Flierman, A.H., 1993, 'Regionalizering in Rotterdam: succesfactoren', *Openbaar Bestuur* Vol.3, pp.5–10.

Foesser, C. and J. Robert, 1989, *Principales politiques communautaires et implications de l'acte unique d'intérêt pour les régions* (Strasbourg: Centre Européen du Développement Régional).

Forth, T. P. and N. Wohlfahrt, 1992, 'Politische Regionalisierung. Zur Paradoxie eines modernen Diskurses', *Staatswissenschaften und Staatspraxis*, Vol. 3, No.4, pp.556–77.

Fouéré, Y., 1984, *L'Europe des Régions* (St Brieuc: Les Cahiers de l'Avenir, 14).

François-Poncet, J. (sous la présidence de), 1994, *Refaire la France. Les propositions de la mission d'information sur l'aménagement du territoire* (Paris: Rapport au Sénat).

Frankel, B., 1992, 'Habermas Meets C. Wright Mills', *Arena*, No. 98, pp. 153–158.

Franklin, S.H., 1969, *The European Peasantry: the Final Phase* (London: Methuen & Co. Ltd.).

Fraser, G., 1984, *René Lévesque and the Parti Québécois in Power* (Toronto: Macmillan).

Fraser, G., 1989, *Playing for Keeps: the making of the Prime Minister, 1988* (Toronto: McClelland & Stewart).

Friedmann, J., 1963, 'Regional planning as a field of study', *Journal of the American Institute of Planners* Vol.29.

Friedmann, J. and Weaver, C., 1979, *Territory and Function: the evolution of regional planning* (London: Edward Arnold).

Fulop, L., 1992, 'How the West was Won and Lost: The Politicization of Needs in Western Sydney', Unpublished PhD thesis, Faculty of Sociology, University of New South Wales, Australia.

Fulop, L., 1993, 'The Western Sydney Regional Organization of Councils (WSROC) and the Economic Development of Western Sydney: A Case Study of a Quasi-ENGO', in C.F. Bonser, A. Ringeling and B. Wijeweera (eds.), *The Role of Non Government Organizations (NGOs) in National Development Strategy in the Asia and Pacific Region*, IIAS Monograph, Brussels.

Fulop, L., 1995, 'Regional Organisations in Australia and their Emerging Roles in National Strategies', *The Role of NGOs in Economic Development "State of the Art" International Research Conference*, Indiana University, Bloomington, April 10–12 (Proceedings forthcoming).

Fulop, L. and D. Sheppard, 1988, 'Life and Death of Regional Initiatives in Western Sydney', *International Journal of Urban and Regional Research*, Vol. 12, No. 4, pp. 609–626.

Fulop, L., J. Noesjirwan, and C. Smith, 1988, 'Heartburn Burn in Labor's Heartland: political lessons from Western Sydney', *The Australian Quarterly*, Vol. 60, No. 33, pp. 337–346.

Furlong, P., 1994, *Modern Italy: representation and reform* (London: Routledge).

Gagnon, A.-G. (ed.), 1993, *Québec: state and society* (Toronto: Nelson Canada).

Gagnon, A.-G. and M. B. Montcalm, 1990, *Quebec Beyond the Quiet Revolution* (Scarborough, ON: Nelson Canada).

Gahan, C., 1989, *Arolwg o agweddau at fenter a busnes ymysg siaradnyr Cymareg* (Aberystwyth: Menter a Busnes).

Gale, D. E., 1992, 'Eight State-Sponsored Growth Management Programs', *Journal of the American Planning Association*, Vol.58, No.4, Autumn.

Galtung, J., 1980, *The True Worlds: a Transnational Perspective* (New York: Free Press).

Gambetta, Diego (ed.), 1988, *Trust. Making and Breaking Co-operative Relations* (Oxford: Blackwell).

Gardiner, W., 1987, 'How the West was lost: urban development in the western Sydney region', *The Australian Quarterly*, Vol. 59, No. 2, pp. 234–244.

Garofoli, G., 1986, 'Squilibri regionali e sviluppo del Mezzogiorno', *Delta*, No.21.

Garraud, P., 1989, *Profession: homme politique* (Paris: L'Harmattan).

Garreau, J., 1981, *The Nine Nations of North America* (New York: Avon Books).

Garten, J. E., 1992, *A Cold Peace: America, Japan, Germany and the Struggle for Supremacy* (New York: Times Books).

Gellner, E., 1964, *Thought and Change* (London: Weidenfeld & Nicolson).

Gellner, E., 1983, *Nations and Nationalism* (Oxford: Basil Blackwell).

Gellner, E., 1977, 'Patrons and clients', in Ernest Gellner and John Waterbury (eds.)

Gellner, E. and J. Waterbury (eds.), 1977, *Patrons and Clients in Mediterranean Societies* (London: Duckworth).

George, S., 1994, 'Review of R. Leonardi (ed.)., 'The regions and the European Community', *Public Administration*, Vol.72, pp.144–5.

Georgiou, G., 1993, 'From Policy to Action: the implementation of European Community regional programmes in Greece', *Regional Politics and Policy* Vol.3, No.2, Summer.

Gestenlauer, H. G., 1985, 'German Länder in the European Community' in M. Keating and B. Jones (eds.), pp.173–90.

Girvin, B., 1989, 'Change and continuity in liberal democratic political culture', in John R. Gibbins, (ed.), *Contemporary Political Culture* (London: Sage).

Gladdish, K., 1991, *Governing from the Centre: politics and policy-making in the Netherlands* (London: Hurst & Company).

Glenny, M., 1993, *The Fall of Yugoslavia* (London: Penguin).

Glickman, N. J. and D. P. Woodward, 1988, *The New Competitors: How Foreign Investors are Changing the US Economy* (New York: Basic Books).

Gluck, C., 1985, *Japan's Modern Myth: ideology in the late Meiji period* (Princeton: Princeton University Press).

Goldsmith, M., 1993, 'The Europeanization of Local Government', *Urban Studies*, Vol.30, No.4–5, pp.683–99.

Goldstein, J., 1988, 'Ideas, institutions, and American trade policy', *International Organization* Vol.42, No.1 (Winter), pp.179–217.

Goodheart, David, 1991, 'For Länder, Brussels poses both threat and opportunity', *Financial Times*, 30 May.

Gordon, M., 1994, 'Relationships Between Regional Economic Theory and Recent Policy Initiatives', Address to 18th Australia New Zealand Regional Science Association Conference, 12–14 December, Perth, Western Australia.

Government of Quebec, Ministère des Affaires internationales, 1991, *Le Québec et l'interdépendance, le monde pour horizon: éléments d'une politique d'affaires internationales* (Québec: Éditeur officiel), pp.40–51.

Granatstein J.L. and R. Bothwell, 1990, *Pirouette: Pierre Trudeau and Canadian Foreign Policy* (Toronto: University of Toronto Press).

Grande, E. and J. Häusler, 1992, *Forschung in der Industrie: Möglichkeiten und Grenzen staatlicher Steuerung* (Köln: MPI für Gesellschaftsforschung, Discussion Paper 3).

Graziano, L. (ed.), 1974, *Clientelismo e mutamento politico* (Milano: Angeli).

Graziano, L., 1980, *Clientelismo e sistema politico. Il caso dell'Italia* (Milano: Angeli).

Greater Western Sydney Economic Development Board, 1994, *Strategic Plan 1994/95*, Parramatta, NSW, November.

Greater Western Sydney Economic Development Board, 1994, *The Economic Powerhouse of Australia.: an Investment Prospectus*, Parramatta, NSW, November.

Greater Western Sydney Economic Development Committee, 1993, *Greater Western Sydney Economic Development Statement*, Parramatta, NSW.

Greer, S., 1967, 'Urbanization, parochialism and foreign policy', in J. N. Rosenau, *Domestic Sources of Foreign Policy* (New York: Free Press).

Greffe, X., 1984, *Territoires en France* (Paris: Economica).

Grémion, C., 1979, *Profession: décideurs* (Paris: Gauthiers Villard).

Grémion, P., 1976, *Le pouvoir périphérique* (Paris: Seuil).

Gribaudi, G., 1980, *Mediatori. Antropologia del potere democristiano nel Mezzogiorno* (Torino: Rosenberg & Sellier).

Grindle, M. S., 1988, *Searching for Rural Development: labor migration and employment in Mexico* (London: Cornell University Press).

Gusfield, J. R., 1989, 'Constructing the Ownership of Social Problems: fun and profits in the welfare state', *Social Problems*, No.36, pp.431–41.

Haas, E. B., 1958, *The Uniting of Europe: political, social and economic forces, 1950-1957* (Stanford, California: Stanford University Press).

Habermas, J., 1981, 'The New Social Movements' in *Telos*, No.51.

Haggard, S., 1988, 'The institutional foundations of hegemony: explaining the Reciprocal Trade Agreements Act of 1934' *International Organization* Vol.42, No.1 (Winter), pp.91–119.

Hainsworth, P. and M. Keating, 1986, *Decentralization and Change in Contemporary France* (Aldershot: Gower).

Hall, P., 1977, *The World Cities* (London: Weidenfeld & Nicolson).

Halperin, M. H. and D. J. Scheffer, with P. L. Small, 1992, *Self-Determination in the New World Order* (Washington, DC: Carnegie Endowment for International Peace).

Hansen, J., 1990, 'Epilogue' in M. Hebbert and J. C. Hansen, *Unfamiliar Territory* (Aldershot: Avebury).

Harrison, B., 1992, 'Industrial Districts: Old Wine in New Bottles?', *Regional Studies*, Vol.26, No.5, pp.469–83.

Harvey, D., 1989, *The Condition of Postmodernity* (Cambridge: Basil Blackwell).

Hathaway, D. A., 1993, *Can Workers Have a Voice?: The politics of deindustrialization in Pittsburgh* (Happy Valley: Penn State University Press).

Haward, M., 1993, 'Intergovernmental Relations and Regional Development Policy: Lessons from the Past, Opportunities for the Future', *17th Australia New Zealand Regional Science Association Conference*, 6–8 December, pp. 1–19, Armidale, NSW.

Hayward, J., 1969, 'From functional regionalism to functional representation in France', *Political Studies*, Vol.17, March, pp.48–75.

Hayward, J., 1983, *France: The One and Indivisible Republic*, 2nd edition (New York: Norton).

Hébert, C., 1991, 'La CSN et la CEQ redeviennent "canadiennes" le temps de faire la guerre aux politiques fédérales', *Le Devoir* (Montreal), 5 April, p.A2.

Hechter, M., 1975, *Internal Colonialism: the Celtic Fringe in British national development* (London: Routledge).

Heinze, R. G. and H. Voelzkow, 1990, *Kommunalpolitik und Verbände: Inszenierter Korporatismus auf lokaler und regionaler Ebene* (Bochum: sit-wp-1).

Helm, S., 1995, 'Paris urges harsh curbs on refugees', *The Independent*, 22 April, p.12.

Hemmens, G. C. and J. McBride, 1993, 'Planning and Development Decision Making in the Chicago Region' in D. N. Rothblatt and A. Sancton (eds.), *Metropolitan Governance: American/Canadian Intergovernmental Perspectives* (Berkeley: Institute of Governmental Studies Press, University of California).

452   *The Political Economy of Regionalism*

Hendriks, F., 1993, 'Regionalizering in de Rijnmond', *Openbaar Bestuur* Vol.3, p.6–10.

Hendriks, F. and Th. A. J. Toonen, 1995, 'The rise and fall of the Rijnmond Authority: an experiment with metro-government in the Netherlands', in Sharpe, L.J. (ed.), *The Government of the World Cities: the future of the metro model* (London: John Wiley & Sons).

Hendriks, F., J. C. N. Raadschelders and Th. A. J. Toonen, 1994, 'Provincial repositioning in the Netherlands: some models and the impact of European integration' in U. Bullmann (ed.), *Die Politik der dritten Ebene: Regionen im Prozess der EG-Integration* (Baden-Baden: Nomos Verlag).

Héraud, G., 1963, *L'Europe des Ethnies* (Paris: Presse d'Europe).

Héraud, G., 1971, *Federalisme et Communautés Ethniques* (Charleroi: Edition J.Destrée).

Hesse, J. J. and R. R. Kleinfeld, 1990, *Die Provinzen im politischen System der Niederlande* (Opladen: Westdeutscher Verlag).

Hilgartner, S. and C. Bosk, 1988, 'The Rise and Fall of Social Problems: A Public Arenas Model', *American Sociological Review*, Vol.94, pp. 53–78.

Hill, S. and J. Keegan, 1993, *Made in Wales: an analysis of Welsh manufacturing performance* (Cardiff: Cardiff Business School), May.

Hilmer, F., 1994, *Principles on National Competition Policy*, (Canberra).

Hintjens, H., J. Loughlin and C. Olivesi, 1995, 'The status of maritime and insular France: the DOM-TOM and Corsica', in J. Loughlin and S. Mazey (eds)., *The End of the French Unitary State: Ten years of Regionalization in France 1982–1992* (London: Frank Cass).

Hirst, P., and G. Thompson, 1992, 'The problem of "globalization": international economic relations, national economic management and the formation of trading blocs', *Economy and Society*, Vol.21, No.4, pp.357–95.

Hocking, B. (ed.), 1993, *Foreign Relations and Federal States* (London: Leicester University Press).

Hocking, B., 1993, *Localizing Foreign Policy: Non-Central Governments and Multilayered Diplomacy* (London and New York: Macmillan/St Martin's Press).

Hocking, B. and M. Smith, 1990, *World Politics: an Introduction to International Relations* (London: Harvester Wheatsheaf).

Hocking, B. and M. Smith, 1994, *Beyond foreign economic policy: the United States, the Single European Market and multilayered diplomacy* (American Politics Group Conference, University of Durham, 4–6 January).

Hofmann, J., 1993, *Implizite Theorien in der Politik. Interpretationsprobleme regionaler Technologiepolitik* (Opladen: Westdeutscher Verlag).

Hogwood, B., 1994, 'Whatever happened to regional government?', *Strathclyde Papers on Government and Politics*, No.97.

Hogwood, B. W. and M. Keating, 1982, *Regional Government in England* (Oxford: Clarendon Press).

Hood, N. and S. Young, 1982, *Multinationals in Retreat: the Scottish experience* (Edinburgh: Edinburgh University Press).

Hooghe, L. and M. Keating, 1994, 'The Politics of EU Regional Policy', *Journal of European Public Policy*, Vol.1, No.3, pp. 53–79.

Hope, Kerin, 1992, 'Farther to go, more to pay', Northern Greece: *Financial Times Survey*, 4 November.

Howe, B., 1994, *Keynote Address (Deputy Prime Minister)*, Regional Development Conference, sponsored by University of Western Sydney, Nepean and Greater Western Sydney Economic Development Board, 30 November, Warwick Farm, NSW.

Hudson, R., 1989, *Wrecking a Region: state policies, party politics and regional change in North East England* (Pion, Ltd.).

Hufbauer, G. C. and J. J. Schott, 1993, *NAFTA: an assessment*, revised edition (Washington: Institute for International Economics).

Hughes, B. B. *et al.*, 1985, *Energy in the Global Arena: Actors, Values, Policies and Futures* (Durham, NC: Duke University Press).

Huntington, S. P., 1968, *Political Order in Changing Society* (New Haven: Yale University Press).

Hurley, F., 1994a, 'The Issue - Attention Cycle and Regional Development: Is it Really Back on the Political Agenda?' *Regional Policy and Practice*, Vol.3, No.2, pp.19–28.

Hurley, F., 1994b, 'Regional Development Policy in the Big Picture', *The Australian Journal of Regional Studies*, No.8, pp.1–11.

Ikenberry G. J., D. A. Lake and M. Mastanduno, 1988, 'Introduction: approaches to explaining American foreign economic policy', *International Organization* Vol.42, No.1 (Winter), pp.1–14.

Industry Commission , 1993, *Impediments to Regional Industry Adjustment*, Report No.35, Canberra, (2 Vols).

Industry Commission, 1995, *The Growth and Revenue Implications of Hilmer and Other Related Reforms*, Canberra.

Istat, 1990, *45 anni di elezioni in Italia*, 1946-90 (Roma).

Istat, 1991, *Le regioni in cifre* (Roma).

Istituto Tagliacarne, 1989, *Il reddito prodotto in Italia. Un'indagine provinciale. Gli anni ottanta* (Milano: Angeli).

Jaensch, D., 1989a, *Power Politics: Australia's Party System*, 2nd ed. (Sydney, Allen & Unwin).

Jaensch, D., 1989b, *The Hawke-Keating Hijack* (Sydney: Allen & Unwin).

Jalbert, P., 1990, *La concertation comme mode de gestion étatique des rapports sociaux*, Ph.D. dissertation, Université de Montréal, Département de science politique.

Jensen, J., 1988, 'The Limits of "and the" Discourse: French Women as Marginal Workers' in Jensen, J., E. Hagen and C. Reddy, (ed.), *Feminization of the Labour Force: Paradoxes and Promises* (New York: Oxford).

Jensen, J., R. Mahon and M. Bienefield (eds.), 1993, *Production, Space Identity: Political Economy Faces the 21st Century* (Toronto: Canadian Scholars' Press).

Jobse, R. B. and S. Musterd, 1994, *De stad in het informatietijdperk: dynamiek, problemen en potenties* (Assen: Van Gorcum).

Johnson, C., 1989, *The Labor Legacy: Curtin, Chifley, Whitlam, Hawke* (Sydney, Allen & Unwin).

Johnston R. J., C. J. Pattie and J. G. Allsopp, 1988, *A Nation Dividing? The Electoral Map of Great Britain 1979–1987* (London: Longman).

Joint Centre for Urban Studies, 1964, *The Effectiveness of Metropolitan Planning* (Washington, DC: US Government Printing Office).

Jones, B., 1985, 'Wales in the European Community', in M. Keating and B. Jones (eds.), *Regions in the European Community* (Oxford: Clarendon Press), pp.89–108.

Jones, B., 1988, 'The development of Welsh territorial institutions' *Contemporary Wales*, Vol.2.

Jones, B., 1990, 'The Welsh Office: a political expedient or an administrative innovation' *The Transactions of the Honourable Society of Cymmrodorion* (Denbigh: Gee & Son), pp.281-92.

Jones, B. and M. Keating (eds.), 1995 *The European Union and the Regions* (Oxford: Clarendon Press)

Jones, B. and R. A. Wilford, 1986, *Parliamentary and Territoriality* (Cardiff: University of Wales Press).

Jones, G., 1988, 'Against Regional Government', *Local Government Studies* September/October.

Jones, G. W., 1989, 'A Revolution in Whitehall? Changes in British central government since 1979', *West European Politics*, Vol.12, pp.238–61.

Jouvenel, H. de and Roque, M.-A. (eds.), *Catalunya a l'Horitzó 2010* (Barcelona: Enciplodèdia Catalana), pp.271–290.

Judt, T., 1979, *Socialism in Provence* (Cambridge: Cambridge University Press).

Kam, C. A. de and J. de Haan, 1991, *Terugtredende overheid: realiteit of retoriek? Een evaluatie van de grote operaties* (Schoonhaven: Academic Service).

Kantor, P., 1995, *The Dependent City Revisited* (Boulder: Westview).

Kapstein, E. B., 1991/92, 'We are us: the myth of the multinational', *The National Interest*, Winter.

Katzenstein, P. J., 1985, *Small States in World Markets: Industrial Policy in Europe* (Ithaca: Cornell University Press).

Katzenstein, P. J., 1987, *Policy and Politics in West Germany* (Philadelphia, PA: Temple University Press).

Keating, M, 1985, 'Introduction', in M. Keating and B. Jones (eds.), *Regions in the European Community* (Oxford: Clarendon Press).

Keating, M, 1986, ' "Revindication and Lamentation"; the failure of Regional Nationalism in Languedoc' in *Journal of Area Studies*, No. 14.

Keating, M., 1988a, 'Does regional government work? The experience of Italy, France and Spain', *Governance*, Vol.1, No.2.

Keating, M., 1988b, *State and Regional Nationalism. Territorial Politics and the European State* (Brighton: Harvester-Wheasheaf).

Keating, M., 1988c, *The City that Refused to Die. Glasgow: The Politics of Urban Regeneration* (Aberdeen: Aberdeen University Press).

Keating, M., 1991, 'The Continental Meso: regions in the European Community' in L. J. Sharpe (ed.), *Between Centre and Locality: Meso Government in Europe* (London: Sage), pp.296–311.

Keating, M., 1992a, 'Do the workers really have no country? Peripheral nationalism and socialism in the United Kingdom, France, Italy and Spain', in J. Coakley (ed.), *The Social Origins of Nationalist Movements. The Contemporary West European Experience* (London: Sage).

Keating, M., 1992b, 'Regional autonomy in the changing state order: a framework of analysis' *Regional Politics and Policy*, Vol.2,No.3, pp.45–61.

Keating, M., 1993a, 'Scottish nationalism and the UK state', Paper presented at the 1993 meeting of the American Political Science Association, Washington, DC, September.

Keating, M., 1993b, *Regionalismo, Autonomía y Regimenes Internacionales*, Working Paper (Barcelona: Institut de Ciències Polítiques i Socials).

Keating, M., 1993c, 'The Politics of Economic Development. Political Change and Local Development Policies in the United States, Britain and France', *Urban Affairs Quarterly*, Vol.28, No.3, pp.373–96.

Keating, M., 1995, 'Local Economic Development: Policy or Politics?', in N. Walzer (ed.), *Economic Development Policies: A Cross-Country Comparison* (Boulder: Westview), pp.13–30.

Keating, M., 1996a, 'La coopération inter-régionale en Amérique du Nord', in R. Balme (ed.), *Cooopération inter-régionale et globalisation économique* (Paris: Economica).

Keating, M., 1996b, *Nations Against The State: the new politics of nationalism in Quebec, Catalonia and Scotland* (London: Macmillan).

Keating, M. and B. Jones, (eds.), 1985, *Regions in the European Community* (Oxford: Clarendon Press).

Keating, M. and B. Jones, 'The Nations and Regions of the United Kingdom and European Integration', in Jones, B. and M. Keating (eds.), 1995.

Keating, M. and Loughlin, J., 1993, *Brief for the Political Economy of Regionalism Project*, Canada and Netherlands.

Keeler, J.T.S., 1979, 'The Defense of Small Farmers in France' in *Peasant Studies*, Vol. 8 No. 4.

Kelty Taskforce, 1993, *Developing Australia: A Regional Perspective: A Report to the Federal Government by the Taskforce on Regional Development*, Canberra (3 volumes).

Kemp, P., 1990, 'Next Steps for the British Civil Service', *Governance*, No.3, pp.186–96.

Kenney, M., L.M. Labao, J. Curry and W.R. Goe, 1989, 'Midwestern Agriculture in U.S. Fordism. From the New Deal to economic restructuring' in *Sociologia Ruralis*, Vol.29, No.2.

Keohane, R. O. and J. S. Nye, 1972, *Transnational Relations and World Politics* (Cambridge, MA: Harvard University Press).

Keohane, R. O. and J. S. Nye, 1988, *Power and Interdependence: World Politics in Transition*, 2nd edition (Boston: Little Brown).

Kernaghan, K., 1992, 'Empowerment and Public Administration: revolutionary advance or passing fancy?', *Canadian Public Administration*, Vol.35, pp.194–214.

Kessler, M.-C., 1986, *Les grands corps de l'Etat* (Paris: Presses de la Fondation nationale des sciences politiques).

Kickert, W. J. M., 1992, 'Administrative Reform in the Dutch Civil Service: organization and management in the last ten years' (Unpublished paper, Department of Public Administration, Erasmus University, Rotterdam).

Kincaid, J., 1993, 'Consumership versus citizenship: is there wiggle for local regulation in the global economy?', in Hocking (ed.).

Klein, N. P. M., 1992, 'De provincies zijn als bestuurlijk orgaan verouderd en moeten worden opgeheven', *Binnenlands Bestuur* 13, 3.

Kloss, H., 1967, 'Abstand languages and Ausbau languages', *Anthropological Linguistics*, No.9, pp.29–41.

Koppenjan, J. F. M., 1993, *Management van de beleidsvorming: een studie naar de totstandkoming van beleid op het terrein van het binnenlands bestuur* (Den Haag: Vuga).

Kraemer, P. E., 1955, *The Societal State* (Meppel: Boom en Zoon).

Krafft, A. and G. Ulrich, 1993, *Chancen und Risiken regionaler Selbstorganisation* (Opladen: Leske + Budrich).

Krasner, S. D., 1988, 'Sovereignty: an institutional perspective', *Comparative Political Studies*, Vol.21, pp.67–82.

Krasnick, M. and R. Simeon, 1986, *Federalism and Economic Union* (Toronto: University of Toronto Press, and Royal Commission on the Economic Union and Development Prospects for Canada).

Kresl, P. K., 1992, 'The response of European cities to EC 1992', *Journal of European Integration*, Vol.15, No.2–3.

Krugman, P. R., 1991, *Geography and Trade* (Cambridge: MIT Press), p.71.

Kuklinski, A., 1993, 'Socio-Political Changes in Central and Eastern European Countries: territorial and economic repercussions and transformations in Europe' in *European Regional Planning*, No.54, The Challenges Facing European Society with the Approach of the Year 2000 (Strasbourg: Council of Europe Press).

Labour Party, 1993, *Who Runs Wales? A briefing paper on Quangos in Wales* (Cardiff: Labour Party publications), January.

Laegreid, P., 1994, 'Norway', in C. Hood and B. G. Peters (eds.), *Rewards of High Public Office* (London: Sage).

Lafont, R., 1967, *La révolution régionaliste* (Paris: Gallimard).

Lajugie, J., P. Delfaud and C. Lacour, 1985, *Espace Régional et Aménagement du Territoire*, second edition (Paris: Dalloz).

Lake, D. A., 1988, *Power, Protection and Free Trade: international sources of US commercial strategy, 1887–1939* (Ithaca: Cornell University Press).

Lancaster, T. D. and M. Lewis-Beck, 1989, 'Regional vote support: the Spanish case' *International Studies Quarterly*, Vol.33, No.1 (March), pp.29–44.

Langlois, S., 1990, *La société québécoise en tendances, 1960-1990* (Québec: Institut québécois de recherche sur la culture)

Lash, S. and J. Urry, 1987, *The End of Organized Capitalism* (London: Polity Press).

Latouche, D., 1993, ' "Québec, See Under Canada": Québec nationalism in the new global age', in A.-G. Gagnon (ed.).

Laux, E., 1986, 'Fuhrung und Verwaltung in der Rechtslehre des Nationalsozialismus', in D. Rebentisch and K. Teppe (eds.), *Verwaltung contra Menschenführung im Staat Hitlers* (Göttingen: Vandenhoeck and Ruprecht).

Lawson, G. and K. Morgan,1991, *Employment Trends in the British Engineering Industry*, (Watford: EITB).

Le Galès, P., 1994, 'Questions sur les villes entrepreneurs', in *Actes du colloque international:'les politiques urbaines'* (Grenoble: Institut d'Etudes Politiques).

Le Roy Ladurie, E., 1977, 'Occitania in Historical Perspective', in *Review*, Vol. 1, No. 1.

Lehmbruch, G., 1991, 'The organization of society, administrative strategies and policy networks', in R. M. Czada and A. Windhoff-Hertier, *Political Choice: Institutions, rules and the limits of rationality* (Frankfurt; Campus).

Lejeune, J.-P., 1991, 'Grands patrons - souveraineté: pas question', *Revue Commerce* (October), pp.76–87.

Lem, W., 1994, 'Class Politics, Cultural Politics: Expressions of Identity in Lower, Languedoc France', *Critique of Anthropology*, Vol.14, No.4.

Lem, W., 1995, 'Identity and History: Class and Regional Consciousness in Rural Languedoc' in *Journal of Historical Sociology*, Vol.8, No.2.

Lem, W., forthcoming, *Cultivating Dissent: Work, Peasants and Politics in Languedoc, France.*

Lequesne, C., 1993, *Paris-Bruxelles. Comment se fait la politique européenne de la France* (Paris: Presses de la Fondation Nationale des Sciences Politiques).

Lessard, D., 1992, 'Jean Campeau met sur pied un regroupement de gens d'affaires souverainistes', *La Presse*, 20 May, p.B1.

Levy, R., 1990, *Scottish Nationalism at the Crossroads* (Edinburgh: Scottish Academic Press)

Lijphart, A., 1975, *The Politics of Accommodation: pluralism and democracy in the Netherlands* (Berkeley: University of California Press).

Lindblom, C., 1977, *Politics and Markets. The World's Political-Economic Systems* (New York: Basic Books).

Lindsay, I., 1992, 'Migration and Motivation: a twentieth-century perspective', in T. M. Devine (ed.), *Scottish Emigration and Scottish Society* (Edinburgh: John Donald).

Lipietz, A, 1987, *Mirages and Miracles* (London: Verso).

Lipietz, A., 1992, *Towards a New Economic Order: post-Fordism, ecology and democracy* (Cambridge: Polity Press).

Lipset, S. M., 1985, 'The Revolt against Modernity', in *Consensus and Conflict. Essays in Political Sociology* (New Brunswick: Transaction).

Litvak, I., 1986, 'Freer trade with the United States: the conflicting views of Canadian business' *Business Quarterly*, Vol.51, No.2 (Spring), pp.22–32.

Lodge, J. (ed.), 1993, *The European Community and the Challenge of the Future* (Pinter Press).

Lodge, J., 1993, 'EC policy-making: institutional dynamics' in Lodge (ed.)., pp.1–36.

Logan, J. and H. Molotch, 1987, *Urban Fortunes. The Political Economy of Place* (Berkeley: University of California Press).

Logan, J. and T. Swanstrom, 1990, *Beyond the City Limits. Urban Policy and Economic Restructuring in Comparative Perspective* (Philadelphia: Temple University Press).

Lohmar, U., 1978, *Staatsburokratie: Das hoheitliche Gewerbe* (Munich: Piper).

Lorrain, D., 1991, 'De l'administration républicaine au gouvernement urbain', *Sociologie du travail*, Vol.3.

Loubère, Leo, 1974, *Radicalism in Mediterranean France: Its Rise and Decline* (Albany: State University of New York Press).

Loubère, Leo, 1990, *The wine Revolution in France: the Twentieth Century* (Princeton: Princeton University Press).

Loughlin, J, 1985, 'Regionalism and Ethnic Nationalism in France', in Y. Mény and V. Wright (eds.), *Centre and Periphery Relations in Western Europe* (London: Allen and Unwin).

Loughlin, J., 1993 (ed.), *Southern European Studies Guide* (London: Bowker Saur).

Loughlin, J., 1994, 'Nation, State and Region in Western Europe', in L. Beckemans (ed.), *Culture: the Building-Stone of Europe 2002 (Reflections and Perspectives)* (Brussels: Presses Interuniversitaires).

Loughlin, J., 1996a, 'Nationalism, regionalism and regionalization in Ireland', in G. Färber and M. Forsyth (eds.), *Regions: factors of integration and disintegration in Western Europe?* (Baden-Baden: Nomos Verslag).

Loughlin, J., 1996b, 'Regional Policy in the European Union', in S. Stravidis, E. Mossialos, R. Morgan and H. Machin (eds.), *New Challenges to the European Union: policies and policy-making at the end of the century* (Aldershot: Dartmouth).

Loughlin, J, 1996c, 'Europe of the Regions and the Federalization of Europe', *Publius: the Journal of Federation*, November.

Loughlin, J. and S. Mazey (eds.), 1995, *The End of the French Unitary State: Ten years of Regionalization in France 1982–1992* (London: Frank Cass).

Lundquist, L. and K. Stahlberg, 1983, *Byrakrater i Norden* (Abo: Abo Akademi).

Lysenko, V., 1993, 'Development of local government in Russia and the CIS' in R. J. Bennett (ed.).

Mabileau, A., 1991, *Le système local en France* (Paris: Montchrestien).

Mabileau, A. and C. Sorbets (eds.), 1989, *Gouverner les villes moyennes* (Paris: Pédone).

Macartney, A., 1990, 'Independence in Europe', in A. Brown and R. Parry (eds.), *The Scottish Govenment Yearbook, 1990* (Edinburgh: Unit for the Study of Government in Scotland), pp.281–6.

MacLaughlin, J., 1986, 'The political geography of nation-building and nationalism in the social sciences: structural versus dialectical accounts', *Political Geography Quarterly*, Vol.3, No.4, pp.299–329.

MacLaughlin, J., 1993, 'Defending the frontiers: the political geography of race and racism in the European Community', in C. H. Williams (ed.), *The Political Geography of the New World Order* (London: Wiley), pp.20–46.

Maddox, G., 1989, *The Hawke Government and Labor Tradition* (Victoria: Penguin Books).

Magas, B., 1993, *The Destruction of Yugoslavia: tracing the break-up, 1980–92* (London: Verso).

Magee, S. P. and L. Young, 1987, 'Endogenous Protection in the United States', in R. M. Stern (ed.), *US Trade Policies in a Changing World Economy* (Cambridge: MIT Press), pp.291–322.

Magee, S. P., W. A. Brock and L. Young, 1989, *Black Hole Tariffs and Endogenous Policy Theory: political economy in general equilibrium* (Cambridge: Cambridge University Press).

Majone, G., 1994, 'Communauté Economique Européenne: déréglémentation ou re-réglementation? La conduite des politiques publiques depuis l'acte Unique', in B. Jobert (ed.), *Le tournant néo-libéral en Europe* (Paris: L'Harmattan).

Malanczuk, P., 1985, 'Les Politiques Communautaires et les Länder en République Fédérale d'Allemagne' *Revue Française d'Administration Publique*, Vol.34, pp.283–302.

Mar-Molinero, C., 1994, 'Linguistic nationalism and minority language groups in the "new" Europe', *Journal of Multilingual and Multicultural Development*, Vol.15, No.3.

March, J. G. and J. P. Olsen, 1984, 'The New Institutionalism: organizational factors in political life, *American Political Science Review*, Vol.78, pp.734ñ49.

March, J. G. and J. P. Olsen, 1989, *Rediscovering Institutions: the organizational basis of politics* (New York: The Free Press).

Marin, B. and R. Mayntz (eds.), 1991, *Policy Networks: empirical evidence and theoretical considerations* (Boulder: Westview Press).

Marks, G., 1992, 'Structural Policy in the European Community', in A. Sbragia (ed.), *Europolitics: institutions and policy-making in the 'new' European Community* (Washington DC: The Brookings Institution).

Markusen, A., 1987, *Regions: the economics and politics of territory* (Totowa, NJ: Rowman and Littlefield).

Martin, P., 1994, 'Free trade and party politics in Quebec', in Doran and Marchildon (eds.), pp.143–72.

Martin, P., 1994, 'Générations politiques, rationalité économique et appui à la souveraineté au Québec', *Revue canadienne de science politique/Canadian Journal of Political Science* Vol.27, No.2 (June), pp.345–59.

Martin, P., 1995, 'Association after Sovereignty? Canadian views on economic association with a sovereign Quebec' *Canadian Public Policy* Vol.21, No.1 (March), pp.53–71.

Martin, R. C., 1963, *Metropolis in Transition: Local Government Adaptation to Changing Urban Needs* (Washington, DC: US Housing and Home Finance Agency).

Mawson J., M. R. Martins and J. T. Gibney, 1985, 'The Development of the European Community Regional Policy' in M. Keating and B. Jones (eds.), pp.20–60.

Maynard, G., 1988, *The Economy Under Mrs Thatcher* (Oxford: Blackwell).

Mayntz, R., 1993, 'Governing Failures and the Problem of Governability: some comments on a theoretical paradigm', in J. Kooiman (ed.), *Modern Governance. New Government–Society Interactions* (London: Sage).

Mazey, S., 1986, 'Decentralization: la grande affaire du septennat', in S. Mazey and M. Newman (eds.), *Mitterand's France* (London: Croom Helm).

Mazey, S., 1993, 'Developments at the French meso level: modernizing the French state', in L. J. Sharpe (ed.), *The Rise of Meso Government in Europe* (London: Sage).

Mazey, S. and J. Mitchell, 1993, 'Europe of the Regions: Territorial Interests and European Integration: The Scottish Experience', in S. Mazey and J. Richardson (eds.), *Lobbying in the European Community* (Oxford: Oxford University Press, 1993).

Mazey, S. and J. Richardson (eds.), 1993, *Lobbying in the European Community* (Oxford: Oxford University Press).

McConnell, G., 1993, 'La dynamique des langues en Europe: partie théorique, partie empirique', in C. Truchot (ed.), *Le Plurilinguisme Europen: Théorie et Practiques en Politique Linguistique* (Paris: Henri Champion).

McCrone, D., 1990, 'Opinion Polls in Scotland: August, 1988 – July, 1989', in A. Brown and R. Parry (eds.), *The Scottish Government Yearbook, 1990* (Edinburgh: Unit for the Study of Government in Scotland).

McDowall, D., 1994, 'The trade policies of Canada's Grits and Tories, 1840–1988', in Doran and Marchildon (eds.), pp.87-116.

McDowell, B. 1985, *Regional Planning Without Federal Aid* (Paper to the 27th Annual Conference of the Association of Collegiate Schools of Planning, 1 November).

McIldoon, Douglas, 1993, 'The view from the EC', in Burch and Rhodes (eds.).

McKinsey & Company (1994), *Lead Local Compete Global: Unlocking the Growth Potential of Australia's Regions*, Office of Regional Development, Department of Housing and Regional Development, Canberra.

McRoberts, K., 1988, *Quebec: Social Change and Political Crisis*, 3rd edition (Toronto: McClelland & Stewart).

McRoberts, K., 1995, *Beyond Quebec: Taking Stock of Canada* (Montreal and Kingston: McGill-Queen's University Press).

Meadwell, H., 1993a, 'The Politics of Nationalism in Quebec' *World Politics*, Vol. 45, No.2 (January), pp.203–41.

Meadwell, H., 1993b, 'Transitions to Independence and Ethnic Nationalist Mobilization', in W. J. Booth, P. James and H. Meadwell (eds.), *Politics and Rationality* (New York: Cambridge University Press), p.191–213.

Meadwell, H., & Pierre Martin, 1996, 'Economic Integration and the Politics of Independence', *Nations and Nationalism*, Vol.2, No.1, pp.67-87.

Meekosha, H., 1993, 'The Bodies Politic - Equality, Difference and Community Practice', in H. Butcher, *et al.* (ed), *Community and Public Policy* (London: Pluto Press).

Meer, F. M. Van der, and J. C. N. Raadschelders, 1988, 'Urbane problematiek in Nederland', *Bestuurswetenschappen*, Vol.41, pp.487–98.

Melucci, Alberto, 1980, 'The New Social Movements: A Theoretical Approach', *Social Science Information*, Vol 19.

Mendlovitz, Saul H. and Walker R. B. J. (eds.), 1987, *Towards a Just World Peace: Perspectives From Social Movements* (London: Butterworth).

Mendras, H., 1970, *The Vanishing Peasant: Innovation and Change in French Agriculture* (Cambridge: MIT Press).

Menter a Busnes, 1993, *Nodweddion siaradwyr Cymraeg mewn busnes* (Aberystwyth: Menter a Busnes).

Menter a Busnes, 1994, *A Quiet Revolution : The framework of the academic report* (Aberystwyth: Menter a Busnes).

Mény, Y., 1974, *Centralisation et décentralisation dans le débat politique français: 1945–1969* (Paris: Fondation Nationale des Sciences politiques).

Mény, Y., 1982, *Dix ans de régionalisation en Europe. Bilan et perspectives 1970–1980* (Paris: Cujas).

Mény, Y. (ed.), 1984, *La Réforme des Collectivités Locales en Europe: Stratégies et Résultats* (Paris: La Documentation Française).

Messina, S., 1992, 'L'immortale fabbrica. I tre miracoli di Gaspari', *La Repubblica*, 11 March.

Miles, R., 1992, 'Migration, racism and the nation-state in contemporary Europe', in V. Satzewich (ed.), *Deconstructing a Nation* (Nova Scotia: Fernwood Publishing).

Miller, R. and M. Cote, 1987, *Growing the Next Silicon Valley: a guide for successful regional planning* (Lexington, MA: D. C. Heath, Lexington Books).

Miller, W., 1977, *Manufacturing: a study of industrial location* (University Park, PA: Pennsylvania University Press).

Millon, C., 1992, 'L'imbrication des pouvoirs, limite pour la démocratie', *Pouvoirs*, Vol.60.

Milner, H. V., 1988, *Resisting Protectionism: global industries and the politics of international trade* (Princeton: Princeton University Press).

Mingione, E., and N. Redclift, 1985 *Beyond Employment: Household, Gender and Subsistence* (Oxford: Basil Blackwell).

Ministère de l'Intérieur, 1994, *Les collectivités locales en chiffres* (Paris: Direction Générale des Collectivités Locales).

Ministry of Home Affairs, 1990, *Bestuur op Niveau, deel 1 (BON-1)* (Den Haag: SDU).

Ministry of Home Affairs, 1990, *Bestuur op Niveau, deel 2 (BON-2)* (Den Haag: SDU).

Ministry of Home Affairs, 1993, *Bestuur op Niveau, deel 3 (BON-3)* (Den Haag: SDU).

Minority Rights Group, 1991, *Minorities and Autonomy in Western Europe* (London: Minority Rights Group).

Mlinar, Z. (ed.), 1992, *Globalization and Territorial Identities* (Aldershot: Avebury Press).

Mlinar, Z., 1994, *Transnational Flows and Language Identity of a Small Nation (The Case of Slovenia)*. Paper presented to the conference on 'Nation and Languages and the Construction of Europe', Katholieke Universiteit, Leuven, November.

Molle, W., 1990, *The Economics of European Integration (Theory, Practice, Policy)* (Aldershot: Dartmouth).

Moore, C. and S. Booth, 1989, *Managing Competition: meso-corporatism, pluralism, and the negotiated order in Scotland* (Oxford: Clarendon Press).

Morata, F., 1991, La Implementacion Regional de las Políticas Comunitarias, *Quaderns de Treball de l'Institut Universitari d'Estudis Europeus*, Vol.7.

Morata, F., 1992a, 'Pla Estratègic, Xarxes Polítiques i Macroregió', in F. Morata (ed.), *Govern Local* (Barcelona: Departament de Ciència Política de la UAB-PPU).

Morata, F., 1992b, 'Regions and the European Community: a comparative analysis of four Spanish regions', *Regional Politics and Policy*, Vols. 1 and 2, pp.187ñ216.

Morata, F., 1993, 'Regions and the European Community: a comparative analysis of four Spanish regions', in R. Leonardi (ed.), *The Regions and the European Community* (London: Frank Cass).

Moreno, L., 1995, 'Multiple Ethnoterritorial Concurrence in Spain', *Nationalism and Ethnic Politics*, Vol.1, No.1, pp.11–32.

Morgan, K., 1992, 'Innovating by networking: new models of corporate and regional development', in M. Dunford and G. Kafkalas (eds.), *Cities and Regions in the New Europe* (London: Belhaven Press).

Morgan, K., 1994, 'Development from Within: Economic renewal and the Welsh Parliament', in J. Osmond (ed.), *A Parliament for Wales* (Gomer Press).

Morgan, K. and C. Roberts, 1993, 'The democratic deficit: a guide to Quangoland', *Papers in Planning and Research*, No.144, (Cardiff: University of Wales).

Morgan, R. (ed.), 1986, *Regionalism in European Politics* (London: Policy Studies Institute).

Morris, D., 1989, 'A study of language contact and social networks in Ynys Mon', *Contemporary Wales*, Vol.3, pp.99–117.

Mouvement des Caisses Desjardins, 1990, *Consultation des dirigeants du Réseau Desjardins sur l'avenir politique et constitutionnel du Québec* (annex 2 of the brief presented by the Mouvement des Caisses Desjardins to the Commission on Quebec's Political and Constitutional Future, November).

Mouvement Québec Français, 1987, *Le libre-échange: une grave menace* (brief presented to the Parliamentary Commission on Canada–US Free Trade, September).

Murray, R. 1990 'Fordism and Post-Fordism' in S. Hall and M. Jacques (eds.), *New Times: The Changing Face of Politics in the 1990s* (London: Verso).

Murray, R. 1992: 'Europe and the new regionalism', in M. Dunford and G. Kafkalis (ed.), *Cities and Regions in the New Europe* (Belhaven: London).

Mutti, A., 1994, 'Il particolarismo come risorsa. Politica ed economia nello sviluppo abruzzese', *Rassegna Italiana di Sociologia*, Vol.35, No.4 (December).

Nadeau, R., 1992, 'Le virage souverainiste des Québécois, 1980-1990', *Recherches sociographiques*, Vol.33 (September), pp.9–28.

Nanton, P., 1991, 'National Frameworks and the Implementation of Local Policies', *Policy and Politics*, Vol.19, No.3, pp.191–7.

Napier, J., 1988, 'La coalition québécoise contre le libre-échange rame seule', *La Presse*, 13 October.

National Audit Office (NAO), 1989, *Locate in Scotland*, Report of the Comptroller and Auditor General, HC 300.

Nelson, D. R., 1989, 'Domestic political preconditions of US trade policy: liberal structures, protectionist dynamics', *Journal of Public Policy*, Vol.9, No.1 (March), pp.83–108.

Noël, A., 1993, 'Politics in a high-unemployment society', in A.-G. Gagnon (ed.), pp.422–49.

North, D., 1990, *Institutions, Institutional Change and Economic Performance* (Cambridge: Cambridge University Press).

Northern Network for Public Policy, 1992, *Questionnaire Survey of Local Authority Council Leaders and Chief Executive Officers in the North-East of England* (Northumbria University at Newcastle).

O'Riagain, D., 1989, 'The EBLUL: its role in creating a Europe united in diversity', in T. Veiter (ed.), *Fédéralisme, Régionalisme et Droit des Groupes Ethniques en Europe* (Vienna: Braümuller).

Ohmae, K., 1993, 'The rise of the region-state', *Foreign Affairs*, Spring.

Olivesi, C., 1994, 'L'avenir du binôme institutionnel Union européenne – Régions', *Pouvoirs*, Vol.64.

Olson, M., 1971, *The Logic of Collective Action* (Cambridge, MA: Harvard University Press).

OOR (Consultation Council for the Rijnmond Region), 1991, *De Inzet* (Rapport van het overlegorgaan Rijnmondgemeenten).

OOR (Consultation Council for the Rijnmond Region), 1992, *De Inzet-2* (rapport van het overlegorgaan Rijnmondgemeenten).

Orchard, L. and L. Sandercock, 1959, 'Urban and Regional Policy', in B. Head and A. Patience (eds.), *From Fraser to Hawke, Australian Public Policy in the 1980s* (Melbourne: Longman Cheshire).

Organization for Economic Co-operation and Development (OECD), 1992, 'Globalisation and Local and Regional Competitiveness Report', *Working Party No. 6, Regional Development Policies*, September (Paris: OECD).

Organization for Economic Cooperation and Development, 1993, *Market Type Mechanisms Series* (Paris: OECD, PUMA Group).

Orridge, A. W. and C. H. Williams, 1982, 'Autonomist nationalism: a theoretical framework for spatial variations in its genesis and development', *Political Geography Quarterly*, Vol.1, No.1, pp.18–39.

Osborne, D. and T. Gaebler, 1993, *Reinventing Government: How the Entrepreneurial Spirit is Transforming the Public Sector* (Plume Book).

Osmond, J., 1994, 'Remaking Wales', in J. Osmond (ed.), *A Parliament for Wales* (Gomer Press)

Ostrom, E., 1991, 'Rational Choice Theory and Institutional Analysis: toward complementarity', *American Political Science Review*, Vol.85, pp.237–43.

Owen, R. G., 1990, 'Assembly of Welsh Counties: inter-regional relations', in *Regions d'Europe 2* (Paris: Assemblé des Régions d'Europe), pp.17–19.

Pahl, R., 1985, *On Work* (Oxford: Basil Blackwell).

Pahl, R., 1993, *Divisions of Labour* (Oxford: Basil Blackwell).

Palard, J., 1993, 'Structural and regional planning confronted with decentralization and European integration', *Regional Politics and Policy*, Vol.3, No.3.

Papageorgiou, F. and S. Verney, 1992, 'Regional Planning and the Integrated Mediterranean Programmes in Greece', *Regional Politics and Policy*, Vol.2, Nos.1 and 2), pp.139ñ61.

Parks, R. and R. Oakerson, 1989, 'Metropolitan Organization and Governance. A Local Public Economy Approach', *Urban Affairs Quarterly*, Vol.25, No.1.

Pascallon, P., 1990, Historique de la politique communautaire d'aménagement du territoire, *Revue d'Economie Régionale et Urbaine*, Vol.5, pp.681–93.

Paul, J. K. (ed.), 1984, *High Technology: international trade and competition* (Park Ridge, NJ: Prentice Hall).

Pech, R., 1975, *Entreprise viticole et capitalisme en Languedoc-Roussillon du phylloxera aux crises de mévente* (Toulouse: Publication de l'Université de Toulouse-le-Mirail).

PEES, 1990, *Pla Estratratègic Econòmic i Social-Barcelona 2000* (Barcelona: Ajuntament de Barcelona).

Pelling, H.M., 1963, *A History of British Trade Unionism* (London: Penguin Books).

Pempel, T. J. and K. Tsunekawa, 1979, 'Corporatism Without Labour: The Japanese Anomaly', in P. C. Schmitter and G. Lehmbruch (eds.), *Trends Toward Corporatist Intermediation* (London: Sage).

Percheron, A., 1992, 'L'opinion et la décentralisation ou la décentralisation apprivoisée', *Pouvoirs*, Vol.60.

Perez-Diaz, V. M., 1993, *The Return of Civil Society* (Cambridge, MA: Harvard University Press).

Peschel, K., 1990, 'Spatial effects of the completion of the European Single Market', *Built Environment*, Vol.16, No.1, pp.11–29.

Peters, B. G., 1986, 'The Politics of Industrial Policy in the United States', in S.A. Shull and J.E. Cohen (eds.), *The Economics and Politics of Industrial Policy* (Boulder, CO: Westview).

Peters, B. G., 1990, 'Government reforms and reorganization in an era of retrenchment and conviction politics', in A. Farazmand (ed.), *Handbook of Comparative and Development Public Administration* (New York: Marcel Dekker).

Peters, B. G., 1992, 'Public bureaucracy and public policy', D. E. Ashford (ed.), *History and Context in Comparative Public Policy* (Pittsburgh: University of Pittsburgh Press).

Peters, B. G., 1994, 'Weder Programmemplanung von unten noch Programmemplanung von oben' *Politische Vierteilsjahrschrift* (forthcoming).

Peters, B. G., forthcoming a, 'Administration in the year 2000: serving the client', *International Journal of Public Administration*.

Peters, B. G., forthcoming b, 'The failure of managerialism in a managerial society', *Revue Francaise d'administration publique*.

Peterson, P., 1981, *City Limits* (Chicago: University of Chicago Press).

Pierre, J., 1994, *Den locala staten* (Stockholm: Allmanna Forlaget).

Piore, M., and C. Sabel, 1984, *The Second Industrial Divide* (New York: Basic Books).

Pirro, F., 1983, *Il laboratorio di Aldo Moro* (Bari: Dedalo).

Plaid Cymru, 1984, *A Voice for Wales in Europe* (Cardiff: Plaid Cymru publications).

Porter, M., 1990a, *The Competitive Advantage of Nations* (London: Macmillan).

Porter, M., 1990b, 'The Competitive Advantage of Nations', *Harvard Business Review*, March-April.

Prud'homme, R., 1994, 'New Goals for Regional Policy', *The OECD OBSERVER*, Vol.193, pp.26–8.

Pugel, T. A. and I. Walter, 1985, 'US corporate interests and the political economy of trade policy' *Review of Economics and Statistics* Vol.67 (August), pp.465–73

Pujol, J., 1993, *Paraules del President de la Generalitat* (Barcelona: Departament de la Presidència).

Pusey, M. (1991), *Economic Rationalism in Canberra: A Nation Building State Changes Its Mind* (Cambridge, Cambridge University Press).

Putnam, R. D., 1988, 'Diplomacy and domestic politics: the logic of two-level games', *International Organization*, Vol.42, No.3.

Putnam, R. D., 1993, *Making Democracy Work: civic traditions in modern Italy* (Princeton: Princeton University Press).

Putten, J. van., 1982, 'Policy styles in the Netherlands', in J. Richardson (ed.), *Policy Styles in Western Europe* (London: Allen & Unwin).

Quah, J. T. S., 1987, *The Government and Politics of Singapore*, 2nd edition (Singapore: Oxford University Press).

Québec, Assemblée nationale, 1992, 'Les Implications de la mise en oeuvre de la souveraineté: les aspects économiques et les finances publiques (Première partie)', Volume 3 of *Studies presented to the Commission on Issues Related to Quebec's Accession to Sovereignty* (Québec: Éditeur officiel).

Québec, Ministère de l'Industrie, du Commerce et de la Technologie, 1990, *Impact sur les secteurs manufacturiers relevant de la compétence du ministère de l'Industrie, du Commerce et de la Technologie d'un accord de libre-échange Canada-États-Unis-Mexique* (Québec: MICT).

Raich, S., 1995, *Grenzüberschreitende und interregionale Zusammenarbeit im 'Europa der Regionen' anhand der Fallbeispiele Grossregion Saar-Lor-Lux, EUREGIO und 'Vier Motoren für Europa'* (Baden-Baden: Nomos).

RBB (the Advisory Council for Home Administration), 1989, *Advies over het bestuur in grootstedelijke gebieden* (Rapport van de Raad voor het Binnenlands Bestuur, Den Haag).

Rea, S., 1973, 'I gemelli d'Abruzzo', *L'Espresso*, 18 November.

Regulski, J., 1993, 'Rebuilding local government in Poland', *Local Government in the New Europe*, R. J. Bennett (ed.).

Reich, R. B., 1983, *The Next American Frontier* (New York: Times Books).

Reich, R. B. 1991, *The Work of Nations: Preparing Ourselves for 21st-Century Capitalism* (New York: Knopf).

Rémond, B. and J. Blanc, 1989, *Les collectivités locales* (Paris: Presses de la Fondation Nationale des Sciences Politiques, Dalloz).

Rhodes, R. A. W., 1992, 'Local Government Finance', in R. A. W. Rhodes and D. Marsh, *Implementing Thatcherite Policies: audit of an era* (Buckingham: Open University Press).

Rhodes, R., and D. Marsh, 1992, 'New directions in the study of policy networks', *European Journal of Political Research*, Vol.21, Nos.1–2.

Ribaud, R., 1986, 'La région contre les Jacobins', *Revue politique et parlementaire*, 921.

Rieken, J. G. P. and J. J. M. Baaijens, 1986, *De provincie als bestuurlijk midden* (Deventer: Van Lochem Slaterus).

Ritaine, E., 1989, 'La modernité localisée? Leçons italiennes sur le développement régional', *Revue Française de Science Politique*, 39.2, pp.154-77.

Ritchie, G., R. J. Wonnacott, W. H. Furtan, R. S. Gray, R.G. Lipsey and R. Tremblay, 1991, *Broken Links: trade relations after a Quebec secession* (Toronto: C.D. Howe Institute).

Robinson, F., 1993, 'The North-East: problems of developing a regional strategy', in M. Burch and M. Rhodes (eds.), pp.58–62.

Rochefort, D. A. and R. W. Cobb, 1994, *The Politics of Problem Definition: Shaping the Public Agenda* (Lawrence: University of Kansas Press).

Rocher, F., 1993, 'Continental Strategy: Québec in North America', in A.-G. Gagnon (ed.), pp.450–68.

Rogowski, R., 1989, *Commerce and Coalition: How Trade Affects Domestic Political Alignments* (Princeton: Princeton University Press).

Rokkan, S. and D. Urwin, 1982, 'Centres and peripheries in Western Europe', in S. Rokkan and D. Urwin (eds.), *The Politics of Territorial Identity* (London: Sage).

Rokkan, S. and D. Urwin, 1982a, 'Introduction' in Rokkan, S. and D. Urwin (eds.), *The Politics of Territorial Identity* (London: Sage).

Rondin, J., 1985, *Le sacre des notables* (Paris: Fayard).

Rondinelli, D., 1975, *Urban and Regional Development and Planning – Policy and Administration* (Ithaca: Cornell University Press).

Rosanvallon, P., 1993, 'Entretien', *Pouvoirs locaux*, No.18.

Rose, R., 1982, *Understanding the United Kingdom: the territorial dimension in government* (London: Longman).

Rose, R., 1993, *Lesson-Drawing in Comparative Policy Research* (Chatham, NJ: Chatham House).

Rosenau, J. N., 1988, 'Patterned chaos in global life: structure and process in the two worlds of world politics', *International Political Science Review* Vol.9, No.4.

Rosenau, J. N., 1990, *Turbulence in World Politics, a Theory of Change and Continuity* (London: Harvester Wheatsheaf).

Rossem, V. van, 1995, *Randstad Holland: variaties op het thema stad* (Rotterdam, Nai Uitgevers).

Rousseau, M. and R. Zariski, 1987, *Regionalism and Regional Devolution in Comparative Perspective* (New York: Praeger).

Royal Town Planning Institute, 1986, *Strategic Planning for Regional Potential* (London: Royal Town Planning Institute).

RPD (National Planning Department), 1995, *Ruimte voor Regio's. Nota van de Rijksplanologische Dienst betreffende het ruimtelijk-economisch rijksbeleid tot 2000* (Den Haag: VROM).

Rutan, G. F., 1988, 'Micro-diplomatic relations in the Pacific Northwest: Washington State-British Columbia interactions', in Duchacek, Latouche and Stevenson (eds.).

Sabatier, P.A., 1987, 'Knowledge, policy-oriented learning and policy change: an advocacy coalition framework', *Knowledge*, Vol.8, p.649–92.

Sabel, C., 1993, 'Constitutional ordering in historical context', in F. Scharpf (ed.), *Games in Hierarchies and Networks* (Frankfurt: Campus).

Sabel, D., 1989 'Flexible Specialization and the Re-emergence of Regional Economies' in P. Hirst and J. Zeitlin (ed.) *Reversing Industrial Decline* (London: Macmillan).

Sack, R. D., 1986, *Human Territoriality* (Cambridge: Cambridge University Press).

Safran, W., 1995, 'Nationalism, ethnic groups and politics: a preface and an agenda', *Nationalism and Ethnic Politics*, Vol.1, No.1, pp.1–10.

Salet, W. G. M., 1994, *Gegrond Bestuur: een internationale ijking van bestuurlijke betrekkingen* (Inaugural Speech at Delft University).

Savy, M., 1993, 'Quarante ans de géographie économique française', in M. Savy and P. Veltz (eds.), *Les nouveaux espaces de l'entreprise* (La Tour d'Aigues: Aube).

Scharpf, F. W., 1988, 'The joint decision-trap: lessons from German federalism and European integration' *Public Administration*, Vol.66, pp.239–78.

Scharpf, F. W. (ed.), 1993, *Games in Hierarchies and Networks. Analytical and Empirical Approaches to the Study of Governance Institutions* (Frankfurt am Main: Campus Verlag).

Schattschneider, E. E., 1960, *The Semi-Sovereign People: a realist's view of democracy in America* (New York: Holt Rinehart and Winston).

Schendelen, M. P. C. M. van, 1984, 'Consociationalism, pillarization and conflict management in the Low Countries' *Acta Politica*, Vol.14, pp.5–177.

Schendelen, M. P. C. M. van, 1987, 'Naar opheffing van de provincie', *Namens*, Vol.2, pp.256–61

Schendelen, M. P. C. M. van, 1995, 'Hoedt U voor de actievoerende regenten', *Intermediair*, Vol.3, No.15.

Schmenner, R.W., 1982, *Making Business Location Decisions* (Englewood Cliffs, NJ: Prentice Hall).

Schmid, J., 1994, ' "Wirtschaft 2000" - Der Bericht der Baden-Württembergischen Zukunftskommission', *Die Mitbestimmung* No.1, pp. 58–62.

Schmid, J., H. Tiemann and H. Kohler, 1991, *Wissenschaftsstadt Ulm: Ein neues Konzept zur Förderung industrieller Innovation und Wettbewerbsfähigkeit* (Bochum: sit-wp-3).

Schneider, M., 1989, *The Competitive City. The Political Economy of Suburbia* (Pittsburgh: University of Pittsburgh Press).

Schrecker, T. and J. Dalgleish (eds.), 1994, *Growth, Trade and Environmental Values* (London, Ont.: Westminster Institute for Ethics and Human Values).

Schulman, B. J., 1991, *From Cotton Belt to Sunbelt* (New York: Oxford University Press).

Scott, J., 1977, 'Patronage or exploitation?', in E. Gellner and J. Waterbury (eds.).

Scottish Development Agency, 1991, *Scottish Enterprise and the European Commission, Final Report and Appendices* (Edinburgh: ECOTEC).

Scottish Enterprise, 1991, *Scotland Europa* (Glasgow: Scottish Enterprise).

Scottish Enterprise, 1993, *The Competitive Advantage of Scotland: Identifying Potential for Competitiveness* (Glasgow: Scottish Enterprise).

Scottish Office, 1993, *Scotland in the Union: a partnership for good* (Edinburgh: HMSO).

Scowen, R., 1993, 'We are all Americans now: free trade deal has created a single market', *The Gazette*, 2 February, p. B3.

Seip, J. A., 1964, *Fra embedsmannsstat til ettpertistat.* (Oslo).

Self, P., 1982, *Planning the Urban Region* (London: George Allen and Unwin).

Seligson, M. A. and E. J. Williams, 1981, *Maquiladora and Migration Workers in the Mexico-United States Border Industrialization Program* (Mexico-United States Border Research Program, University of Texas at Austin).

Sharpe, L. J. (ed.), 1980, *Decentralizing Trends in Western Democracies* (London: Croom Helm).

Sharpe, L. J. (ed.), 1993, *The Rise of Meso Government in Europe* (London: Sage).

Sheth, D. L., 1983, 'Grass roots stirrings and the future of politics', *Alternatives*, No.9.

Shils, E., 1975, *Center and Periphery. Essays in Macrosociology* (Chicago: University of Chicago Press).

Shiner, P., 1995, *Local Work* (Manchester: Centre for Local and Economic Strategies).

Shuman, M. H., 1986–7, 'Dateline Main Street: local foreign policies', *Foreign Policy*, No.65.

Silverman, S., 1965, 'Patronage and community-national relationships in central Italy', *Ethnology*, Vol.4, No.2, April (reprinted in S. Schmidt *et al.*

(eds.), 1977, *Friends, Followers and Factions. A Reader in Political Clientelism* (Berkeley: University of California Press) .

Silverman, S., 1977, 'Patronage as myth', in E. Gellner and J. Waterbury (eds).

Simeon, R., 1991, 'Concluding comments' in D. M. Brown and M. G. Smith (eds.), *Canadian Federalism: Meeting Global Economic Challenges?* (Kingston, Ont.: Institute of Intergovernmental Relations; Halifax, NS: Institute for Research on Public Policy).

Skelcher, C., 1993, 'Involvement and Empowerment in Local Public Service', *Public Money and Management* Vol.13, No.3, pp.13–20.

Smelser, N., 1966, 'Mechanisms of Change and Adjustment to Change', in J. L. Finkle and R. W. Gable (eds.), *Political Development and Social Change* (New York: Wiley).

Smith, A. D., 1981, *The Ethnic Revival in the Modern World*, (Cambridge: Cambridge University Press).

Smith, A. D., 1991, *National Identity* (London: Penguin).

Smith, A. D., 1993, 'Ties that bind', *LSE Magazine*, Spring, pp.8–11.

Smith, A., 1995, 'La Commission, le térritoire et l'innovation: la mise en place du programme LEADER', in Y. Mény, P. Muller and J.-L. Quermonne (eds.), *Les politiques publiques en Europe* (Paris: L'Harmattan).

Smith, G., 1991, 'The Production of Culture in Local Rebellion' in W. Roseberry and J. O'Brien (eds.), *Golden Ages, Dark Ages: Imagining the Past in Anthropology and History* (Berkeley: University of California Press).

Smith, J.H., 1978, 'The French Wine-growers' Revolt of 1907' in *Past and Present*, 1979.

Sørensen, T., 1993, 'Key Recommendations in the Draft Industry Commission Report', *Regional Policy and Practice*, Vol.2, No.2, pp.21–23.

Sørensen, T., 1994, 'On the White Paper: "Working Nation"', *Regional Policy and Practice*, Vol. 3, No. 1, pp. 2–4.

Sørensen, T. and R. Epps, 1994, 'The Links Between Leadership and Local Economic Development', *18th Australia New Zealand Regional Science Association Conference*, 12–14 December, Perth, W.A.

Sortia, J. R., Ch. Vandermotten and J. Vandalaer, 1986, *Atlas Economique de l'Europe* (SRBG: Université Libre de Bruxelles).

SOU, 1992, *Demokrati och makt* (Stockholm: Statens offentliga utredningar).

Spooner, D., 1995, 'Regional Development in the UK', *Geography*, Vol.80, No.1, pp.72–9.

Staatsministerium Baden-Württemberg, 1993, *Aufbruch aus der Krise. Bericht der Zukunftskommission Wirtschaft 2000* (Stuttgart: Staatsministerium).

Standing Committee on State Development, 1993, *Regional Business Development in N.S.W., Trends, Policies and Issues, Discussion Paper No. 4* (N.S.W.: Standing Committee)

Steed, G. P. F., 1987, 'Policy and High Technology Complexes: Ottawa's Silicon Valley North', in F.E. Hamilton (ed.), *Industrial Change in Advanced Economies* (London: Croom Helm).

Steiner, M. and Sturn, D., 1992, 'New dimensions of regional policy in times of accelerated change', in G. Gorzelak and A. Kuklinski (eds.), *Dilemmas of Regional Policies in Eastern and Central Europe* (Warsaw: University of Warsaw).

Steinmo, S., K. Thelen and F. Longstreth, 1992, *Structuring Politics: historical institutionalism in comparative analysis* (Cambridge: Cambridge University Press).

Steketee, M. and M. Cockburn, 1986, *Wran: An Unauthorised Biography* (Sydney: Allen & Unwin Australia).

Stewart, M.,1983, 'The Inner Area Planning System', *Policy and Politics*, Vol.2, No.2, pp.203–214.

Stewart, M., 1986, *Ten Years of Inner Cities Policy* (Bristol: School for Advanced Urban Studies).

Stillman, R. J.,1991, *A Preface to Public Administration* (New York: St. Martin's).

Stilwell, F., 1989, 'Regional Economic Policy and Local Enterprise', *Journal of Australian Political Economy*, No.25, October, pp.70–91.

Stilwell, F., 1994a, 'Economic Rationalism, Cities and Regions', *The Australian Journal of Regional Studies*, No.7, October, pp.54–65.

Stilwell, F., 1994b, 'Regional Policy Initiatives: A Political Economy Perspective', *The Australian Journal of Regional Studies*, No.8, pp.49–63.

Stone, C., 1987, 'The Study of the Politics of Urban Development', in C. Stone and H. Sanders (eds.), *The Politics of Urban Development* (Lawrence: University of Kansas Press).

Stone, C., 1989, *Regime Politics. Governing Atlanta, 1946-86* (Lawrence: University of Kansas Press).

Streeck, W. and P. C. Schmitter, 1991, 'From National Corporatism to Transnational Pluralism: organized interests in the Single European Market, *Politics and Society* Vol.19, No.2, pp.133–164.

Stretton, H., 1975, *Ideas for Australian Cities* (Melbourne: Georgian House).

Sturm, R., 1991a, *Die Industriepolitik der Bundesländer und die Europäische Integration* (Baden-Baden: Nomos).

Sturm, R., 1991b, 'Westeuropäischer Regionalismus und deutscher Föderalismus', in G. Hirscher (ed.), *Die Zukunft des kooperativen Föderalismus in Deutschland* (München: Hanns-Seidel-Stiftung), pp.205–21.

Sturm, R., 1994, 'Integration ohne Dezentralisierung. Die ökonomische Modernisierung der ostdeutschen Länder', in U. Bullmann (ed.), *Die Politik der dritten Ebene* (Baden-Baden: Nomos), pp.378–89.

Suleiman, E. N., 1978, *Elites in French Society* (Princeton: Princeton University Press).

Tanguay, B. A., 1993, 'Québec's political system in the 1990s: from polarization to convergence', in A.-G. Gagnon (ed.), pp.174-98.

Tarrow, S., 1967, *Peasant Communism in Southern Italy* (New Haven: Yale University Press).

The Western Sydney Economic Development Strategy, 1988, Sydney: Premier's Department.

Thijn, E. van, 1991, *Democratie als hartstocht: commentaren en pleidooien 1966-1991* (Amsterdam: Van Gennip).

Thurow, L., 1993, *Head to Head: the Coming Economic Battle among Japan, Europe and America* (London: Brealey, 1993).

Todd, E., 1990, *L'invention de l'Europe* (Paris: Seuil).

Toonen, T. A. J., 1990, 'The unitary state as a system of co-governance: the case of the Netherlands' *Public Administration*, Vol.68 pp.281-96.

Toonen, T. A. J., 1993, 'Dutch provinces and the struggle for the meso', in L. J. Sharpe (ed.), *The Rise of the Meso in Europe* (London: Sage).

Touraine, A., 1987, *The Voice and the Eye* (Cambridge: Cambridge University Press).

Touraine, A., 1992, 'L'état et la question nationale', in R. Lenoir and J. Lesourne (eds.), *Où va l'état?* (Paris: Le Monde éditions).

Touraine, A., 1995, *A Critique of Modernity* (Oxford: Basil Blackwell).

Touraine, A. *et al.*, 1981, *Le pays contre l'Etat* (Paris: Seuil).

Trigilia, C., 1991 'The paradox of the region: economic regulation and the representation of interests', *Economy and Society*, Vol.20, No.3.

Trudgill, P., 1993, *The Ausbau Sociolinguistics of Minority Languages in Greece* (Mimeo: Lausanne University).

Turone, S., 1993, *Agonia di un regime. Il caso Abruzzo* (Bari: Laterza).

Urry, J. , 1990, 'The End of Organised Capitalism', in P. Hall, M. Stuart and M. Jacques (eds.) *New Times: The Changing Face of Politics in the 1990s* (London, Verso).

Ushkalov, I. G., 1993, 'Regional development in the former USSR', in R. J. Bennett (ed.).

Vaillancourt, F. and J. Carpentier, 1989, *Le contrôle de l'économie du Québec: la place des francophones en 1987 et son évolution depuis 1961* (Québec: Gouvernement du Québec, Office de la langue française).

Van Horn, C. E. (ed.), 1993, *The State of the States* (Washington, DC: Congressional Quarterly Press).

Vanhove, N. and L. H. Klaassen, 1987, *Regional Policy: a European approach* (Aldershot: Avebury).

Vega-Canovas, G. M., 1994, 'The free trade policy "revolution" and party politics in Mexico', in C. F. Doran and R. Marchildon (eds.), pp.197–222.

Walker R. B. J. and S. H. Mendlowitz, 1987 'Peace, politics and contemporary social movements', in S. H. Mendlovitz and R. B. J.Walker (eds.).

Walle, M. van de, 1988, 'Des Québécois lancent une campagne de $300 000 dollars en faveur du libre-échange', *La Presse* (Montreal), 9 November.

Wallerstein, M., 1987, 'Unemployment, collective bargaining, and the demand for protection' *American Journal of Political Science*, Vol.1, No.4, (November), pp.729–52.

Walsh, J. H., 1992, 'Migration and European nationalism', *Migration World*, Vol.20, No.4, pp.19-22.

Waniek, R., 1993, 'A new approach to decentralization in North-Rhine Westphalia', *Regional Studies*, Vol.27, No.5, pp.467–74.

Wannop, U., 1984, 'The Evolution and Roles of the Scottish Development Agency', *Town Planning Review*, Vol.55, No.3, pp.313–21.

Wannop, U., 1990, 'The Glasgow Eastern Area Renewal (GEAR) Project', *Town Planning Review*, Vol.6, No.4, pp.455-74.

Wannop, U., 1993, 'Regional Planning and Governance in the United States' *Regional Politics and Policy*, Vol.3, No.3.

Wannop, U., 1995, *The Regional Imperative* (London: Jessica Kingsley Publishers).

Waterbury, J., 1977, 'An attempt to put patrons and clients in their place', in E. Gellner and J. Waterbury (eds.).

Weber, E., 1976 *Peasants into Frenchmen: The Modernization of Rural France 1870–1914* (Stanford: Stanford University Press).

Weber, M. P., 1988, *Don't Call Me Boss: David L. Lawrence, Pittsburgh's Renaissance Mayor* (Pittsburgh: University of Pittsburgh Press).

Weiler, Conrad, 1994, 'Free-trade agreements: a new federal partner?' *Publius* Vol.24, No.3.

Weintraub, S., 1990, *A Marriage of Convenience: relations between Mexico and the United States* (New York: Oxford University Press).

Weir, L., 1993, 'What so New in the New Social Movements?', in *Studies in Political Economy*, Vol 40.

Welch, R., 1993, 'Economic restructuring and the capitalist periphery: implications for eastern Europe' in R. J. Bennett (ed.).

Welsh Council of Labour, 1978, *The Common Market and Wales* (Cardiff).

Welsh Economic Council, 1971, *Wales and the Common Market* (Cardiff).

Welsh Office, 1994, Press Releases: W94222, 25 April; W94344, 21 April

Western Sydney Regional Organisation of Councils (WSROC) and MSJ K. Young, 1985, *Regional Community Development Program, West Sydney 2000*, Vols. 1 and 2 (Blacktown, N.S.W.), March.

Western Sydney Regional Organisation of Councils (WSROC), and C. McNamara Consultants in association with Dr. E. Blakely, 1986, *Advanced Technology Development Strategy for Western Sydney*, (Blacktown, N.S.W.), September.

Western Sydney Regional Organisation of Councils Ltd, 1994a, *Western Sydney - A Vision for the Next 20 Years*, (Blacktown, N.S.W.), April.

Western Sydney Regional Organisation of Councils Ltd, 1994b, *WSROC UPDATE*, (Blacktown, N.S.W.), August, p.1.

Wettenhall, R., 1987, 'Local Governments as Innovators', *Australian Journal of Public Administration*, Vol.47, No.4, pp. 351–374.

Whebell, C. F. J., 1988, *A Non-Deterministic Metaprocess Model of Political-Territorial Change*. (London, Ont.: Department of Geography, University of Western Ontario).

Williams, C. H., 1980, 'Language contact and language change in Wales, 1901–1971: a study in historical geolinguistics', *The Welsh History Review*, Vol.10, No.2, pp.207–38.

Williams, C. H. (ed.), 1982, *National Separatism* (Cardiff: The University of Wales Press; Vancouver: The University of British Columbia Press).

Williams, C. H., 1984, 'More than tongue can tell: linguistic factor in ethnic separatism', in J. Edwards (ed.), *Linguistic Minorities, Policies and Pluralism* (London: Academic Press).

Williams, C. H. (ed.), 1988, *Language in Geographic Context* (Clevedon, Avon: Multilingual Matters).

Williams, C. H, 1989a, 'The question of national congruence', in R. J. Johnston and P. Taylor (eds.), *A World in Crisis?* (Oxford: Blackwell).

Williams, C. H., 1989b, 'New domains of the Welsh language: education, planning and the law. *Contemporary Wales*, Vol.3, pp.41–76.

Williams, C. H., 1990b, 'Political expressions of underdevelopment in the West European periphery', in H. Buller and S. Wright (eds.), *Rural Development: problems and practices* (Aldershot: Avebury).

Williams, C. H. (ed.), 1991b, *Linguistic Minorities, Society and Territory* (Clevedon, Avon: Multilingual Matters).

Williams, C. H., 1992, 'Agencies of language reproduction in celtic societies', in W. Fase *et al.* (ed.), *Maintenance and Loss of Minority Languages* (Amsterdam: J. Benjamins).

Williams, C. H., 1993a, 'Towards a new world order: European and American perspectives', in C. H. Williams (ed.), *The Political Geography of the New World Order* (London: Wiley), pp.1–19.

Williams, C. H., 1993b, 'The European Community's lesser used languages', *Rivista Geografica Italiana*, Vol.100, pp.531–64.

Williams, C. H., 1994, *Called Unto Liberty: on language and nationalism* (Clevedon, Avon: Multilingual Matters).

Williams, C. H. and A. D. Smith, 1983, 'The national construction of social space', *Progress in Human Geography*, Vol.7, pp.502–18.

Williams, R., 1993, 'Spatial planning for an integrated Europe', in J. Lodge (ed.), pp.348–59.

Wishlade, F., 1993, 'Competition policy, cohesion and the coordination of regional aids in the European Community', *European Competition Law Review*, Vol.14, No.4, pp.143–50.

Wood, J. R., 1981, 'Secession', *Canadian Journal of Political Science*, Vol.14, pp.107–34.

Worms, J.-P., 1966, 'Le Préfet et ses notables', *Sociologie du travail*, No.3.

Wright V. (ed.), 1994, *Privatization in Western Europe: pressures, problems and paradoxes* (London: Pinter Publishers).

WRR (Scientific Council for Government Policy), 1992, *Van de stad en de rand* (Den Haag: SDU).

WRR (Scientific Council for Government Policy), 1994, *Besluiten over grote projecten* (Den Haag: SDU).

Yarbrough, B. V. and R. M. Yarbrough, 1992, *Cooperation and Governance in International Trade: the strategic organizational approach* (Princeton: Princeton University Press).

Young, K. and P. Garside, 1982, *Metropolitan London. Politics and urban change 1837–1981* (London: Edward Arnold).

Young, R. A., 1995, *The Secession of Quebec and the Future of Canada* (Montreal and Kingston: McGill-Queen's University Press).

Young, S., 1982, 'The regional offices of the Department of the Environment', in B. W. Hogwood and M. Keating (eds.), pp.75–95.

Yuill, D., K. Allen, J. Bachtler, K. Clement and F. Wishlade, 1995, *European Regional Incentives, 1994–95*, (London: Bowker-Saur).

Index